Edwin L. (Edwin Lewis) Jewell

Jewell's Crescent City Illustrated

New Orleans

Edwin L. (Edwin Lewis) Jewell

Jewell's Crescent City Illustrated
New Orleans

ISBN/EAN: 9783743315013

Manufactured in Europe, USA, Canada, Australia, Japa

Cover: Foto ©ninafisch / pixelio.de

Manufactured and distributed by brebook publishing software
(www.brebook.com)

Edwin L. (Edwin Lewis) Jewell

Jewell's Crescent City Illustrated

Jewell's Crescent City Illustrated

New Orleans

CRESCENT CITY ILLUSTRATED.

EDITED AND COMPLIED BY

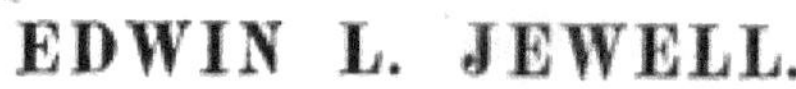

The Commercial, Social, Political and General History

—OF—

INCLUDING

Biographical Sketches of its Distinguished Citizens,

JEWELL'S

CRESCENT CITY ILLUSTRATED.

INTRODUCTION.

NO City in the United States, of equal population, commercial importance and material wealth, is so little known by the outside world as New Orleans. And yet its history, full of romantic incident and legendary lore is in itself sufficient to fill a volume, whilst its peculiar characteristics, local institutions, and singular manners and customs of its people would furnish material for a work of larger scope than is designed by the author of this publication.

It is, however, his object and desire to present to the reader, in an attractive and succinct form, a brief historical outline of the most prominent features that contribute to make the Crescent City the great metropolis of the South and South-West, and prove the intelligence, enterprise and progressive spirit of its citizens. It is also his design to produce such a work as will disseminate a more general knowledge of the local history of New Orleans and will, in a great degree, demonstrate its immense resources, advantages and attractions, and at the same time furnish such information as will engage the attention of the casual reader and command the serious consideration of capitalists, immigrants and the commercial world.

In the preparation of this volume, comprising as it does, a vast amount of information and a great variety of subjects, the author has been materially assisted by the contributions of a number of literary friends whose valuable services he desires to publicly acknowledge. The Hon. Charles Gayarre, Prof. D. K. Whittaker, Prof. Alex. Dimitry, Hon. Wm. M. Burwell, Albert Fabre, Esq., E. W. Halsey, Esq., Judge Alexander Walker *and* Mr. E. C. Hancock, *of the New Orleans "Times," and* Mr. J. A. Quintero, *of the "Picayune," have all lent the aid of their graceful pens to the pages of the* Crescent City Illustrated. *To say that all of these gentlemen are recognized as writers of the highest order of literary talent would only be to accord them their well-merited reputation. Extracts also have been made from "Norman's History of New Orleans," and other volumes have contributed interesting statistics which have been carefully compiled and arranged.*

If this volume, prepared with much care and labor, will in any way contribute towards giving additional information or throwing more light upon the general history of New Orleans and tend to remove the unreasonable and unjust prejudices that exist through ignorance of its true character, the highest object in view will have been fully attained and the richest reward obtained by

THE AUTHOR.

NEW ORLEANS, Jan. 1st, 1873.

To

E. J. HART, Esq.,

The successful and highly esteemed Merchant;

The enterprising, liberal, and public-spirited Citizen;

The honorable, high-toned, and exemplary Man;

The generous Friend and devoted Father and Husband,

THIS WORK IS

Respectfully Dedicated,

AS AN

Evidence of Appreciation of True Moral Worth, and as a Token of Remembrance of years gone by so fondly cherished

BY THE AUTHOR.

New Orleans, January, 1873.

THE CRESCENT CITY.

Slow sweeping from a bleak northwestern clime,
Where snow-storms beat and forests rise sublime,
Till, gathering strength, as southward rolls his course,
To Mexicana's Gulf descends his force;
Monarch of streams! great Mississippi flows,
While on his breast the fervid sunbeam flows.

And, rising near his disemboguing tide,
The Crescent City sits in queenly pride;
The spires ascend, a coronet on high,
Her gardens bloom with every floral dye;
Her thronging marts a varied crowd display,
The merchant prince, the dame in rich array,
The wan-eyed beggar, and the tradesman keen,
The brisk attorney with his eager mien,
And sapient age, with tottering step and slow,
Walks side by side with youth in freshest glow;
From different lands collected strangers meet,
Are borne in cars or move along the street.

But white and solemn, midst the ceaseless tread,
Rise, here and there, the dwellings of the dead!
Whose peopled mansions never sound repeat,
Save song-birds' wail, at evening, clear and sweet.

The floating palace on the grand old stream,
The thundering iron horse impelled by steam,
Pour in her lap rich treasures from all lands,
As, Queen of Trade, the Crescent Empress stands!

New Orleans, January, 1873.

BIRD'S EYE VIEW OF NEW ORLEANS.

THE CITY OF NEW ORLEANS.

New Orleans, the Metropolis of the South, stands on the right side of the Mississippi, in ascending, ninety-two miles from its mouth. The river here makes a considerable bend to the northeast, and the city occupies the northwestern side, although its situation is east of the general course of the stream. It is in latitude 29° 57′ north, longitude 90° 8′ west; by the river 301 miles below Natchez; 1220 miles below St. Louis; 1040 below Cairo, at the mouth of the Ohio; 2004 below Pittsburg; and 1244 southwest from Washington city.

In 1718, Bienville, then Governor of the province, explored the banks of the Mississippi, in order to choose a spot for the chief settlement, which had hitherto been at Biloxi. He selected the present site, and left fifty men to clear the ground, and erect the necessary buildings. Much opposition was made, both by the military and the directors of the Western Company, in removing the seat of government to this place. Another obstacle, for a while, threatened almost insurmountable difficulties to his design. In 1719, the Mississippi rose to an extraordinary height; and, as the company did not possess sufficient force to protect the spot from inundation, by dykes and levees, it was for a time abandoned. In the November of 1722, however, in pursuance of orders, Delorme removed the principal establishment to New Orleans. In the following year, agreeably to Charlevoix, it consisted only of one hundred cabins, placed with little order, a large wooden warehouse, two or three dwelling-houses, and a miserable store-house, which had been used as a chapel, a mere shed being then the only accommodation afforded for a house of prayer. The population did not exceed two hundred. Thus commenced what is now called the "Crescent City;" which, in a commercial point of view, and in proportion to the number of its inhabitants, has not an equal on the face of the globe.

During the same year, a party of German emigrants, who had been disappointed by the financier, Law, of settling on lands granted to him in Arkansas, descended the river to New Orleans, in the hope of obtaining passage to France; but the government being either unwilling or unable to grant it, small allotments of land were apportioned them, on what is now called the German Coast. These people supplied the city with garden stuffs; and most of their descendants, with large accessions from the old country, still cultivate the same land, upon a much improved scale.

In September of this year, the capital was visited by a terrible hurricane, which levelled to the ground the church, if such it might be called, the hospital, and thirty houses; and three vessels that lay in the river were driven ashore. So destructive was it to the crops and gardens, that a scarcity of provisions was the consequence; and such was the distress, that several of the inhabitants seriously thought of abandoning the colony.

In the summer of 1727, the Jesuits and Ursuline nuns arrived. The fathers were placed on a tract of land now forming the lowest part of the fauxbourg St. Mary. The nuns were temporarily lodged in a house in the corner of Chartres and Bienville streets—but, soon after, the company laid the foundation of the edifice in Conde and Ursuline streets, to which they were removed in 1730; this place was occupied by them until the great value of the land induced them to divide the larger portion of it into lots. Their new convent was erected about two miles below the city, and there they removed in 1824. At this period, the council house and jail were built, on the upper side of the Cathedral.

In 1763, Clement XIII expelled the Jesuits from the dominions of the kings of France, Spain and Naples. They were, consequently, obliged to leave Louisiana. Their property in New Orleans was seized, and sold for about one hundred and eighty thousand dollars. At the time of the expulsion of this order, they owned the grounds which are now occupied by the first District. The valuable buildings in which they dwelt, were situated in Gravier and Magazine streets. Some of them were pulled down to make room for the late banking-house of the Canal bank, on the corner of those streets. It is computed, that more than one half of the real estate in this city, is derived from the confiscation of the property of the Jesuits, under legal proceedings had by order of the French government. The archives of the city contain many interesting and curious documents in relation to these proceedings, that are well worth examination.

The first visitation of the yellow fever was in 1769. Since that time it has continued to be almost an annual visitor. It was introduced into this continent, in the above named year, *by a British vessel*, from the coast of Africa, *with a cargo of slaves*. In addition to this affliction, (the yellow fever above alluded to,) the colony was, during the year 1769, transferred to Spain, and the capital was taken possession of by O'Reilly, with a show of military power, and an individual disposition to oppress, that brought equal disgrace upon himself, and upon the government that commissioned him. The commerce of this city suffered very much from the restrictive colonial system of Spain. This, however, was removed in 1778, (a year memorable for a fire that burnt nine hundred houses at one time) and, in 1782, the mercantile interest of the place was benefited by still farther extended privileges of trade.

The census of 1785 gives to the city a population of 4,780, exclusive of the settlements in the immediate vicinity.

In consequence of the commercial advantages above alluded to, a number of merchants from France established themselves here, and British trading vessels navigated the Mississippi. They were a species of marine pedlers, stopping to trade at any house, by making fast to a tree, and receiving in payment for merchandize, whatever the planter had to spare, or giving him long credits. The Americans, at that time, commenced the establishment of that trade from the west to New Orleans, which has been steadily increasing ever since. The idea of this traffic was first conceived by General Wilkinson. A lucrative business was also conducted by the Philadelphians, which the colonial authorities winked at for a while; but the Spanish minister, finding that he did not participate in the profits of it, as the Americans refused to comply with his hints to consign to his friends, put a stop to it. He procured a list of the names of the vessels, severely reprimanded the intendant, Navarro, and so worked upon his fears that he began to prosecute all infringements of the revenue laws, seizing the vessels, confiscating the goods and imprisoning the owners, captains and crews. The venal minister, perceiving that he had rendered himself extremely unpopular by his intermeddling with the commerce between Philadelphia and New Orleans, finally released all the individuals he had imprisoned, restoring the confiscated property, and discontinuing any further interference. The trade immediately received a new impulse and was greatly increased. General Wilkinson at the same time obtained permission to send one or more launches loaded with tobacco, from Kentucky.

Soon after, many Americans availed themselves of a privilege which was granted, of settling in the country.

The first company of French comedians arrived here in 1791. They came from Cape Francois, whence they made their escape from the revolted slaves. Others from the same quarter opened academies—the education of youth having hitherto been confined to the priests and nuns.

The baron Carondelet, in 1792, divided the city into four wards. He recommended lighting it, and employing watchmen. The revenue did not amount to seven thousand dollars, and to meet the charges for the purchases of lamps and oil, and to pay watchmen, a tax of one dollar and an eighth was levied upon chimneys.

He also commenced new fortifications around the capital. A fort was erected where the mint now stands, and another at the foot of Canal street. A strong redoubt was built in Rampart street, and at each of the angles of the now city proper. The Baron also paid some attention to training the militia. In the city, there were four companies of volunteers, one of artillery, and two of riflemen, consisting of one hundred men each, making an aggregate force of 700 men.

A great extension was given to business in February of this year. The inhabitants were now permitted to trade freely in Europe and America, wherever Spain had formed treaties for the regulation of commerce. The merchandise thus imported, was subject to a duty of fifteen per cent.; and exports to six per cent. With the Peninsula it was free.

In 1795 permission was granted by the king to citizens of the United States, during a period of ten years, to deposit merchandise at New Orleans. The succeeding year, the city was visited by another conflagration, which destroyed many houses. This reduced the tax upon chimneys so much, that recourse was had to assessing wheat bread and meat, to defray the expense of the city light and watch.

At the time of the transfer to the United States, the public property consisted of two large brick stores, running from the levee on each side of Main street, (which were burnt in 1822,)—a government house, at the corner of Levee and Toulouse streets, (which also suffered a similar fate in 1826,)—a military hospital, and a powder magazine, on the opposite side of the river, which was abandoned some years since—an old frame custom house—extensive barracks below those now remaining—five miserable redoubts, a town house, market house, assembly room and prison, a cathedral and presbytery, and a charity hospital. At this memorable era, the grounds which now constitute that thriving portion of the city, then known as the second municipality, were mostly used as a plantation. It was the property of a wealthy citizen named Gravier, after whom one of the principal streets that runs through the property has been called. How has the scene changed! At this moment it contains a population of nearly fifty thousand, and has become the centre of the business, and enterprise, and beauty of the city.

In 1804, New Orleans was made a port of entry and delivery, and Bayou St. John a port of delivery. The first act of incorporation was granted to the city, by the legislative council of the territory, in 1805, under the style of "the Mayor, Aldermen and inhabitants of the city of New Orleans." The officers were a mayor, a recorder, fourteen aldermen and a treasurer. This year a branch of the United States Bank was established in this capital.

The population of the city and suburbs in 1810, amounted to 24,552; having been trebled in seven years, under the administration of its new government. The prosperity of its trade increased in an equal ratio.

At that time the city extended no further down than Esplanade street, with the exception of here and there a villa scattered along the levee; nor above, further than Canal street, unless occasionally a house occupying a square of ground. A few dwellings had been erected on Canal and Magazine streets, but it was considered to be getting quite into the country, to go beyond the *Polar Star Lodge*, which was at the corner of Camp and Gravier streets.

There was not then a paved street in the city. The late Benjamin Morgan, who, some time after, made the first attempt, was looked upon as a visionary. The circumstance which gave an impulse to improvements in the second municipality, was the erection of the American theatre, on Camp street, by James H. Caldwell, Esq., the only access to which, for a long time, was over flatboat gunwales. This was in 1823—4. He was ridiculed for his folly, and derided as a madman—but time proved his foresight. He was soon followed by a crowd that gave life and energy to that section; and, in a few years, through the enterprise of others of a similar spirit, the then suburb of St. Mary reached its present advanced state of elegance and prosperity.

FRENCH MARKET AND SHIPPING.

The block where the Auctioneer's Exchange has since been built, was then occupied by a row of frail wooden shanties; and the corner of Royal and Custom house streets, where the bank now stands, was tenanted by Scott, who furnished food for his hundreds a day directly opposite, and who laid the foundation of his fortune in the tenement that was removed to make room for the present beautiful edifice.

ARCHITECTURE.

The houses are chiefly constructed with bricks, except a few ancient and dilapidated dwellings in the heart of the city, and some new ones in the outskirts. Wooden buildings are not permitted to be built, under present regulations, within what are denominated the fire limits. The modern structures, particularly in the First District, are generally three and four stories high, and are embellished with handsome and substantial granite, marble or iron fronts. The public buildings are numerous; and many of them will vie with any of the kind in our sister cities.

The view of New Orleans from the river, in ascending or descending, is beautiful and imposing—seen from the spire of St. Patrick's Church, it presents a panorama at once magnificent and surprising. In taking a lounge through the lower part of the city, the stranger finds a difficulty in believing himself to be in an American city. The older buildings are of ancient and foreign construction, and the manners, customs and language are various—the population being composed, in nearly equal proportions, of Americans, French, Creoles, and Spaniards, together with a large portion of Germans and Irish and a good sprinkling from almost every other nation upon the globe.

In the summer of 1844, a fire destroyed about seven blocks of buildings between Common and Canal streets, near the charity Hospital. The ground has since been occupied with much better buildings, and presents a very improved appearance.

POPULATION.

The population of New Orleans, after it was ceded to the United States, increased very rapidly. At the time of the transfer, there were not eight thousand inhabitants.

	Blacks.	*Whites.*	*Total.*
In 1810	8,001	16,551	24,552
1815	——	——	32,947
1820	19,737	21,614	41,350
1825	——	——	45,336
1830	21,280	28,530	49,826
1840	——	59,519	102,191
1850	——	91,431	119,460
1860	——	149,063	174,491
1870	——	149,923	191,418

and at the present period there are, probably two hundred and twenty thousand. During 1844 there were more buildings erected than any previous year—notwithstanding which, tenements are in great demand, and rents continue high.

BOARD OF HEALTH.

The first ordinance for the establishment of a board of health in this city, (so far as known,) was passed by the general council in June, of 1841. The board consisted of nine members—three aldermen, three physicians, and three private citizens. It was invested with ample powers to adopt and enforce such sanitary regulations as were thought conducive to the health of the city. This board performed all its functions well during the first year of its existence. The second year there was a falling off; but a dissolution did not take place till 1843. In 1844, the board of health having ceased to officiate, the general council invited the medico-chirurgical society to take charge of this duty. This proposition was accepted, and a committee of nine members appointed, with full power to act as a board of health.

SOCIETY.

Society, as at present constituted in New Orleans, has very little resemblance to that of any other city in the Union. It is made up of a heterogeneous mixture of almost all nations. First, and foremost, is the Creole population. All who are born here, come under this designation, without reference to the birth place of their parents. They form the foundation, on which the superstructure of what is termed "society," is erected. They are remarkably exclusive in their intercourse with others, and, with strangers, enter into business arrangements with extreme caution. They were once, and very properly, considered as the patricians of the land. But they are not more distinguished for their exclusiveness, and pride of family, than for their habits of punctuality, temperance and good faith.

CHARACTER OF THE POPULATION.

Till about the commencement of the present century, the period of the transfer of Louisiana to the United States, the Creoles were almost entirely of French and Spanish parentage. Now, the industrious Germans, the shrewd and persevering Irishmen, are beginning to be quite numerous, and many of them have advanced to a condition of wealth and respectability.

Next come the emigrants from the sister States, from the mighty west, from the older sections of the south, and (last not least) from the colder regions of the north, the enterprising, calculating, hardy Yankee.

Then come the nondescript watermen. Our river steam navigation, averaging, during half the year, some three hundred arrivals per month, furnishes a class of fifteen thousand men, who have few if any parallels in the world. The numberless flatboats that throng the levees for an immense distance, are peopled and managed by an amphibious race of human beings, whose mode of living is much like that of the alligator, with whom they ironically claim relationship, but who carry under their rough exterior and uncouth manners, a heart as generous and noble as beats in any human breast. They are the children of the Mississippi, as the Arabs are of the great desert, and, like them, accustomed to encounter danger in every shape. Combining all the most striking peculiarities of the common sailor, the whaleman, the backwoodsman, and the Yankee, without imitating, or particularly resembling any one of them, they are a class entirely by themselves, unique, eccentric, original, a distinct and unmistakeable feature in the floating mass that swarms on the levees, and treads the streets, of the Cresent City.

Among them may be found the representatives of nearly all the states. Some are descendants of the Pilgrims, and have carried with them the industrious habits, and the strict moral principles, of their Puritan forefathers, into the wilds of the West. They are all active, enterprising, fearless, shrewd, independent, and self-sufficient, and often aspiring and ambitious, as our halls of legislation, and our business circles can testify. They are just the stuff to lay the broad foundations of freedom in a new country—able to clear the forest, and till the soil, in time of peace, to defend it in war, and to govern it at all times.

SOCIAL CHARACTERISTICS.

Of the two hundred and fifty thousand souls, who now occupy this capital, about twenty thousand may be estimated as migratory. These are principally males, engaged in the various departments of business. Some of them have families at the North, where they pass the summer. Many are bachelors, who have no home for one half the year, and, if the poets are to be believed, less than half a home for the remainder. As these two classes of migratory citizens, who live at the hotels and boarding-houses, embrace nearly, if not quite, one third the business men of the city, it may serve to some extent, to accout for the seemingly severe restrictions by which the avenues to good native society are protected. Unexceptionable character, certified beyond mistake, is the only passport to the domestic circle of the Creole. With such credentials their hospitality knows no limits. The resident Americans are less suspicious in admitting you to their hospitality, though not more liberal than their Creole neighbors, when once their confidence is secured.

The restrictions thus thrown around society, and the great difficulty which the new comer experiences in securing a share in those social enjoyments to which he has been accustomed in other places, have had an unfavorable effect upon the morals of the place. Having no other resource for pastime, when the hours of business are over, he flies to such public entertainments as the city affords. And if these are not always what they should be, it behooves us to provide better. Public libraries, reading rooms, galleries for the exhibition of the fine arts, lyceums for lectures, and other kindred rational amusements, would do much to establish a new and better order, and to break down those artificial barriers, which separate so many refined and pure minded men from the pleasures and advantages of general society, condemning them to live alone and secluded, in the midst of all that is lovely and attractive in the social relations of life.

HEALTH OF THE CITY.

The character of New Orleans, in respect to health, has been much and unjustly abused. At the north, in ratio to their population, the consumption annually destroys more than the yellow fever of the south. Patients with pulmonary complaints, resort to these latitudes for relief, where such diseases are otherwise rarely known. In truth, this capital shows a more favorable bill of mortality, than any seaport town in the United States.

MORALS.

There is little to be said in favor of the morals of New Orleans, during the first few years after its cession. Report made them much worse than they were. As the community was composed of some of the worst classes of society, gathered from every region under the sun, nothing very good was to be expected. But circumstances have changed. A system of wholesome police regulations has been introduced and enforced, which has either brought the desperate and the lawless under subjection, or expelled them from the community. By reference to the statistics of crime, in other commercial cities in proportion to the number of inhabitants, the stranger will be convinced that this City has reason to be proud of her standing. Personal security in the public streets, at all hours, is never endangered—and females may venture out after dark, without a protector, and be free from insult and molestation.

THE PROFESSIONS.

The learned professions here, generally, stand preeminently high. The science of medicine may boast of a talent and a skill, that would confer honor upon any city in the Union—and the few empirics that disgrace the practice, are so well known that the evil is circumscribed within very narrow limits. The clergy are proverbial for their learning and eloquence—and the same remarks will apply with equal force to members of the bar.

PUBLIC LIBRARY.

This city, at the present time, possesses no public library. Considering the population, and their ability, this must be regarded as a blot upon the intelligence of its citizens. This is completely a commercial community, however, and money is the universal ambition. Thence springs that acknowledged deficiency in literature and the fine arts, observable to the stranger. But shall it still remain? Is there no Girard—no Astor—among our millionaires, who will leave behind them a monument which shall make their names dearer and more honored in all coming time, than those of heroes and conquerors!

SOCIETIES.

The Masonic fraternity in New Orleans appears to enjoy all their ancient privileges. There are some sixty-five lodges, besides a grand lodge and an encampement. Here is a large number of the order of Odd Fellows, and one of Equal Fellows—a Typographical Union, and Mechanics, Hibernian, St. Andrews, German, and Swiss societies. These are all, more or less, of a benevolent nature; and within their own circles, have all been extremely serviceable.

THE MISSISIPPI.

The navigation of the Missisipi, even by steamboats, in 1818, was extremely tedious. The Etna is recorded as arriving at Shipping port, a few miles below Louisville, in

DR. WARREN STONE.

Louisiana National Bank,

—OF—

NEW ORLEANS.

United States Depository & Financial Agent,

OFFICERS:

JOSEPH H. OGLESBY, President,
A. LURIA, Cashier.

DIRECTORS:

J. F. D. LANIER,	W. A. JOHNSON,
J. N. LEA,	T. L. AIREY,
JULIUS VAIRIN,	W. J. FRIERSON,

JOSEPH H. OGLESBY.

Incorporated, December 30th, 1865.

Commenced Business, January 18th, 1866.

CAPITAL STOCK, $1,000,000.

SURPLUS FUND, $150,000.

Total Net Earnings, Commencement of Business, (exclusive of taxes) to July 1, 1872, $712,272.[illegible]

Total Dividends, Commencement of Business, (exclusive of taxes) to July 1, 1872, $530,000.

thirty-two days. The Governor Shelby in *twenty-two* days, was considered as a remarkably short passage. An hermaphrodite brig was *seventy one* days from New Orleans—and a keel boat *one hundred and one*; the latter to Louisville. Now the time occupied is *four* to *five* days.

During the business season, which continues from the first of November to July, the levee, to the extent of five miles, is crowded with vessels of all sizes, but more especially ships, from every part of the world—with hundreds of immense floating castles and palaces, called steamboats; and barges and flatboats innumerable. No place can present a more busy, bustling scene. The loading and unloading of vessels and steamboats—the transportation, by some three thousand drays, of cotton, sugar, tobacco and the various and extensive produce of the great West, strikes the stranger with wonder and admiration. The levee and piers that range along the whole length of the city, extending back on an average of some two hundred feet, are continually covered with moving merchandize. This was once a pleasant promenade, where the citizen enjoyed his delightful morning and evening walk; but now there is scarcely room amid hogsheads, boxes and bales, for the business men to crowd along, without a sharp lookout for his personal safety.

COMMERCIAL EMPORIUM.

The position of New Orleans, as a vast commercial emporium, is unrivalled—as will be seen by a single glance at the map of the United States. As the depot of the West, and the half-way house of foreign trade, it is almost impossible to anticipate its future magnitude.

Take a view, for instance, of the immense regions known under the name of the Mississippi valley. Its boundaries on the West are the Rocky Mountains, and Mexico; on the South, the Gulf of Mexico; on the East the Alleghany mountains; and, on the North, the Lakes and British possessions. It contains nearly as many square miles, and more tillable ground, than all continental Europe, and, if peopled as densely as England, would sustain a population of five hundred millions—more than half of the present inhabitants of the earth. Its surface is generally cultivable, and its soil rich, with a climate varying to suit all products, for home consumption or a foreign market. The Mississippi is navigable twenty-one hundred miles—passing a small portage three thousand may be achieved. It embraces the productions of many climates, and a mining country abounding in coal, lead, iron and copper ore, all in veins of wonderful richness. The Missouri stretches thirty-nine hundred miles to the Great Falls, among the Flat Foot Indians, and five thousand miles from New Orleans. The Yellow Stone, navigable for eleven hundred miles, the Platte for sixteen hundred, and the Kansas for twelve hundred, are only tributaries to the latter river. The Ohio is two thousand miles to Pittsburgh, receiving into her bosom from numerous streams, the products of New York, Pennsylvania, Ohio, Kentucky, Western Virginia, Tennessee, Indiana, and Illinois. The Arkansas, Big Black, Yazoo, Red River, and many others, all pouring their wealth into the main artery, the Mississippi, upon whose mighty current it floats down to its grand reservoir, New Orleans.

ALGIERS

DRY DOCKS.

For the repair of shipping and river craft, our port is supplied with several extensive dry docks along the Algiers Levee.

THE OCEAN DOCK.

This is located near the landing of the First and Second District ferryboats at Bartholomew street. It is [illegible] feet long in the clear and 60 feet beam, with capacity for a ship of a thousand tons, 225 feet keel and drawing fifteen feet. For the service of the dock there is a steam saw mill, and a smith's shop is also attached. The number of mechanics and laborers employed during a busy season is from fifty to one hundred. The officers of the Ocean Dock company for 1872 were Messrs. Spencer Field, President and Treasurer, J. B. Williams, Secretary and F. G. Mackie and J. F. Follett, Managers.

THE MARINE DOCK.

This adjoins the Ocean Dock below, and has a front of 500 feet by 250 feet deep. It has capacity for a ship of 1600 tons. The two Peruvian Monitors were recently repaired in this dock. The officers of the company are Messrs. S. Hopkins, Jr., President; C. E. Morrison, Secretary and J. Geddes, Treasurer.

THE VALLETTE DOCK.

This is located at the foot of Vallette street, a block below the landing of the Third District ferry. It has a frontage of about 100 feet on Patterson street, with a depth of 290 feet to the river. The dock is 315 feet long by 84 feet beam, with capacity for the largest ships that come into this port. It employs a blacksmith shop and a saw mill, with several gangs of saws. From 75 to 150 men are employed in ship building and repairing. The dock is owned by a joint stock company, under the special management of Messrs. François Vallette and Octave F. Vallette, Paul Fouchy, President; and Roger T. Boyle, Secretary.

THE GOOD INTENT DRY DOCK.

This is located just above the Algiers landing of the Canal street ferry. The grounds of the company have a river frontage of one and a half squares and a depth of 150 feet. The dock measures 200 feet in length by 50 feet in breadth inboard. The works employ from 60 to 100 men. The affairs of the company are managed by four directors, the present being Messrs. S. Hopkins, Jr., G. Busing, Hermann Schroeder, Secretary, and John H. Reiners.

The manufacture of ice, in New Orleans, is now successfully and profitably carried on. A view of the works is to be found on another page, and will give some idea of the extensive scale on which the business is conducted.

HON. CHARLES GAYARRE.

THIS distinguished Louisianian, whose historical and literary labors have made his name familiar to the *literati* of this country and of Europe, was born in New Orleans in 1805. He is of mixed Spanish and French descent, his paternal ancestor, Don Esteban Gayarré, having come here in 1766 with Governor Ulloa as *Contad* or Comptroller of the province of Louisiana, which had just then been ceded by France to Spain. His grand-mother in the female line was the daughter of Destrehan, who, for a long time, had been the treasurer of the colony under the French, and his maternal grand-father was Etienne Boré, who was the first to make sugar in Louisiana in 1795, and was Mayor of New Orleans under the French Republic in 1803. Among his ancestors were also the Grandpré's who were the companions of Bienville and Iberville, and whose descendants occupied important military positions under the French and Spanish dominions. Charles Gayarré was educated at the "College d'Orléans" then conducted by Lakanal, the celebrated member of the French Convention, who was then an exile in Louisiana. In this college some of the most distinguished men of this state received their diplomas. In 1826, Mr. Gayarré went to Philadelphia and studied law in the office of William Rawle, then at the head of the bar of that city and well known as the author of an excellent work on the constitution of the United States. In 1829 the subject of this sketch was admitted to the bar, and in 1830 he returned to Louisiana, where he published, in French, an "Historical Essay on Louisiana." In the same year, he was almost unanimously elected to the State Legislature, and was chosen by that body to write the complimentary address sent by them to the French people on the occasion of the Revolution of 1830. He was appointed assistant Attorney General in 1831, and two years later, he was called to the office of presiding judge of the City Court of New Orleans. In 1835, although he was a Democr and the Whigs had a majority of the legislature, Mr. Ga arre was elected to the Senate of the U. S. for six yea three of his political opponents having voted for him. U fortunately the wretched condition of Mr. Gayarré's hea prevented him from taking his seat, and in obedience to t advice of his physicians, he had to go to Europe, where remained until the end of 1843. Shortly after his retu he was elected to the legislature from the city of N. O., a carried several important measures, among others a bill provide for the liabilities of the State, whereby a reducti of two millions and a half of the State debt was effect during Gov. Mouton's administration. Having been elected in 1846, he accepted the office of Secretary of St tendered to him by Gov. Isaac Johnson, an office of ve great importance and responsibility at the time, as in ad tion to his other duties, the Secretary of State was *ex off* Superintendent of Public Education, and constituted join with the State Treasurer, the "Board of Currency." In t laborious position, the multifarious duties of which he c charged with great benefit to the State, Mr. Gayarré mained till 1853, having been re-appointed by Govern Walker in 1850. During that period, Mr. Gayarré pu lished in two volumes a "History of Louisiana," in French language, and in which all the most interesting c curious documents he had collected from the archives France were textually reproduced. He also publish through Harper & Co., of New York, a series of lectu in English under the title of the "Romance of the Hist of Louisiana."

The State library of Baton Rouge, with its valuable h torical works and documents collected by Mr. Gaya during his seven years term of office, was almost tota destroyed during the war. A few years before that eve Mr. Gayarré had succeeded in obtaining from the Span government important documents from the archives the Kingdom, the substance of which he embodied in "History of Louisiana," in three volumes, octavo, embr ing the French, Spanish and American régimes, from earliest settlement of the colony to the year 1861—a wo which may justly be considered as the most valuable c tribution ever made to the history of our State. This wo has already passed through several editions. After a b connection with the American or Know-nothing par which he left at once when his efforts to strike out the an catholic plank of their platform proved unavailing, and unsuccessful run for Congress as an independent candid Mr. Gayarré supported the candidacy of President Pier and his name was prominently mentioned in connect with the Mission to Spain on the accession of the new ministration. That appointment, however, having b first tendered to Senator Soulé, Mr. Marcy, then Secret of State, offered to Mr. Gayarré the position of Assist Secretary, just then created, and in which his extens knowledge of European affairs and fine linguistic atta ments would have proved eminently useful to the Adm istration. His offer, however, was declined by Mr. G arre. In 1861, Mr. Gayarré, having been called upon his views on the right of Secession, addressed an imme meeting of citizens at Odd Fellows' Hall, taking a stro

THE STEAMBOAT LANDING.

State rights view of the subject. During the war, Mr. Gayarré advocated the arming of the slaves and the conclusion of a treaty with England and France recognizing the independence of the Southern Confederacy on the basis of a gradual emancipation of the African race. In 1866, when Louisiana was presumed to be reconstructed, Mr. Gayarré's name was put forward by his friends in the Legislature, and came within a few votes of obtaining the honor of an election to the United States Senate—Messrs. Randal Hunt and G. Williamson, his successful competitors, having been denied admittance to that body. Since the war, Mr. Gayarré, besides the last volume of his great historical work on Louisiana, has published a "*History of Philip II.*" of Spain—a work of great research and sound historical philosophy and a novel based on the early history of Louisiana, "*Fernando de Lemos*," which has elicited great praise from all the literary journals of the country. He is now preparing for publication another historical novel, "Aubert Dubayet," in which the hero goes through the American Revolution of 1776 and the French revolution of 1789. It will doubtless prove highly interesting, and give ample scope to the writer's wide field of information and fertility of conception.

HON. MILES TAYLOR.

This gentleman, who is one of the best civil lawyers in this State, was born in New York about sixty years ago. He is small of stature, gray haired, fair complexioned and bright eyed.

When quite young he came to this State and devoted his attention to the study of the law. He passed an excellent examination before the Supreme Court, and obtained his license to practice. As Mr. Taylor had previously studied pharmacy, old Judge Eisley with naiveté said at the time of his admission to the bar, that Mr. Taylor would be unrivaled in bringing an apothecary (hypothecary) action.

Mr. Taylor has proved to be one of our most eminent lawyers. He is certainly a gentleman of vast talents, profoundly read in law, and trained to grapple closely with every question. He is distinguished for grace and ease of manner, and for happy and polished address.

He exerts great influence on the mind and affection of those who know him.

He is a good speaker, clear and correct in diction. Endowed by nature with a quick and vigorous understanding, his arguments are vivid, and he shows in all the cases intrusted to him, honesty of purpose, earnestness and faithfulness. Even at his advanced age he is most diligent and attentive to business.

Mr. Taylor has represented Louisiana in the Congress of the United States when that body contained the most brilliant array of ability ever seen in any deliberate assembly. He there distinguished himself as a polished debater, achieved a high position, and stood on the same plane as the most prominent statesman who adorned the halls of the National Legislature.

THE ST. MARY'S MARKET fronts on Tchoupitoulas street and runs to New Levee. It was completed in 1836 in the rusticated Doric order at a cost of about $48,000.

MAYOR JOHN L. LEWIS.

Of all the members of the old population of New Orleans, there is no one who is better known, and more universally esteemed by all classes than the subject of this sketch. John Lawson Lewis is the son of Judge Lewis, who was appointed to the Supreme Bench of the then Territory of Orleans by Thomas Jefferson, immediately after the purchase of Louisiana from France. Mr. Lewis was then only three years old, and was brought up at the school of Mr. D'Hebecourt, on the old Bayou Road, where he had for his schoolmates many of the creoles who afterward took a leading part in the politics of the State, and afterward completed his studies at the Academy of the Rev. James F. Hull, on Canal street. In 1819, young Lewis left school and read law under his father, entering shortly after the office of Martin Gordon, Sr., then Chief Clerk of the First District Court, to which position he succeeded upon the resignation of Mr. Gordon, in 1826. In 1842, John L. Lewis was unanimously elected Commanding General of the First Division of the Louisiana Militia, an office for which he was peculiarly fitted by his previous military training and his great personal influence, and to which he was invariable re-elected without the shadow of an opposition. In 1845, he ran as an independent candidate for the Shrievalty of the Parish of Orleans, and though opposed by several of our most popular citizens, was returned at the head of the poll. So ably did he administer the office, that on three successive occasions he was re-elected by handsome majorities, sometimes in the face of a formidable party opposition, and when, some years later, an effort was made to defeat the hitherto invincible A. D. Crossman, Gen. Lewis accepted the nomination of the Democratic Party for the Mayoralty, and although the ticket upon which he ran was beaten, so great was his personal popularity that he was returned over his competitor by a small majority. When the war broke out Gen. Lewis, although not liable to military service, promptly offered his sword to the Confederate Government, and served throughout the war with great gallantry and distinction in the Trans-Mississippi Department. As a public officer, Gen. Lewis has always maintained the reputation of an able, courteous and incorruptible public servant. A high-toned, affable gentleman, ever generous and open-handed whenever his means allowed him to indulge the warm impulses of his nature, few men of his generation can claim a larger circle of attached friends, or after occupying so many responsible positions, are able to exhibit more unexceptionable record than John L. Lewis.

The following letter, written by Gov. H. W. Allen to Gen. Lewis, soon after the battle of Mansfield, shows the high estimation in which Gen. Lewis's services were held by that distinguished official :—

SHREVEPORT, LA., April 27, 1864.

GEN. LEWIS:

MY DEAR SIR,—I have just heard from you through Mr. Wagner. I am rejoiced to hear that you are doing well. I sent my surgeon-General down to take care of you. He reported that you were doing well.

Receive my thanks, my dear sir, and the thanks of Louisiana for your gallant conduct on the battle-field of one of the best fought battles of this war. If you visit Shreveport do not fail to call on me. I shall be glad to receive you at the Executive Mansion and extend all the courtesy that a brave patriot and gallant soldier.

Very truly your obedient servant,

(Signed.) HENRY W. ALLEN, Gov. Louisiana.

To Gen. John L. Lewis, Mansfield, La.

ROBERT MOTT ESQ.

Is a native of Baltimore, Md., of fair complexion, classical features, of commanding appearance and about fifty-seven years of age. He is open and above everything like dissimulation, warmly affectionate and steadfast in friendship.

As a lawyer, the clearness of his statement presents at once a picture to the mind. In his arguments he appeals forcibly to strict reason, and his tone, though deferential and courtly, is manly. He indulges very sparingly in declamation.

He is one of the best civil, commercial and chancery lawyers in this State, with an uncommon capacity for effective and untiring industry. His legal studies have been comprehensive. He writes with great facility and clearness, exhibiting philosophical research and maturity of judgment.

Several years ago, he served as a member in the State Legislature of Louisiana with much ability. After our late war, he went to Europe and visited the principal cities of the Old World.

Mr. Mott is now in the full vigor of all his faculties, active in his movements and in turning off business with as much ease as when he entered public life thirty years ago. He is kindly in his disposition, so as to devote some of his time and resources to making others happy—domestic and affectionate in his habits, and religious without intolerance.

He is a cautious and safe counsellor, a diligent man of business, punctual to his appointments, regular in the distribution of his time, never suffering pleasure or distraction of any kind to interfere with his duties.

JOSEPH H. OGLESBY

IS DESCENDED from Scottish ancestry. His father, the Rev. Joseph Oglesby, D.D., was born in West Moreland, Virginia, the native county of Washington and Lee. His mother, Elizabeth Hite, was born in the Valley of the Shenandoah. His grandfather removed to Kentucky, and the father and mother of Mr. Oglesby subsequently removed from Kentucky to Madison, in Indiana, at which place the subject of this sketch was born September 14, 1822. In 1839, Mr. Oglesby came to New Orleans, and was employed as a clerk in the house of Hyde & Comstock, Poydras street. In the year 1842, Mr. Comstock retired, and at the early age of twenty, Mr. Oglesby became a partner in the Western produce commission house of Hyde & Oglesby. The house did a large and profitable business, and upon the withdrawal of Mr. Hyde, was continued under the style of Oglesby & McCaulay, which was a leading house in the Western trade, at the declaration of civil hostilities in 1861.

Upon the termination of the war, Mr. Oglesby resumed business under his own name, in the same street in which he has been engaged in the same trade for a period of about thirty years. Perhaps few cities have undergone the same mutations of commerce within the same period. An inspection of the Directory of 1846, shows that of about 300 firms engaged in the commission business at that date, only eleven exist at present under the same style, while very few of the members who composed these firms are in business at all. To have pursued the same business, in the same community, amid such vicissitudes of commerce, and for so long a period, displays a sound texture of character and systematic business habits. After a period of mercantile probation so long and so successful, it was natural that Mr. Oglesby should have been promoted to the charge of the associated interests of his fellow merchants. The highest and most disinterested evidence of commercial ap-

WM. H. BELL, ESQ.,

CITY SURVEYOR

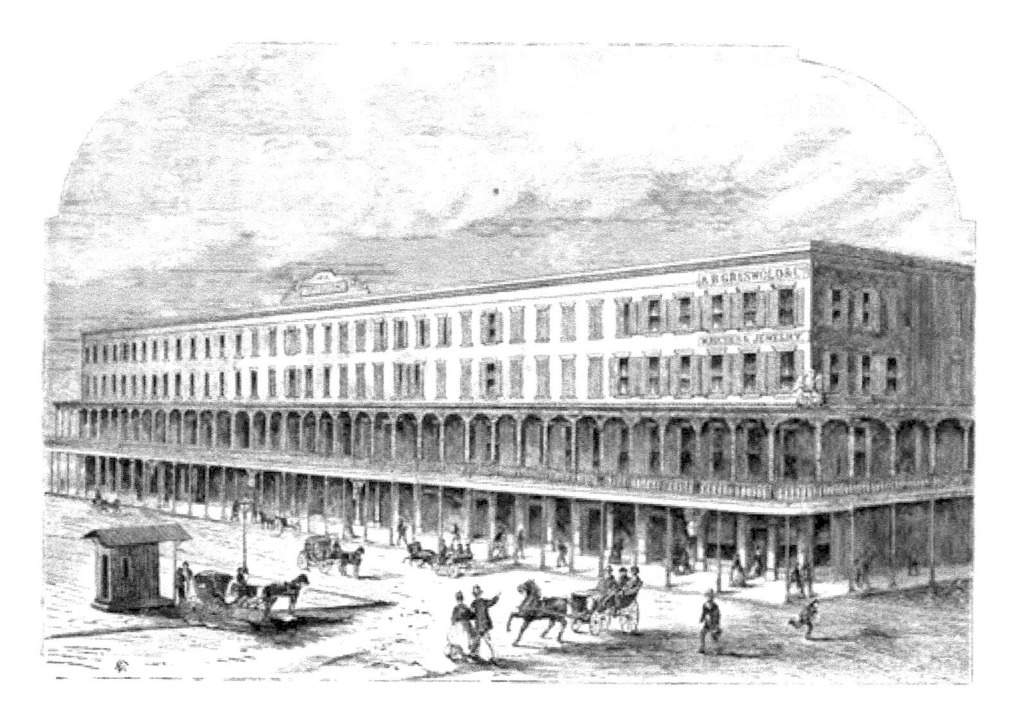

TOURO BUILDINGS.

preciation was, of course, his election as President of the Chamber of Commerce, in which office he is now serving his second term.

In 1869, he was elected President of the Louisiana National Bank, one of our largest financial institutions. As we believe much of the capital stock has been subscribed abroad, the appointment shows that the reputation of Mr. Oglesby is appreciated by other commercial communities besides his own. In the same year he was chosen President of the Commercial Insurance Company, of New Orleans. He was also tendered, at the same period, the office of Mayor of the City of New Orleans, and was solicited by citizens, without distinction of party, to accept it. This important position he was, after much deliberation and in consequence of official and domestic obligations, compelled to decline. The discharge of the trusts accepted by Mr. Oglesby with the superintendence and consultations of his own commercial house demands very unusual faculties. It requires moreover that extended experience which, by knowing and being known to the men and commerce of a community, secures accuracy and dispatch of administration. Nothing except the combination of those qualities could enable Mr. Oglesby to wield the vast and complicated duties so conferred upon him. This, however, he seems to do with comparative ease. He has even, by dint of systematic organization and judicious choice of subordinates, been enabled to spare extended portions of the years 1869-70-71 to be devoted to a tour in Europe. In addition to the education of his children and the care of the health of Mrs. Oglesby, he has thus had an opportunity to observe the commercial and social systems of other countries. It may be mentioned at this point that Mr. Oglesby married Miss Margaret Hendricks. This estimable lady died August 24, 1871, at Paris, France, leaving to her afflicted husband the comparative consolation of a family of interesting and well-reared children.

Mr. Oglesby has been enabled by his experience at home and his observations abroad to render to New Orleans invaluable services toward the restoration of her commerce. The extraordinary result to which we have adverted elsewhere, by which an artificial system of transportation has wrested from New Orleans so much of her natural and immediate territory, has compelled her to adopt a countervailing economy and dispatch in conducting the trade of this debateable region; no one has been more sagacious than Mr. Oglesby in perceiving this inevitable conflict, or more prompt in adopting a counteracting commercial strategy. The ancient mode of receiving, storing, and forwarding by produce sail vessels, no longer met the demands of the interior. Even a part of the cotton crop immediately adjacent to our market began to feel the influence of these competing facilities. The Western surplus of provisions once exclusively exported, foreign and coastwise, through our port, was taken across direct to Eastern Atlantic ports for exportation, while the European imports, consumed in the interior, took the same route. This formidable invasion rendered necessary the construction of new and the extension of incomplete railroads into Louisiana, Texas, and Mexico. It also required improved facilities of importation and transmission of goods in bond. It was also necessary to establish close connection between the rail and river, with all other facilities for protection and dispatch of commodities in transit, as employed by our competitors elsewhere.

It became necessary to establish a cheap and certain transportation by river barges, the storage, transfer, and shelter of bulk grain and other products by elevator, with an organization of ocean steam line adequate to the dispatch of our staple crops, and other commerce. To each and all of these Mr. Oglesby has given the influence of his approbation and the aid of his capital. It is under such auspices that New Orleans bids fair to replace the commerce of which she has been despoiled, with an infinitely greater, for which she can never fear a rival. In enumerating the men who have contributed signally to maintain and advance the commercial destinies of our city, it is our duty to assign a most prominent position to Joseph H. Oglesby, Esq. With unimpaired health and energies, and enlarged capacity for continued usefulness, we may enjoy the benefit of his counsel and action until the crisis of commercial competition shall have passed from New Orleans, and the object of her restoration effected.

THOMAS H. KENNEDY, ESQ.

Judge Thomas H. Kennedy is an eminent jurist and a man of unblemished honor.

He was born in New Orleans, and is now nearly fifty years old. He is of slight but manly form, black haired, with high and broad forehead and eagle eyes.

He is thoroughly acquainted with the ancient and modern writers, and speaks several foreign languages fluently.

With culture, a keen intellect and much force of character, he is always prepared for a full discharge of his duties.

The genial current of his soul is not frozen by calculating policy. He loathes the cold and sordid propensity of clinging to power so epidemic in our day.

Endowed with the highest faculties of the understanding, despising all the surface accomplishments that dazzle the vulgar, he has an immovable fortitude in all those situations in which human weakness is most apt to yield.

His devotion to the maintenance of principle is embellished by modesty. These rare qualities are not only worthy of admiration, but of imitation in this degenerate age.

This true and worthy gentleman acts always so as to satisfy his own conscience. How very few like him!

Judge Kennedy is not only a man of firm mind and steadily fixed principles, but he is also a person of great accomplishments and excellent abilities as a lawyer.

Educated in the study of the civil law at one of our best colleges, he resided long enough in Europe to perfect his learning in all the ordinary branches of education.

Those of our readers who are personally acquainted with him will bear me witness that he is the most unpretending of men. His abilities and virtues make him an ornament of society.

He was for many years before our late war Judge of the Third District Court. At that time it was a high honor to occupy such a position, because the judicial ermine was then kept in all its purity. Since then how many changes!

LA. EQUITABLE LIFE INSURANCE COMPANY.

The business of Life Insurance in this country is of such recent growth that few people appreciate its importance and greatness. Beginning only about a quarter of a century ago from the most slender foundation it has grown into mammoth proportions. The combined assets of the various companies is estimated to exceed $250,000,000 with an amount of insurance at risk exceeding $2,000,000,000. The annual income exceeds a hundred millions of dollars. The influence of these corporations outside of the good they do to the widows and orphans of deceased policy holders, is paramount in every place that they are located. Their funds requiring prompt and speedy investment furnish means for commercial and industrial enterprises that otherwise might not have been initiated.

It was plainly seen after the war that one of the surest ways of rebuilding the prosperity of the South was the establishment of Home Life Insurance Cos. It was with this view that in the year 1869 a number of the most prominent gentlemen in New Orleans formed the Louisiana Equitable Life Insurance Co. under the management of Joseph Ellison Esq. an old time merchant of this city and one of its best known citizens as President, and Wm. P. Harper as Secretary, the Company began its career and notwithstanding the opposition it met with it steadily kept on its way, daily adding to its list of customers, and finding fresh favor in the eyes of the community and particularly of those who felt it their interest and duty to support Home Institutions. In the latter part of 1870 the official staff of the Company was increased by the appointment of Mr. Wm. C. Robbins as Manager of Agencies. Mr. Robbins' long experience in the business was of great value to the Company, and under his intelligent management its business grew rapidly and was extended into the adjacent states. In September 1872, owing to the resignation of Messrs. Ellison and Harper, Mr. James H. Low, formerly of the firm of Wood & Low, and Wm. Henderson, Esq., were respectively elected to the positions of President and Secretary. These gentlemen, in conjunction with Mr. Robbins have, by their earnest efforts, placed the Company in a position worthy of the city that gave it birth. The Board of Directors are composed of the first business men of the city. Their names are known throughout the whole country and give it a standing wherever it may be introduced. The Company has, by its promptness in settlement of claims, and the liberality of its plans earned a widely-spread reputation and it would be safe to prophesy that the day is not far distant when the Louisiana Equitable Life will stand among the foremost companies of the country.

TIVOLI CIRCLE is an unornamented public ground, circular in form and about 150 yards in diameter. It is surrounded by a wide pavement and is enclosed in an iron railing with four gateways. The circle is capable of such improvement as will add greatly to the attractiveness of the locality and to the comfort of citizens. From this point St. Charles street expands to double its width below the circle and becomes a broad and magnificent avenue. The New Masonic Temple, the Temple Sinai and the residence of Andrew Smith Esq overlook this Circle.

NEW ORLEANS GAS-LIGHT COMPANY.

In 1822, when Baltimore was the only American city lighted by gas, James H. Caldwell, Esq., an enterprising citizen of New Orleans, constructed works here for lighting his theatre, the old American. A gas company was formed in 1828, but failing in compliance with the terms of its charter, it was soon dissolved. In 1833 Mr. Caldwell obtained a charter, and in the face of many difficulties, and by his own resources, he established the Gas Works on a large scale and on a permanent basis. Mr. Caldwell also introduced gas in Cincinnati and Havana. He was long a member of the City Council, and foremost in measures of enterprise and public benefaction. The oddly sounding and usually mispronounced classical and mythological names of many of our streets above canal, were chiefly of Mr. Caldwell's suggestion while he was an alderman and our Fourth District a swamp.

The New Orleans Gaslight and Banking Company was chartered by the General Assembly in 1835, with a capital stock of six million dollars. By this charter it was provided that the Gas Works might be bought by the City after forty years. The charge for gas was at first regulated by the time of burning; afterwards meters were introduced. In 1860 an amendment to the charter limited the charge to $4 per thousand cubic feet of gas, required gas to be supplied to the Charity Hospital free, extended the term of the Company to 1895 and withdrew the exclusive privilege of furnishing gas. The capital of the Company is now about two millions. The works, a mile from the river, are bounded by Gravier, Perdido, Magnolia and Locust streets, the slate roofed brick buildings occupying the entire square. On the grounds are shops for blacksmiths, carpenters, and machinists, for the manufacture and repair of articles and implements used, except the clay retorts, which are brought from Belgium, of which there are 290 in operation. The interesting process of making gas, differs in no essential respect from the well-known method employed elsewhere, the coke and coal tar being utilized. To remove the carbonic acid and sulphuretted hydrogen gas, quick-lime is used made entirely of oyster shells. The Pittsburgh coal employed produces 10,500 cubic feet of gas per ton. The reservoirs are six in number the largest being of more than half a million cubic feet.

The gas consumed in 1846 was 31,252,000 feet; in 1856, 85,421,000 feet; in 1866, 174,649,000 feet; in 1871, 289,417,000 feet. The present number of street lamps is 3476; of meters over 10,000. The gas pipe in 1836, was eight miles in length; in 1846, 23 miles; in 1856, 61½ miles; in 1866, 100 miles; and in 1872, 134½ miles.

The Presidents of the company were: in 1835 James H. Caldwell; in 1835-36, E. Yorke; in 1836, Samuel Hermann, Jr.; in 1836-37 and '38, Thomas Barrett; in 1838-39 and '40, Thomas C. [illegible]; from 1840 to 1856, James Robb; from 1856 to 1863, J. H. Wood; in 1863, W. H. Mercer; from 1863 to 1869, G. C. Duncan; from 1869 and present incumbent, James Jackson.

D. H. HOLMES,

155 Canal and 15 Bourbon Streets,

NEW ORLEANS.

FOUNDED APRIL 22, 1842.

DIRECT IMPORTATION

OF

Dry Goods.

Dealer in

ALL KINDS OF

American Dry Goods,

AT

WHOLESALE & RETAIL.

41 RUE DE LE CHIQUIER,
PARIS.

94 CHURCH STREET,
NEW YORK.

MAYOR JOHN R. CONWAY.

JOHN R. CONWAY was born in Alexandria, Virginia, August 24th 1825. His ancestors were from Wales, and emigrated to the State of his nativity in the reign of Charles the Second. Their exists now among their descendants, family portraits brought over from England at the time of their settlement on the Potomac, antique relics of the days of the Stuarts, and prized as mementoes of the men who, in common with all Virginia, repudiated Cromwell and his Roundheads, adhering under all circumstances to the fortunes and dynasty of Charles the First and Charles the Second, and the Cavaliers of the Restoration.

Mr. Conway came to New Orleans in December 1843, and actively engaged in a mercantile life, being connected with one of the largest Commission and Cotton firms in a position of great trust and responsibility to the time of the capture of the City, in April 1862, by the Federal forces. Business being thenceforth suspended in all of its legitimate branches, and in common with his Southern friends and neighbors, he made no effort to resume his own during the military occupation of the city.

At the close of hostilities in 1865 he again embarked in mercantile business as a Wholesale Grocer and Commission Merchant, which was successfully carried on up to 1867. During this time, and at all times since his residence in New Orleans, it was well known that he never considered it inconsistent with the business of a merchant to take an active part in public affairs, but on the other hand regarded it a duty to do so. Hence always acting in concert with the Democracy, he was selected Chairman of the Democratic Parish Committee on its first reorganization after the war. Cooperating with the State Executive Committee the way was prepared for returning the State and City to the representatives of the people, the latter at least having been for more than four years wholly under Military rulers.

On the reorganization of the City Government, he was appointed by Governor Wells a member of the Police Board, presided over by the newly selected Mayor, John T. Monroe. He served in this capacity until removed by General Sheridan under the Reconstruction Act. Under the Supplemental Reconstruction Act of Congress an election was held for municipal officers on the 17th and 18th of April 1868. Mr. Conway having received the Democratic nomination for Mayor of New Orleans was elected by seven hundred majority.

Mr. Conway being the first Mayor elected by the people since the occupation of the city by the Federal authorities, necessarily found the affairs of the city in a complicated condition, and his administration of the city government was unavoidably attended by serious difficulties. The finances were in a deplorable condition and the credit of the city at a very low ebb. But with the substitution of the civil for military law, confidence was restored and gradually city securities improved in value, and fair promise was held out that the financial *status* of New Orleans would again reach that eminent standard it enjoyed before the war.

HON. JOHN A. CAMPBELL.

HON. JOHN A. CAMPBELL was born in the State of Georgia. He graduated at Athens, in that State, in 1830, when twenty years of age. He is now sixty-five. He is above the medium size, has blue eyes, light complexion, expansive forehead and classical features.

He was, before our late war for independence, one of the Judges of the Supreme Court of the United States, and in 1865 represented the Confederate States, together with Mr. Hunter, of Virginia, and Mr. Stephens, of Georgia, in the interview had by them with Mr. Lincoln and Secretary Seward, at Hampton Roads, in order to bring about a compromise between the North and the South.

He possesses a most extraordinary memory, and frequently refers, when consulted upon a decision or authority, to the number of volume and page in books he has not handled for years.

Judge Campbell is one of the greatest lawyers in the United States. He is certainly a most accomplished advocate. He confines himself to powerful argument and never indulges in declamation. His clearness of statement and the force and precision of his language are remarkable. His manner is above the common order of forensic delivery. His wit is not genial or playful, but sarcastic.

It is related of Judge Campbell that being asked by a young attorney of New Orleans, not distinguished for his talents, whether he (Judge C.) had any objection to the attorney joining in a great case at that time conducted by Judge Campbell and other eminent lawyers, he answered: "Most certainly not, my dear sir, provided you do not appear on m side."

His mind is eminently fertile in resources. He compresses his matter vigorously and reasons cogently.

He is known to be, in his personal character, of scrupulous integrity and unsullied honor.

EDWARD H. SUMMERS, ESQ.

If enterprise, public spirit, liberality, firmness and devotion to the great interests of commerce, entitle any individual to respect and consideration in this community, no one is more richly deserving of them, than the unpretending but influential gentleman, whose name stands at the head of this notice.

Mr. Summers was born in Bullitt County, Kentucky, September 28th, 1827. We presume his father was in easy circumstances, able to give his son the advantages of a liberal education, for, after completing his preparatory studies, we find that he entered Bethany College, Virginia, where he graduated in July, 1846, at the early age of nineteen years.

His first intention was to pursue the law as a profession, for which he accordingly prepared himself, and graduated in the Law Department of Transylvania University, Lexington, Ky., in 1848.

On attaining majority, he abandoned the law, and, in 1850, devoted himself to mercantile business in Louisville.

In 1857, he removed to New Orleans, where he has remained ever since, engaged in the commission business.

In 1869, he was elected President of the Crescent City National Bank, which position he now holds.

In 1871 Mr. Summers was chiefly instrumental in organizing the New Orleans Cotton Exchange—the most important movement that has yet been made in this great court of commerce. In consequence of the energy which he displayed in originating this important association, Mr. Summers was elected its first President, and, at the annual election the second year, he was again elected. After two years service, he declined a reelection. On which occasion he made a speech distinguished for its ability and eloquence, and which exhibits in glowing colors the important consequences which have resulted from this great movement of our merchants and which will be likely still further to flow from it in promoting our commercial prosperity.

We cannot better portray the traits which distinguish the character of this high-toned merchant than by giving some extracts from this admirable speech. The wretched condition to which New Orleans was reduced by the late unhappy war, and the necessity of resorting to some extraordinary measures for the extrication and the restoration of its commerce is thus eloquently referred to by him.

"When that long and devastating war," said Mr. Summers, "was ended, we found our beloved city crippled in her commerce on every side. The necessities of a mighty nation, battling against us, had greatly aided in tapping, at many points, the great artery of our commerce, the grand old Father of Waters, and our products were being taken from our very doors to the great Atlantic cities, where wealth, capital and prosperity all invited them, our cotton factors, at the same time, found themselves embarrassed by the indorsement of planters' paper, the main security having vanished by the fate of war.

"But we went to work with a will, settled our debts as best we could, and launched our little barks again into the great sea of commerce.

"Scarcely had we emerged into the open sea before the great storm of 1867 struck us with all its force. Our planters, with the pittance left them, had gone to work in good earnest, and with the brightest hopes of a good harvest. The disastrous results you all know. Suffice it to say that this unexpected and most lamentable failure of crops, together with the levels of Federal, State and Parish Collectors, was more than our poverty-stricken planters could endure, and the result was wide-spread demoralization, bad faith and diversion of crops on all sides; but the cotton factors of this city had to breast this storm. We had to stand by our posts—to succumb was inevitable ruin. Our chief capital was our untarnished names, and I am proud to say that but few fell by the wayside.

"This year, however, gentlemen, taught us a wise but sad lesson, and that was, in the then disorganized and demoralized condition of our country, our main reliance was in the integrity, capacity, industry and good management of our constituents.

"It was absolutely necessary to separate the good from the bad; and to accomplish this, union and good faith and harmony among ourselves were indispensable. And, this, gentlemen, was the main and direct cause of the establishment of this Exchange.

"I am proud to say we were nobly seconded in our efforts by many of our prominent cotton buyers and cotton brokers, who, realizing that they had an interest in common with the cotton factor in the prosperity of our city, and feeling moreover the necessity of proper rules and regulations for the government of the cotton trade, which could only be accomplished by union of all, most heartily aided us in our efforts. And though we were met at the threshold by difficulties which would have disheartened and deterred a less resolute set of men, we never faltered. Every previous effort towards establishing an Exchange in this city had been a failure.

* * * * * *

"But nothing daunted, we worked faithfully, and manfully explained the necessity, and expatiated upon the advantages of union, and we finally succeeded in getting together a sufficient number to justify an organization.

"You honored me, at your first meeting, by electing me as your presiding officer; and whilst appreciating your motives, I am free to say that I entered upon the discharge of my duties with many misgivings. But, gentlemen, you surrounded me with godfathers over this infant institution—merchants of large business experience and sagacity, all animated by the same zeal, and fully conscious of the charge intrusted to them.

"Then, gentlemen, after two years of service, I deliver back into your hands this predicted abortion, this weakly suckling, a two years old commercial giant.

"During less than two years back, with an empty treasury, and a limited membership, we have regularly, daily, and, I may say, almost by the minute, furnished you with telegraphic news, embracing every point of the habitable globe where cotton was a prominent article of commerce. And, besides this, we have furnished you daily a table of statistics unsurpassed, if not unequalled, by any Exchange either in Europe or America.

A. S. BADGER,

CHIEF OF POLICE.

ST. CHARLES HOTEL.

RIVERS & LONSDALE, Proprietors.

"And whilst we have accomplished this at a necessarily heavy outlay, we return you to-night, as shown by the report of the Finance Committee, a surplus in our treasury of $43,234,80.

"I proclaim it to-night, and with just grounds for the assertion, that, under the auspices of the Cotton Exchange, which now embraces almost every respectable dealer in cotton, that no city, on this or any other continent, can handle this great staple with the same economy, the same ease, the same impartial justice as can the city of New Orleans.

"I reiterate to-night what I said twelve months ago, that this Exchange presents an 'anomaly' in the commercial history of the world, and to prove this, I have only to refer you to the report of our venerable Chief Justice of the Board of Errors and Appeals, read in your hearing this evening.

"Just think of it, gentlemen, receiving, storing and shipping one agricultural product, at our port, to the value annually of one hundred and twenty million dollars; having control of this staple from the time the seed is assigned to mother earth, until the gathering of the harvest, and the final disposition of the product; and yet, in all the various vicissitudes of this transposition, there is scarcely a ripple of contention or dispute among three hundred merchants handling and turning over the vast product.

"I defy the Exchanges of the world to produce such a record; and this, gentlemen, with our great cosmopolitan trade, embracing every nation known to the category of civilization. I say the City of New Orleans can have no prouder escutcheon than the records of this Exchange.

"But, gentlemen, this Exchange has not confined the sphere of its usefulness to the cotton interest alone. It has ever had a watchful eye to the great general commercial interest of this city, which is inseparably connected with the cotton interest of this great Southern emporium.

"In evidence of this, need I point you to the great iron barge enterprise, which had its origin in this Exchange and though it now sleeps with a subscription of $800,000, is, just as sure as time rolls on, to be revived and culminate in a magnificent fleet of cheap and safe and prosperous public carriers, bringing to us from the Alleghanies on the East to the Rocky Mountains on the West, the untold and most inestimable wealth of this great valley.

"This grand enterprise had its origin, its support and its partial success under the auspices of this Exchange. Who, gentlemen, was it that set on foot the great iron highway that is destined to connect us with that vast domain of wealth, the State of Texas? Was it not this Exchange that took Col. Scott, the great railroad king, by the hand, had him welcomed in our midst, and pledged ourselves, individually and collectively, that we would span the chasm that separated us from this great highway to the Pacific Ocean?

"Was it not within the walls of this Exchange that the noted and efficient Rail Road Committee of Fifty had its birth? And was it not through their unceasing labors that this great highway is guaranteed to us within the next twelve months?

"I have thus, gentlemen, passed in review the origin, advantages, labors and fruits of this Exchange—the first example in this city of the effect of union and energy and self-reliance amongst ourselves.

"After a service of two years, I beg, this night, to bid you an affectionate adieu as your presiding officer, my business engagements, as also my ideas of rotation in office, rendering it necessary and proper."

Should the "Cotton Exchange," in its future results to our commerce, sustain the well-founded expectations of its public-spirited projector, (as it has done in its past brief career), he will be well entitled to the lasting gratitude of this community as a public benefactor. Though he has declined to act longer as its President, the same public considerations which, in the midst of doubt and discouragement, led him to embark fearlessly in the enterprise, will, we are assured, induce him still to watch over its interests with ceaseless vigilance, and will enable him and the large body of intelligent merchants associated with him to redeem New Orleans from the sad consequences of the late war, and make her what, from her position, the spirit that animates her, and the energy and ability of her merchants, she is well entitled to be, the great cotton market of the world. He has himself only just reached the meridian of life, and a long career of usefulness still lies open before him.

FATHER J. MOYNAHAN.

This distinguished ecclesiastic was born in the Parish of Kontork, County of Cork, Ireland, on January 1st 1815. He received his English and Classical education at Missionary College, Youghal, County of Cork, Ireland.

In the year 1841, he emigrated to the United States of America, and finished his theological course of studies in the Diocese of New Orleans; was ordained Priest on the 24th of November 1846; and spent four years as Curate of the Parish of St. Joseph. He was afterwards deputed by the most Reverend Arch-Bishop Blanc to build a church in what now constitutes one of the most flourishing Parishes in New Orleans in a locality which was originally a swamp, but, at the present time, one of the most thronged portions of this great metropolis.

On the 1st of January 1851, he embarked on his arduous mission. People of every denomination rallied around him and contributed liberally to the sacred object which he had at heart. The result has been the erection of two churches, one of them a brick edifice, now nearly completed, which is one of the most substantial and beautiful in the South.

He has also established in the city two convents, and a parochial school for both sexes. Recently he has been clothed by Arch-Bishop Perché, with the functions of Canon, his duty as such, being to attend his Grace on all important occasions, be present at the Chapters of the Diocese, and act as one of his counsellors.

Father Moynahan, notwithstanding his intense devotion to the interests of the Roman Catholic Church, has, by his fine social qualities, the urbanity of his manners, the liberality of his opinions, and the deep interest he has exhibited in objects promotive of the public welfare, secured in a large degree, the homage as well as affections of his fellow citizens of all classes and denominations. His pulpit eloquence partakes of the controlling elements of his character, and is marked by boldness and intrepidity.

NEW MASONIC TEMPLE.

On the 15th February 1872, was laid the corner-stone of the new Masonic Temple by the Grand Master, officers and members of the Grand Lodge of Louisiana in the presence of many hundreds of visiting brethren and citizens. After the solemn and ancient ceremonies, eloquent addresses were delivered by the Rev. W. V. Tudor and Grand Master Todd. The Grand Lodge being in session, the imposing rites attracted a large assembly of Masons and a vast concourse of citizens. The corner-stone was a block of granite from one of the mountains of Georgia and a present from the Masonic Grand Lodge of that State. The foundation walls have been laid in brick, resting on a basis of blue clay.

The New Temple will be built according to the design and plans of S. H. Haggart, Esq., the architect selected to supervise its construction. It will front on St. Charles street, near the Tivoli Circle. Its dimensions will be as follows:—Front, 137 feet; depth, 92 feet; two wings 38 feet wide and 84 feet deep, extending back nearly to the rear of Temple Sinai; main portico, 30 feet wide, 9 feet projection, extending through a vestibule 24 feet wide, 12 feet deep and 20 feet high, having a beautiful tesselated floor and latticed doors. From these doors the passage, 24 feet wide and 20 feet high, extends to the staircase 42 feet, by which the second story is reached. On each side of the main entrance are to be two stores 70x27½ feet. At the rear, on each side, are porticos leading by stairways to the corridor on the second floor and to the lodge rooms on the third floor, as well as to the ladies' parlor and ball-room. In the north wing will be the office of the Grand Secretary, 28x42, two library rooms 22x28 and 38x21 connected by arches, and in the rear the office of the Grand Master, 18 feet square. In the south wing will be a kitchen, supper room, lumber room, etc. On the second floor of the main building is the ball-room or hall, 140 feet long, 70 feet wide, 36 feet high, lighted by 19 windows, which extend from floor to ceiling and opening on broad balconies. By three vast doors the hall connects with the broad corridor across which, in the north wing, is the ladies' parlor, 28x42, which communicates with 3 large dressing rooms, a retiring room and a cloak room. From these, by brick walls, will be a gentlemen's parlor, 30x21 feet, a hat room and staircase extending to the saloon below. In the south wing, second story, is the supper room, 70x28, with butler's pantry and cook's pantry connecting with the kitchen below by dumb waiters and a staircase. Over the hall are 5 lodge rooms, each 27x50 and 16 feet high. The Grand Lodge room, 65x38 and 20 feet high, is the third story of the south wing with a raised gallery for music. In the north wing, over the parlors, are the appropriate rooms of the Grand Commandery.

The Temple, when completed, will have an airy, graceful and elegant appearance, owing to the manner in which the walls are gathered up into columns and pilasters and to vast windows and balconies. It will thus become a lofty and conspicuous ornament to that part of the city, and a monument worthy of the ancient fraternity and the noble cause to which it is to be dedicated.

The details of structure may vary from the plans and dimensions as given above, according to the materials used and the funds available.

Under the jurisdiction of the Masonic Grand Lodge of Louisiana there are now 152 subordinate lodges, with an aggregate membership of 7,557. Thirty of these are located and working in New Orleans, named as follows:—Perfect Union, Polar Star, Concorde, Perseverance, St. André, Los Amigos del Orden, Silencio, Foyer Maçonique, Germania, Friends of Harmony, Mount Moriah, George Washington, Dudley, Marion, Hiram, Alpha Home, Quitman, Orleans, Hermitage, Louisiana, Ocean, Excelsior, Linnwood, Orus, Kosmos, Union, Orient, Dante, Perfect Harmony and Corinthian. The members of the city lodges number 2,700, or an average of 90 members to each lodge. The dates of the charters of the above-named city lodges are as follows:—Perfect Union, July 12, 1812; Polar Star, July 12, 1812; Concorde, July 12, 181_; Perseverance, July 12, 1812; St. André (originally Disciples du Senate Maçonique), chartered June 3, 1829; took its present name Feb. 14, 1865; Los Amigos del Orden, Sept. 24, 1842; Silencio, Feb. 12, 1861; Foyer Maçonique, Oct. 6, 1838; Germania, April 18, 1844; Friends of Harmony, April 22, 1848; Mount Moriah, March 24, 1849; George Washington, Dudley, Marion and Hiram, March 3, 1850; Alpha Home (a union of Alpha, organized in 1848 with Home, organized in 1855), chartered Feb. 14, 1860; Quitman and Orleans, March 4, 1850; Hermitage, Jan. 21, 1851; Louisiana, Jan. 22, 1851; Ocean, Feb. 10, 1857; Excelsior, Feb. 12, 1861; Linnwood, Feb. 13, 1861; Ours, Feb. 9, 1864; Kosmos, Feb. 9, 1864; Union and Orient, Feb. 17, 1865; Dante, Feb. 14, 1866; Perfect Harmony, Feb. 14, 1867; and Corinthian, Feb. 9, 1865.

The Grand Lodge was founded by Perfect Union, Polar Star, Charité (extinct), Concord and Perseverance, in 1812, since which the Grand Lodge granted charters to these original lodges and to 218 others. Twenty-three lodges, including Charité, have become extinct. Seventeen lodges have forfeited charters and 21 surrendered them. The oldest lodge in the State is Perfect Union, founded in 1793.

The Grand Masters of the Grand Lodge have been as follows:—P. Francis Du Bourg, 1812-13-14; J. Soulié, 1815-16-17; L. C. Moreau Lislet, 1818; J. B. Modeste, Lefebvre, 1819; y. Lemonnier, 1820; Aug. Macarty, 1821; J. F. Canonge, 1822-24-29; D. F. Burthe, 1823; John H. Holland, 1825-26-27-28-30-31-32-33-34-36-38-39; L. H. Ferand, 1836-37; A. W. Pichot, 1840-41; Jean Lamathe, 1842; E. A. Canon, 1843-44; Robert Preaux, 1845; Felix Garcia, 1846-47-48; M. R. Dudley, Lucien Hermann, 1849; John Gedge and Lucien Hermann, 1850; Jno. Gedge, 1851; H. R. W. Hill, 1852-53; Wm. M. Perkins, 1854-55-56-57-66; Amos Adams, 1858; Samuel Manning Todd, 1859-69-70-71-72; A. J. Norwood, 1867; H. R. Swasey, 1868; J. Q. A. Fellows, 1860-1-2-3-4-5. Of the Past Grand Masters five only are living—Perkins, Fellows, Norwood, Swasey and Todd.

The Grand Secretaries of the Grand Lodge have been as follows:—J. B. Gregoire Veron, 1812-13-14; Auguste Guibert, 1815-16-17-18; N. Visinier (part of) 1819; F.

TRINITY CHURCH.

Dissard, remainder of 1819 and until 1840; L. H. Feraud (part of) 1840; P. Dubayle, 1841–42 and part of 1843; F. J. Verrier, 1843–44–45–46–47; W. H. Howard, 1848; J. J. E. Massicott, 1850 and part of 1851; Edward Barrett, 1850–51–52–53; Samuel G. Risk, 1854–5–6–7–8–9–60–61; Samuel M. Todd, 1862–3–4–5–6; and Dr. Jas. C. Bachelor, 1867–8–9–70–1–2. Barrett, Todd and Bachelor are the only living Past Grand Secretaries.

The offices of Deputy Grand Masters, Senior and Junior Grand Warden and Grand Treasurer have been filled variously by the following:—L. C. Moreau Lislet, J. Blanque, Francis Pernot, Jean Baptiste Pinta, Jean B. Des Bats, Dominique Roquetté, G. Dubuys, A. Peychaud, G. W. Morgan, G. Lesmount, L. A. de Boitin, A. Langer, Charles Maurain, C. Miltenberger, M. Flertas, A. Morphy, D. F. Barthe, J. B. Fagot, M. Fouche Cougot, Seth W. Nye, Jean Lamathe, Aug. Douce, Thomas Blois, Alexander Phillips, J. B. F. Giquel, Charles Revoille, F. J. Verrier, Joaquin Viosca, François Cougot, J. J. Mercie, J. B. Lambert, Zenon Cobson, Perez Snell, Cotton Henry, G. A. Montmain, Ramon Vionnet, Fleury Generelly, A. D. Guesnon, Paul Bertus, Francis Calonge, H. Kidd, Joseph Liskony, François Meilleur, Roman Bragier, Thomas B. Paxton, Alexander Derbes, Thomas H. Lewis, W. P. Coleman, G. Gorin, Daniel Blair, Antoine Mondelli, Simon Meilleur, John W. Crockett, J. W. McNamara, George W. Catlett, R. P. McGuire, W. L. Isaacs, S. Herriman, S. M. Hart, H. W. Huntington, George B. Shadburn, D. Goodman, M. H. Dowson, Law P. Crain, Stephen C. Mitchell, Louis Texada, S. O. Scruggs, A. S. Washburn, Joseph Santini, A. G. Carter, John C. Gordy, Henry Regenburg, B. G. Thibodaux, S. J. Powell, Harmon Doane, George A. Pike, John Booth, John C. Jones, John A. Stevenson, Sy. G. Parsons, William McDuff, Amos Kent, John L. Barrett, William Robson, John Scraparn, Joseph P. Hornor, Michel E. Girard, Edwin Marks.

Fifty-two of those who have held elective offices in the Grand Lodge are dead, and forty were living in 1872.

COTTON SEED OIL WORKS.

The manufacture of oil from cotton seed has been chiefly developed since the close of the war, and now every considerable Southern town has one or more factories, while New Orleans has six, employing a capital of a million and a half, and with capacity to use a hundred thousand tons a year. The largest of these (and the largest in the world) is in the Fifth District or Algiers (New Orleans Right Bank), owned by a company and controlled by a Board of Directors, of which Col. C. E. Girardey, Auctioneer, is President. The conspicuous buildings occupied formerly constituted Clark's Foundry. This factory will produce 300 barrels of oil and 400 tons of oil cake per week. The four brick buildings are connected and occupy a square of about four acres. Here the seed, which costs about $15 per ton, is reginned to divest it of lint, often in sufficient quantity to be worth as much as the seed cost. The seed is next passed through a simple huller, consisting of a grooved cylinder by which the seed is crushed, and a sieve by which the hulls are separated from the kernels. The kernels are mashed or ground, roasted, placed in cats and pressed by steam, the oil running off into tanks, whence it is pumped into vats for purifying. The oil cake is exported and is used for feeding cattle. The hulls are burned in the furnaces of the two 75 horse power engines or sold as fertilizers. The oil is purified by carbonate of soda and barrelled for shipment. What is precipitated by the process is re-boiled and is used in the manufacture of soap. The oil finds a ready market in Great Britain at prices ranging about fifty cents per gallon, where it is variously employed for chemical, mechanical, medicinal and household purposes, no small quantity finding its way back to America in the form of Olive Oil for table use.

The only check to this lucrative industry is the difficulty of obtaining the cotton seed in sufficient quantity.

THE TOURO ALMS HOUSE.

About eighty thousand dollars were left by the late opulent and public-spirited Judah Touro, Esq., for the erection of an Alms House in this city. By judicious management this munificent bequest was increased, after the death of Mr. Touro, by R. D. Shepherd, Esq., to the amount of about $130,000, besides his making a donation of land worth about $45,000. The amount of cash in hand not being sufficient to meet the cost of the contemplated building (estimated at from $165,000 to $200,000), Mr. Shepherd proposed to make up the deficiency. War interrupted the work, and the edifice, as far as completed, was destroyed by fire on the last day of its occupation by negro troops. Some evidence existed to show that the disaster was attributable to the use of an intended ventilation flue as a chimney for a large bake oven, by which fire was communicated to the roof timbers.

The ground donated by Mr. Shepherd was about 318 feet wide from Piety to Desire street, Third District, and facing the river, extending about 746 feet. The main kitchen buildings, at the time of their destruction, were roofed in and floored, but not completed inside. They were three stories high, in the Gothic style, ranging from the pointed or early Gothic, in the centre, to square headed, or late Gothic, at the extreme wings, with the flattened arch or intermediate between, and stood 100 feet from the river road. The main building was 290 feet long by about 60 feet deep in the body of the structure, and 75 feet at the wings.

The centre pavilion contained the main entrance, parlors, offices, etc., between which and the extreme wings were three stories of iron galleries on the river front. The kitchen building contained the dependencies. The design further contemplated surrounding the ground with workshops for different industries, in which the inmates were to be kept occupied, while the intermediate space was laid off for orchards and vegetable gardens.

It was also contemplated to light the buildings with gas manufactured on the premises.

An unsuccessful effort has been made, since the war, to obtain an appropriation from the General Government for the restitution of this expensive structure, destroyed while in the occupancy of Federal colored troops.

GEN. RANDALL LEE GIBSON.

GEN. RANDALL LEE GIBSON was born on the 10th of September 1832, at the residence of his maternal grandfather, Spring Hill, Woodford County, Ky. He is descended from the Harts of Kentucky and the Prestons of Virginia, on his maternal side and from the McKinleys of Virginia, and Gibsons of Mississippi and South Carolina, on his paternal side. His father was the Honorable Tobias Gibson, of Terrebonne Parish, La., one of the largest planters of our State, and a gentleman of high character and intelligence. He was educated at Yale College, where he graduated in 1853, with the highest honors of his class—the valedictory.

After receiving his diploma from the law department of our State University, he travelled several years throughout Europe and remained nearly a year as an attaché of the American Legation at Madrid, where his personal accomplishments rendered him a welcome attendant. On his return his fondness for country life led him to become a planter, but he found time to contribute occasional articles to our leading reviews, characterized by fullness, accuracy and vigor, and he acquired a reputation as an effective and eloquent speaker, both in the English and French languages.

At the outbreak of the war between the States, he joined one of the first companies raised in his Parish, as a private soldier, and was elected captain. He afterwards, however, accepted the appointment of captain in the 1st Regiment Louisiana Artillery. He stood steadfastly by the colors of the Southern Confederacy until they were furled away, and rose successively through the various grades under such officers as Breckinridge, Hardee and Johnston, with whom he was an especial favorite, until he was assigned to the command of a division. He was the commander of the 13th Regiment Louisiana Infantry, and Gibbon's Louisiana Brigade, which became renowned as one of the *corps d'elite* of the army.

Much credit is due to General Gibson for the glorious reputation his brigade acquired. Unappreciated at first, because of his quiet reserve and shy isolation of manner, combined with rigid views of discipline as the true traits of his character were developed by events, he became one of the most beloved officers in the army—

> "Lofty and sour to those who love him not,
> But to such as seek him, sweet as summer."

His firm hand gradually impressed upon his brigade that iron discipline and unyielding steadiness that no reverse could impair. His impartial justice enabled him to exact implicit obedience, for his orders were conceived in kindness, and founded upon necessity and reason. And it was his chivalric bearing and unselfish devotion to his troops and the service, and his uncommon energy and spirit, that, assisted by his meritorious subordinates, built up a command that became celebrated in an army of veterans, and by every title was fairly included in that incomparable and unconquerable infantry of the Confederacy, that though they might sometimes be compelled to recoil from ill-advised or impossible assaults were never driven from their positions by front attack, and were never surpassed in the history of war, in any age or country in all soldierly virtues. Gen. Gibson in his address of adieu, truthfully observed: "The old brigade has stood before the enemy for more than four years, and had never lowered its colors save over the bier of a comrade fallen." He was selected by General Lee to command the rear guard of Hood's Army, for the first day after Nashville, having command of his own, Holtzclaw's Alabama, and Stoval's Georgia brigades. No higher tribute could have been paid to his merits. He was warmly complimented and recommended to the Government, both by Generals Lee and Hood, for his services in this campaign. They regarded him as one of the best officers in the army.

He was assigned to the defence at Mobile and conducted the operations near the water battery of the Spanish Fort, with a Division of Infantry and about forty pieces of artillery; Gibson's Louisiana, Holtzclaw's Alabama, Thomas' Alabama and Ector's Texas Brigades, with Col. Patton's 22nd Louisiana Artillery.

After the war he returned to his plantation, in Terrebonne Parish, but found it a wreck. In 1866 he came to this city and began the practice of that profession he had acquired years before, when young and prosperous. He has achieved an enviable position for exact methods of attending to business, and as a jurist and orator. He is admired and esteemed for his genuine goodness of heart, his perfect naturalness, his unfailing courtesy, his high sense of honor, his unflinching devotion to duty, and the wide range of his learning. Although a resident of this city, his tastes and sympathies are those of the country, and his plantation in Terrebonne parish, shows the evidences of his love and knowledge of agriculture. In all questions concerning the public welfare, without being a politician, he manifests a lively interest and takes an active and decided part. He is broad and liberal and non-partisan in his view.

In 1868 he was married to the eldest daughter of the late R. W. Montgomery, a prominent merchant of this city.

In June 1872, the name of General Gibson was prominently before the Democratic State Convention for nomination for the office of Governor of Louisiana, and but for the dissension in the party at that time, he would have been selected as its standard bearer.

THE Firemen's Charitable Association was incorporated in 1835, and managed by a board of directors chosen from each company, subject to certain restrictions. The officers, (a president, vice-president, secretary and treasurer,) are elected by the board from members of the association, on the first Monday of January, of each year. The object of this society is the relief of its members, who are incapacitated from attending to business from sickness or misfortunes not arising from improper causes. It makes provisions also for the benefit of their families—particularly widows and orphans. This is a very laudable association, and every way deserving of the excellent fire department from which it originated.

GEO. S. LACEY, ESQ.,

CITY ATTORNEY.

SLOCOMB, BALDWIN & CO.

HARDWARE IMPORTERS.

Dealers in

Agricultural Implements.

Iron, Steel,

Nails, Castings,

Tin Ware,

Paints, Oils,

Metals, &c., &c.

Rail Road Supplies,

Blacksmiths' and

Carpenters' Tools,

Carriage Hardware,

Cutlery,

Guns, &c., &c.

74 CANAL AND 91 TO 95 COMMON STREETS,

Adjoining the City Hotel.

WAREHOUSES.—PETERS and CROSSMAN Streets, NEW ORLEANS

Our Importations are all direct and prices guaranteed as low as any market North or South

MAYOR BENJAMIN FRANKLIN FLANDERS.

The career of the late Mayor of New Orleans has been a very checkered one; but if office in the United States is indicative of merit, he is entitled to much praise. It is both interesting and instructive to trace his history up to the period when he became the chief executive officer of this city.

Mr. Flanders was born in New Hampshire in 1816, and, from the time of his arrival in New Orleans in 1842, he has been prominently before the public in situations which required ability, and which have served to test the extent of his powers. His first employment in New Orleans was that of a teacher in our public schools, and he appears to have been a principal teacher in what was then the First Municipality, but is now the Second District. How long precisely he remained connected with the schools we are unable to say, but it was not long, inasmuch as in 1844 we find him occupying the position of co-editor and proprietor of the Tropic newspaper. In 1848 and 1849 he began to be connected with municipal affairs, serving in the Council of the Third Municipality and again in 1851.

In 1852 he was elected Secretary and Treasurer of the Opelousas Rail Road, a position which he held till January, 1862. In July of the latter year, he was appointed City Treasurer by military authority, and was elected to Congress the following November. In 1863 he received from Mr. Chase the appointment of Supervising Special Agent of the Treasury Department, which he held, without interruption, till the year 1866. In 1864 he occupied for some time the post of President of the First National Bank of New Orleans.

In June 1867, he was appointed Governor of the State by General Sheridan, but resigned the office the following December.

In 1870 he became Mayor of the city, first by the appointment of the Governor, and subsequently, in November 1871, by election of the people.

GABRIEL DE FERIET.

Mr. Gabriel De Fériet is the oldest auctioneer and real estate agent now in the business in New Orleans, his connection as such dating as far back as 1828. Mr. De Fériet is the oldest son of Louis Claude, Baron of Fériet, a French nobleman who came here during the Colonial period, and attained the rank of Captain under the Spanish dominion. A native of Nancy, (Lorraine,) he married Marcelite de St. Maxent, a native of New Orleans, whose progenitors had settled here when Bienville laid the foundation of our city. Of this marriage Mr. G. de Fériet is the only surviving male issue. He received his education at the College of Father Martial, and subsequently went North in 1825, and completed his studies at the Lewisville Military Academy, in Lewis County, New York, then presided over by Col. Taylor. Returning to New Orleans in 1827, he went into the lumber business, and soon after received the appointment of Controller of the Treasury of the Third Municipality, which office he held with great satisfaction to his constituents, till 1856, when he was commissioned by Governor Hébert, auctioneer for the City and Parish of New Orleans, a branch of business of which he is still one of the most prominent and successful members in this city. Although born in 1807, Mr. de Fériet retains all the ardor and energy of youth, and there is no one of a later generation who brings greater enthusiasm into all matters of public interest. His ardent temperament and patriotic impulses, got him into trouble during the Butler regime, and he had to pay the penalty of his unyielding integrity by a long imprisonment in the city, and was subsequently banished with many other estimable citizens, to the sand bank of Ship Island, by the "hero" of Fort Fisher. Mr. de Fériet is one of our most energetic, public spirited citizens, and deservedly enjoys the confidence and support of the old inhabitants of New Orleans, who understand and appreciate his many sterling qualities of head and heart.

MR. JULES TUYES,

President of the N. O. Mutual Insurance Co., was born in New Orleans in 1821, and after receiving his collegiate education in Paris, commenced business as a clerk in the commission house of Messrs. Blanchard, Elmer & Co., a position he afterwards exchanged for a more responsible one in the Banking House of F. de Lizardi & Co., from which last situation he was promoted in 1845 to the office of Secretary of the Company, to preside over which he was elected in 1854. Mr. Tuyes is a gentleman of cultivated mind and refined habits, in whom great suavity of manners and kindness of heart, unite with strict integrity, and a nice sense of honor. These qualities have endeared him to a large circle of friends and acquaintances, who look upon him as the genuine type of the Creole gentleman, ever courteous and straight forward in all his actions, and whose fair fame the breath of envy has never dared to touch. To his sterling qualities of heart and head much of the prosperity and success of the institution over which he so ably presides may be fairly attributed.

THE HOWARD ASSOCIATION OF NEW ORLEANS.

No pleasanter duty can be assumed than that of recording the organization and progress of the Howard Association of New Orleans, incontestably one of the noblest and worthiest of the philanthropic institutions of the civilized world. The name of the illustrious English philanthropist, Howard, has, in many instances, in his own native country and in the United States, been the leading title of various charitable and humane institutions, but it is doubtful whether as much honor has been conferred upon the memory of that great and good samaritan as by its adoption by the Howard Association of this city. Perhaps the field of labor has contributed largely in entitling the city of New Orleans to claim superiority in this matter; but whatever the causes, we are none the less gratified at the belief that we possess an institution whose deeds by far surpass those of any other similar one.

Together with the Sisters of Charity—that exalted organization of the Catholic Church—the Howard Association shares the highest praise of our citizens and of many strangers whose lives have been saved or wants supplied through the ministrations of this body of self-sacrificing gentlemen. While the Sisters of Mercy have a vaster mission, it is nevertheless true that the Howard Association is a constant institution, the members of which are ready, at any moment, to answer the call of suffering humanity. Months, and, with the steadily improving wealth of New Orleans, years may come and pass, without even hearing the name of the Association referred to, until suddenly the dark cloud of disease lowers upon the city when the welcome Samaritans, forgetting self, rush forward to brave the tempest and pour forth sunshine from their glowing hearts.

It was in 1837, in the month of August, when the Yellow Fever of that year became epidemic, that Farquhar Mathewson, a young man, aged some twenty-two or three years, then a clerk in the establishment of Messrs Henderson & Gaines, a young man of active mind and ardent temperament, such as fitted him to be a leader among the young men with whom he associated, suggested to his associates the propriety of forming an association of young men, for the purpose of affording relief to the poor and distressed victims of the epidemic, who were without the means of procuring medicine or nurses. His suggestion was immediately acted upon, and a meeting of young men was held at the Planter's Hotel, on Canal street, for the purpose of organizing the proposed association. Among those participating at this meeting, and active members of the association in that memorable year (1837) were the following:

F. Mathewson, Virgil Boulemont, Milton Boulmet, Wm. B. Rotta, Jno. C. Page, Jno. F. Delan, Chas. H. Wabbe, E. Hiestand, J. P. Breedlove, Simon Green, Ed. L. Nimmo, Jas F. Rusha, J. D. Kenton, Thos. A. James, Thomas Y. James, L. C. Dillard, Alex. Levy, Almon Parsons, Thos. Love, Alex. Hazlett, F. W. Leslie and Jno. Leslie, Jr. Others were at the organization and active participants in the association, but owing to the destruction of the books of the Association by the burning of Odd Fellow's Hall in 1866, it is impossible to give their names.

Nearly if not all of those whose names are enumerated, were members of Protection Hose Fire Company, of which Mathewson was also a leading member. When the name of the society came up for consideration, that of "Howard," the great English Philanthropist, was suggested by Mathewson, who supported it by a few well chosen and pithy remarks, which led to its immediate adoption. Farquhar Mathewson was elected President, and Virgil Boulmont, Vice President; the other officers elected at the organization are not now recollected.

The operations of the Association were confined to searching out the poor and helpless victims of the epidemic, appointing Committees of members to set up with and nurse the sick, which duty was most cheerfully acquiesced in by each member when his time came, whilst the duty of the Stewards were to visit each Committee during the night with refreshments.

The first two weeks operation of the Association developed the fact, that the poor and helpless victims of the epidemic were vastly too numerous to be aided solely by the limited means of the Association, when it was resolved to appeal to the well known liberality of the citizens of New Orleans, and in every instance their appeals have been responded to in the most liberal manner.

The Association, during the epidemic of 1853 disbursed over $159,000 on some 11,000 sick and destitute. During the epidemic of 1867, over $78,000 were expended on some 5,000 sick and destitute.

The number of members is limited to 50, but there are not that number at present.

The first President of the Association was F. Mathewson. At a subsequent date, Mr. D. I. Ricardo was elected Secretary, which office he continued to fill until his death in 1863.

The present officers are: E. F. Schmidt, President; W. S. Pike, Vice-President; John F. Caldwell, Secretary; R. S. Robertson, Treasurer.

CITY WATER WORKS.

An Act of the General Assembly, approved April 1 1833, incorporated the Commercial Water Works and Banking Co. of New Orleans, and among the conditions of their charter was the right and duty of supplying the city and its faubourgs with water at specific charges, except public institutions, which they were to supply with water free of charge. To the city was reserved the right to buy at the end of thirty-five years such Water Works as the company might construct, in accordance with which condition the city bought the Water Works in 1868 for thirteen hundred thousand dollars in city bonds, and the administration of the Water Works now forms a branch of the city government.

The engine buildings are in the First District one and one-half miles from Canal street, about two hundred yards from the Mississippi River. Two engines of 700 horse power each drive four double acting pumps of the united capacity of a million gallons per hour. The water, in consequence of the falling of a wall of one of the reservoirs, is pumped directly into the pipes during the day.

RESIDENCE OF W. E. SCHMIDT.

There are 56 miles of main pipe, formerly of wood or cement, but now in process of replacement by iron. The pipe from the river to the reservoir is 48 inches in diameter, that extending from Calliope to Canal street is 30 inches. The rest are smaller. The hydrants number 11,000, many of which are now closed. For fires and street cleansing there are more than a thousand fire-plugs, which being frequently opened during hot weather add much to the health and comfort of citizens.

The water rate is, for one hydrant supplying a family of four persons, $12 per annum, and $1 more for each additional member. The supply to each hydrant is more than twice as much as it is in any other city. General Braxton Bragg, in his report for 1859, shows that the daily average to each person (allowing ten persons to each hydrant), was 95 gallons. The water of the Mississippi, when filtered or settled, is entirely pure and free from organic matter. Seamen find that it remains fresh longer than any other water taken on board their vessels.

When the Water Works Company was chartered all that region above Felicity road was swamp or plantations. What is now Melpomene street was a bayou, the delight of half the boys of the city for hunting and fishing. What were then frog ponds and almost impenetrable swamp thickets, are now the sites of elegant residences.

From 1845 to 1868, the Water Works were under the control of a Board of Directors, of which Felix Labatut was the honored, able and very efficient President. He was aided by Paulin Durel, A. Carrière, George A. Freret, Frank Perret and D. Lacata, members of the Board.

FIRST PRESBYTERIAN CHURCH.

This large and time-honored church, situated on Lafayette Street, opposite the fine square that bears the same name, is a brick edifice, 75 feet by 90 in length, and 42 feet in height. The main tower is 115 in height, the spire with pinnacle is 104 feet, and the entire height 219 feet.

The body of the church contains 1311 sittings, and is usually filled to its utmost capacity.

Attached to the church is a lecture room, 25 feet by 78 in length, and 18 feet in height, which has 218 sittings; also a school-room with the same number of sittings, and two session rooms and a library. The architect of this fine edifice was Henry Howard; the builder, G. Purvis; and the artist, P. Gualdi, Esquires.

The rostrum or pulpit, slightly elevated (in modern style) above the pews, is tastefully designed and elegantly furnished. The church, throughout, is richly, though not gorgeously, equipped. The orchestra, opposite the pulpit, accommodates a large choir, whose music, whether in hymns, psalms or anthems, always of a high order, is of the grave and noble style adapted to Protestant worship in the Presbyterian churches of America. Lofty and commodious galleries, on a level with the orchestra, and to the right and left of the minister, are, especially at the morning service, and in the Winter season, crowded with attentive listeners of all classes and colors.

HANCOCK LITERARY ASSOCIATION.

This Association was chartered under the general laws of the State, June 1st 1872, to exist for a period of twenty-five years from the first Friday in March 1868, the date of its organization.

The objects of the Society are: the cultivation of polite literature, oratory and elocution, by discourses from history and the Belle-lettres and by recitations from the poets. It is an Association identical in its character and aims with the Raven Club of Washington city, which, composed of the *elite* of the National Capital, met weekly antecedent to the late war at the residence of D. K. Whitaker, Esq., on 11th street, and whose meetings were, by that gentleman, regularly reported for the press, he being historiographer and presiding officer of that well-known club.

Mr. Whitaker is President of the Hancock club, and J. J. Foley, Esq., Vice-President. Both these gentlemen have been accustomed to deliver weekly lectures on recondite subjects in the more elevated branches of literature, in which much learning is embodied. Distinguished visitors frequently take part in the discussions—always welcome and always appreciated. Since its commencement the Society has slowly but steadily advanced. *Recherche* in character, it is happily free from blatant demagogism in politics, and absurd bigotry in religion; indeed both these much-vexed and agitating subjects are excluded from its debates.

The President, drawing on his large and matured resources, is accustomed to open the meetings, handling at will, various epochs of the English literature, and dealing with them as familiar things.

Mr. Foley, Vice-President of the Association, has, during the years of his membership, dating from its organization, delivered discourses on the Lord Chancellors and Chief Justices of England, the Chief Justices of the United States—on epic poetry—the ancient and modern drama—on forensic eloquence, and the corrupt practices of the judicial tribunals of the past and present. These lectures have been marked by distinguished ability proving their author at once the able advocate and astute reasoner.

An agreeable feature of the Society consists in recitations, original and selected, by its lady members, who, though entirely ignoring the woman's rights dogma, as something unnatural and unbecoming, are still willing, in a quiet and modest way, to aid the cause of letters.

Mr. Overall, a much admired and highly esteemed poet and journalist, is critic of the Association and one of its most brilliant orators.

Weekly meetings take place at the residence of the President, and, on those occasions, as in the groves of Academus, leaving the work-day world behind, intellectuality may revel in its higher sphere, and mind and heart be alike cultivated.

It is the wish of its members to foster an especial *esprit de corps*, a love of letters in the Crescent City, which must always go hand in hand with refinement and civilization.

The original and interesting matter presented at different times, before this Association, would furnish volumes of valuable and useful information.

THE MISTICK KREWE OF COMUS.

HISTORY OF THE KREWE AND THEIR VARIOUS FESTIVALS FROM 1857 TO 1873.

MARDI GRAS has ever been a memorable day in the social annals of New Orleans, and since the year 1857, its joys and festivities have been inseparably connected with the revels of the Mistick Krewe. Where they came from, what their history, and who compose the mysterious band, are as impenetrable mysteries now as they were fourteen years ago. This fact we do know, however, that the Krewe have become so much a part of Mardi Gras, that were they to drop out of the events of the day, the very life of that merry time would seem as dead.

The near approach of the time when they will "walk" again, and the general awakening of public interest and anticipation—which ever recurs when Mardi Gras draws nigh—prompts us to relate the history of the Mistick Krewe and their festivals from their inception to the present time.

In 1857, for some time before Mardi Gras, there were whispers that a fresh and novel entertainment would be offered to our people. Nobody at first knew what it would be, but by some means it leaked out that an organization calling itself the Mistick Krewe of Comus, would appear upon the streets on Mardi Gras night in all sorts of fanciful masks and costumes; that they would form in procession, march through the principal streets, and then retire to the Varieties, (then called the Gaiety) Theatre, where certain tableaux of a mythological character would be exhibited, after which a grand ball would be given, to which only a certain select company would be invited. The affair created great interest and excitement, the greater from the profound secrecy and mystery which surrounded it, the beautiful cards of invitation which were issued to the ball, and the complete ignorance of each invited guest of the source from whence the invitation came.

After the first celebration of 1857, enough was known to satisfy the public that the Krewe were composed of precisely the right sort of persons to make the affair a complete success. Their identity was apparently known to no one, and to this day the impenetrable veil which has covered them so long has never been lifted. All sorts of speculations concerning them have been indulged in. Yet no one can say that he is positive of knowing a single individual connected with the Krewe. Thus far their incognito has been sacredly preserved. Without a doubt, however, they are all gentlemen of intelligence, wealth and social position, as the magnificent and select character of their entertainments fully testify.

It was decidedly noticeable that the interest in the forthcoming celebration shows itself long before the day arrives, and there is always an eager desire to procure tickets of admission to the tableaux and ball. In the year 1866, a gentleman of this city, in his eagerness, advertised for a ticket, offering to pay therefor a large sum of money—but no one has been known to procure a ticket through his own exertions, or to use one not intended for him—the lucky individual receiving his card of admission in a manner that leaves him in a most delightful state of uncertainty as to how it reached him.

The cards of admission and invitations to the annual balls of the Krewe are magnificent specimens of the engraver's art, and by the receivers are highly prized and preserved as treasures.

Having explained as much as we or any one knows about the M. K. C., we come to

THE FIRST FESTIVAL—1857.

Mardi Gras fell this year on the 24th of February, and the festival of the Krewe was described "as the great feature of the night." It can readily be conceived that curiosity concerning their appearing was at fever heat. They made their appearance in the streets—dressed in the most fantastic costumes accompanied by torchlights—which with the fearful looking masks they wore—made them as much resemble a deputation from the lower regions as the mind could well conceive. After marching through the principle thoroughfares to the intense gratification and astonishment of the throng gathered to see them, they repaired to the Gaiety Theatre, which was soon filled with invited guests.

In due time the Krewe appeared upon the stage in the tableaux, of which there were four. The first represented Tartarus. The characters in this scene were Pluto and Proserpine, presiding over the three Fates, Clotho, Lachesis and Atropos; the three Furies, Alecto, Tisiphone and Megaera; the three Harpies, Aello, Ocypete and Celeno; the three Gorgons, Medusa, Stheno and Euryale, with Ixion, Sisyphus, Tantalus, Minotaur, Cerberus, Charon and Chimera.

The second tableaux was the Expulsion. In this were represented Satan, Beelzebub, Moloch, Dagon, Belial, Isis, Osiris, Mammon, and a host of other infernals.

The third tableaux represented the conference of Satan and Beelzebub.

The fourth represented Pandemonium. This was described as a most magnificent spectacle, in which Gluttony, Drunkenness, Indolence, Avarice, Murder, Vanity, Theft, Discord, Licentiousness and Jealousy were personated, all being presided over by Satan, and flanked by Sin and Death.

The different tableaux were arranged in accordance with descriptions in Milton's Paradise Lost, and the truthful manner in which they were represented reflected the highest credit upon the poetic taste and judgment of the gentlemen composing the Krewe.

After the tableaux the ball commenced, being joined in by the mysterious hosts and their guests. Upon the stroke of midnight the Krewe silently disappeared, leaving their friends to continue the festivities. Thus commenced and ended the first festival of the M. K. C., which, from its brilliancy, gave promise of much in store for the future.

SECOND FESTIVAL—1858.

February 16th.

As may be imagined, the interest and pleasure excited by the first appearance of the Krewe, created a lively expectation as the time approached for their second appear-

COL. J. B. PRICE

THE SUGAR SHEDS

ance. From the records, we learn that this festival exceeded in brilliancy and splendor anything which had until then ever been presented in New Orleans. The Krewe, upon this occasion, revived the mythology of the olden time in all its classic glory, presenting the pictures of the different deities which have for so many ages afforded material to the poet, the painter, and the sculptor.

The richness of the costumes and perfection of the appointments, were subjects alike for wonder and admiration. The characters represented in the procession were: Comus, Momus, Janus, Spring, Summer, Autumn, Winter, Flora, Pomona, Vertumnus, Ceres, Pan, Fauns, Bacchus, Silenus, Satyr, Diana, The Muses, Vesta, Harpocrates, Hygeria, Esculapius, Fortune, Plutus, Destiny, Nemesis, Saturn, Cybele, Jupiter, Juno, Aurora, Phœbus, Apollo, Night, Æolus, Neptune, Amphritrite, Pluto, Proserpine, Hecate, The Furies.

As before, the procession wound its way to the theatre, which was crowded to its utmost with the beauty and fashion of the city.

The tableaux presented were, as on previous occasion, four in number.

The first represented Minerva's victory over Neptune, before an assemblage of the gods.

The second portrayed the flight of time, the characters represented being Castor, Pollux, the Hours, Time and Destiny.

The third tableaux shewed a Bacchanalian revel, represented by Bacchus, Silenus, Faunus, Fauns and Satyrs—Comus the Seasons, Flora and Momus.

Tableaux Fourth was a procession by the Krewe around the Theatre, by which the assembly was enabled to look closely upon the rich and beautiful costumes which had delighted them so much.

After the procession, the assemblage joined in the merry dance, and at midnight the Mistick Krewe "folded their tents and silently stole away."

THIRD FESTIVAL—1859.

This year, March 8, was Mardi Gras, and the two previous exhibitions having assured the people that the celebrations by the Mistick Krewe of Comus were firmly fixed as objects of the greatest interest, expectation was on tiptoe for a repetition of the glorious pageants which even now lingered like a sweet memory.

The procession this year represented the four old English holidays, May Day, Midsummer Eve, Christmas and Twelfth Night.

TWELFTH NIGHT was represented by two trumpeters, carrying trumpets of a most peculiar design. Herald and Ensign of the Lord of Misrule, followed by an enormous chicken cock. Page, bearing the crown; Lord of Misrule, attended by his Jester, and the Abbott of Unreason as his chief adviser. Two Ushers and a group representing various games and sports.

IN MAY DAY—were Jack in green, Tom the piper, the Tabor man, Scarlet and Mock, May Queen, Robin Hood, Friar Tuck and Stokesley.

MIDSUMMER EVE—introduced most odd and startling characters. St. George, followed by the Dragon, Puck, the Bear, Moth, Mustard Seed, Pea Blossom, and the other fairies of Midsummer Eve, surrounding Queen Titania, with Bottom transformed into a donkey. The Lion and Unicorn. The great giants Gog and Magog.

CHRISTMAS presented Harlequin following a grotesque group of Christmas carollers performing upon silent instruments of most ridiculous design; Bell man, Christmas tree, Santa Claus, boar's head, plum pudding, mince pie, wassail bowl, barrel of ale, bottle of champagne, bottle of port.

Arriving at the theatre, the tableaux were presented, and embraced the four seasons described, and in a manner most charming to behold.

The ball and disappearance of the mystical crew followed as before, and the Sons of Comus lived once more but in the memories of those who had gazed upon their glory.

FOURTH FESTIVAL—1860.

By this time the Mistick Krewe of Comus had become a fixed institution, and their festival was looked forward to as a part of domestic history. It was expected that the Krewe having gone on from year to year, increasing in grandness of display, would this year present an exhibition superior to all their previous efforts, nor was the public disappointed. The procession eclipsed everything that had been attempted before. A tablet at the front expressed the design upon it the inscription of the display, bearing "Statues of the great men of our country."

Following were fifteen cars, each representing a block of granite, and containing groups of living statues of famous historic persons.

FIRST CAR—Christopher Columbus.

SECOND CAR—Sebastian Cabot, Vespucci and Carter.

THIRD CAR—Ponce De Leon, Narvaez and Alvaro, the early adventurers of Florida.

FOURTH CAR—Ferdinand De Soto, Vanusno Menendez, Vasquez and De Gourgues.

FIFTH CAR—De Bienville De La Salle, Father Hennepin, Laudoinere, Jean Ribault, Lacaille and Nicolas Bone.

SIXTH CAR—Sir Walter Raleigh, Martin, Frobisher, Gerold, Archer, Greenville and Ratcliffe, early settlers in Virginia.

SEVENTH CAR—Captain John Smith and Pocahontas.

EIGHTH CAR—William Penn in the midst of a group of Indians.

NINTH CAR—Hendrick Hudson and Peter Stuyvesant, the Dutch discoverer of the Hudson River, and the Dutch Governor of New York.

TENTH CAR—Edward Winslow, John Carver, Miles Standish, John Alden, William Bradford, Edward Filly, Isaac Allerton and Roger Williams, the pilgrim founders of New England.

ELEVENTH CAR—Heroes of the American Revolution—George Washington, Lafayette, Marion, Putnam and Knox.

TWELFTH CAR—Gens. Lincoln, Wayne, Gates, Montgomery, Schuyler, Lee, and Green—Generals of the American Revolution.

THIRTEENTH CAR—The great statesmen of the American Revolution—Benjamin Franklin, John Adams, Robert Livingston, Thos. Jefferson, Patrick Henry, Roger Sherman, Richard Henry Lee, and John Hancock.

FOURTEENTH CAR—General Andrew Jackson.

FIFTEENTH CAR—Illustration of the compromise of 1833, Henry Clay, J. C. Calhoun and Daniel Webster. The Statues, while dressed to represent the various characters, were white as marble from top to toe.

As heretofore the Theatre was the scene of the crowning glories of the night, the tableaux were beautiful in design and faithful in execution.

"The historic sculpture of America," was the general design of the tableaux, represented by ten different groups, embracing "Landing of Christopher Columbus at San Salvador," Ferdinand De Soto discovering the Mississippi, Pocahontas saving the life of Capt. Smith, Landing of the Pilgrims at Plymouth Rock, William Penn's treaty with the Indians, Declaration of American Independence, Monument to the Generals of the American Revolution. The Compromise of 1833, The Hero of Chalmette—Andrew Jackson.

The tableaux concluded, Terpsichore reigned supreme. True to their faith, the Mistick Krewe vanished at the sound of the midnight bell, and were seen no more.

FIFTH FESTIVAL—1861.

The troubled state of the country, and the foreshadowing of civil war, led many to believe that the festivities of the Mistick Krewe would be held in abeyance; but, true as the needle to the pole, the revellers appeared on Mardi Gras night, the date this year being February 14. The line of procession was on Camp, Julia, St. Charles, Royal, St. Louis, Chartres, Canal and Carondelet, to the theatre, the crowds on the street making the affair a complete ovation. The representation was "Scenes from Life," embracing the four divisions—childhood, youth, manhood and old age.

The costumes were gorgeous, and the characteristics of each age faithfully poetrayed. Childhood was an infant in a cradle, followed by a nurse. Boyhood was surrounded by maskers, representing a kite, top, sweet cake, marbles and other boyish things. Youth was attended by the representations of virtues, aspirations, temptations and trials incident to that era. Manhood then came with the vices, follies and better qualities of mature life, all represented by maskers. Old Age was accompanied by a similar band, and following all came Death. As usual, the events of the night were the tableaux and ball; of the former there were five, as follows:

The Innocence of Childhood. The virtues and aspirations of Youth.

The vices and follies of Manhood,

Conflict between Virtue and Vice in Old Age.

The triumph of Virtue over Vice, in which was represented Childhood, Youth, Manhood and Old Age, leaving Vice and Folly behind and ascending toward fame.

The tableaux being concluded, the maskers joined in the merry dance which was continued far into the night; but after the witching hour of 12 the Krewe were no more seen, having faded away as they had done in every instance before.

AN INTERLUDE.

The war had now burst in all its fury, and in the contemplation of the bitter train of realities following in its wake, the Mistick Krewe dropped from out the local history of the city; their memory was dimmed by the terrible strife which ruled the land; for four years the Krewe roamed no more; where they went, or what they did, is known to none but themselves. However, with the return of peace, they once more appeared before the delighted gaze of assembled multitudes, and we chronicle the

SIXTH FESTIVAL—1866.

The announcement that the celebration of the Krewe would be revived, created the utmost enthusiasm, and kindled anew the happy recollections of the splendors which had always characterized their displays. The day (Feb. 13) was anxiously looked forward to, and when the night arrived the populace *en masse* thronged the streets to obtain a sight of the pageant which was about to resurrect itself from the ashes of the past. Their appearance was hailed with every demonstration of delight, and the people congratulated themselves upon the return of that spectacle which had come to be considered as an object of particular and peculiar pride.

The features of the procession were appropriately symbolical of the return of peace. At the theatre, as of old, was assembled the wealth and beauty of our city. The tableaux were four in number, as follows:

THE PAST—represented by the characteristic Strife, Destruction, Want, Grief and Terror.

THE PRESENT—Washington approving the blessings of peace, surrounded by Industry, Commerce, Science, Agriculture, History, Mechanism and Art.

THE FUTURE—Peace and Plenty.

THE COURT OF COMUS—represents the King of the Court entertaining his beasts in an unknown language.

The ball followed as of yore, and again did the Mistick Krewe vanish from the gaze of the world ere the new-born day was ushered in.

SEVENTH FESTIVAL—1867.

Mardi Gras came this year on the 5th of March, and as the grand firemen's celebration had taken place but the day before, the city was more than ever crowded with eager expectants for the forthcoming festivities of the Krewe. As suddenly and mysteriously as had ever been their custom, they appeared in procession, coming no one seemed to know from where.

The design of the display was the "FEAST OF EPICURUS," the costumes as gorgeous, their appointments as perfect as before, and their numbers somewhat increased. First came the Heralds of Appetite—Absynthe, Sherry and Bitters—followed by special aids, Oysters and Johannisberger; Lords of the Ladle, with soups, led on the Knights of the Shell, such as shrimps, crabs, etc. Pages of the household our codfish aristocracy, followed by the Hog. The Rulers of the Roast, King Comus leading the Boeuf Gras, surrounded by all the vegetables of the table; next came a basket of flowers, followed by the Salt Cellar, Maccaroni Italienne, Canard Grecque, Paté des Oiseaux, Grenouille Francais, Snipe au Diable, Sausage a la bow-wow.

Then came the Knight and Lady of the Green Crests,

followed by a Salad Fork, Lettuce and Castors. The Knight of the White Crest, attended by Cold Slaugh, Cauliflowers, Artichokes and Asparagus, were followed by the Stewards in waiting, flanked by Jelly and Plum Pudding.

Next in order were seen the Grand Equerry and Lady, supported by Ice Cream and Strawberries, Ushers of the Court, Maccaroon, Meringue and Champagne. The Fruits of Victory now appeared, aided by Apples, Peaches and Plums. The Gentlemen of Cultivation were represented by Bananas, Pineapples, Oranges, Grapes, Melons and Burgundy. The "Triflers of the Council" were Nuts, Confections, Omelettes, etc. The "Peacemakers"—Coffee and Cigars, Curacoa and Kirschwasser—concluded the Feast of Epicurus.

The affair was of the most magnificent character, and excited wonder and admiration, not only because of the elegance of the costumes, but for the very correct manner in which the many difficult characters were portrayed.

At the Theatre the crush was as great as ever, and expectation was at its highest for the presentation of the Tableau, on this occasion consisting of a single display—"The Gourmand's Vision of Two Courses and a Dessert." This tableaux was most elaborately gotten up, and embraced all of the members of the Mistick Krewe, who represented at the banquet the various dishes known to civilization. The press of the day pronounced it the most beautiful and appropriate of all the Tableaux which the Krewe had ever given.

Again did Terpsichore rule Queen of the night, and again did the Krewe melt into thin air, as they did on so many occasions before. Whether they remained there, or whether they reappeared in mortal form we cannot say, but we do know that they came again upon the occasion of the

EIGHTH FESTIVAL.—1868.

February 25th ushered in Mardi Gras, and the return of the Krewe to the scenes of their former triumphs. The subject chosen for the display of this year was Moore's Lalla Rookh, one requiring a full appreciation of the poet's theme, and a particular attention to detail, and which, at the hands of its faithful expounders, met with such portrayal, that none could be at a loss to know and feel the perpetuation of the beautiful story.

The pageant was formed to represent the entrance of Lalla Rookh into Delhi—and she could not have been more thoroughly welcomed than was the Mistick Krewe by the thousands who thronged the streets upon this occasion. Leading the procession came a cavalcade of horsemen bearing aloft the blazing insignia of royalty, and blazing with jewels and gaudy colors.

In their train were the mighty Fadladeen, young Feramorz and the rest of the courtiers appointed to accompany "Tulip Cheek" to her bridal. Then came the elephants, bearing aloft in the palanquins the princess and her attendant houris. Interspersed in the procession were foot soldiers and attendants, bearing aloft many colored lanterns of strange and fanciful shape, and drooping garlands on their lances.

The line of horsemen was closed by a similar body, such as in the olden time galloped through the streets of Stamboul, and bore the banner of Islam to victory.

As the glorious vision passes from view, with its wealth of roses, light, fair women, and brave men, the spell was over all, that Comus was yet monarch of his own phantom realm, with all its dazzling glory and mystery.

The selections of Tableaux for this year exhibited the refined taste of the gentlemen composing the Krewe, and nothing which they had presented before was richer or rarer.

We give the list of tableaux as embodied in the immortal poem.

The Veiled Prophet of Khorassan—His Court; The Oath; The Banquet.

Paradise and the Peri—Gates of Heaven; Patriotism; Devotion; Contrition; The Gift Most Dear to Heaven.

The Fire Worshippers—Discovery; Death of Hafed.

The Light of the Harem—Feast of Roses.

"At the end of the hall stood two thrones as precious as the Cerulean Throne Koolburga, on one of which sat Aliris, the youthful King of Bucharia, and on the other was in a few minutes to be placed the most beautiful princess in the world.

"Immediately upon the entrance of Lalla Rookh into the saloon, the monarch descended from his throne to meet her, but scarcely had he time to take her hand in his, when she screamed with surprise and fainted at his feet.

"It was Feramorz himself that stood before her. Feramorz was himself the sovereign of Bucharia, who, in this disguise had accompanied his young bride from Delhi, and having won her love as an humble minstrel, now amply deserved to enjoy it as a King."

The march by the Krewe, the ball and the flitting away of the mysterious shadows completed this most successful display of 1868.

NINTH FESTIVAL.—1869.

Mardi Gras came early this year falling on the 9th of February. The procession of the Mistick Krewe upon this occasion represented the Five Senses, or Sight, Sound, Smell, Taste and Touch.

Each sense was represented by a pallid antique statue in character. The first personated Phœbus in his car of light drawn by four coursers. Then followed Ceres as the Goddess of fruit, Orpheus as the Type of Music, Flora as the representative of Smell, and Venus as the personator of Touch. These emblematic representations gave the performers an opportunity of representing in a fantastic and amusing manner, various species of animals, insects, fruits and flowers.

During the procession a serious accident occurred, occasioned by the falling of a gallery on Camp street, precipitating many people into the street, resulting in serious injury to quite a number.

The usual route was passed through—the customary call upon the Mayor was made—and the pageant wended its way to the Opera House where the tableaux and ball were to crown the festivities of the night.

The Tableaux were as follows:

Phœbus and his types of Light.

Orpheus and the types of Sound.

Flora, the Goddess of Flowers, with her types of Smell.

Ceres, daughter of Saturn, and Rhea, bursting like a ripe peach from her types of Taste.

Venus, the child of Jupiter and Dione, with her types of Touch.

The last scene, the Revel of the Passions, embodied a melange of all the characters, with the Genius of Decay in strong contrast.

Thus ended the Ninth Festival of the Mistick Krewe, which, like those which had preceded it, furnished a source of delight and sweet remembrance to the multitude, and maintained the well-earned reputation of the merry King Comus.

TENTH FESTIVAL—1870.

Shrove Tuesday entered the year on the first of March, and found the eager and excited populace anxious to live over again the pleasant dreams which the revels of the Mistick Krewe had now made a part of existence.

The subject chosen for the display this year was the HISTORY OF LOUISIANA, and was represented most beautifully and appropriately in statuary.

First came old "Mische-Sepe," the Father of Waters, mounted on a ghostly-looking horse, followed by sixteen cars, bearing the representatives of the different eras in the History of the State.

CAR No. 1—Louisiana, wearing as a crown a coat of arms, and in her hand a shield; standing near her New Orleans wearing a crown with a crescent. Next to these stood the personators of Sugar, Cotton and Rice.

CAR No. 2—YEAR 1539.—Ferdinand De Soto, surrounded by Juan D. Guzman, Pedro Calderon, Nuno Tobar and Musco de Alvarado.

CAR No. 3—YEAR 1539.—Seven figures on this car: Vasconcellos De Silva, Gonzalo De Cordova and the five Spanish soldiers who made with De Soto that wondrous march from Florida to the Mississippi.

CAR No 4.—The central figure is the Indian Princess who made the gallant Fernando welcome to the country of Cofachiqui. She is surrounded by representations of the different tribes of Indians, upon whom fell the burden of the vindication of their race.

CAR No. 5—YEAR 1673.—Two priests are seen teaching to the Indians by whom they are surrounded, the truths of the Gospel.

CAR No. 6.—La Salle, on horseback, stands forward a representative of another phase of civilization. His faithful friends, Tontin and Father Hennipen, are with him.

CAR No. 7—YEAR 1700.—In this are Iberville and Joinville, Counts Pontchartrain, De Maurepas, Crozate de la Vente and Marigny de Mandeville, honored names in the history of Louisiana.

CAR No. 8.—The central figure is Bienville—the true French chevalier. With him are the Sieur Denis and Dona Marie; around him is a trio of Governors, who represented, with varying credit, His Most Christian Majesty in Louisiana. Their names are Lamoth Cadillac, De L'Epinay and Perier.

CAR No. 9—YEAR 1727.—Religion heads the list, with the figure of a Jesuit Priest and two nuns.

In striking contrast is the martial figure of General Grondel, a dashing French officer, flanked by the Marquis Vaudrieul and Gov. Kerleree.

CAR No. 10.—There is presented here Gen. O'Reilly and Don Juan Ulloa, first Spanish Governor of the Territory. At the side of Don Juan is the Marchioness D'Abrado, a beauty of the period. Next to them is La Frenier. Father Dagobert, a noted priest of the day, closes the picture.

CAR No. 11—YEAR 1772 to 1797.—The Governors of the Territory from 1792 to 1797. Don Luis Ungaso, Governor in 1772; Don Bernardo de Galvez, in 1777; Miro, in 1784; Baron Carondelet, in 1790; and General Gayoso, in 1797.

CAR No. 12—1799 TO 1803.—Marquis Casacalvo, who ruled the State in 1799, and Don Manuel de Lalado, who governed in 1803. Next to them, Robert Livingston, Jas. Madison and James Monroe, the distinguished characters in the history of our country, who were charged by the Government with the purchasing of Louisiana from the French.

CAR No. 13, 1803.—This is a sequel to the last design. Napoleon has resolved to accept the $15,000,000 from the United States, and the group represents Gov. Claiborne and Gen. Wilkinson receiving the territory from the French Commissioner Laussat. The two remaining figures are Etienne Bore, first Mayor of New Orleans, and Girod, the second Mayor.

CAR No. 14, 1815.—General Jackson on horseback, surrounded by his staff, Major Latour, a gallant Frenchman, Major Thomas Butler and Generals Coffee and Carroll.

CAR No. 15, 1815.—In this are seen Pierre and John Lafitte famous in history as the Pirate Brothers, but who earned the names of patriots when they offered themselves with six hundred comrades to the service of Jackson. With them are seen Generals Thomas, Winchester, Labatut and Morgan. These men tell the story of the army of deliverance of Louisiana.

CAR No. 16.—This is the last, and contains General Villere, a gallant looking man, representing worthily one of the highest and most ancient of creole families. With him are General Adair, of Kentucky, Major Plauche, Col. Edward Livingston and Commodore Patterson.

The design of this year's display was not only rich but it was historically valuable. It recalled to the people the deeds and names of those who for them fought with savage tribes, and hazarded life and comfort in a dream of empire, to result, in after years, to the benefit of their descendants.

The procession closed, the Theatre was the future scene of the closing revels, where the Tableaux and ball were to take place—which we give as follows:

TABLEAU FIRST—Louisiana; her Daughter, New Orleans; her Wealth, Cotton, Sugar, Rice; Miche-Sepe, the Father of Waters.

TABLEAU SECOND—Death of De Soto at the mouth of the Red River, in 1542.

RESIDENCE OF JOS. ELLISON, ESQ.

TABLEAU THIRD—Reception of Father Marquet and Joliet by the Indians, in 1673.

TABLEAU FOURTH—La Salle taking possession of Louisiana in 1682, "In the name of the Most Puissant, Most High, Most Invincible, and Victorious Prince Louis, the Great King of France."

TABLEAU FIFTH—Crowning the Hero.—On a raised platform the "man of iron will," glorious old Jackson, was seen standing, while the maiden Louisiana held out her hand over his head in the act of crowning him with the laurel wreath of victory, mingled with the olive leaves of devotion and love. Other figures were grouped around.

TABLEAU SIXTH—Louisiana—Her Founders and Defenders—The grandest effort of the evening, and pronounced by all who saw it the most perfect, beautifully conceived, and handsomely grouped tableau ever beheld. Words cannot convey the beauty and expression of the group. Louisiana appeared on a pedestal, with her daughter, New Orleans, and her friend Miche-Sepe on either hand, while in front stood the representatives of her wealth—Cotton, Sugar and Rice. Lower down were grouped the different characters who had appeared in the previous tableaux, while on her right and left, a little retired, mounted on their favorite horses, were those great heroes and our nation's idols, Washington and Jackson.

The tableaux concluded, the ball followed, and thus for the tenth time the Mistick Krewe flashed across the common-placed existence of mortality.

MECHANICS' INSTITUTE AND NEW ORLEANS MECHANICS' SOCIETY.

THE Mechanics' Institute is among the largest and most imposing of the public buildings of New Orleans. It is built of brick, painted and stuccoed in imitation of granite. It is well lighted on both sides and in front. The lower floor is occupied as the Library and Committee room of the New Orleans Mechanics' Society; two large rooms are occupied as the State Executive office; the Secretary of State has his office in another, and the Hall, intended as the lecture room of the Society, is appropriated to the State Senate. The second story, reached by two broad staircases, is lofty, light and airy. It contains besides, two large apartments, the vast assembly room now employed as the Hall of the Louisiana House of Representatives. The third story is used now as committee rooms, the windows of which command a view of a large part of the city, being higher than the roofs of houses in the vicinity.

This substantial and stately building was the work of the New Orleans Mechanics Society, and it occupies the site of the original institute, which was burned in 1854. The Society was instituted in 1806, the officers for the year 1807 being, H. M. Dobbs, President, Peter Craig, Vice-President, Nicholas Sinnot, Treasurer, and James Armitage, Secretary. The corporators announced in their Constitution, that their objects were: "to relieve the wants, comfort the sufferings and promote the happiness of their fellow creatures," which they held to be essentially the duty of all. The Society was incorporated by an act of the legislature of 1821, H. M. Dobbs, Nicholas Sinnott, Moses Duffy, Peter K. Wagner, Hugh Carr, W. Liddell, John Veasey and Martin Gordon being the first incorporators as named in the act.

The term, (20 years,) was extended by an act of 1838 for thirty years more. By an act of 1850, the State gave to the Society a lot, seventy feet front on Philippa, (now Dryades) Street, and one hundred and fifty feet deep, on condition of erecting a suitable Hall thereon. This is the site of the present Institute. In 1863 the Fisk Free Library, originally presented by Mr. Fisk to the City of New Orleans, was transferred to the care, possession and control of the Mechanic's Society, to be used as a Free Library according to the bequest of the philanthropic donor, to be kept open to the public six hours each day. At the same time the Library Building at the corner of Custom House square and Bourbon streets, was transferred to the Society in order that its rents might be applied to the preservation and enlargement of the library.

This library was nearly destroyed by the fire of 1854, but the few thousand volumes which were saved have since grown into a respectable collection, enjoyed daily by many visitors.

In 1870 the Register of the Society bore 867 names of members, of whom 516 are dead and 71 resigned. Among these members have been some of the worthiest of the public-spirited men of the city who have contributed to its prosperity and honor by their intelligence, virtue, learning and high character. The charitable and useful works of the Society are beyond all estimate, while the scope and extent of its usefulness are continually increasing.

Among the adjunct institutions of the Society is a Savings Bank, authorised by an act of the Legislature of 1863. The Bank is under the management of a Board of twelve trustees.

The officers of the Society for the year 1872, were: John McIntyre, President; H. R. Swasey, Treasurer; Luther Homes, Secretary; and S. Jamison, E. M. Rusha, F. Wing W. McCulloch, Williamson Smith, John A. Shakespeare, Robert Roberts, Peter Ross, J. P. Coulon, James D. Edwards, E. Claren and Thomas O'Neil, the Executive Committee.

COLISEUM PLACE.—This is a long, irregular triangle, having Race street for its base, and Camp and Coliseum streets for its sides, its apex being near Melpomene street. It is planted with shade trees, and is provided with seats. A drainage canal extends along the Camp street side and flows into the larger Melpomene canal. Many fine buildings surround this Park (usually called a "Square,") among which are the homes of Mrs. Stickney, and of Messrs. Peale, Wilson, Hendry, Seeds, Moore, Renshaw and Vincent. The square is overlooked by the new Baptist Church, remarkable for its substantial structure and the graceful spire which is one of the first seen by the traveler as he approaches the city by the river. The small "Church of the New Jerusalem" is on Coliseum street just below the "square."

MAYOR L. A. WILTZ.

Mr. Louis Alfred Wiltz is a native of New Orleans, and, we believe, enjoys the distinction of being the youngest man ever elected in this country to the chief magistracy of a city of the size and importance of the Southern Metropolis. Mr. Wiltz was born in 1843, and is therefore under thirty years of age. He received his education in the Public Schools of this city at a time when they were much better organized and conducted than they have been since. When the State of Louisiana seceded from the Union in 1861, Mr. Wiltz, although not yet of age, entered the Confederate service and was elected captain of a company of infantry, and after the fall of New Orleans, he went into the Trans-Mississippi Department, where he remained on active duty during the war, performing every obligation imposed upon him with characteristic intelligence and conspicuous gallantry.

In 1868, Mr. Wiltz was elected to the House of Representatives from the ninth ward of New Orleans, and the next year he was also elected to the Board of Aldermen, of which body he was made the President by a unanimous vote. Mr. Wiltz's course as a legislator and a city administrator was marked by strict integrity and great vigilance in guarding the interests and vindicating the rights of his constituents, and the Democratic Parish Convention which met in 1869 acknowledged the value of his services by tendering to him the unanimous nomination for the Mayoralty. The municipal election which was to have been held that year having been postponed by an act of the Legislature, Mr. Wiltz was again unanimously chosen for the same position in 1870, and although he did not receive his certificate of election, it was generally believed at the time that he had obtained a majority of the votes cast, and that he was unfairly "counted out."

In 1872, Mr. Wiltz was again nominated for the Mayoralty by the Democratic, Liberal and Reform parties, and was elected by a very large majority over Mr. Fish, the radical candidate.

Although he has always taken a lively interest in public affairs, Mr Wiltz is not a politician, in the vulgar sense of the word, and in his case it may truly be said that the office sought the man, not the man the office. Since the war he has been engaged in commercial pursuits, and is a member of the well-known and highly respected firm of P. S. Wiltz & Co., commission merchants on Carondelet street.

Mr. Wiltz has also devoted much time to the Public Schools of his section of the city, and is also an active and zealous member of our Volunteer Fire Department. This intelligence, knowledge of the wants of the people and thorough acquaintance with the affairs of the city, admirably qualify him for the task of introducing order and economy into every branch of the municipal administration, and his well known integrity and firmness of character are guaranties that the supervisory powers of the office shall be wielded by the new Mayor in such a manner as to hold every member of the city government to a faithful performance of their duty.

E. B. BENTON.

The President of the Accommodation Bank, was born in Vermont in the year 1822. His early occupation was that of a farmer, a pursuit he continued to follow in his native State until 1858, when he removed to Tennessee, and purchased the site now known as Fort Pillow. Here, through indomitable energy and unceasing labor, he succeeded in establishing a trading point, and attracting thither a number of settlers to locate with a view of building up a town. Wishing to enlarge his sphere of business, Mr. Benton visited Europe for the purpose of making contracts for the delivery of oak staves. Whilst absent the war broke out, and all kinds of business being suspended, he returned to New York, and there engaged in the practice of the law in Albany. After the occupation of Tennessee by the Federal authorities, he returned to Fort Pillow, and there re-established the trading post. Enjoying the confidence of the military commanders, he was enabled thereby to render many and valuable services to the Southern people in the vicinity, whom he knew by a previous residence in their midst, and whose respect and esteem he had secured by uniform kindness and correct deportment. After the capture of Fort Pillow by Gen. Forrest, Mr. Benton, who lost all of his property by the fall of the place, went to St. Louis, and there resumed the practice of his profession. He, however, did not remain there long, before finding an opportunity to make an investment of a large amount of capital in the town of Shreveport, La.

Having secured the confidence and assistance of a wealthy gentleman in St. Louis, Mr. Benton established one of the largest and most successful business houses in Shreveport, and conducted it until 1867, when he came to New Orleans, where he has since resided. By industry, frugality and discreet judgment, Mr. Benton has succeeded in accu-

U. S. CUSTOM HOUSE,

(FRONTING ON CANAL STREET,)

NEW ORLEANS.

mulating an independent position, and his sagacity displayed in the purchase of stocks has secured for him the directorship of several companies, and the Presidency of the Accommodation Bank, a position to which he has been twice elected. His management of this institution has been eminently successful, profitable to the stockholders and satisfactory to its patrons. This bank is established upon a firm basis, and its dividends will compare favorably with any similar institution in the country. As Cashier, President Benton has the valuable assistance and services of Mr. Richard Wood, an experienced accountant and business man, whose devotion to the affairs of the Company has contributed not a little to its success. Although a Northern man by birth, Mr. Benton has become thoroughly identified with the South, and is as devoted to its welfare and prosperity as the most ultra Southerner. He married the daughter of the late Barton Lee of Mississippi, and since his residence in this State has become a large land owner. Never having been a politician or a partisan, he has avoided making enemies and he now enjoys the satisfaction of feeling and knowing that the community in which he lives cherishes no bitter animosities against him. On the contrary, those who know him recognize and appreciate his sterling qualities, whilst his general reputation is that of an honest, upright, and enterprising citizen, and a generous and benevolent man. Though comparatively just embarking in business in this city, a bright and prosperous future is in store for all who possess the industry, perseverance and integrity of Mr. E. B. Benton.

BENJAMIN MORGAN PALMER, D. D. LL. D.

Rev. Dr. Palmer, one of the most distinguished divines of this city and of the age in which he lives, was born January 25th, 1818, in the City of Charleston, S. C., where his ancestors were settled prior to the Revolution, and where his father before him was born.

The family was well known in that city, the grandfather living to the advanced age of 98 years, and one of the last links connecting with the Colonial History of South Carolina. The uncle, whose full name was transmitted to the nephew, was, for a quarter of a century, a leading pastor in one of its churches. The father, Rev. Edward Palmer, survives, at the age of 84 years, and is still a laborious pastor in the town of Walterboro, S. C., having always maintained the character of an accomplished divine and most urbane gentleman. It is not too much to say that he has transmitted to his still more eminent son, as an invaluable inheritance, much of the grace which marked the character of the beloved disciple of the Great Founder of the Christian Faith.

Dr. Palmer graduated, with the highest distinction, at the University of Georgia, August, 1838; entered upon the study of Divinity in the Theological Seminary at Columbia, S. C., and was licensed to preach the gospel by the Presbytery of Charleston, April, 1841.

He was married in October of the same year, to Miss Mary A. McConnell, a native of Liberty County, Georgia, and was, soon after, ordained and installed pastor of the First Presbyterian Church in Savannah, Ga.

His ecclesiastical relation was dissolved a year after, by transfer to the pastoral charge of the church in Columbia, S. C. In this connection he remained fourteen years, 1842–1856, during the last three of which, 1853–1856, he filled the chair of Church History and Government in the Theological School at Columbia, in connection with his pastoral duties.

A visit to the South West, in the interest of this Divinity School, during the Winter of 1855, brought him into acquaintance with the First Presbyterian Church, New Orleans, then vacant by the removal to California of its former pastor, Rev. W. A. Scott, D. D., and resulted, after negotiations protracted through a portion of two years, in his settlement in this important church, in December, 1856. Here his labors have been continued to the present time.

In the year 1847, in connection with the Rev. Drs. Thornwell, Howe, Smythe, and other distinguished men, he became one of the projectors and editors of "*The Southern Presbyterian Review*," an able religious quarterly, published at Columbia, S. C., and which has maintained an almost uninterrupted existence, being now in its 23d volume.

The Honorary Degree of Doctor of Divinity was conferred on him, in 1852, by Oglethorpe University in the State of Georgia, and that of Doctor of Laws, in 1870, by Westminster College, in the State of Missouri.

At the formation of the General Assembly of the Southern Presbyterian Church, in 1861, he was called to preside over that venerable Court at its first sessions in the city of Augusta, Ga.

Few American divines, North, South, East or West, have obtained a reputation for eloquence equal to that of Dr. Palmer, none surpass him in theological or secular lore. To intellectual powers of a high order, admirably trained and disciplined, he unites an amount and variety of learning seldom attained. Literary associations and even Universities receive, rather than confer, honor, by his acceptance of their appointments to address them on important occasions. Envy and jealousy are silenced and overcome by the singular modesty and thorough absence of all assumption, which are characteristic traits of this distinguished scholar. In the respect that is entertained for him, in the secret and overt influence he exerts, no divine belonging to the great Presbyterian Church of the United States stands in advance of Dr. Palmer. Even those sects, denominations and churches in New Orleans, which occupy other platforms of religious faith, acknowledge his rare genius, his profound learning, his wondrous eloquence, his possession of all those fine qualities of mind and heart, and his manifestation of all those christian virtues and sympathies, which constitute the model divine. The Crescent City is proud of his reputation, and his own numerous, intelligent and wealthy congregation regards him with enthusiastic devotion.

PAUL FOURCHY.

Mr. P. Fourchy, President of the Merchant's Mutual Insurance Co., and of the Mutual National Bank of New Orleans, is the youngest of our Bank Presidents, having been born in 1832. Mr. Fourchy is a native of New Orleans, and an excellent home education was the only inheritance he received from his father, a distinguished French officer, who commanded a cavalry regiment under the first Napoleon. Commencing life without any of the adventitious influences which usually lead to success, Mr. P. Fourchy owes his present high position to his own industry and good conduct, united with a remarkably clear and well disciplined intellect. In addition to his fine business abilities, Mr. Fourchy is a man of liberal and enlarged views, always ready to take the initiative in all improvements and to lend his assistance to every enterprise calculated to promote the public good; nor is he to be turned aside from what he deems the right course, by outside pressure or popular clamor, his rule of conduct being, "*Fais ce que dois, advienne que pourra.*" Mr. P. Fourchy commenced life as clerk in the well known banking house of Messrs. Jeannet, Quertier & Co., and was subsequently connected in the same capacity with that of Mr. Pierre Poutz, of this city. In 1857, he received the appointment of general accountant of the Merchants's Mutual Insurance Co., was promoted in 1864 to the position of Secretary, and finally on death of the esteemed President of that company, the late John Pemberton, he was unanimously selected as his successor. During the few leisure hours allowed to him, by his laborious duties, Mr. Fourchy found time to qualify himself for admission to the bar, and received his diploma in 1854; and although the engrossing nature of his avocations never permitted him to engage into active practice he is generally admitted by competent judges to be very accurate in all questions relating to the laws of Insurance.

THOMAS A. ADAMS, ESQ.

This gentleman, a native of Boston, Mass., came to New Orleans in the winter of 1842-3, as the representative of the Mutual Safety Insurance Company of New York, and introduced here the Mutual Scrip System of Insurance.

At the time of the arrival of Mr. Adams, five local stock companies were doing the entire insurance business of the city.

The Fireman's Insurance Company soon failed. *The Western* and the *Ocean*, in a few years, went into liquidation. The *Merchants'* and the *New Orleans*, which completed the list, continued with greatly impaired capitals, and with limited business, mostly fire; but they continue to this day, with amended charters, converted into mutual companies, and with enlarged capitals, and greatly increased business.

Soon, other agencies followed, and they so multiplied that they controlled the principal business of the city.

On reviewing the history of insurance in New Orleans, Mr. Adams discovered the important fact that ultimate success had never attended any local insurance company, or any agency. Pursuing his research, another fact was developed, viz: that there had never been any bond of union with the underwriters; and believing this to be the true cause of failure in connection with the leading insurers, he sought, and, in 1846, obtained, the formation of a Board of Underwriters, and to that association he attributes the large and general success that has attended the Insurance interest of New Orleans. Aug. Martin, Esq., the highly respectable President of the New Orleans Insurance Company, was its first President. On his removal to France, Leonard Mathews, Esq., was his successor; and on his death in 1854, Mr. Adams was elected President, and has annually been unanimously reelected during the eighteen following years.

The Crescent Mutual Insurance Company was incorporated in 1849, Mr. Adams as its Vice-President. In 1850, he was unanimously elected its President, which position he still holds.

Other local companies, chartered under the Mutual Insurance system, succeeded each other, all important agencies gradually retiring; and the insurances which, for a series of years, had been transacted by agencies, were now again in the hands of the local companies, who have since controlled them to a large extent.

Before the war, Mr. Adams was, for a number of years, President of the New England Society, composed of many of our leading citizens, a society purely social and charitable, and, we may add, doing great good in its day, aiding the poor, visiting the sick, and relieving the distressed.

Mr. Adams was an active member and trustee, for many years, of the Church of the Messiah, and was one of the largest contributors to the building of the new and beautiful church which bears that name.

In the establishment of a savings bank for the laboring poor, upon a strong and sure basis, Mr. Adams worked assiduously—was an original Trustee in the New Orleans Savings Institution, the leading association of the kind in

HON. L. A. WILTZ,

MAYOR OF THE CITY.

F. A. GONZALES. A. GONZALES.

GONZALES BROS.

Importers of

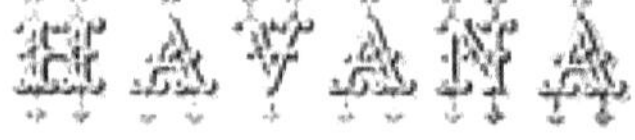

Corner of Camp and Common Streets,

OPPOSITE THE CITY HOTEL.

No. 2 Carondelet St., near Canal, and cor. Union and Carondelet Sts.

New Orleans, La.

All Cigars fully guaranteed imported and genuine brands.

PARTAGAS, UPMANN LA CARONA, LA ESCEPCION, ETC., ETC.

the South. He is, now, its first Vice President—also Vice President of the Printing Institution of the Blind.

With most of the various charitable institutions of the city, the name of Mr. Adams is associated.

Quiet and retired in his habits and tastes, he has uniformly declined any proposition of a political or public nature—shrinking always from attracting any kind of publicity. With a large and well selected library, a devotee to his profession, he may be said to seek his happiness with his books, and in the refined domestic intercourse which awaits him, at his elegant mansion of Prytania street. Here he is the earnest and sincere friend, the courtly host, and the frank, genial companion, fully informed on all subjects.

An ardent and unpretending student, his compeers readily esteem him authority in questions of Insurance Law, and he is never happier than when giving them the advantage of his experience. It is not too much to name him among the leading financiers of New Orleans, yet one who seldom volunteers an opinion in monetary matters, until summoned from his privacy, and then pronounces a judgment which is accepted as law, and remains unreversed.

Thirty years have nearly passed since Mr. Adams became a citizen of New Orleans. His life has been an open book, read of all men. Its pages have been stainless, and its records, in which manliness, virtue and integrity are predominant, have gone forth to eternity. Of him, we may say, in sincerity, what was said of the acts of Addison: "His logic fed his morality, and the uprightness of his mind carried out the justice of his heart!"

COL. JAMES T. TUCKER.

Was born in Salem, Massachusetts, March 16 1838, educated in the public schools, and at the age of sixteen was taken into the service of the Illinois Central R. R. Co., at the principal office in Chicago, then under the administration of President J. M. Douglas. At the opening of the war, he entered the federal army as aid-de-camp on the staff of Major-General Banks, U. S. A., with the rank of Colonel in which capacity he served until the close of the war. He was acting Chief of Staff and private secretary to the same general officers during the Louisiana campaign. After the war he settled in New Orleans, as the general agent of the Illinois Central Railroad Company. In this capacity he has brought to bear an unusual degree of energy and business training. The particular commercial problem which he has undertaken to solve, is the establishment of a direct trade between the Lakes and the Atlantic States, with an extension to the Spanish America or Tropical trade. He has exercised his influence with the Presidents of the Company who have visited New Orleans to inspect personally the feasibility of his views. As a result it has been determined to connect with the Illinois Central Steamboat and Barge navigation at Cairo; and second to extend the Mississippi Central, or the Mobile and Ohio R. R. from Columbus, Kentucky, along the river to a crossing of the Ohio at or near Cairo. This will make a through rail from New Orleans to Chicago without break of grade or change of car. These connections completed, the Illinois Central can now bill freights through between Chicago and New York, Havana, Vera Cruz and Rio Janeiro, or other points having connection with New Orleans. It is undoubtedly the establishment of a longitudinal commerce which will connect the ever-expanding north-west with the American Continent, and its islands. Mr. Tucker is a representative man who brings the enterprise and capital of the northwest to develop the commercial future of the South. He has chosen the South as a permanent residence, and has united himself in marriage with a young lady of one of our oldest and most respected Creole families. As a young man he has a biography to make, but with his character, energy and the confidence of one of the largest and most influential Railroad Corporations in the West he may achieve much honor to himself and usefulness to the section whose interests he has done so much to harmonize.

PIERRE SEVÈRE WILTZ.

Mr. P. S. Wiltz was born in 1818, and is undeniably one of the most influential men of the race to which he belongs, particularly in the Third District of New Orleans, where he has resided uninterruptedly for the last forty-five years. Mr. P. S. Wiltz was born in the Parish of St. Charles, his father and mother being also Louisianians by birth, but tracing their respective ancestry to Germany and France. Leaving school when he was only thirteen years old, Mr. Wiltz went at once into the hardware business, which he subsequently left for the Cotton and Sugar Factorage, completing his studies by his own unaided exertions, during his leisure moments at home. The rudiments of the strong, sturdy, self-reliant character of the man, were thus laid down in early life, and the subsequent career of Mr. Wiltz has shown that the seed was not sown in barren soil. In 1844, Mr. Wiltz first entered public life, being elected to the City Council as a Democrat from a hitherto strong Whig district, nor was it possible for his political opponents to unseat him at subsequent elections, although they carried the district by large majorities for all their other candidates. When the city was consolidated in 1854, Mr. Wiltz was also four times elected to the Common Council, by an almost unanimous vote. He was also sent to the House of Representatives, and was one of the leading members of the Secession Convention in 1861. In 1855, Mr. Wiltz was elected Clerk of the Second Court, over a very formidable competitor, and was again reelected to the same office in 1859. Mr. Wiltz is now engaged in the Factorage business, and is also a director in two of the most flourishing Insurance Companies in New Orleans, the Merchant's Insurance Co., and the New Orleans Insurance Co. One of his partners in business, is his nephew, Mr. L. A. Wiltz, a rising young Creole, who, after gallantly serving his country in the field, received the high compliment of a nomination for the Mayoralty of New Orleans, in 1870, and who is generally believed to have received a large majority of the legal votes, although his opponent was *counted in* by the returning officers.

THE KING OF THE CARNIVAL'S STORY.

His Royal Highness, the King of the Carnival, sprang into existence like Minerva, from the brain of Jove, full armed, on January 31st, 1872. The project was at first a novel one, lacking both men and means to carry it to a successful issue, and, as usual in such cases, a little ruse was employed to secure these two necessary adjuncts for its triumph. The first public intimation given of the project appeared in an editorial in the New Orleans *Times* of that date, as follows:

According to Mr. Greeley and all other great public lights, the raw material should never be wasted, and so think a few respectable and public spirited young citizens in regard to the annual display of Mardi Gras. Heretofore the maskers, who are generally out in goodly numbers upon that day, have wandered round in small bands loosely all over the city. These they propose to collect together on Canal street, at 3 o'clock in the afternoon, and arrange into a procession. Bands of music will be provided, and at the specified hour the Chief Marshal and his aids propose to be in waiting at the Clay Statue to take charge of all arrangements. Orders will be issued in time for more direct guidance, and it is expected that the officers holding their commissions from the shadowy King of the Carnival will be obeyed in all respects with cheerfulness and alacrity.

No doubt the announcement will stimulate the young people to greater efforts, and New Orleans will, this year, revel in a day procession almost equal to the gorgeous night display of the Mystic Krew of Comus.

The services of several gentlemen were now privately enlisted, and with such good prospects, that the same evening appeared the following advertisement:

NOTICE.—The King of the Carnival herewith notifies all parties desirous of taking part in the Carnival Celebration to report to him immediately through their Marshals, stating character of display, probable number, and whether with or without music.

In due time, positions will be assigned, and such arrangements completed as best calculated to make the contemplated procession a complete success.

For the present, his Majesty's address will be "King of the Carnival," New Orleans postoffice. REX.

New Orleans, January 31, 1872.

Meanwhile, friends had been at work with subscription lists, encouraged by the liberality of a gentleman thus referred to in the *Times* of the following day:

Col. Charles T. Howard, having read in yesterday's *Times* of the laudable intention entertained by a band of enterprising young men to organize the wandering maskers of Mardi Gras "into an army with music and banners," has placed in our hands one hundred dollars to further the merry purpose. This sum now awaits the personal order of the "King of the Carnival." Mr. Howard's prompt and liberal action, while creditable to him as a citizen, gives assurance that the enterprise will be accepted and encouraged in a proper spirit by the public, for whose benefit and amusement it has been improvised.

The project was already on the high road to success; subscriptions flowed in liberally, and on February 1st the campaign was opened with the following publication:

MARDI GRAS.

As will be seen by the following correspondence, "The King of the Carnival" allows no grass to grow beneath his royal feet, and by proceeding in a systematic manner has already established his usurping authority in the cause of fun and frolic.

All our people will be delighted at the prospect of thus having one of our olden glories revived, and what has heretofore been a day of vagrant mummery turned into one of grandeur and magnificent display, in which the fanciful tastes of the people will be allowed full license.

His Majesty, though a king, is yet the most liberal one alive, and welcomes all to his revel, whether on foot or horseback, in carriage or in cart, though they come in numbers like organized armies, or singly as spies, all are his subjects, and can share his glory. Let them beware, however, how they disobey his orders, as he is said to be a very choleric, though a very good old party. And so "Long live the King," and may his reign be a merry one.

NEW ORLEANS, Jan. 31, 1872.

To the Hon. B. F. Flanders, Mayor:

His Royal Highness the "King of the Carnival," believing that both the peace and prosperity of the city could be better secured by organizing the wandering maskers of Mardi Gras into a procession on Canal street, respectfully requests your permission to carry out his views, and the co-operation of the police in enforcing his "self-assumed" authority. An early answer is respectfully requested. REX.

To A. S. Badger, Superintendent of Police:

The permission asked for above is granted, and I would respectfully request that the police assist and protect the procession.

BENJ. F. FLANDERS, Mayor.

NEW ORLEANS, January 31, 1872.

To His Royal Highness the "King of the Carnival":

The request referred to me (as above) by his Honor Mayor Flanders, is cheerfully acquiesced in. I will do all in my power, and that of the force under my command (as far as consistent with public duty), to make your Majesty's fleeting reign as powerful and pleasant as it no doubt deserves to be.

In accordance therewith, I hereby order all maskers of Mardi Gras to join in the procession under your Majesty's direction.

Respectfully yours, A. S. BADGER,
Sup't of Police.

The only difficulty remaining was a serious one. An unknown, yet efficient, authority had to be established over the people to which all would yield unquestioned obedience, while yet in ignorance of its character or personality. To achieve this, it was decided to issue a series of "edicts," the first of which appeared on February 2d, in the New Orleans *Times*, as follows:

THE KING OF THE CARNIVAL.

In the language of Louis Napoleon, if there are men who do not comprehend their epoch, the royal personage whose title heads this article, is evidently not of them. His steps at usurpation betray as much daring as enterprise, and from the meek manner in which his encroachments on supreme power are met, it is very plain that he will reign monarch of all he surveys on Mardi Gras. By the annexed correspondence, it will be observed that the military arm of the State yields without question to his shadowy authority, and will do all in its power to add to the glory of his evanescent reign:

EDICT I.

To Whom it may Concern, Greeting:—Our beloved subject, Charles W. Squire, Colonel Commanding Louisiana Field Artillery, is hereby ordered to hold himself in readiness with a battery of artillery at the foot of Canal street, on Mardi Gras, February 13, 1872.

Then and there to fire such salutes as may be deemed by his

VARIETIES THEATRE.

Royal Highness, the "King of the Carnival," necessary to the proper maintenance of his state and dignity.

Given under our hand and seal at Carnival Palace, February 1, 1872. REX.

HEADQUARTERS REGIMENT LOUISIANA VOLUNTEER FIELD ARTILLERY,
NEW ORLEANS, Feb. 1, 1872.

To His Royal Highness the King of the Carnival:

Fully recognizing the supreme power and glory of your Majesty's authority, I respectfully submit to its mandate, and will forthwith take the necessary measures to station a battery of Napoleons at the foot of Canal street on Mardi Gras, February 13, and there await your Majesty's orders.

Kissing your royal hand, I remain with much respect your obedient servant.
CHAS. W. SQUIRES,
Colonel Commanding La. Artillery.

In addition to the above information, it has pleased his Mightiness to request from us a public notification to the following effect:

That large or distinct organizations need only communicate with him officially, previous to Mardi Gras. Small parties, or single maskers, in whatever guise they choose to appear, will find themselves provided for, and their positions assigned in the general edict, containing the programme of the procession, which will be issued in good time. All are welcome. God save the King.

This was speedily followed by other edicts, as will be seen by the following extract from the *Times* of Feb. 3:

"VIVE LE ROI!"

As an usurper the "King of the Carnival" is evidently a success, since history furnishes but rare examples in which ambition has met with so few obstacles in the pathway to power.

If His Majesty possesses one shining qualification superior to all others, it certainly consists in what vulgar people would denominate "check." By a few well directed movements and judicious orders he has achieved a successful coup d'etat and will reign on Mardi Gras, with a title none dare dispute.

With the example of obedience thus set in high places, it is expected that the people, who are more directly interested, will yield an equally prompt and willing submission to all His Majesty's orders.

The following edicts were yesterday promulgated by His Royal Highness:

EDICT II.

To His Excellency the Governor of the State of Louisiana:

In order to avoid any unpleasant complications which might arise through conflict of authority, you are hereby directed to close your office on Mardi Gras and during that period to refrain from the exercise, or attempt to exercise, any gubernatorial privileges or duties whatever.

Further—In order to better preserve the peace and maintain the dignity of the realm, you are also directed to disperse that riotous body known as the Louisiana State Legislature, and close their halls of meeting during the same period of time.

A prompt acknowledgment of your Excellency's submission will be esteemed a favor.

Given under our hand and seal, at Carnival Palace, on this the 2d day of February, 1872. REX.

STATE OF LOUISIANA, EXECUTIVE DEPARTMENT,
NEW ORLEANS, Feb. 2, 1872.

To His Royal Highness the King of the Carnival:

The Governor of the State of Louisiana, entertaining the highest regard for your Majesty's person and authority, will feel honored in obeying your Royal mandates as far as lies in his power.

He regrets that his influence with the State Legislature is not sufficient to control their action to the extent demanded, but will cheerfully transmit to that body your Majesty's gracious communication.

With a high sense of the honor conferred, he remains obediently,
H. C. WARMOTH,
Governor of Louisiana.

Subsequent to the occurrence of the above important correspondence, His Majesty was pleased to order the promulgation of the following:

EDICT III.

To all whom it may Concern, Greeting:

In view of numerous petitions laid at the foot of the throne—all to the following tenor:

NEW ORLEANS, Feb. 1, 1872.

Your Majesty would confer a great favor on a large number of employees, if you could succeed in having business suspended on the evening when your dictum will be the acknowledged law of the city. Wishing you abundance of fun, and hoping through your aid to be able to assist in the frolic, I remain your subject,
EMPLOYEE.

Now, therefore, we, the "King of the Carnival," do hereby order and ordain, That all private places of business in this city BE CLOSED AT ONE O'CLOCK, P. M. ON TUESDAY, February 13, 1872, (Old Probabilities permitting), so that none of our beloved subjects may be debarred from participating in the honors to be accorded their liege Sovereign.

Given under our hand and seal, at Carnival Palace, this the 2d day of February, 1872. REX.

In addition to the above we learn from one of the King's Chamberlains that the procession promises to be not only a complete success, but perhaps one of the grandest affairs that ever occurred in New Orleans. Masking parties are everywhere forming, among which are some composed of the wealthiest and most respectable young men in the city. All seem to have caught the spirit of the thing, and are reporting as directed to headquarters. The system thus introduced cannot fail to add greatly to the enjoyment of all parties concerned, including the public, and Mardi Gras promises to be this year an "upside down" day of the most comical yet orderly character.

Next day the following notice appeared:

"AYE, EVERY INCH A KING!"

Is His Majesty of the Carnival. All day yesterday his cabinet was crowded with secretaries answering communications and completing preparations for the grand organization of Mardi Gras, his Majesty personally superintending the duties of his ministers. Two edicts were issued during the day, which have not yet been promulgated. It was rumored however, around the court yard of the Palace, that one was aimed at suppressing an important judicial body, and that the other was issued in behalf of the school children.

The cheerful alacrity with which his Majesty's edicts have been obeyed has not been without a beneficial effect upon his health and spirits. He properly regards this as not only flattering to his dignity, but as attesting a mark of approval on the part of his beloved subjects promising well for his reign.

The Keeper of the Royal Boot-Jack reported to his Majesty at a late hour last night holding a Council of State upon the subject of the Committee of Fifty-one, which he is inclined to view as an insurrectionary body, he being overheard to say that they reminded him of an old flint-lock musket that would never "report and go off" when it was wanted to.

It was officially announced during the day that five bands of music have already been engaged, and that organizations are daily reporting in greater numbers. Everything is now in train for a happy and successful issue. God save the King.

Excitement had now been fired, and all the necessary preparations for the display were under way in competent hands. His Majesty's coffers were full to plethora, and nothing remained but to keep public attention aroused. With this design, the following appeared in the *Times* of the 6th:

H. R. H. THE KING OF THE CARNIVAL.

ANOTHER EDICT.

The following edict, issued by His Majesty on Saturday, now for the first time officially promulgated:

EDICT IV.

To the Hon. Chairman of the Congressional Investigating Committee, Greeting:

His Royal Highness the "King of the Carnival," having a firm belief in the doctrine "Pleasure first and business afterward," hereby interdicts any session of your honorable body being held on Mardi Gras, February 13, 1872, and respectfully invites its members to witness the glory of his regal state during his reign upon that day.

He now awaits a signification of your acquiescence in this Royal mandate.

Given under our hand and seal, at Carnival Palace, February 3, 1872.
REX.

New Orleans, Feb. 3, 1872.

To His Royal Highness the King of the Carnival:

Bowing to your royal will the members of the Congressional Investigating Committee will obediently comply with your command.

With many wishes for a successful reign, we remain your Majesty's grateful servants.

By order JAS. R. YOUNG,
Secretary of Congressional Investigating Committee.

COURT JOURNAL.

His Majesty was in session nearly all day yesterday with his Council, and was pleased to signify his approbation of the conduct of the Recorders in deciding to adjourn their courts on Mardi Gras, without waiting for a royal edict to that effect. He expresse himself so warmly in consideration of this delicate recognition of authority, that he was obliged to be vigorously fanned by the Lord of the Meerschaum in waiting. His Majesty also completed the appointments of his royal household, assigning the new officials their final duties in providing for his reign. He subsequently, during the afternoon, retired to the Divan, where he passed the evening in meditation, puffing vigorously at one of Don Jose Domingo's cigars.

His Majesty, it was rumored, is somewhat perplexed in regard to the precise and proper relations to be established between himself and his royal cousin, the Grand Duke Alexis, who will be in the city during his reign. Upon this subject he is profoundly reticent, his silence being almost Grant-like in its grandeur, but as His Majesty has already proven himself a poor hand at making mistakes, no doubt the problem will be solved to the mutual satisfaction of both distinguished personages.

In the course of the afternoon, many of his principal subjects called and earnestly solicited an audience with the King; among them Col. J. B. Walton, Judge Cooley, D. F. Kenner, Judge Howe, Dr. Mercer, John Burnside, Chas. Cavaroc, Robert Moore, Mayor Flanders, Pat. Irwin, C. A. Weed, T. A. Adams, Jno. G. Gaines, W. S. Pike, E. Salomon, and many others. All these gentlemen were respectfully but firmly denied an audience, His Majesty having fully determined to hold no public levee until Mardi Gras. Of course the reception of this determination was received with profound regret by the applicants, all of whom desired to have their compliments conveyed to His Royal Highness, by the Groom of the Royal Velocipedes, who was in attendance.

Toward 10 o'clock P. M., His Majesty, as always his custom of an afternoon, commanded the attendance of one of his Under Secretaries, who proceeded, as usual, to read him to sleep with the proceedings of the City Council. He was noticed to yawn repeatedly under the infliction, and at 11 P. M. fell off into a gentle slumber.

At 11.30, a peaceful smile stole like an exhalation over his childlike and bland features, and the Royal Bootjack signified to his brother of the Dressing-gown, that "an Angel whispered to the King." This the latter, who is not much given to the melting mood, refused to "see," saying "More like he was dreamin' he'd drawn a prize in the State Lottery."

At midnight the gates of the Palace were closed, when the sentinel's watchword went echoing from battlement to battlement, "Long live the King."

Next morning the following short biography of His Majesty was laid before the public:

H. R. H.

SOMETHING ABOUT HIM.

The King of the Carnival is the offspring of Old King Cole and the Goddess Terpsichore, whom, in imitation of Jove, he wooed and carried off, in the form of an Irish Bull. He is, therefore, gifted with immortality by virtue of his Olympian origin on his mother's side. He was born somewhere upon the shores of the Mediterranean, about the eighth century, and in consequence is now, though hale and hearty, somewhat advanced in years. Upon arriving at man's estate he speedily conquered the whole of Southern Europe, which he held under dominion for a long period of time. About two centuries ago he declared war against his cousin, King Gambrinus, who at that time held all Northern Europe under sway, and after fighting that monarch desperately a long time was finally conquered and driven into obscurity. During these dark days of misfortune, he sought refuge in England, where he assumed the

NEW ORLEANS GRAIN ELEVATOR.

name of Joseph Miller, familiarly known as "Old Joe Miller," and devoted himself to politics, in which he subsequently achieved some fame as the author of the Junius Letters and the founder of the London *Punch*. A few years since he returned to Rome, where he established a race course on the Corso, and made a desperate attempt to reclaim his dynasty. Failing in this, through the machinations of Count Cavour and Victor Emmanuel, he set sail for the United States, where he landed in 1866, and has since been living in seclusion at the South, managing the political affairs of its people. The prince of mischief-makers and jokers, he is credited with having inspired the queer governments and social relations existing in this benighted section. Only a few days have elapsed since his successful attempt at overthrowing the government of Louisiana, one of the most remarkable occurrences on record—in a cheeky point of view.

His Majesty, in personal appearance, is more interesting than commanding. Rather below the medium height, an erect form surmounted with a well set head, covered with a profusion of snow white hair, and a long patriarchal beard, his aspect is at once venerable and imposing. His brow is wide and expansive, his eyes dark and glittering, always fixed, as it were, on a dreamy futurity. His mouth firm set and stamped with a perpetual smile. His face bronzed with the exposure of centuries, and his entire appearance and bearing are calculated to inspire the most profound awe and respect.

His Majesty has never married, giving as an excuse that this state should not be entered into until experience has sobered the liveliness of youth and all the wild oats have been sown. We give this latter piece of information for the benefit of the ladies who are already overwhelming His Majesty with billet-doux.

It is well to note in this latter connection that the national air or anthem of the Carnival Dynasty, for many centuries past, has been, as is at present, "If ever I cease to love."

A bold stroke was now resolved upon, no less than a general edict closing the District Courts on Mardi Gras. In every instance the order was acquiesced in, eliciting in some instances letters in reply. We quote from the *Times* of the sixth instant:

"*REX.*"

THE KING OF THE CARNIVAL ISSUES HIS EDICTS TO THE DISTRICT JUDGES.

This (Monday) morning, the Judges of our several District Courts were served with a royal edict emanating from His Highness the King of the Carnival, by which it will be seen that "Rex," with an assumption of sovereignty as sweeping as that of the most elevated monarch, has but to command his faithful subjects, even to the dignified Judiciary, fall down and obey. Annexed is a copy of the edict, a *fac-simile* of which was received by each Judge:

EDICT V.

To our Beloved Brother, Judge ———:

Greeting—His Royal Highness the King of the Carnival, by virtue of authority in him vested, does hereby ordain and decree;

1. That the ——— District Court stand adjourned on or before the hour of 12 M., on Tuesday, February 13, 1872.

2. That the Honorable Judge thereof immediately notify the officers thereof, and the bar practitioners of this royal mandate.

All for the glory and state of their sovereign liege, whom God preserve.

Given under our hand and seal at Carnival Palace, this the fifth day of February, 1872. REX.

In response thereunto the judges have signified their cheerful willingness to obey the royal commands, and have addressed His Royal Highness, by hand, as follows:

FROM JUDGE ABELL.

First District Court, Parish of Orleans.

To His Majesty the King of the Carnival:

Your royal authority is fully recognized and will be cheerfully obeyed. Respectfully,

EDMUND ABELL, Judge.

FROM JUDGE COOLEY.

To His Royal Highness, the "King of the Carnival:"

Your Majesty—I have received your communication, enclosing your Majesty's edicts, to the effect that the Sixth District Court be closed on Tuesday, the 13th instant, from the hour of 12 M., and also that I, as Judge of that court, notify the officers thereof, and the members of the Bar, of your royal mandate.

I beg to assure your Majesty that I am anxious to comply with your desires; that instead of adjourning my court as you order, at 12 M., on the 13th, I shall have it hermetically closed at 3 o'clock P. M., the day preceding, and shall so advise the officers and members of the Bar.

Tendering to your Majesty my best wishes for a prosperous and joyful reign, I remain your Royal Highness' most obedient servant,

W. H. COOLEY,
Judge Sixth District Court.

FROM JUDGE DUVIGNEAUD.

To His Majesty the King of the Carnival:

Sire—I cheerfully acknowledge the receipt of your royal mandate, and beg leave to inform your amiable Majesty that I will faithfully, as a loyal subject, comply with your request. Praying Almighty God that you may live thousands of years in our beloved city, I have the honor to be, of your Majesty, the most humble and obedient servant, J. S. DUVIGNEAUD,

Judge of the Second District Court, by the grace of your Majesty and the free people of this city.

FROM JUDGE LEAUMONT.

To His Royal Highness, King of the Carnival:

Sire—A significant nod of the judicial cranium has just brought me near—nearer to the somewhat antique bench of his Honor, Don Cesar Leaumont, holding forth as Major Domo, sole Judge of the Fifth District Court for the parish of Orleans.

That functionary now affectionately hands me your peremptory order and decree, directing the closing of his infirmary on Tuesday, February 13, 1872, and begs me to assure you that—

He deems it not only a duty, but a pleasure to strictly comply with your Royal behests, feeling as he does that "the Court is in full accord with Mercuries," and that this case "presents no difficulty."

I am further enjoined by Don Cesar to renew the assurance of his eternal loyalty.

Thrice saluting, oh! King, I am thine.

LOUIS POWER,
Clerk Fifth District Court, parish of Orleans.

FROM JUDGE DIBBLE.

Palace of Justice,
Department of Prerogative Writs.

To His Royal Highness, King of the Carnival:

I am directed by his Honor the Judge of this our Court, to inform your Highness that in obedience to your royal command, our court will be adjourned on the occasion of the entrance of your Majesty into this city, and that all of your Majesty's commands thereunto will be strictly obeyed.

I am further directed by his Honor the Judge, to make his pledges of fealty to your Majesty.

I have the honor to be your Majesty's most obedient servant,

O. M. TENNISON,
Register of Decrees.

In addition to above, Judges Theard and Collens have given the bearer of His Majesty's edicts personal assurance of their compliance.

Another batch of edicts appeared the following morning, and it was now very plain that His Majesty's authority was established beyond all cavil or dispute. We quote from the daily papers of the seventh:

IMPORTANT EDICTS.

FROM H. R. H. THE KING OF THE CARNIVAL.

Now, by St. Paul, the work goes bravely on, and all the realm is alive with preparation. Never before was a conqueror more thoroughly successful. He has but to speak, and lo! all hasten to obey. Below we publish the four last edicts of the King of the Carnival, which give holiday to a vast number of public employees, and all the public school children:

EDICT VI.

To A. B. Carter, Esq., Superintendent Public Schools, Parish of Orleans:

Greeting—His Royal Highness the King of the Carnival, being desirous that the children of the realm should be afforded an opportunity of participating in the honors to their liege Sovereign on Mardi Gras, February 13, 1872, hereby ordains and decrees, that all the schools under your jurisdiction be closed upon that day, and that you immediately take the necessary steps to secure the enforcement of this royal mandate.

A prompt acknowledgment of your acquiescence in this order will be esteemed a favor.

Given under our hand and seal, at Carnival Palace, this, the third day of February, 1872. REX.

OFFICE OF DIVISION SUPERINTENDENT PUBLIC SCHOOLS,
Sixth Division, 20 City Hall,
NEW ORLEANS, February 6, 1872.

To His Royal Highness, the King of the Carnival:

The kingly decree of your Majesty as to the public schools of this division, has been received, and in due submission to the sovereign mandate the schools will be closed on the thirteenth instant—Mardi Gras.

I crave permission to add that your Majesty has no more faithful subjects than the "children of the realm" in the schools, albeit they themselves are, to a degree, sovereigns and rulers with unbounded, if not constitutional sway, in the home dominion.

Wealth, prosperity and great wit and wisdom to your Majesty.

A. B. CARTER, Superintendent.

WM. ROLLINSON, Secretary Board Directors.

EDICT VII.

To the Hon. C. W. Lowell, Postmaster, New Orleans:

Greeting—His Royal Highness, King of the Carnival, by virtue of authority in him vested, and in consideration of communications received in the following tenor:

To His Royal Highness the King of the Carnival:

Wishing to take an active part in the festivities on the thirteenth instant, I trust Your Majesty will request the Postmaster to excuse his employees from slinging literature on that day. I am very respectfully, etc., yours, EMPLOYEE.

It is hereby ordained and decreed that you conform as closely to the above request as consistent with your public duties. This for the honor and glory of the King, who awaits a signification of your obedience.

Given under our hand and seal, at Carnival Palace, this, the fifth day of February, 1872. REX.

POST OFFICE,
Corner Canal and Old Levee streets,
NEW ORLEANS, February 6, 1872.

His Royal Highness, the "King of the Carnival:"

Sire—Your decree of the fifth instant has been duly communicated to me, and I have the honor to inform you, that in obedience to your command, this office will be closed on Tuesday, the 13th instant, at 12 o'clock M.

Your Majesty's most loyal subject,

C. W. LOWELL, Postmaster,
New Orleans, La.

EDICT VIII.

To James F. Casey, Esq., Collector of the Port of New Orleans:

Greeting—His Royal Highness, King of the Carnival, having been informed that a large number of his well beloved subjects are under your authority and control, hereby ordains and decrees—

First—That they be released from duty at noon, on Mardi Gras, under penalty of our Royal displeasure.

Second—That the revenue cutter "Wilderness" remain in port during the entire day.

His Majesty now awaits notification of your compliance with this Royal mandate.

Given under our hand and seal at Carnival Palace, the fifth day of February, 1872. REX.

CUSTOM HOUSE, NEW ORLEANS,
Collector's Office, February 6, 1872.

To His Majesty, the "King of the Carnival:"

I am instructed by Collector Casey to acknowledge the receipt of your royal command, directing the suspension of the collection of customs and the detention of the United States revenue steamer "Wilderness" in port during the Mardi Gras festivities, and to assure you that it will be his pleasure for to faithfully execute the decrees of your Majesty. Your loyal subject,

E. P. CHAMPLIN, Deputy Collector.

EDICT IX.

To Charles T. Howard, President Louisiana State Lottery:

Greeting—It having come to the knowledge of his Royal Highness, the King of the Carnival, that some three hundred of his loyal subjects are temporarily under your control, therefore,

Know ye, that this mandate hereby interdicts the transaction of any business whatever, connected with the Louisiana State Lottery, on the day, (February 13, 1872) consecrated to His Majesty's reign.

Given under our hand and seal at Carnival Palace, this, the sixth day of February, 1872. REX.

NEW ORLEANS, Feb. 6, 1872.

To His Royal Highness, King of the Carnival:

Sire—Bowing in mute allegiance to your royal authority, I hereby notify the public and all employees connected with the Louisiana State Lottery, that the regular day drawing of the same will be omitted on February 13, 1872, (Mardi Gras), and at the same time entreat them to do everything in their power to contribute to your Majesty's state and glory on that occasion. With the best wishes for the health, power and prosperity of your Royal Highness, I remain your humble servant,

CHARLES T. HOWARD,
President L. S. L.

His Majesty desires us to state that in consequence of his secretaries and attendants being overwhelmed with preparations for Mardi Gras, he will issue no more special edicts.

The public for all future information is referred to the general edict of His Majesty, which will appear in all the papers on Friday morning. Meanwhile he can be addressed as usual through the post office.

A day's rest was now taken, but on the 9th the work again commenced, as witnessed by the following extracts from the papers of that date:

H. R. H.

THE KING OF THE CARNIVAL.

This potent Monarch, who seems to be as considerate as he is mighty, who tempers the exercise of unlimited power with profound judgment, yesterday sent as a Minister of the Royal Household to request, through the press, an explanation to the public.

Among the many prayers laid at the foot of his throne is one signed by nearly all the bank clerks and tellers in the city, praying the issuance of a royal edict closing all banks and banking houses at 12 M. on Tuesday, the 13th inst.

While maintaining direct personal sway over all public officials, and exacting the strictest obedience, he has so far avoided touching arbitrarily on any private or business relations of his well-beloved subjects, and is therefore compelled to withhold the special mandate prayed for. At the same time, feeling assured that in a community so loyal, his slightest wish expressed, will be esteemed law, he expresses a firm belief that the closing of all banks and banking-houses, and, he might also add, insurance offices, at 12 M., on the day of his reign, is one of the necessities of the times; and he feels sure that the officers of the same, in whom such authority may rest, will not willingly incur his royal displeasure by committing such an unpardonable impropriety as to keep them open. The early action of the parties referred to, upon this hint, will not fail to find favor in His Majesty's eyes.

THE BŒUF GRAS.

One of the most interesting features of the Carnival procession on Tuesday will be the *Bœuf Gras*, accompanying the butchers. The ox selected for the honor is a remarkable one. He belongs to Messrs. C. Mehle & Co., who intend decorating and parading him in return for his valuable services. "Jeff. Davis" or "Old Jeff," as he is more familiarly known around the stock yard, is the leader who beguiles all the beeves on board vessels and steamboats, transfers them to the pens and maintains a general supervision over the doomed captives on their way to execution. He is a splendid animal, milk white in color, and exhibits extraordinary intelligence. He is said to hold conversation with his friend and keeper, whom he follows about like a spaniel, obeying the slightest word or direction. Messrs. C. Mehle & Co. think that "Old Jeff" is entitled to some public honor, before he goes the way that all good oxen go, and have accordingly selected the present occasion as an appropriate one. He will be beautifully decorated and surrounded with a guard of honor composed of cooks with shining cleavers and Vaqueros with their lariats. So success to "Old Jeff."

The following was given to the public on the 10th inst.:

H. R. H.

THE KING OF THE CARNIVAL.

Held a State Council Thursday night, which was attended by the entire Court. About 9 o'clock, His Majesty, accompanied by his Lords in waiting, entered the audience chamber and mounted the throne. He looked paler than usual, as though somewhat jaded with the immense labors lately undergone, but still preserved that calm demeanor under which sleeps the wild and fury of the lion, when aroused. All matters connected with the approaching display were there submitted to His Majesty, who manifested his gracious assent to the arrangements made by the Grand Marshal of the Empire in the premises. He also made an affectionate inquiry in regard to the state of the royal exchequer, which was answered by the Lord High Treasurer in such encouraging terms, that His Majesty actually smiled. After this the ceremony of presentation and kissing hands took place, which over, His Majesty addressed a few words to his courtiers concerning their duties. During the course of his remarks he alluded in high terms to the loyalty manifested by his subjects, and the willing manner in which they had all aided his efforts.

He said, that although an exceedingly mild and unexacting monarch, prone always to err upon the side of good nature, there was one point upon which he wished to be distinctly understood, and he trusted all the gentlemen attached to his Royal person would take particular pains to make him so.

The persons living along the route of pageant laid down by the Grand Marshal of the Empire, should consider themselves, not only highly but exceptionally honored; and that he expects them to display a due sense of appreciation of kingly favor, by having their galleries and houses appropriately decorated on the occasion of his reign. Any omission in this wise would be surely noted as a mark of gross disrespect to his royal person and dignity; and unless the entire route be appropriately decorated, the royal pageant of the ensuing year would certainly avoid all such streets and localities.

It will thus be seen that the persons living along the route of the procession have an important responsibility devolving upon them, and if they wish to propitiate his Royal Highness the King of the Carnival, each and every one had better take immediate steps to have their galleries appropriately festooned. They must recollect that in all well ordered empires, and none is more so than that of his Majesty of the Carnival, the King's will is law.

THE ANTHEM.

His Royal Highness, the King of the Carnival, requests us to notify all organizations provided with their own music, that while passing in review before His Majesty, each band is expected to play the Royal anthem of the most puissant House of Carnival. Said anthem being familiar to modern ear under the title of

"If ever I cease to love."

On the 12th inst. the General Edict laying down the programme of the projected celebration, was promulgated in all the city papers as follows:

EDICT NO. X.

BY H. R. H., THE KING OF THE CARNIVAL.

To all whom it may Concern—Greeting:

The thirteenth day of February, 1872, having been set apart as one dedicated to His Majesty's glory, for the better guidance of his loyal subjects, it is hereby ordained and decreed, that all persons or parties owing allegiance to his dynasty will join according to the following rules and regulations, to

GRAND STATE PAGEANT.

His Royal Highness, the King of the Carnival, will command in person, assisted by the Grand Marshal of the Empire, and the Lords of the Horse, Carriages, Vans, Yeomanry and the Unattached—all of whom, with their Aids, will appear at Clay Statue at 2 o'clock P. M.

Upon arrival, the Lords herein named will immediately take position at the points assigned for the rights of their respective Divisions, in the manner laid down in this our Royal mandate, taking care to place and hold in line their several bodies, subject to the orders of the Chief Marshal of the Empire.

HOW IT WILL FORM.

The pageant will be divided in Five Grand Divisions, which will form as follows:

THE FIRST DIVISION—Will comprise all foot maskers, (in ranks of four), and will form on the South side of Canal street, their right resting on St. Charles street, extending toward the swamp.

THE SECOND DIVISION—Comprising all maskers in open or private carriages, will form on St. Charles street, the right resting on Canal street.

THE THIRD DIVISION—Comprising all maskers in vans, floats, milk-carts and other public vehicles, will form on Camp street, their right resting upon Canal street.

THE FOURTH DIVISION—Comprising all masked horsemen in sections of four, will form on the south side of Canal street, their right resting upon Camp street, and rear extending toward the river.

THE FIFTH DIVISION—Comprising all stragglers, late comers and subjects not elsewhere provided for, will form on the North side of Canal street, their right resting upon Chartres street, and rear extending toward the river.

All the above are required to be in line by 2 o'clock P. M.

HOW IT WILL MOVE.

At precisely three o'clock P. M. a Royal Salute of thirteen guns will be fired from the foot of Canal street, by Col. C. W. Squires, Commander-in-Chief of his Majesty's forces, when the King and Court will immediately move from the Clay Statue, taking up the line of march, followed by the First Division, down the south side of Canal street to the intersection of Camp and Chartres streets, up the south side of Canal street to Royal, and down Royal street.

When the left of the First Division passes St. Charles street, the Second Division will move into line; when its rear passes Camp street, the Third Division will move into line; the Fourth Division following next in order, and the Fifth Division last.

Each Division will be provided with a Band of Music, and its and its Lord Marshal attended by a Standard Bearer.

ORDER OF PROCESSION.

Squadron of Mounted Police.

Grand Marshal of the Empire.

H. R. H., THE KING OF THE CARNIVAL, with attendants.

Music.

Lord of the Yeomanry.

Boeuf Gras.

FIRST DIVISION—Music; Lord of the Carriages.

SECOND DIVISION—Music; Lord of the Vans.

THIRD DIVISION—Music; Lord of the Horse.

FOURTH DIVISION—Music; Lord of the Unattached.

FIFTH DIVISION—Platoon of Police.

THE ROUTE OF MARCH.

Down Royal street to Esplanade street; down Esplanade street to Rampart street; up Rampart street, north side, to Canal street; up Canal street, south side, to St. Charles street; up St. Charles street to St. Joseph street, to Camp street; down Camp street to Canal, to Clay Statue, where His Royal Highness will graciously review his subjects and dismiss the pageant to their own enjoyment—a Band of Music being placed in each square between Rampart and Camp, to better secure this end.

GENERAL ORDERS.

1. All organizations and subjects intending to participate must report to the Lords Marshal of Division, at 2 o'clock P. M.

2. All places of business, public and private, are hereby ordered to be closed at 12 o'clock M.

3. Owners and drivers of public and private vehicles, are required to keep out of the highways in which the Divisions of the Royal pageant will form and through which it will pass.

4. Owners and masters of vessels and steamboats in port, the proprietors of public buildings, the Consuls of all foreign nations at peace with His Majesty, are directed to display their colors during the entire day.

5. The City Authorities are hereby ordered, under penalty of Royal displeasure, to remove all obstructions from the highways on which the pageant is to form or pass.

6. All malicious mischief upon the part of his loyal subjects, such as throwing flour, is interdicted and forbidden under the severest penalty.

7. The Lords Marshal will be distinguished as follows: Grand Marshal of the Empire, purple and gold rosette and baton; Division Lords Marshal, red and gold ditto; Aids, to correspond.

At Sunset another Royal Salute will be fired by the Commander-in-Chief of His Majesty's forces, when all his subjects will immediately disperse, in order to give place, and do appropriate honor to our Cousin COMUS, who visits His Majesty after that time.

And now, enjoining strict obedience upon the part of his beloved subjects, His Royal Highness trusts his honor and glory in their loyal hands.

Given under our hand and seal, at Carnival Palace, this the 5th day of February, in the year of our Lord, 1872. REX.

Preparations had now advanced to such a point, that nearly everything was in readiness; and, on the 12th, the following proclamation was issued by the Lord Grand Marshal:

PROCLAMATION

By the Grand Marshal of the Empire.

CARNIVAL PALACE, FEBRUARY THE TWELFTH,
Anno Domini, 1872.

I. In obedience to H. R. Highness' Edict No. X, and to carry out its provisions and commands promptly and harmoniously, the Grand Marshal of the Empire, call upon all loyal and obedient subjects, to form at their respective places of rendezvous, precisely at one o'clock, on Tuesday, (Mardi Gras,) 1872, in order that they may report to the Lord Division Marshal, to whose division the character of the organization belongs.

The prompt carrying out of this command alone will prevent confusion and unnecessary delay. As the Royal State Pageant will move punctually at 3 o'clock, all organizations and subjects will have to be in line at 3 P. M.

II. The Lords of Yeomanry, of Carriages, of Vans, of the Horse and of the Unattached, together with their Aids, are commanded to report in person to the Lord Grand Marshal, at his department of State, at 12 M.

III. Col. A. S. BADGER, commanding His Majesty's Household Guard, is commanded to report to the Grand Marshal of the Empire at the same hour and place.

BY THE LORD GRAND MARSHAL.

Approved, REX.

On the same day the following notices appeared in the *Times*:

THE KING OF THE CARNIVAL.

COURT JOURNAL.

The calm which invariably precedes the storm, prevailed at the palace yesterday, and but little work was done. The guards lounged around the galleries and ante-chambers in a listless manner, occasionally gathering into knots listening to the jovial yarns of Col. Jack Wharton, Chief Equerry in waiting to His Majesty, or exciting stories of the chase as related by Billy Connor, Lord Groom of the

CAPT. T. P. LEATHERS,

STEAMBOAT NATCHEZ.

CHURCH OF THE IMMACULATE CONCEPTION.

Royal Stables. During the entire morning His Majesty remained in seclusion, only granting an audience to a deputation of loyal ladies, who desired some information concerning the Royal colors, with a view to using them in the decorations of Tuesday. His Majesty received them graciously, and summoned Garter King-at-Arms, to his presence. The latter explained that the Royal colors were Green, Gold and Purple; regretting that the subjugation of the State had been too recent to prepare a Royal Standard, but that upon all His Majesty's future fete days it would invariably be displayed. An hour was subsequently spent in completing additional arrangements for the reception of the Grand Duke; His Majesty, who of course understands all languages, inditing the following autograph letter, to be handed to his Royal cousin upon arrival. We give it in the vernacular;

His Royal [illegible] Highness [illegible] The King of the Carnival, [illegible] Alexis Alexandrovitch Romanoff [illegible] Mardi Gras.

REX.

In the evening a grand State banquet was given. Among the guests attending which were to be found Gen. H. S. McComb, Gen. Beauregard, Col. Sam Boyd, Norbert Trepagnier, F. O. Hebert, Samuel Smith, J. W. Burbridge, I. N. Marks, C. A. Whitney, and C. H. Slocomb, Esquires. The approaching festivities were here discussed at length with the viands and wines until [illegible] o'clock, when His Majesty, attended by his Lords in waiting and Gentlemen of the Bed Chamber, retired, leaving the guests to their own enjoyment. His Majesty was subsequently read to sleep by one of the Under Secretaries, but with some difficulty. The proceedings of the City Council usually productive of somnolency being found upon this occasion ineffectual, through their unusual brevity of late; resort was then had to the minutes of the Academy of Natural Sciences, under the soothing influence of which nature shortly succumbed.

Many additional applications for position were filed during the day at the office of the Grand Marshal of the Empire, and another heavy batch of correspondence was being opened up to a late hour of night, all testifying greater promise of gorgeous magnificence of the Royal State Pageant. God save the King.

A CARD.

More Honors to H. R. H.

New Orleans, Feb. 10, 1872.

To His Royal Highness, the King of the Carnival:

Sir—Hearing that some three hundred employees of the New Orleans, Jackson & Great Northern Railroad have addressed a petition to your throne, praying a special edict releasing them from duty upon the occasion of your reign, February 13, 1872, I hasten to forestall that necessity.

Proud of being ranked among your Majesty's most loyal subjects, and fully appreciating the wisdom and profound judgment which characterizes your rule, I herewith announce the intention of the New Orleans, Jackson and Great Northern Railroad to release all employees from duty upon your fete day, except those actually necessary to bring the throngs of subjects daily arriving to do honor to your Royal Highness.

I hope that all said employees may join in the pageant, and thereby publicly testify the high and loving estimation in which you are held by your honored and submissive subjects.

H. S. McCOMB,

President New Orleans, Jackson & Great Northern Railroad.

On the 13th dawned the memorable day of His Majesty's first triumph, on the morning of which he issued his last edict, through his official journal, as follows:

THE KING RIDES FORTH TO-DAY.

Yesterday at Carnival Palace.—Another Edict.—Preparations for the Display Being Actively Pushed Forward.

"VIVE LE ROI!"

His Majesty remained in his private apartments throughout the entire day yesterday, absorbed in meditation and the inevitable Gonzales cigar. Having been apprised the evening previous of the arrival of his royal cousin, the Grand Duke Alexis, at 10 A. M., he ordered the State carriage, with outriders and chasseurs, and dispatched it with the Lord Chamberlain, Chief Equerry in waiting, and his Honor the Lord Mayor of the Corporation, to conduct His Highness to the apartments arranged for him in the north wing of the Imperial Palace of St. Charles.

To-day having been set aside for the official reception of the Grand Duke, of course great quiet and seclusion prevailed around His Majesty's apartments. The offices of the Grand Marshal, the Grand Almoner, and the Secretaries were, however, very busy all day making preparations for to-day's celebration, and from what we could glean, everything promised a happy consummation.

The following letter from a prominent firm in the railroad and steamship interests was handed to His Majesty's Secretary while just upon the point of issuing a special edict in the premises:

New Orleans, Feb. 12, 1872.

To His Royal Highness, the King of the Carnival:

Sire: In obedience to your Royal mandate, contained in Edict X, we beg leave to announce our intention of releasing all employees from duty, on February 13th, 1872, who may wish to participate in the honors to be accorded your Royal Highness, and who can be conveniently spared from the exigencies of business.

With highest esteem, we remain, your obedient servants,

C. A. WHITNEY & CO.

As night wore on, the gates of the Palace were closed, the portcullis lowered and the draw-bridge raised. All strangers and newspaper reporters were exiled beyond the moat, but long into the silent watches of the night, the flickering lights waving to and fro, and clink of hammers closing rivetings, gave evidence that the work of preparation was being pushed on with unabated zeal.

During the course of the day, the following edict was ordered promulgated by His Royal Highness the King:

EDICT No. XI.

To all Whom it may Concern:

His Royal Highness, the King of the Carnival, being deeply impressed with the enthusiastic loyalty manifested by his beloved subjects of all degrees and conditions, upon this, his most blessed *fete* day, has resolved—

That a proper consideration for the glory of his regal state and sovereign care for his loyal subjects, demands the abrogation of all laws, and the removal of all impediments of whatsoever kind or nature, that may impair or interfere with public enjoyment.

In pursuance of this determination, he, therefore, solemnly enacts the following decrees to rule the law of the land during the entire reign of his illustrious and glorious Majesty:

First—Whereas, It having come to our Royal knowledge that one Stockdale, Collector of Internal Revenue, intends taking advantage of His Majesty's preoccupation in affairs of State connected with the Royal Pageant, to collect all the taxes of the Realm, his office is hereby abolished.

Second—The following laws enacted by a previous government having been found to weigh grievously upon His Majesty's subjects—The Registration Law, Constabulary Law, Election Law, Printing Law, Taxes and Judge H. C. Dibble—all of the same are hereby abrogated and abolished.

Third—The credit of the Realm is hereby re-established on a specie bank, and all securities, of whatever nature, are declared to rule at par value. Any person, subject or foreign, detected at any attempt at their depreciation will be immediately incarcerated in the lowest dungeon of the Donjon-keep.

Fourth.—All subjects guilty of any breach of the peace, working at and any description of disorder or offence against good taste and decency, in the display of entire or improper costumes, will be immediately conveyed to the barracks of the household troops; and our well beloved servant, Col. A. S. Badger, Captain of the Guard, near to the person of His Majesty, is hereby charged with the strict enforcement of this order under penalty in default thereof of being forced to attend the meeting of the Academy of Natural Sciences for the entire year.

Fifth.—The market rate of cotton is hereby established for this day at fifty cents per pound, low middling grade, and for sugar at 25 cents per pound, other products of the realm to grade in proportion. Any subject violating this order will, upon trial and conviction be sentenced to serve not more than one term at hard labor in the Louisiana State Legislature.

Sixth.—All punishments incurred by the children of the realm for any offences of whatever nature, committed anterior to this date, are hereby cancelled in honor of the fete of His Royal Highness. Parents or guardians disregarding the provisions of this order are hereby sentenced to a perpetual deprivation of their night latch keys.

Seventh.—All quarrels, hatreds, jealousies and vendettas heretofore existing between any of His Majesty's subjects are hereby cancelled, as nothing but the most unalloyed good humor and jollity will be allowed to prevail throughout the realm during the glorious reign of His Majesty.

Eighth.—All persons residing along the route of the royal pageant, are ordered to provide proper extra supports for their galleries, to festoon and decorate the same with the royal colors, (green, gold and purple,) and to pay due obeisance to His Royal Highness, in passing, under penalty in default thereof of perpetual exile to the Balize.

Lastly.—Sir Warren A. Stone, the Right Hon. D. C. Holliday, the Hon. J. T. Scott, and Sir Howard Smith, Physicians in Ordinary to His Majesty's household, having recommended a change of air and scene, the King of the Carnival will therefore be under the unpleasant and regretful necessity of leaving his loyal subjects after at sunset today, for a brief period of time; promising to return again when his health, in the opinion of the Royal Physicians, shall have been fully re-established.

In doing so, it is with a profound and gratifying sense of the loyalty displayed by his subjects, of the cheerful and prompt alacrity with which his orders have been obeyed, and with the promise that on the occasion of his next entry into his capital, the splendors of today's pageant shall be far outdone in magnificence and gorgeous state.

And now, with the best wishes for their health, prosperity and happiness, he bids them, in anticipation of his rather sudden departure, an affectionate adieu. Enjoining upon them during his absence, unswerving loyalty in their allegiance to the Royal House of Carnival, and an unimpaired continuance of that loving affection already manifest for its reigning head, which is above all price. God save the King.

Given under our hand and seal, at Carnival Palace, this, the 13th day of February, in the year of our Lord, 1872.

REX.

The unprecedented success of the Procession is yet too fresh in the recollection of our readers, to need elaboration in this short story; it can, however, be readily referred to if desired, in all, or any of the New Orleans daily papers of February 14, 1872; from which the following short comments are extracted:

It is with pleasure that the chronicler reflects that the work of this article was to record the dawning of a new era in the long history of Mardi Gras festivities, and that the advent has been not only brilliant but successful, the thousands of delighted people who were not slow to express their enthusiasm, can fully testify. It is no easy matter to conduct such a spectacle satisfactorily, and it is therefore a cause for much gratification that in every respect the Procession of Rex, his court and kingdom, will be looked forward to as one, if not as the great event of Mardi Gras, and when he again "rides forth" the king of the Carnival, his loyal subjects will greet him with a welcome made stronger and heartier by reason of his achieved success, and the assurance of additional pleasure, which have by his means entered into the glorious and festal time.

It has opened a new era to New Orleans; one we trust to see cultivated, and the little plant of only ten day's growth which yielded so bountifully of blossoms, we trust to see expand, in the future, to a lusty tree, hung with the golden fruit, that all will be glad without exception to pluck and enjoy. In the old language of the sectional unpleasantness, the association of gentlemen who managed this affair, "covered themselves with glory."

The benign yet firm reign of His Majesty on this occasion, developed one remarkable result. Although 5,000 maskers were assembled in Procession, yet the police statistics of disorder and arrests were notably smaller on that occasion than any preceding Mardi Gras; while the jollity and enthusiasm was immensely augmented. Not the slightest break or delay occurred in the programme, and at sunset, His Majesty and escort left the city, via Carrollton, en route for Assyria.

Previous to leaving, His Majesty ordered the Legislature of Louisiana to constitute his fete day a legal holiday. Which order was promptly complied with, as will be seen by the following extract from the daily press of April 4th, at which point the King of the Carnival story closes for the present.

MARDI GRAS.

H. R. H. HEARD FROM.

Yesterday the bill passed by the last Legislature, making Mardi Gras a legal holiday, was signed by Governor Warmoth and has now become a law; in compliance with the last strict orders issued by his Majesty of the Carnival before leaving our city on the 13th of February last. Notice of this act of submission and homage to his supreme domination was immediately dispatched to the Governor of the State, after affixing his signature, to the office of the Lord High Chamberlain at Carnival Palace. Upon its reception the guard was immediately turned out, the Royal standard was displayed upon the battlements, and the guns of the Citadel fired a Royal salvo in honor of the act of obeisance.

In the evening, a bearer of dispatches, duly attended, left the city with the notification for His Majesty, who is now on his way to Assyria, where he proposes to spend the summer in travelling for the benefit of his health.

The last information received at the Palace, was to the effect that his majesty was then at Malta, recuperating for his further journey. He was at the time engaged in the preparation and perfection of many Patents of Nobility; it being his royal intention to create a Peerage in his newly conquered dominions, in order to add still further to the magnificence of his reign and state. The commission bearing these graceful evidences of royal condescension were expected to leave for New Orleans in the course of three or four weeks, and pending their arrival, his ambitious subjects who aspire to share their honors, must restrain impatience.

It was also given out at Malta, that his Majesty's army was now actively recruiting in Assyria, with a view to immediately placing his realm upon a war footing, impelled thereto by the warlike preparations going on throughout Europe, and the threatening attitude of the United States army towards the South under the operation of the Kuklux law.

His Majesty, at last accounts, was reported much improved in health, but somewhat jaded by the fatigues of travel. Although in his 1025th year, he is said to have grown both in stature and weight since leaving New Or-

New Odd Fellows' Hall.

beams, and now presents a most imposing appearance. His Majesty's leisure moments are constantly occupied with making plans for his next *fête*, to which he looks forward to with pride and satisfaction. Having definitely settled upon the final transfer of his seat of government from the shores of the Mediterranean to those of the Mississippi, it is to be expected that his entry on the ensuing Mardi Gras in 1873, will far surpass in splendor and ceremony, anything ever witnessed in any country during the present age. The preparations are certainly upon a stupendous scale, and with the active co-operation of his loyal, loving subjects, so freely and cordially extended, he feels that nothing is impossible.

GOD SAVE THE KING!

[NOTE.—In excellent and responsible hands, embracing a large number of our most highly esteemed and responsible citizens, the King of the Carnival, whose origin is herein related, has now become a permanent institution of New Orleans. Its design and objects while pleasurable and æsthetic have still a practical and ulterior object in benefitting the City of New Orleans, commercially and socially. It not only offers increased attractions to visitors from abroad, but in all the festivities arranged, or consequent thereupon, the entertainment and accommodation of the Mardi Gras visitors are primarily considered in the true spirit of hospitality. It is to be hoped that it will ever meet with the good wishes and encouragement which have so far marked every step of its progress.

THE EXPOSITION BUILDING.

THIS beautiful and imposing structure has lately been added to the ornaments of our city by the South Western Exposition Association.

The purpose for which it was erected was to establish a PERMANENT and attractive place for the exhibition and sale of all manufactured articles used in the South.

The fact that New Orleans is the commercial centre of the Southwest, and that through her is supplied a vast agricultural population, requiring the manufactures of other sections, pointed out the great advantage to the consumers of the articles, as well as to the manufacturers, of the establishment of the permanent Exposition and manufacturers salesroom in the Exposition building. The Planter or the Merchant here sees collected under one immense roof every article he can need, from the steam engine, cotton gin or sugar mill, down to the smallest article needed in his household, all of the latest and most improved style.

The manufacturer here has an opportunity for bringing the article *itself* which he makes directly before the attention of the consumer, a far more effective plan of introducing and selling than by trusting only to descriptive circulars and engravings. In short the manufacturer is thus brought face to face with the consumer, and the latter is enabled to decide satisfactorily upon the merits of any article he may need, because he has an opportunity of personally examining and testing it before purchasing. It will thus be seen that the enterprise is one of great importance to the trade of this section.

The association was incorporated in October 1871. Early in the Spring of that year the originator of the enterprise, Mr. Henry Shaw, first suggested its advantages to some of our leading capitalists. The first to take an active part in it, was the late John Davidson, Esq., a gentleman always ready to use his large means and influence in the furtherance of any enterprise promising public benefit. Amongst the other incorporators were Messrs. Richard Lloyd, Charles J. Leeds, Jas. D. Hill, Geo. Purves, Samuel H. Kennedy, Harmon Doane, L. F. Generes, John G. Fleming, all prominent and well known gentlemen of this city.

Immediately after the organization of the association a large property on St. Charles and Carondelet, between Julia and Girod Street, was purchased, and the services of Mr. Albert Diettel, architect, were engaged to prepare plans for the Exposition Building.

The contract was awarded on the 21st of December, 1871, and by the 1st of May 1872, the association was able to give their inaugurating exposition of the manufactures of the country, the building being by that time sufficiently finished for their purpose. The inaugurating exhibition was continued until June 1st, at which time the permanent exposition opened under most favorable auspices and is now an assured success.

The following dimensions will give an idea of the scale upon which the Exposition building is constructed.

Occupying a front of 85 feet on both St. Charles and Carondelet streets, it runs through the Square by straight lines 341 feet. The entire building is built of brick, with a slate roof, and in its exterior appearance as well as its interior arrangement and adornment, is an ornament to the City of New Orleans, of which her people may well be proud. The whole of the first floor, a hall of 341 feet by 85, is devoted to the exhibition and sale of heavy machinery and agricultural implements, a line of shafting, driven by a powerful engine, traverses this hall from end to end, furnishing facilities for showing machinery in motion. In the second story, Carondelet street end, is located the Fine Arts and Miscellaneous Departments, a hall 170 feet long by 81 feet wide, filled with all kinds of useful and ornamental articles. In addition to these two large and elegant exhibition rooms for the display of manufacturers articles, a Concert Hall 170 feet long by 81 in width, with a 40 foot ceiling was constructed. Decidedly the handsomest room of the kind in the South. And over the Fine Arts Hall on Carondelet street are two Halls, one 60x60 feet for use in connection with the Grand Concert Hall, and the other 90 feet by 60 feet, to be used as a Lecture Room, etc.

The beautiful fresco work and interior adornment of these Halls is done under the direction of Mr. F. Hang, and reflects great credit upon his artistic skill and taste.

This entire enterprise has been carried forward from the beginning with an energy and determination on the part of the managers of the Association, which was worthy of the success which it has already attained, and which is a sure augury of its future stability.

E. A. TYLER, ESQ.

The life of this gentleman, who has been the architect of his own fortune, has been marked by adventure and a spirit of enterprise peculiar to the natives of New England, and been crowned by remarkable success. Few citizens of New Orleans have been more distinguished for devotion to business, in his particular department of Art, for reliability, intelligence and public spirit. By the steadfastness, manliness and energy, which have constituted leading traits of his character, by the loftiness of his aims, and the purity of his motives, he has acquired a multitude of friends and admirers, and has left the impress of his history on that of the great metropolis with whose fortunes his own have blended for more than a quarter of a century.

Mr. Tyler was born in Boston, Mass., on the 22nd of April 1815, commencing life at the date of the declaration of peace after the second war with Great Britain. His early education was pursued in the Boston schools, always remarkable for the advantages they offered for moral and mental culture—if not superior than of any other American city. From the age of twelve years, he earned his own living. When he reached fourteen, he became apprenticed to the watch-making and jewelry business, which has ever since been his vocation. In 1834, he went to Belfast, Maine, where he remained four years in the same occupation. At the expiration of that period, he determined to remove to New Orleans, where fortunes, he understood, were readily made by young men of intelligence, enterprise and steady habits. The journey before him was an expensive one, and he had but little money; but nothing daunted by the fact, he resolved, by obtaining business on the route, as he had opportunity, to work his way hither.

It was the commencement of his great life struggles, but he was animated by youthful hope and a courage fitted to the emergency. He accordingly, in April 1838, left Belfast, and started from Boston, his native city, early the following May, with only forty-two dollars in his pocket. After remaining a few days in New York and Philadelphia, he left for the West by the way of Pittsburg, thence to Cincinnati. Here he lingered a few days, looking around for business, but, not obtaining any, paid his hotel bill, and found he had only eighteen cents left for the prosecution of his journey; whereupon he packed his tools in his valise, left his trunk with an old schoolmate, and, with valise in his hand, crossed the Ohio river to Covington. Here he struck the turnpike road to Lexington—walked twelve miles to the first village, stopped there a few days, repaired watches, clocks and jewelry, and in a week made seventeen dollars beyond expenses. He then went to the next village, Crittenden, where he made sixteen dollars over expenses; thence to Williamsburgh, where he only paid his expenses. There he took the stage to Lexington, where, after remaining several days and finding nothing to do, he gratified his curiosity by visiting Henry Clay, the servant of the nation, with whom every citizen had a right to be acquainted. He also went to see the celebrated Irving Estates. Thence he proceeded to Nicholasville, where he did not do much that increased his resources, but received a letter from a gentleman in Cynthiana, holding out some promises to him if he would visit that place. He returned to Lexington, and, after making friends, and spending most of his money in sight-seeing, went to Paris by stage, and thence walked, a distance of twelve miles, to Cynthiana, got a ducking in a stream which he had to ford, besides being thoroughly soaked in a shower—arrived late in the day at the hotel kept by a gentleman named Boyd, and knowing, from certain premonitions, that he was going to be sick, frankly told his host of the fact, informing him at the same time of his inability to defray his expenses. The latter assured him with true Kentucky liberality, that he need give himself no uneasiness about the matter, and that he was quite welcome to the best that could be done for him under the circumstances.

A comfortable room was assigned him in the hotel, and a doctor immediately sent for to whom he was equally frank in making known his circumstances. This Kentucky Doctor told him that he never asked people if they had money; all that he had to do was to take the medicine he gave him, and obey orders; if he did not recover, it would be no fault of his. Mr. Tyler, in referring to this part of his history, testifies that he never knew a nobler or better hearted man than Dr. Desha, (son of ex-Governor Desha) and Mr. Boyd, the hotel keeper. On his recovery, he commenced business in earnest. It accummulated on his hands. His friends increased in number—among others—A. Broadwell, Esq., one of the wealthiest citizens in Kentucky.

Early in October he left Cynthiana for the South. The Ohio river being so low that no boats could be run upon it, he returned to Lexington; thence he went, by stage, to Nashville, Tenn., where he met with a friend who accompanied him to Mill's Point, Ky., the nearest point at which to take a boat for New Orleans. This little town was

115 CANAL STREET,

Has on hand, and is constantly receiving from the best manufactories in the world, a large and well-selected stock of

Watches, Clocks, Jewelry,

Silver and Plated Ware,

Masonic and Odd Fellows' Jewels,

AND

Fancy Goods,

All of which are offered at reduced prices.

Sole Agent for the celebrated Watches of Thos Russell & Son, Chas E. Jacot, Albert Gerard, David F. Magnin, and Henry Hoffman.

Southern Agent for the celebrated Whiting Manufacturing Company, *Manufacturers of Sterling Silver Ware only.*

Our stock of Silver Ware is very large, and our prices defy competition.

crowded with parties waiting to obtain a passage. Among them were those whole souled planters, Duncan F. Kenner, Alexander Barrow, and several others, with their families. After waiting four days, two boats came down the river, when all embarked, late in the evening, on board the Somerville, except himself and friend, who took passage in the Prairie, (Capt. Freligh,) which, encountering a fog, was obliged to lay up during the night. Next morning, coming up with the Somerville, found she had run on a snag—worked with all hands, all day, to get her off. Finally, the passengers on the Somerville came on board the Prairie, and on the ninth day of their embarkation, reached New Orleans.

On his arrival in the Crescent City, Mr. Tyler was so fortunate as to find an old friend and acquaintance, a jeweler at 13 Chartres street. He induced this artisan to rent him his window fronting on the street, and immediately commenced business, retaining the locality four years, when he removed to 37 Camp street, with better accommodations, and where he remained with varying fortunes, the good however attaining the ascendancy, when, through the influence of Rev Father Mullen, he was so fortunate as to secure his present elegant and extensive establishment on Canal street, in the most thronged and fashionable part of the city—certainly an excellent stand for his business, and where, by his enterprise, he has succeeded in amassing a large fortune.

Mr. Tyler is a model American, who, like most of our people engaged in various branches of commerce, is doubtless fond of accumulation, but who eschews avarice and employs his wealth to noble ends, the advancement of all our social interests, including all public and private charities, relieving distress whenever brought to his notice, lending a helping hand to the unfortunate, and always anxious to recognize and reward merit. No object of great public utility is started in the community that does not find in him a zealous and liberal supporter. He was one of the original projectors and proprietors of the Fair Grounds, whose annual exhibitions have done so much to the advancement of our agricultural, mechanical, commercial and manufacturing interests.

During the inundation of the city which occurred somewhat upwards of a year ago, he proved himself equal to the crisis, being one of the largest contributors for the relief of the houseless sufferers. He has been, for many years, one of the most prominent leaders in the Church of the Messiah, on St. Charles street, and an influential individual in commercial circles as Director of the Bank of Lafayette. During the late war, he acted earnestly with the State of his adoption, to which his allegiance was due. He was guilty of no offense, but, being one of our most prominent citizens, General Butler regarded his opinions dangerous, and accordingly applied the gag of imprisonment, and had him sent to Fort Jackson, where he was confined four months. His friends, who were permitted to have no communication with him, and hearing nothing from him, supposed that he was dead, and when it was supposed that he actually would die, he was released on a bond for ten thousand dollars. His arrest took place on the same day with that of the late Dr. Warren Stone.

On the 22nd of September 1840, he married Miss Julia A. Barnes, of Cambridge, Mass. The ceremony was performed by Rev. Dr. Charles Lowell, of Boston, at Lynde street church. He has had five children, of whom three are still living.

Without pride or ostentation, he has yet surrounded himself with all the comforts and elegancies of life. His residence on St. Charles street, is one of the most beautiful in the city. Its garden, filled with the choicest flowers and shrubbery, and all its appointments, bespeak the man of taste and refinement. His energy, his public virtues, the wealth acquired by his own skill and industry, and the uses to which he employs it, entitle him in fine, to be regarded one of the merchant princes of this great emporium.

CHARLES CAVAROC, ESQ.

Mr. C. Cavaroc, President of the New Orleans National Banking Association, of the New Orleans Mutual Insurance Association, and of several other companies organized for industrial or commercial purposes, is one of the representative men of the Latin race in Louisiana.

Mr. Cavaroc was born in New Orleans in 1828, of French parents, and received his education in the mother country of his progenitors. He first entered into business as clerk in the general wine importing house of T. M. Lucas on Royal street, and upon the death of Mr. Lucas, which occurred in 1851, he took charge of the business in which his success was both steady and rapid. This was owing no less to the strict integrity than to the thorough knowledge of this branch of trade possessed by the able merchant who is the subject of this sketch. In 1866, Mr. Cavaroc was called to the Presidency of the Bank of New Orleans at a very critical period of the career of that bank, whose stock was then much depressed owing to heavy losses consequent upon the late civil war. Under the skillful management of its new President, this institution soon recovered from its disasters, and the stock rose in a few months from $16 to $30. A year ago the New Orleans Bank was reorganized as a National Bank, with a capital of $600,000, and under its present title of the New Orleans National Banking Association, and it now stands in the front rank of our financial institutions. In 1870, the New Orleans Mutual Insurance Association was organized by Mr. Cavaroc upon an entirely new plan, the particulars of which are given elsewhere, and its success has been such as to realize the most sanguine anticipations of its founder and stockholders.

Mr. Cavaroc is not only one of the most successful and enterprising merchants of New Orleans, but also one of its most public spirited and liberal citizens. There is hardly an undertaking calculated to enhance the prosperity of our city or State in which he has not taken a prominent part, and in private life his charities have all been munificent as well as judiciously bestowed.

He is emphatically a pushing, go-ahead, live merchant, a useful citizen, and an honorable, high-toned gentleman. There are few men whose loss would be more universally felt in this community than Charles Cavaroc.

THE ACADEMY OF SCIENCES.

The New Orleans Academy of Sciences was founded in 1853 by a number of gentlemen belonging exclusively to the medical profession. The first meeting, held on the 21st of March of that year, was presided over by Dr. Bennet Dowler, whose devotion to scientific pursuits is well known. On the 25th of April following, Dr. Josiah Hale was elected President and a constitution was adopted. In May, correspondence with the Smithsonian Institute at Washington was opened, and a promise of its co-operation obtained. That promise, commencing with contributions in the following October, has been constantly and liberally fulfilled, and now the Academy is in communication with most of the great scientific institutions of various parts of this continent and Europe. At first the meetings of the Academy were held at the private residences of members. Subsequently, the gratuitous use of a room was obtained in the City Hall, then the hall of the Mechanic's Institute was rented, and on the 21st of November of the same year, a hall at the southeast corner of Poydras and Carondelet streets, rented for the purpose, became the place of meeting. On the 5th of December, the Academy subscribed for fourteen scientific publications, the members assessing themselves for this expense, as they had for all others. On the 6th of March following, the Academy ordered the publication of its proceedings, and on the same day Dr. E. H. Barton was elected President.

The object of the Academy is the promotion of science by lectures, papers, and discussions on scientific subjects, and by the collection of a library and museum. The year 1853, it will be recollected, was one in which fearful havoc was made by an epidemic; but the Academy, nevertheless, persevered in its prescribed course, and progressed to a firm establishment, without any material aid or sympathy or aid from either the authorities or the general public. The first paper was read by Dr. B. Dowler, on the 30th of May. On the 27th March 1854, the late Professor J. L. Riddell exhibited before the Academy one of the most interesting and useful improvements yet achieved in aid of scientific research. This was a binocular microscope which he had constructed, and the honor of inventing which is universally conceded to him. As since improved and simplified, under the designs of Mr. Wenham, and the manufacture of the famous Beck, this instrument has now become the great microscope of the world. On the same day the Academy earnestly discussed the necessity for a geological survey of the State, and adopted a resolution to present to the Legislature a recommendation that it should be made. Although this has not been done, Professor Hilgard has, under the auspices of the Academy, made some surveys of parts of the State, the results of which have been given to the public through the newspapers.

On November 6th 1854, the Academy again changed its place of meeting to a room in the City Hall, which the Council had appropriated for the purpose, this room being subsequently changed for another. On the 5th of March 1856, Dr. Riddell was elected President. A few days afterward the Academy was incorporated, and made a branch of the University of Louisiana, subject, in a great measure, to the discretion of the administrators of the University. On the 26th of May, with this status, the Academy met in the east wing of the University buildings, although it was not till 1869 that the administrators formally acknowledged the Academy as a branch of the University, and then with a condition that they might disconnect it by giving a year's written notice.

During the war, the buildings were taken possession of by the military, and much of the property of the Academy was lost, destroyed and injured; that it was not all sacrificed was due to the exertions and influence of Dr. Riddell. After the war, the Academy, not without much struggling, however, soon re-established itself in its efforts and regained its former position without any outside aid whatever. On the death of Dr. Riddle, in 1866, Dr. Copes was elected President, as he still remains.

The Academy gives weekly lectures, except during the summer, besides holding general discussions on scientific subjects, politics and religion being excluded. These are open to the public gratuitously, under invitation from members, which, however, is all but nominal, and the hall of the Academy is open to visitors daily in the same manner. The records of the Academy contain a great deal of very interesting and instructive information upon a great variety of subjects, many of them of the highest importance in connection with the welfare and progress of the city and State. The library contains very valuable contributions from leading scientific societies in various parts of the world. The Museum, though comparatively small, contains conchological, geological, palaeontological and other collections well worthy of examination.

Election to membership, under the rules, requires recognized scientific acquirements, nomination and recommendation by two or more Fellows, posting for one month and ballot.

The institution is one which needs and deserves much more consideration from the authorities and the public of the city and State than it has yet received, and we hope yet to see it recognized as worthy of liberal countenance and support.

THE SYNAGOGUE ON CARONDELET STREET.

This beautiful house of worship is owned and used by the Hebrew Congregation, "Dispersed of Judah," whose charter of incorporation dates from 4th June 1847, though its organization had taken place some years previously. Its present vitality and prosperity are, however, mainly due to the benevolence of the late Judah Touro, who made the congregation a free gift of the church edifice which stood on Canal and Bourbon streets, and at his own cost fitted it up and converted it into a synagogue.

A few years later, this building requiring extensive repairs, it was decided to pull it down and build another place of worship located further up-town. Accordingly, the present edifice was erected on Carondelet street, on six lots of ground which had, at one time, formed a portion of the Poydras Estate.

The mode of service is according to the Sephardic ritual, known commonly as that of the Spanish and Portuguese Jews, though with some modernization.

The present minister is the Rev. Henry S. Jacobs.

CITIZENS' BANK.

GEORGE A FOSDICK, ESQ.

THIS enterprising merchant, largely identified with the shipping interests of New Orleans, affords in his career a striking illustration of the influence exerted by talent, energy and perseverance, in a country like ours, in overcoming difficulties, and of attaining, in the end, to success, fortune and independence. From childhood up to manhood, he wasted no golden moments in frivolous occupations and idle amusements, but regarding labor as the great law of life, first with a view to subsistence and next to comfort and elegance, exerted all his physical and intellectual powers in order to the attainment of these ends. Exemplary success has crowned his well-directed efforts.

He was the son of Capt. W. R. Fosdick, who, for a series of years, commanded one of the first packet ships running between New York and New Orleans, and was born at the former city, May 3, 1820. At the early age of twelve years, he had the misfortune to lose his father, and was thus suddenly thrown on his own resources. Of a respectable family, active and intelligent, and with no indisposition to labor for a living, he found little difficulty in obtaining employment in the commission house of James Hamilton & Son, of New York city, who paid him a salary of fifty dollars for the first year; and the American boy, who could command fifty dollars a year, when he was not yet in his teens, was somebody, and he felt that he was. So he went to work with a will, looking to the future. Here he remained for five years, until the crisis of 1837, which swept off most of the mercantile houses of the country—during which period he worked in the daytime and continued his educational studies at night, his salary being increased from year to year, as he grew older and more capable of being of service to his employers. He was not yet in the way of making a fortune, but certainly—which was far better—was passing through the preliminary stages necessary to make him a man of business and a thorough merchant.

In 1837, the calamitous year referred to, he left New York and came South, first stopping for a while at Mobile, seeking business in vain, and then coming to New Orleans, where he was equally unsuccessful. He now embarked on the Tombigbee, which seemed to invite the adventurer, sailing up as high as Westport, Miss., a small town situated about two miles above Columbus, on the other side of the river. Here he was employed, for the space of eighteen months, by Dunstan Banks, doing a supply business.

In the meantime, his brother had established himself at New Orleans in the shipping and commission business, and, knowing his industrious habits, at once took him into the concern in the capacity of a clerk. This was in 1839. In 1840, he became associated with him as a partner in the business, which he has prosecuted with singular energy and success ever since. Taught in the school of hard experience, making the most of his opportunities, taking no step forward without being sure of his footing, he has attained the enviable position he occupies, and the fame he has achieved of an accomplished and prosperous merchant, by relying mainly on his own exertions, and depending but little on the uncertain, however well meant, advice and fluctuating assistance of others. In other words, he furnishes a fine example of the self-made man, who thinks for himself and acts for himself, and who entertains opinions and prosecutes enterprises which reflect credit on the age and country in which he lives.

Such men, in a community of high-toned merchants like New Orleans, are advanced to places of honor and responsibility, and may command almost any position that they please. For two years Mr. Fosdick occupied the high post of President of the Chamber of Commerce, to which no individual could have been appointed who was not at once a thorough merchant and a perfect gentleman. The pressure of his business, after his service in that capacity for the term mentioned, led him to decline a re-election; but he is still an influential member of the Chamber, and a perspicuity and forethought that lead him to investigate the past and anticipate the future, he seizes on every occasion calculated to advance the interests of this great mart of commerce.

Again, he was the first delegate elected to the National Board of Trade at Philadelphia, where he exerted a decided influence in securing the passage of a resolution of that body, calling on Congress to grant immediate aid to improve the mouth of the Mississippi river.

He has always taken a lively interest in politics, having acted as Chairman of the Democratic Committee since the war, and Chairman of the Douglas State Democratic Committee and Co-operative Committee before the war.

He has never held any public office except that of State Registrar on the First Board of Registration, a position which he accepted solely at the request of the State and Parish Democratic Committees, in the hope of accomplishing some good for our people, though at a sacrifice to his personal interests. He was nominated for Congress by the Second District Convention in 1870, but withdrew at the request of the Democratic State Committee, to enable them to carry out a fusion which they contemplated.

HENRY HOWARD, ESQ.

This well-known and accomplished architect was born in the city of Cork, Ireland, February 8th 1818, where he remained till he reached the age of eighteen years. He pursued his education at the Mechanics' Institute of that city, and received from his father, Thomas Howard, a noted builder, of Cork, the first rudiments of Architectural drawing and a knowledge of Mechanics. Owing to his father's death which took place when he was sixteen years of age, he emigrated, in the Spring of 1836, from his native city to New York, with a view to continuing the study of architecture with an American architect. In this particular he was at first disappointed. Arriving in New York on the 8th of May 1836, after the great fire, he had to go into a Looking-glass and Picture-Frame Maker's establishment, where he remained eighteen months.

Being desirous of seeing an older brother living, at that time in New Orleans, he left New York for the South, and arrived here on the 29th of September 1837, in the height of the prevalence of the Yellow Fever, a disease, which, notwithstanding its frequent occurrence in New Orleans, he has hitherto fortunately escaped. On arriving in this city, he undertook all kinds of carpenter's and joiner's work, including the most difficult branch of it, viz, stair building, commanding at first, only journeyman's wages. He shrank from no task on account of its difficulty, worked with diligence and rapidity, and always studied the welfare of his employers. After being engaged in this way about five years, he was promoted to a foremanship under the late E. W. Sewell, a well-known builder.

In 1839, he pursued the study of Architecture for a short time, with the late Col. James H. Dakin, an able architect of this city; also, during the same year, with Henry Mollhausen, a Prussian, a good surveyor and civil engineer.

In 1845, Mr. Howard commenced the erection of a large brick country residence on Bayou Lafourche, for the late Thomas Pugh, Esq. After its completion, he opened in 1848, an Architect's office in Exchange Place, and, in order to execute and finish with despatch the large amount of business entrusted to his care, he was in the habit, during the first few years of his professional practice, of working and studying from eighteen to twenty hours a day. His employment and success were uninterrupted till the occurrence of the late war, during the continuance of which he was employed as principal draught-man in the Confederate States Naval Iron Works at Columbus, Georgia.

After the war was over, he returned to New Orleans and resumed the practice of his profession, and, notwithstanding dull times, high taxation and other troubles, has had, up to the present time, a fair share of business, sufficient to give himself and his numerous family a handsome living.

In the year 1839, while working at stair-building, he married in this city Miss Richards, a native of New York, by whom he has had eleven children—eight girls and three boys. Of these, there are surviving six daughters and two sons; also grand-children, the oldest being eleven years of age.

The following is a list of the buildings erected in this city from designs and specifications furnished by Mr. Howard, and, in most instances, under his personal supervision.

PUBLIC BUILDINGS IN THE CITY:

First Presbyterian Church, Lafayette Square;
Second Presbyterian Church, Washington Square;
St. Peter's Roman Catholic Church, Third District;
* Importers' Bonded Warehouse, Second District;
Hale's Warehouse, First District;
Buildings for Louisiana Fair Grounds;
Engine House and Engine Foundations for Commercial Water Works;
Zoelly's Brewery Buildings, corner of Magazine and Delord street;
Home Mutual Insurance Buildings, First District;
Crescent Mutual Insurance Building, First District;
Conery's Stores, corner of Common and Water streets;
Avendano's Store, corner of Delta and Common streets;
Remodelling Equitable (late Tulane) Building, Camp st.;
Extensive addition to Jewish Widows' and Orphans' Home, corner of Jackson and Chippewa sts., Fourth Dist.;
St. Elizabeth Asylum, Magazine street, Fourth District;
Protestant Boys' Orphan Asylum, on St. Charles avenue, Sixth District;
Catholic Orphan Boys' Asylum, Third District;
New Syphilitic Wards and Dissecting Rooms at the Charity Hospital, Common Street.

PRIVATE BUILDINGS IN THE CITY:

Pontalba Buildings, Jackson Square, Second District;
Hale's Five Dwellings, Camp Street, First District;
Conery's Dwellings, Prytania Street, First District;
Cyprien Dufour's Dwelling, Esplanade street;
Freslenburg's Dwelling, Esplanade street;
Barthe's Suburban Residence, St. Charles avenue;
Palacio's Suburban Residence, St. Charles avenue;
Miltenberger's Dwelling, St. Charles avenue;
Grinnan & Short's Villa, Prytania street, Fourth Dist.;
Buildings Nos. 8, 9 and 13 Commercial place.

PUBLIC AND PRIVATE BUILDINGS IN THE COUNTRY.

Thomas Pugh's Residence, Bayou Lafourche, Parish of Assumption;
W. W. Pugh's Residence, Bayou Goula, Parish of Iberville;
John H. Randolph's Residence, Bayou Goula, Parish of Iberville;
General R. Camp's Residence, Bayou Goula, Parish of Iberville;
Remodelling Louis La Bourgeois' Residence, Parish of St. James;
Court House and Prison, Carrollton, Parish of Jefferson;
Court House and Prison, Thibodeaux, Parish of Lafourche;
Court House, Donaldsonville, Parish of Terrebonne;
Presbyterian Church, Houma, Parish of Terrebone;
Episcopal Church, Houma, Parish of Terrebone;
Episcopal Church, Bayou Goula, Parish of Iberville.

JUDGE JOHN A. CAMPBELL,

B. T. WALSHE,

Importer of and Dealer in

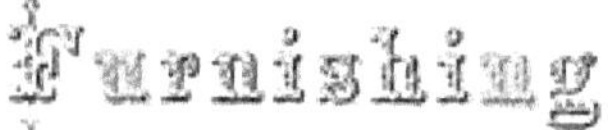

Men's Shirts,

Underwear,

Gloves,

AND

Hosiery,

Boys' Shirts,

AND

Underwear.

For all ages.

Umbrellas &c.

—and—

BOYS' AND CHILDREN'S CLOTHING.

110 CANAL STREET,

NEW ORLEANS.

S. B. PACKARD, Esq.

STEPHEN B. PACKARD, United States Marshal, born at Auburn, Maine, May 25th, 1839, entered the United States service Nov. 27th, 1861, as First Lieutenant Company G, Twelfth Regiment Maine Volunteers. In 1863 served as Judge Advocate on the staff of Gen. J. J. Reynolds; mustered out of service at Portland, Me., February 7th, 1865.

Upon leaving the army Captain Packard came to New Orleans, where he had previously married, and entered business as a Government claim agent, in partnership with Cyrus Hamlin, son of ex-President Hamlin.

Mr. Packard at once took an active part in the organization of the Republican party in Louisiana, and was elected Chairman of the First State Central Committee of that party, to which position he has ever since been re-elected. He was a member of the Constitutional Convention, Chairman of the Board of Supervisors at the election of 1868, at which time he was arrested by General Buchanan, but released by order of the then Gen'l of the Army, the present President of the United States.

Subsequent to the election of that year, Captain Packard was appointed by Governor Warmoth, Register of Conveyances, which office he resigned upon his appointment by President Grant in April, 1869, as United States Marshal for this District. He entered upon the duties of this office May 5th, 1869, and was re-appointed by the President in March, 1873, being the first United States Marshal appointed during the second term of President Grant.

JACOB C. VAN WICKLE.

THE subject of this sketch was born in Middlesex County, New Jersey, on the 20th of October 1805. At an early age he left his native State with a view of making for himself both a fortune and a name. He came to Louisiana and settled in the Parish of Point Coupee, in December 1827. His temperate and industrious habits, favorably impressed the people among whom he had cast his lot, and it was not long before he received the appointment of Deputy Sheriff of the Parish, in which capacity he served from 1828 to 1833. He was then appointed Sheriff by Gov. White and subsequently re-appointed by Gov. Roman, retaining this office from 1833 to 1842. In 1845, Mr. Van Wickle was elected to the Lower House of the Legislature, on the Whig ticket and served his constituents with zeal and fidelity. His political affiliations have always been with the Whig Party, of which he was a consistent and devoted member, but political prejudices could never induce him to ignore or neglect the interests of his opponents or make him intolerant, and the reputation he acquired as a politician was that of an honorable, just and liberal gentleman. By prudence and economy, Mr. Van Wickle had succeeded in amassing a sufficient amount of money to purchase a sugar plantation in 1846, and from that time until 1869, he devoted himself entirely to the cultivation of sugar-cane. A series of successful crops soon made him a rich man. Surrounded by all the comforts and luxuries of life, he dispensed the hospitalities of his house with a liberal hand. Naturally of a very kind and generous disposition, he was never deaf to appeals for assistance from those in distress; and in all the relations of life he was an exemplary citizen and highly esteemed by all who knew him. In 1836, he married Miss Eloise Ledoux, the daughter of Mr. Valerien Ledoux, one of the most respectable and wealthy planters in the State, and became the father of two lovely daughters, one only of whom lived to womanhood, the elder, Julia, having died at the age of thirteen years, whilst at school at Nazareth, Ky. The younger, Miss Amanda, an interesting and handsome lady, married Mr. Ogden K. Dunning, of the house of J. B. Burnside & Co., of this city, but soon became a widow by the death of her husband, about three years after her marriage. In 1841, Mrs Van Wickle died, and Mr. Van Wickle married the widow Dayries, also a member of the Ledoux family, and who is now in the full vigor of health, a devoted wife, and a most excellent and charitable lady. Like most of the Southern planters, Mr. Van Wickle sustained heavy losses by the ravages of war, and after its close, finding the labor system so demoralized and uncertain that he concluded to abandon the cultivation of his plantation, and finding a purchaser for it, he removed to New Orleans to reside permanently. In 1868, his name was prominently before the Democratic Convention of this city for Mayor, and was defeated in the Convention by only two votes by his successful opponent, Mayor Conway. Subsequently, his friends presented him as a candidate before the Legislature for the position of United States Senator, but it was withdrawn when it was ascertained that a sufficient Republican majority had been obtained to elect Hon. W. P. Kellogg. His large experience as a successful planter, and his thorough knowledge of the Levee system of the State, eminently qualified him for a position on the Board of Public Works, and in 1869, Gov. Warmoth appointed him to represent the Second Levee District, extending from the Balize to the Atchafalaya river. During his administration, and under his supervision, the largest levee in the State, known as the Grand Levee, was substantially built, and through his energy and perseverance, other public levees were constructed and a large area of country saved from overflow. To these works he can point with pride and satisfaction to himself, feeling conscious that his official career has ever been without reproach and universally commended. For the last twenty years Mr. Van Wickle has been the lessee of Wood's Cotton Press, one of the largest institutions of the kind in the city, an illustration of which will be found on another page of this book. The press is the property of his sister, Mrs. Wood, and under his management has averaged, per annum, about seventy-five thousand bales of cotton compressed for shipment to New York and Europe. Besides being a real estate owner in this city, Mr. Van Wickle is now the proprietor of the old homestead at "Old Bridge," New Jersey, where he was born, and where for many years past he has spent his summers in quiet retirement and in the peaceful contemplation of a long life of usefulness and exemplary character.

LAFAYETTE SQUARE is decidedly the handsomest in the city. It is in the First District, and has St. Charles and Camp streets in front and rear, and several public buildings in its immediate neighborhood. It has a handsome and substantial iron railing around it, based upon well laid blocks of granite; is well laid off in regular walks, and is ornamented with beautiful trees and a statue of Franklin, presented to the city by Mr. Charles A. Weed, proprietor of the N. O. *Times*.

ALFRED PHILIPS, ESQ.

THE gentleman whose name heads these lines was born in 1832. He was partly educated in this city and at St. Mary's College, in Baltimore, Md.

He began the study of the law with Mr. Christian Roselius, and after attending three courses of lectures in the Law Department of the University of Louisiana, graduated from the same in 1853; but not being of age, he did not commence the practice of his profession until 1858.

In 1865 he was elected a professor in the Law Department of the University, to fill the chair made vacant by the death of the lamented Judge Theo. H. McCaleb. He continued to act as professor down to 1870, when he resigned.

Mr. Philips was a member of the House of Representatives of the State Legislature in 1866 and 1867, which was distinguished as an upright and very able body.

He was, of course, carried away by the patriotic ardor which filled the heart of every young man in the South during the late war for independence, and rendered valuable services to the Confederacy as a Captain in one of the Louisiana regiments.

Mr. Philips is an unfortunate bachelor, but has been most happy in all his relations in life. He has been peculiarly fortunate in his profession, and his exertions have been rewarded by a fortune of respectable dimensions.

In 1864 he became Mr. Roselius's partner, and has continued to practice law, associated with him, ever since.

As a lawyer, Mr. Philips is one of the most accomplished in this city, being thoroughly learned in jurisprudence and literature. He is an elegant speaker, and his arguments reveal his vigorous and logical mind.

Those who are well acquainted with him will bear witness to the fact that it has ever been his aim since he was first admitted to the bar to endeavor to cultivate friendly relations with his brother lawyers and to look accordingly with warm approval upon all their exertions to elevate themselves in the ranks of the profession; never to envy or detract, but always to encourage and applaud. He has always by liberality and frankness sought to encourage an *esprit de corps* among the members of the bar, never taking improper advantage of the weakness or want of preparation of his adversary, but on all occasions granting and very rarely asking favors.

He has never failed to recognize that the vocation of the lawyer is to assist, instruct and guide courts of justice in arriving at truth and administering right, and that he should never undertake to mislead a judge or jury; that he is an officer of justice and should faithfully exert all his talent and energies in aid of justice.

The lawyer should be a gentleman; that is, no man can be a lawyer, in the proper acceptation of the term, unless he is a gentleman, which implies, necessarily, high integrity, unsullied honor, charity of heart and mind, sensibility and regard for all animated nature, polished address and polite demeanor to all, as well as the possession and exercise of all those elevated mental faculties which stamp humanity as the master animal. All these qualities mark the gentleman and should be recognized in the lawyer, and his efforts should be directed to the cultivation of all these graces and qualities.

In personal appearance Mr. Philips is of the medium height, with brown hair and light blue eyes. He is very social and genial in his feelings, aspiring to no praise except that of being regarded as an honest, upright man, all of which he deserves, as he is remarkable for his candor and truthfulness.

W. M. RANDOLPH, ESQ.

NO LAWYER in this or any State more fully commands the respect and confidence of the members of the bar, and the public, than Judge W. M. Randolph. He is a native of Virginia, about fifty years old, and a near relative of the great defender of State Rights, John Randolph of Roanoke.

A learned and upright man, no worldly consideration can turn him from the strict path of honor and duty. He is amiable, courteous, gentlemanly and chivalrous.

Descended from a noble line, he commanded from his birth all that wealth and family influence could give, with the best opportunities for education.

In his youth he resided in one of the mountain districts of Virginia, and his constant application to the study of the law impaired seriously his health. His grandmother, who was devotedly attached to him, requested him to take a horse and travel, for exercise and recreation, in the neighborhood of the place where they resided.

Randolph, who was an excellent rider, did as he was instructed. A few miles from his residence there was a circus with an excellent equestrian company. He joined them, and after traveling with them seven days, returned, home much improved in health. Upon being asked what he had done during his absence, he frankly stated the truth. His grandmother, who was an aristocratic lady and a strict Presbyterian, confessed that the young acrobat had done more than she had bargained for.

It has been said that to genius irregularity is incident, and great men are often marked by eccentricity, as if they disdained to move in the vulgar orbit. Judge Randolph does not seem to pay much attention to appearances. His flowing beard resembles that of a Capuchin friar, and his hair, uncommonly long, hangs down over his coat collar, after the old cavalier fashion.

He is tall and well-formed, his features are regular and his eyes grey and brilliant.

His familiarity with the principles of jurisprudence is as ample as his application of them is masterly. He has great intensity and directness of purpose and meets difficulties boldly. Accomplished as a scholar, he is unhesitating in his conduct, although polite in demeanor. His powers as an advocate are great. He is one of our best speakers. He has a refined classical wit and loves harmless pleasantry.

Unlike his great relative, John Randolph, of Roanoke, his spirit is cheerful and his temper mild.

LOUISIANA ICE WORKS.

THOMAS J. SEMMES, ESQ.

Hon. Thomas J. Semmes was born at Georgetown, D. C., in 1824. He springs from one of the oldest families in Maryland, his ancestors having emigrated to that State with Lord Baltimore.

He graduated with the highest honors at Georgetown College in 1842. He read law in the office of Clement Coxe, of that city, and entered the law school of Harvard University, where Judge Story and Simon Greenleaf were professors. He graduated in 1845, and was admitted to the bar of Washington the same year.

In 1850, he removed to New Orleans. Five years after he was appointed a member of the Democratic State Central Committee of the State Convention. During the gubernatorial canvas of '55 he had a controversy with a committee of the American party as to the right of naturalized citizens to vote. He distinguished himself at that time for his strong intellect and firmness of character.

In the same year he was elected a member of the Legislature, and in this body he became Chairman of the Judiciary Committee.

In July, 1857, he was appointed U. S. District Attorney, and in November, 1859, elected Attorney General of Louisiana.

In 1862, he was elected Confederate States Senator, and in this body he was made a member of the Judiciary and Finance Committee. He prepared the tax bill in conjunction Hon. R. M. T. Hunter, of Virginia, and wrote the report on retaliation and the resolutions from the Judiciary Committee on martial law.

His palatial residence on Annunciation street, in this city, was, after the capture of New Orleans, confiscated, together with its fine furniture, paintings, mirrors, carpets, etc., which amounted to a considerable sum of money. His law library was stolen by soldiers under Gen. Butler, and at the end of the war, when he returned home and resumed the practice of his profession, he was quite poor.

Since that time Mr. Semmes, by close application to business, has been accumulating property, and he is now on the road to fortune. It is generally believed that he and his partner, Mr. Robert Mott, have an excellent practice in the city.

In person, Mr. Semmes is of the middle size; he has eyes of the color of the waters of the sea, that grow with promethean fire, regular features, and moustache and goatee, in which assiduous labor and long nights of study have interspersed not a few silver threads. His bald head is a capital one—unrivaled; still, he scorns to wear a wig.

His exterior is apparently cold, probably from the fact that he is not demonstrative. Yet he is a true and reliable friend. His countenance is serious, but when excited in speech it grows articulate with the emotions that thrill his soul. His voice is musical and fits every intonation and cadence.

His penetrative intellect possesses a perspicuity, as quick as it is vivid, and his conclusions do not wait upon labored induction. He darts at once upon the core of the subject, and starts where most reasoners end.

He is familiar with the Latin and Greek classes. Tacitus is his favorite author.

Disciplined by such an education his taste is always correct.

In the subtle game of law he is adroit as a practiced general in the field. When he gets into his subject and is warmed with it, he utters words of fire that carry the listener captive along with him. If his argument is close to the point, it is at the same time full of expositions of the adversary's inconsistency. Mr. Semmes is renowned for his ability to sway courts by a logic, almost irresistible, and juries by a fascinating eloquence. He is, no doubt, a man of positive character, of pure reputation, and of untiring energies. He is called by some of our lawyers, "The incarnation of logic." At home he is quite amiable and his spirit buoyant and even playful.

JUDGE THOMAS WHARTON COLLENS.

Hon. Thos. Wharton Collens, who presides over the Seventh District Court for the Parish of Orleans, is a gentleman of unimpeachable integrity and a Judge of great capacity and learning.

He was born in Covington, La., and is fifty-nine years old. He was educated in this city, and has been thirty-nine years at the bar, discharging, at different periods, the offices of District Attorney and Judge of the Criminal Court with great ability. He is acquainted with the ancient and modern languages, and has written several philosophical works, which have been highly praised by the best critics.

In order that the reader may see Judge Wharton Collens in the mind's eye, a brief outline of his outer man is necessary.

In person he is slight and of the middle size. His face is pale, but often kindles up with the light and brilliancy of his dark eye. He has regular features, and iron-gray hair and beard. With fibres and nerves delicately toned, and not enjoying good health, his nervous system is sometimes irritable.

Judge Wharton Collens has a metaphysical turn of mind. Like all men of such bent, he is a stickler for technicalities. If he were a soldier he would be a martinet.

His style is that of the severest reasoning. The language is choice, perfectly clear, and admirably suited to the matters which the words clothe.

His decisions are based upon clear and rational grounds, evincing learning and showing a legal structure of understanding, felicitous statement and profound knowledge.

Over the Seventh District Court he has presided for several years and his administration of its functions has shed a lustre alike upon that tribunal and the Judge.

It may be said, without fear of contradiction, that a long time will elapse before there shall arise in this State such another legal luminary, to adorn the bench as the worthy gentleman I have briefly portrayed.

FRANCIS H. HATCH.

The subject of this sketch, although he has lived in Louisiana for nearly forty years, is a native of New England, his ancestors being among the early settlers of that colony, and having taken part in the Revolutionary struggle inaugurated by Adams, Franklin, and Washington. Mr. Hatch was born in 1815, and came to New Orleans when a mere youth, commencing life as a clerk in the then prominent wholesale grocery house of McLeod & Campbell, in which position he gave so much satisfaction to his employers that, before he was of age, he became a partner of the firm on the withdrawal of McLeod from business. The failing health of the remaining partner, Mr. Campbell, threw the entire management of the business into the hands of Mr. Hatch, and thus, at the early age of twenty-one, he found himself in a position of great responsibility, in which he proved himself equal to the occasion, and became well prepared for the vastly more arduous and responsible public offices he was to be called upon to occupy. In 1848, the failing health of his wife induced him to retire from business and to settle into the Parish of St. Helena, where he soon entered into the arena of politics, being first elected to represent that piney-wood region to the Constitutional Convention of 1852, a body which achieved the very unusual feat of preparing, discussing and adopting a Constitution for the State in the short space of twenty-five days. From 1854 to 1857 Mr. Hatch represented his parish in the Legislature, and in 1857, he received from President Buchanan the appointment of Collector of the Port of New Orleans, an office which he filled to the entire satisfaction of the mercantile community, and with much honor to himself, as well as credit to the general government. Mr. Hatch's long identification with Louisiana led him to embark warmly in the cause of Secession, which he served with devoted fidelity throughout the late struggle, to the great detriment of his private interests. Returning from the war impoverished, but not disheartened, Mr. Hatch again reverted to his old business pursuits, and is now the President of the New Orleans Branch of the Mound City Life Insurance Company, one of the best known and most flourishing institutions of that kind in the South. Mr. Hatch is one of the best specimens of the hardy New England stock grafted upon the Southern stock. For his energy and industry, combined with great prudence, a clear head, and a high sense of honor, he owes the enviable distinction of having passed through the most trying vicissitudes, commercial and political, without ever failing to meet all his obligations, both private and public, and to retain to the fullest extent the esteem and confidence of the population among which he has spent the last forty years of a useful life.

SAMUEL H. KENNEDY, ESQ.

This gentleman was born in Massachusetts, in the year 1816, and brought up as a farmer's boy in a family of eight children. His education was confined to those advantages which most farmers' sons were compelled to accept, who were obliged to till the sterile soil of New England—that is, to go to school in the winter months and work on the farm during the summer. His ambition as a youth was to go to Harvard College, at Cambridge, where his oldest brother graduated in 1826, and his position in all his classes, while at the town school and at the academy, induced his father to promise to send him to that institution. But the death first of his mother and then of his father, while he was yet a boy, prevented the execution of that plan, which was a favorite one with him, and he was taken from his classes at the early age of sixteen, forthwith launched into the world and fitted for American life in the rigid but not profitable school of experience.

He soon obtained a situation in a wholesale grocery store in Boston, where he remained till 1835, when influenced by the attractions of the Western country, which exerted a wondrous spell upon many young men of that region, he turned his steps thitherward. In December of that year he arrived at Alton, Ill., with only a trifle in his pocket, but after looking around him found a situation at fifty dollars a month as book-keeper in a dry goods store. After two years service he embarked in the wholesale grocery business, in which he remained till impaired health compelled him to seek a warmer latitude, in order to avoid a threatened pulmonary disease.

In 1843 he commenced business in New Orleans, under the firm of Kennedy & Foster, as Western commission and produce merchants. The death of Mr. Foster, in 1850, caused a change of the firm to S. H. Kennedy & Co., which name has remained unchanged up to the present time, and he is the only merchant now living in New Orleans, who has continued twenty-nine successive years in the Western business.

Mr. Kennedy has always been devoted to his profession, and by economy and close application has been rewarded with success. His rule has been—and he has found it a good one—to confine expenses in his own private affairs to a sum within his income.

Mr. Kennedy has been one of the most active members of the Chamber of Commerce of New Orleans, and for several years was elected its President.

He was for many years before the war a Director in the Louisiana State Bank, when that institution was the leading bank in the city. It had a capital of $2,000,000, and a deposit of over $5,000,000. Its stock was $190 in gold. The disaster of the war caused the bank to lose over $3,000,000. But under able management it paid all its liabilities. The result, however, was a condition so crippled that it was in 1870 about to go into liquidation when, at the request of a large number of stockholders, Mr. Kennedy was induced to take charge of the institution and resuscitate it. This has been done under his skillful administration of its affairs, and it is now, under the National Bank system, one of the leading banks of the city.

Mr. Kennedy is now in the prime of life and full of business energy. He is distinguished for public spirit, and takes a lively interest in all matters connected with the progress and welfare of the community.

On the corner of First and Camp streets, in the Fourth District, can be seen one of the most elegant houses in this city, surrounded with lovely grounds, laid out in the English lawn style, with a large variety of trees and shrubbery. Here Mr. Kennedy has resided for twenty years, surrounding himself and his family with those comforts and elegancies (the result of a well-earned prosperity) which a refined and cultivated taste can so well appreciate.

THOMAS ALLEN CLARKE, ESQ.

This respected and successful lawyer was born at Albany, in the State of New York, in 1814. His father was in the United States army, and at the close of the second war with Great Britain he moved to Utica. His grandfather was Lieut. Allen, who, not suspecting the treason of Arnold, announced to him the capture of André.

The youth of Mr. Clarke was spent at Utica. One of the oldest boys at school with him was Gov. Horatio Seymour. Among his companions were Professor Dana, of Yale College, the most distinguished living geologist in the United States; Dr. S. Wells Williams, the eminent Orientalist; the late Gen. Morris S. Miller, of the United States army; Capt. Lathrop, of the Texas navy, prepared for College at Utica and Canandaigua.

Mr. Clarke graduated at Hamilton College in 1834. He studied law at Utica, with Judges Kirkland and Bacon.

He came to New Orleans in 1835, and (like Benjamin and other eminent lawyers, whose modesty makes them diffident and distrustful as to their immediate success), engaged in mercantile pursuits. He resumed the study of the law with Judge Slidell, at the same time that he was paying teller in the Canal Bank of this city.

In 1842 he was admitted to the bar, and since that time he has been one of our prominent lawyers.

Mr. Clarke is a gentleman of fine personal appearance, with fair complexion, blue eyes and light hair. He has a striking air and dignified bearing, and is admired both for his talents and sterling integrity.

CHARLES T. HOWARD.

Among the many instances of men in this city who have, by their own exertions, industry and strict attention to their business, elevated themselves from comparative obscurity to positions of influence, wealth and character in the community, there is a no more striking instance of this fact than that represented by the subject of this sketch.

Mr. Howard was born in Baltimore in 1832. It was not his good fortune to enjoy the benefits of a thorough education but such as circumstances permitted, he readily availed himself of every opportunity. At an early age he left school in Philadelphia, after having qualified himself for the ordinary avocations of life. He then engaged in commercial pursuits in that city until 1852, when he came to New Orleans.

His first business connection here was with the steamboat interests of the South and West, with which he was identified until 1854. At this time having demonstrated business qualities of a high degree by an assiduous attention to his duties, he was recommended for and received the appointment of agent in this city for the Alabama State Lottery Company. His management of the affairs of this company, which was highly successful and satisfactory, was terminated by the breaking out of the war, in which Mr. Howard was one of the first to enlist under the banner of the Confederate States.

He first served in the navy and afterward joined the Crescent Regiment, then under command of Col. Marshal J. Smith. In this regiment he was made Orderly Sergeant of Co. G, and served in that capacity until he was discharged on account of sickness. He afterward entered the cavalry service, where he remained on active duty around Mobile until the termination of the war.

Upon returning to this city in 1865, Mr. Howard, like many others who had risked their all upon the issue of the great struggle for State Rights, found himself again upon the threshold of life. Nothing daunted, however, by the reverses of fortune or the loss of time, he again resumed work with the determination to recover all that had been lost. About this time the agency of the Kentucky State Lottery was tendered to and accepted by him. This position he filled with remarkable success until 1868.

Mr. Howard's connection with the Alabama and Kentucky State Lotteries familiarized him thoroughly with the operations of those companies and demonstrated the immense profits accruing to these States under the patronage of which these institutions were conducted. Mr. Howard conceived the idea that Louisiana, too, might be made the beneficiary of a similar corporation and the thousands of dollars annually paid as a tribute to the lottery companies of Alabama, Georgia, Kentucky and Havana might be poured into the coffers of his own State. With this object in view he secured the co-operation of a number of capitalists and citizens and obtained a charter from the State Legislature in 1868, for the incorporation of the Louisiana State Lottery Company. Of this company Mr. Howard was elected President, a position he has filled from 1868 to the present time with marked ability and efficiency. The Louisiana Lottery Company, under his control, has become one of the most substantial and lucrative institutions of the city, the dividends on its stock exceeding those of any of the banks.

Besides the business tact of Mr. Howard, which has made him so successful in life, he is a liberal-minded, generous and public-spirited citizen.

His name will be found connected with many of those public institutions which contribute so largely to the attraction of the city and which, but for the patronage, energy and liberality of a few such active and live men as Mr. Howard, would languish and finally pass away. To him is due in a great degree the establishment of the finest race course and Jockey Club House in the United States, and the success of the "Crescent City Yacht Club" is in like manner attributable to his lively interest in its welfare. Of the La-Jockey Club Mr. Howard is the Vice-President, and is also Vice-Commander of the "Crescent City Yacht Club," and is the owner of the famous yachts "Protos" and "Xiphias," whose fame as fast-sailing crafts is national as well as local.

To all subscriptions for works of public improvement, charitable purposes and all schemes for the welfare of the city, Mr. Howard is always a liberal contributor.

The institution of which he is President pays a tribute annually of $40,000 to the Public School Fund of the State, whilst personally the generous nature of Mr. Howard is evidenced by his many acts of kindness and charity unostentatiously bestowed and hence unknown to any but the grateful recipients.

Mr. Howard is an exempt member of the Fire Department. For a number of years he was Treasurer of the La-Hose Company, and as a testimonial of the high appreciation in which he was held by the members, their elegant steamer is called the "Annie Howard," in honor of the charming little daughter of Mr. Howard.

In 1854, Mr. Howard was married to Miss Floristelle Boulemet, a member of one of the oldest and most respected creole families of New Orleans, and is now the father of four children. His residence (an engraving of which is on another page of this book) is pleasantly situated in the most delightful portion of the city, and is surrounded by all the elegance, luxury and comfort wealth can afford. And here Mr. Howard enjoys life and the fruits of his labor without ostentation, but with liberality in dispensing the hospitalities of his elegant home.

THOMAS L. BAYNE, ESQ.

Thomas Livingston Bayne, a distinguished lawyer of this city, was born in Jones county, Ga., but moved at an early age to Butler county, Ala., and resided there until his education was completed. He is about 45 years of age. I am told by one of his intimate friends that Mr. Bayne entered Yale College in 1843, and graduated with distinction in 1847.

He came to New Orleans in 1848, and studied law with his friend, Mr. Thomas Allen Clarke.

He was admitted to the bar in 1850. Three years afterwards he entered into a partnership with Mr. Clarke, which continues to the present time.

When our late war for the independence of the Southern States broke out, Mr. Bayne entered the 5th Company of the Washington Artillery as a private. He was one of the foremost in the battle of Shiloh, where he was shot through the right arm whilst serving one of the guns of his company. He recovered in a few weeks, and subsequently was appointed captain of artillery for gallant conduct in the field. Soon after he was promoted the rank of Lieutenant Colonel.

At the close of the war, Mr. Bayne returned to New Orleans and resumed the practice of the law with his former partner, Mr. Thos. Allen Clarke.

A few years before the war, he married in Selma, Alabama, the fair and accomplished daughter of Hon. John Gayle, ex-Governor of that State, ex-member of Congress of the Mobile District, and ex-Judge of the United States First District Court.

Mr. Bayne is a gentleman not only highly esteemed in this State for his honesty and profound knowledge of the law, but for his amiability and courtesy towards his fellow members of the bar. This gentleman, together with his partners, Mr. Clarke and Mr. Renshaw, has an excellent and deserved practice in this city.

Mr. Bayne is of the middle size, of slight frame, and with fair complexion.

Washington Square is in the Third District; is bounded by the Elysian Fields, Great Men's, Casa Calvo and Frenchmen streets. Though admirably situated, owing to the distance it stands from the denser portion of the city, it has not yet received those attentions which, at some future day, will render it a beautiful promenade.

NEW ORLEANS ROW BOAT CLUB.

CAPTAIN W. I. HODGSON.

Washington Irving Hodgson was born in Louisville, Kentucky, on the 27th day of November, 1833, and after receiving a very limited education in that State, and at the "Eaton Seminary" in Murfresboro, Tenn., removed to the City of New Orleans, during the Fall of 1847, (then only about fourteen years of age), and began his business career as an under clerk in the well remembered hardware establishment of J. Waterman & Co., corner of Common and Magazine Sts., remaining there some years; he changed to the house of Samuel Locke, as entry clerk, in the same line of business, and afterwards as bookkeeper and cashier with Messrs. Alex. Norton & Macaulay, grocers, and C. C. Bier & Co., stove dealers. We find him in 1858, and up to the breaking out of the war in 1861, occupying the same position with Col. Jas. B. Walton, the well known auctioneer, and after many years service with that distinguished gentleman, in March, 1869, we find him associated with Mr. Charles T. Nash, as the junior partner in the firm of Nash & Hodgson, Auctioneers and Real Estate Agents.

Mr. Hodgson is the youngest son of Captain Henry Hodgson, favorably known from 1815 to 1834, as the commander of some of the largest and finest ships then plying the Atlantic, between New Orleans and the ports of Europe, and it was on one of these, the "Parker & Sons," under his command, that some of our most worthy, enterprising and public-spirited citizens of foreign birth made their first trip to this country. Among whom may be mentioned Robert Stark, John Watt, John D. Bein, Dr. Richard Bein, William and Samuel Bell, and hosts of others, the most of whom, with their old friend, now fill honored graves, Captain Hodgson dying in England at an advanced age, during the recent war.

Mr. Hodgson's mother, Jane Josephine Howard, was born in Dublin, Ireland, of American parents, and was returned to Dublin and educated, and on her final return to America, was married at an early age, while a guest at the hospitable residence of a Louisville gentleman. She was very popular in Washington and Philadelphia society, along from 1825 to 1850, and was noted far and wide for her beauty and accomplishments, speaking fluently five or more languages, and numbered among her particular friends the families of Washington Irving, Henry Clay, Daniel Webster and others.

This esteemed lady died suddenly of cholera in this city in 1853, deeply mourned and regretted by a large circle of friends.

Mr. Hodgson is a direct descendent, on his maternal side, from some of England's great personages, and is a great great grand nephew of Robert Elliott, who so successfully commanded the defences of the "Gibralta," during a seven years seige, by all the combined forces of Europe, and for which His Royal Master knighted him "Lord Elliot Heathfield."

His maternal grandfather was an officer in the U. S. Army during the English war of 1812, and while gallantly leading his troops at the battle of Bladensburg, in the defense of Washington City, received wounds from which he suffered for many years, and which finally resulted in his death.

The subject of our sketch, imbibing somewhat the spirit of excitement and adventure, as it were, of his ancestors, joined the renowned corps, the Battalion Washington Artillery, (then a single company) as far back as the 2nd of April, 1851, and during a series of years, passing through the various grades from private onward. He entered the Confederate service in March, 1862, as captain of the Fifth Company of that famous corps, which office he subsequently resigned, to accept service with his good friend, the late Henry W. Allen, then Governor of Louisiana, as the commander of the State Artillery (doing outpost duty with the Confederate troops and under Confederate authority), and rendered eminent and conspicuous services to the state and government throughout the entire war, remaining in the service until after the last gun was fired, receiving his parole from the U. S. forces, on the surrender of Gen. E. Kirby Smith's army, in the Trans-Mississippi Department, in June, 1865.

Through his checkered and varied life, either as clerk, merchant, soldier, citizen or friend, Captain Hodgson has ever proven himself honorable, just and charitable to his fellow man, with a gay and happy disposition and cheerful pleasant manner with all, he has, through his indomitable energy, capacity and sterling integrity (in connection with his partner), built up a large and prosperous business, second to none in their line, and they enjoy the esteem and confidence of the entire community.

A peculiarity in our city railroads is that there are no conductors. Passengers on entering the cars walk up to the fare-box, and deposit five cents—this being the price for a ride to any portion of the city. The amount saved by the Companies, by salaries for conductors and their perquisites add largely to the increase of dividends on the stock

HENRY ABRAHAM, ESQ.

This gentleman, of Israelitish extraction, was born in Germany in 1836. Having finished his academic course at home, he, at an early age, emigrated to the United States, and the first place where he fixed his residence was the beautiful city of Montgomery, Alabama, where, in 1851, he entered into trade with his brother, who had also left his fatherland for the New World, and where he remained ten years advantageously and prosperously occupied.

In 1862, he removed to New Orleans, the great mart of Southern and South-western commerce. Here he first entered into the wholesale business on a large scale, with F. Goldsmith, Esq., under the firm name of Abraham & Goldsmith, which continued until 1866, when he formed a co-partnership with other parties in the cotton commission business, under the firm name of Lehman, Newgass & Co., New Orleans. He subsequently became partner in the firms of Lehman Brothers, New York, under the name of Lehman, Newgass & Co.; also of Lehman, Durr & Co., Montgomery, Ala., and of B. Newgass & Co., Liverpool, England.

The business of this firm has been prosperous from the start, owing to the mercantile skill, high integrity and general intelligence of the principal at the head of it, and of the gentlemen associated with him in the management of its affairs. It has experienced no reverses, and has rapidly risen to occupy the rank of one of our first commercial houses. It has also extended its branches to other commercial centres.

Mr. Abraham has settled the question, which has provoked skepticism at the North, and been regarded doubtful at the South, of the perfect feasibility of establishing cotton manufactures successfully in this section of the country. Indeed with the staple, machinery, water power and steam power necessary for manufacturing purposes, at our own door, it is surprising that our large capitalists and enterprising citizens have not embarked in this profitable enterprise at an earlier period. His Lane Cotton Mills, beautiful and commodious structures, situated on Tchoupitoulas Street, near Napoleon Avenue, in which yarns, ropes, osnaburgs, sheetings, shirtings and blankets, of the finest texture, are manufactured, equal to any produced in Europe or America, and for which the demand is large, and being continually extended, have introduced an era in this great industrial interest, for which not only New Orleans, but the whole Southern country is greatly indebted to this public-spirited citizen. We have regarded these mills as furnishing so marked a feature in the history of the times and of the *renaissance* of this metropolis, that we have had an accurate engraving of them made for this work. In prosecuting the noble enterprise (a novelty in our midst) with a species of enthusiasm that has been attended with the most encouraging results, the subject of this notice has had a special eye to the condition of a large class of persons among us who have been reduced to poverty and destitution by the late unhappy war. With a humanity that does honor to him, and to the persecuted and distinguished race from which he has descended, he has sought out, in the thoroughfares of the city, this class of persons, by the hundred, and given them a home and occupation. Not only men, but indigent boys and girls, clamoring for bread but willing to work, have been employed by him and rewarded for their labor. The number of operatives daily employed in and about the factory, in various tasks, ranges at from sixty-five to seventy. It forms the nucleus around which similar institutions will, in process of time, spring up, by means of which, as the example spreads, far and wide, from city to city, and from town to country, the South will, at length, become as well known and as noteworthy, for its manufactures, as it now is for its agriculture and its commerce.

In addition to the cotton mills, Mr. Abraham, under the firm of Smith & Goldsmith, started the Commercial Cotton Press, which, with the buildings attached to it, occupies four blocks on Tchoupitoulas street, where cotton is received in large quantities, stored, handled, pressed, prepared for market, and shipped on its destination. This is a great advantage to our planters and to purchasers and shippers of cotton. The Press itself is the most complete piece of workmanship of the kind ever imported into this city, and furnishes occupation, in various ways, for a large number of operatives.

Mr. Abraham is a Director in the Germania National Bank, and also a Director in three of our Insurance Companies, viz: the Crescent Mutual, the Hope, and the Teutonia. When not at his office, where he is generally to be found "from early morn to dewy eve," he is usually to be met with at the Bank, or some of the Insurance offices, or on "'Change, where merchants "most do congregate," receiving or imparting information as to the rise or fall of stocks, and the condition of the market at home and abroad. To politics, such as it has been for the last ten years in this community, he has an extreme aversion and never meddles with it.

This prosperous merchant takes a deep interest in the progress and completion of the new Jewish Temple "Sinai," on Carondelet street, now nearly finished, and has been a liberal contributor to it, as well as an ardent supporter of the cause of the Reformed Israelites, for whose special benefit that elegant structure was originally designed. One of the features which distinguishes their worship from that of the old time Israelites is, that, in accommodation to the spirit of the age, and the requirements of modern civilization, their service, in part at least, is conducted in the English language.

Washington Square.—This fronts on Elysian Fields street and the line of the Pontchartrain and the New Orleans, Mobile and Texas Railways. The square is otherwise bounded by Frenchmen, Dauphine and Casacalvo streets. From the river side it is overlooked by the Third Presbyterian Church, a fine brick building, whose front and steeple are now green with clambering vines. The square is enclosed with an iron fence, is copiously shaded upon the borders and is open for parades in the centre. It is the favorite resort for the children of the vicinage.

WM. S. PIKE, Esq.

N. O. INSURANCE ASSOCIATION BUILDING,

102 CANAL STREET.

NEW ORLEANS

MUT'L INSURANCE

ASSOCIATION.

CHARTERED MAY 7th, 1869.

Capital, $1,000,000

C. Cavaroc, *President,*

G. Lanaux, *Secretary.*

DIRECTORS:

C. Cavaroc,	S. Cambon,
Chas. DeBuys,	A. Pessou,
Leon Haas, Jr.,	J. Egle,
E. F. Mioton,	F. S. Willis,
W. Agar,	L. Querouze
A. Thibaut	

This Insurance Company, although one of the youngest, is already numbered among the most prosperous and popular associations of the same character in New Orleans. It was established in August '69, under the auspices of Mr. C. Cavaroc and a number of well known capitalists and merchants, and in December 1870, the act of incorporation was amended by the adoption of the mutual principal, under which no stockholder can participate in the profit of the company unless he has effected insurance therein and paid premiums accordingly, and then only in the proportion of the earned so paid, and by which also the capital of the Association was fixed at one million of dollars (1,000,000.) The last quarterly statement of the New Orleans Mutual Insurance Association, published Sept. 30th, 1872, shows that during that quarter the Fire, Marine and River premiums received amounted to $316,492.68, the net earned premiums to $130,237,90, from which amount, after deducting losses, expenses, interest on capital paid, etc., there still remained the sum of $70,222,00 as the net profits of the quarter ending Sept. 30th, 1872.

The assets of the Association at the same date amounted to $1,092,-638,25. The above figures show a most flourishing condition of the Association, so ably conducted by Mr. C. Cavaroc, with the efficient aid of Mr. George Lanaux, the accomplished and highly esteemed Secretary of the company. It is proper to add that the magnificent marble front three story building just erected by Mr. H. Howard, architect, on the site formerly occupied in Canal Street by the Mechanics' and Traders' Bank, is the property of the New Orleans Mutual Insurance Association, whose office occupies the front part of the ground floor. The rear part is occupied by the New Orleans National Banking Association, and on the first story is the office of the Crescent City Live Stock Landing and Slaughter House Co., all of which are also presided over by Mr. Cavaroc.

NEW ORLEANS

NATIONAL BANKING

ASSOCIATION.

Chartered as Bank of New Orleans, MAY 14th, 1853.

Converted into the N. O. National Banking Association, JULY 1st, 1871.

Capital, $600,000.

Chas. Cavaroc, *President.*

Numa Augustin, *Cashier.*

DIRECTORS:

E. F. Mioton,	F. S. Willis,
S. Cambon,	Leon Haas, Jr.,
A. Thibaut,	E. F. Converse,
J. Aldige,	C. DeBuys,
A. Tertrou.	

This Bank, formerly called the Bank of New Orleans, was about to go into liquidation at the end of the war, when a few of the stockholders had the happy idea of calling Mr. C. Cavaroc to the helm. Under his auspices a vigorous and altogether successful effort was made to revive this institution, the result of which was soon felt in the highly increased value of its stock, which in 1868 was quoted at $17, and is now [1872] worth $9.50. Under its new title, the New Orleans National Banking Association is now organized as a National Bank, with a capital of $600,000, divided into 20,000 shares of $30 each. The last official report made according to law on the 3d of Oct. 1872, shows the large sum of one million one hundred and ninety-eight thousand five hundred and twenty-eight dollars and twenty cents [$1,198,528.20], as amount of individual deposits at the close of business on that day, from which an accurate conception of the popularity and success of this bank may be formed. To Mr. C. Cavaroc, the able and energetic President, this flourishing condition of the New Orleans National Banking Association is mainly due, nor should we forget to add that he is very efficiently supported by an excellent Board of Directors, and by the gentlemanly cashier of the Association, Col. Numa Augustin, an intelligent merchant who, having left the counting-house for the tented-field during the late war, returned to his former peaceful avocations in 1865, and is now doing good service to the community in his present capacity. The New Orleans Banking Association is one of those financial institutions of which any city might feel justly proud, and it stands second to none in the estimation of the public.

JAMES W. ZACHARIE.

The subject of this sketch was one of the oldest and most respected merchants of this city. He was a native of the city of Baltimore and at the time of his death was in the seventy-fourth year of his age. He arrived in this city on the 1st of January 1803, about the period of the transfer of Louisiana from the French Republic to the United States, and was one of the few survivors who witnessed the event.

Mr. Stephen Zacharie, the father of the present subject, was Cashier of the Bank of Louisiana, the first institution of the kind established in the States, and his family soon became closely connected with the business interests of the newly acquired territory. At the period of the British invasion, James Zacharie, in common with the youths of his age, threw aside his books, to participate in the effort to expel the invaders. He was wounded in the battle of the 23d of December 1814, and was also in the celebrated battle of the 8th of January 1815.

Shortly after his father's death he was summoned from school to take charge of his business affairs, and by his industry and capacity soon became one of the most prominent merchants of this city. He supported with untiring energy every effort to advance the mercantile interests of New Orleans, and during his long and prosperous career, was very active in maintaining the commercial relations with the Spanish West Indies, the Spanish Main, and with Mexico. He was made President of the Chamber of Commerce, and was frequently the director of Banking institutions. Like most men of sterling and positive character he possessed many eccentricities, but withal was exceedingly kind hearted, liberal and honorable. Being one of the most prominent and successful merchants he soon acquired a large fortune and was enabled to retire to private life and enjoy the fruits of his labors. At his death New Orleans lost a most useful and enterprising citizen, and his family a kind, generous and indulgent parent.

LOUIS JANIN, ESQ.

THE subject of this sketch is a living example of a man retaining his physical and mental powers in perfection past seventy years.

He was born in France. In spite of his reticence concerning his origin, his contemporaries know that on his mother's side he belongs to one of the noblest families of the Kingdom of Portugal. His grandmother married one of the generals of Frederick II, of Prussia. The King of Portugal, who admired the genius of this eminent soldier, employed him to instruct his troops in the new military tactics.

The mother of Louis Janin was the issue of that marriage. Mr. Janin became an orphan in his infancy, and was sent to Germany and reared on the estate of his grandfather. After the death of the latter, his tutor settled his accounts and succeeded in getting young Janin to travel through Western Europe.

He saw military service for some time, and at last felt a desire of coming to the United States.

He arrived in 1826 or '27 and visited the West, where he learned the English language, which he now speaks with rare perfection, as well as the German, French, Italian and Spanish.

In 1828 or '29 Janin came to New Orleans and was much pleased with the country and the manners of the people.

He was, a few years afterward, admitted to practice as a lawyer, and has since had no superior competitors in his profession.

He has great professional energy, and his numerous successes in the most complicated cases, mark him as a great lawyer.

Mr. Janin is a cultured gentleman, frank and straightforward, and always ready to assist others.

In 1845 he established a sugar refinery in the neighborhood of New Orleans, in association with Mr. J. P. Benjamin, at that time a famous lawyer in this city. He lost in this undertaking a large capital, which he had accumulated by his untiring industry at the bar.

In 1830 or 1831 he married Miss Covington, one of the daughters of Governor Covington, of Kentucky. He had from that marriage four sons, who have distinguished themselves by their acquirements and honorable character.

Edward, the eldest, died in the field of honor, during our late civil war, whilst in command of a Confederate company. The other three sons are at present practicing law in California, Nevada and Washington City.

Mr. Janin is of small stature and rather stout, with piercing dark eyes.

All those who know him can testify to his amiable disposition and suavity of manner.

It is generally conceded that as a land lawyer he has no superior in the United States.

HON. RANDELL HUNT, ESQ.

HON. RANDELL HUNT was born in Charleston, South Carolina. He is about fifty years of age, and above the middle size.

He has been United States Senator, and is one of the Professors of our University.

He firmly opposed secession and showed at all times his attachment and devotion to the Union; but when the war broke out, he did not hesitate to partake of the destiny of the South, and was true to her cause and interests.

If we have an orator in the highest sense of eloquence—the lofty, the impassioned, not being among us common qualities—it is he. No lawyer ever advanced greater claims to the personal confidence and respect of the bar.

He possesses great depth of voice, speaks with fluency, and displays a confidence both of assertion and tone which seldom fails to take his hearers' judgment captive.

Mr. Hunt is distinguished for a most honorable character in private life, moderate opinions in politics, extensive information upon all subjects in his profession, and talents of a high order.

He is a great constitutional lawyer. The efforts of his genius combine with majestic declamation the deepest pathos, the most lively imagination and the closest reasoning.

When addressing a jury his strength lies in the lofty appeals he makes to the nobler qualities of the heart and in his withering scorn of the sordid and base.

Mr. Hunt is generally admired not only for his high talents, but loved for his generous, charitable, magnanimous and social disposition, frank and direct, with no mean qualities or littleness of mind.

ISAAC N. MARKS, ESQ.

THIS gentleman, of Hebrew descent (as his name indicates) and universally regarded as a distinguished representative of his ancient and highly favored race (in all respects save his adoption of Christianity as constituting a positive fulfilment of Hebrew predictions), was born at Charleston, South Carolina, May 2th, 1817. At the age of nineteen he removed to New Orleans and has resided here ever since, greatly esteemed by all classes of citizens of all creeds, both for his private and his public virtues. None of our merchants have maintained a higher character for integrity than he, none have reached the acme of wealth and prosperity by the exercise of superior skill. Nor does he appear at any time to have been more solicitous for his own advancement than for the public interests.

Soon after his arrival here, the mercantile firm of E. J. Hart & Company was established, of which Mr. Marks was an influential member. The credit, financial ability, and extensive resources of that firm are as well understood at New York, Chicago and St. Louis, as they are at New Orleans, and whenever and wherever the name of Isaac N. Marks is mentioned in connection with it, it has always been considered a synonym for honor, promptitude and efficiency.

Mr. Marks has identified himself very creditably with our public institutions. Officially, he stands in a most responsible position, at the head of the Fire Department of the city—an essential part of our city organization, and probably no city in the Union is more adequately provided with men and means for the prompt extinguishment of destructive fires, and for relief to the sufferers by them, not merely by Insurance Companies, but by the Fire Companies themselves, than the city of New Orleans. In 1840, four years after his arrival here, he was elected President of Perseverance Fire Company No 13, and, from year to year, continued to be reelected to that office. In 1850 he was chosen President of the Firemen's Charitable Association, representing all the Fire Companies of New Orleans, a kind of Masonic brotherhood, whose province it is to minister to the wants of the families of its deceased members. For seventeen years Mr. Marks has been elected to fill this delicate and difficult post by acclamation—an evidence of the fidelity with which he has dispensed the charities of this noble association. During all that time he has also been Chairman of the Board of Commissioners of the Fire Department, and, in that capacity, been often required to settle nice questions, referred to him, growing out of their contract with the City Government.

The thirty-fifth anniversary of the Firemen's Charitable Association will ever be a memorable day in the history of New Orleans, and in the life of the subject of this brief notice. The whole population of the Crescent City took a deep interest in the celebration of this anniversary. The sentiment which pervaded the entire community was one of deep gratitude to the brave and heroic men who were in the habit of exposing their lives to save from destruction the lives and property of their fellow citizens and to their distinguished President. As the Fire Companies moved on through our great thoroughfares, arrayed each in its own uniform, with their glittering engines gaily dressed with flowers, to the sound of martial music, they, by previous arrangement, passed opposite the City Hall, in order to pay their respects to his Honor, the Mayor, and the City Council. The address made by the President of the Fire Department, and the response of the Mayor on this occasion, were equally creditable to the good taste of both those distinguished individuals, and the subsequent presentation to Mr. Marks, at the Varieties Theatre, with imposing ceremonies, of a magnificent silver punch bowl, goblets and salver, testified to the high respect and esteem entertained for him by the Fire Companies, and was recognized as well merited by the approving acclamations of thousands of gentlemen and ladies who were present to witness it.

Soon after his establishment in New Orleans, the interest which he took in public affairs caused him to be elected an Alderman of the Second Municipality, which brought him into association with such men as Samuel J. Peters, James H. Caldwell and Henry Renshaw, who are, to the present day, justly regarded as fathers of the city, and projectors of some of the most important reforms, particularly in the department of education, that have occurred since the foundation of it. In all these enterprises Mr. Marks took a decided and prominent part.

As President of the Louisiana Fair Association for a series of years, he has furnished evidence of an interest in the Agriculture, Mechanic Arts, and Manufactures of the State, such as has probably been displayed by no other individual in our midst. He is President also of the New Orleans, Florida & Havana Steamship Company, President of the New Jerusalem Church Society, Director of the Sun Mutual Insurance Company and President of the Mutual Aid and Benevolent Life Association.

Mr. Marks was always, in politics, an old Line Whig, belonging to a party that embraced many of the purest patriots and ablest statesmen in the Union. In our late troubles he adhered steadfastly to the cause of the South. Two of his sons were in the Confederate army. One of them (Henry Clay) died at Malvern Hill, fighting valiantly at the head of his own company. The other, Rev. Alexanders Marks, is a highly esteemed Episcopal clergyman of this city. Mr. Marks is one of nine brothers, all of them still living, save one. He is said to have been eminently fortunate in all the relations of domestic life.

THE MECHANIC'S INSTITUTE.

CHARLES W. RINGGOLD.

Charles W. Ringgold is a native of this city, and perhaps the most youthful Federal official in the building. He has very decided ability, and makes a most excellent officer, being perfectly courteous and respectful to everybody, and at the same time watchful of the interests of the Government—a decided improvement on his predecessor.

Mr. Ringgold acquired his business education in the old hardware establishment of McCutcheon, Howell & Co., before the war. In 1865 he received his first official appointment, being made chief clerk of the Appraiser's Department. He was elected to the Legislature from the Fourth Ward in 1870, and was appointed State assessor of the Sixth District in 1872. In March, of the present year, he was appointed Postmaster to succeed C. W. Lowell.

CAPT. BLAYNEY T. WALSHE.

Among the young and rising merchants of New Orleans there is none whose success has been so marked and so rapid as that of Mr. B. T. Walshe, nor is there any one more highly esteemed in the community than he is for high social character and sterling integrity. Born in New Ross, Co., Wexford, Ireland in 1840, Mr. Walshe, with his parents, came to New Orleans at the early age of thirteen years, and soon after his arrival here found employment in the house of Lagay & Lecaun, then the leading boys' and children's clothing establishment of the city. Here he remained for a series of years, and by diligence, industry and close application prepared himself for the discharge of more responsible duties and for a wider field of labor. At the opening of the war Mr. Walshe was engaged in the well-known clothing house of Norris, Maull & Co., but like hosts of his countrymen, when his adopted State claimed his services in the army, he promptly responded to the appeal, and in 1861 joined the famous Washington Artillery. In May of the same year he was elected Lieutenant of Company A, of the Irish Brigade, subsequently incorporated in the Sixth La. Regiment, commanded by Colonel I. G. Seymour. In the record of this regiment, made famous by its bravery and efficiency and by its proud position in Hay's Brigade and Stonewall Jackson's Corps, he fully participated in all of its glories until, at Gaines's Mills, Captain Walshe was severely wounded in the ankle during the seven days' fight before Richmond. Thus being made unfit for active duty in the field, he was assigned to duty in Richmond as Chief of the Passport Office of the Department of Henrico. About a year after, when able to dispense with the use of crutches, he was assigned to staff duty as Chief Provost Marshal of South Mississippi and East Louisiana, and served until the termination of the war.

Having discharged well and faithfully his duties as a soldier he returned to New Orleans poor in pocket, but full of hope, and with a determination to begin anew as it were the battle of life, but not upon such blood-stained fields as those he had so recently abandoned. Peace once more blessed the land; the avenues of trade and commerce were once more opened. For these avocations the early training of Mr. Walshe had cultivated a taste and developed a talent that subsequently crowned his efforts with abundant success. In October 1868, by industry and economy, Mr. Walshe was enabled to embark in business on his own account. His knowledge of the business of gentlemen's furnishing goods and boys' and children's clothing prompted him to make this line a specialty, and to say that he has been eminently successful would only be to re-echo the public verdict. As one thoroughly identified with all of the interests of New Orleans, coming from a foreign country and adopting this as his home, there is no better specimen of a stranger possessing all of the attributes of an exemplary and valuable citizen than Mr. Walshe. In 1863, he married a most estimable lady of New Orleans, and is now the father of five interesting children, three boys and two girls. In his pleasant but unpretending home he is surrounded by all the comforts and pleasures a devoted family and the fruits of an industrious life can alone procure. In the various relations of life Mr. Walshe is by every one recognized as worthy of confidence, respect and esteem. As a citizen he is public-spirited, enterprising and liberal. The improvement of the city, public works, and private enterprises for the general good all meet with his hearty support and substantial assistance, whilst his social character is that of an upright and honorable man, a true friend and a generous benefactor.

AMILCAR FORTIER.

The President of the Bank of America has filled the position up to the present time with great honor to himself and great acceptability to the Stockholders, having already declared during the last three years of his administration, dividends exceeding *ninety per cent* on the original capital of the Bank, after paying all its cash balances since the war in gold. Mr. Fortier is a native Louisianian and traces his ancestry to two of the oldest, best-known, and most esteemed families in the State. Although still in the prime of life, (he was born in 18[illegible]), Mr. Fortier has the reputation of being one of the most prudent, cautious and conservative of our Bank Presidents, and his judgement, being guided by a very accurate as well as extensive knowledge of the business men of New Orleans, the Bank of America, under his administration, has suffered fewer losses than it ever did before, whilst its deposits have gradually increased, until they now surpass in amount those of every other Banking Institution in the city.

Place d'Armes.—This is an open parade ground commonly known as "Congo Square," fronting on Rampart street, between St. Peter and St. Anne streets, with St. Claude street in the rear. It differs in no essential respect from the other public squares of the city.

JOSEPH A. MAYBIN, ESQ.

THIS eminent citizen and able lawyer came to New Orleans from Philadelphia, his native city, in the year 1817, and has resided here ever since, greatly respected by all classes of citizens among us. Learned, faithful, conscientious, judicious, no member of the profession has commanded more of the confidence of the community, and he has enjoyed an uniform and respectable practice.

He has been forty-four years a ruling elder in the First Presbyterian Church of this city, over which the Rev. Dr. Palmer is now pastor. This office is one of great trust and importance in the Presbyterian denomination,—the duties being to assist the pastor in visiting the sick, dying and bereaved members of the church, and in other most important spiritual matters, and, on account of his want of legal practice for a number of years past, Mr. Maybin has been enabled to execute this trust with great assiduity and fidelity.

He prefers the Presbyterian Church from education, and the conviction that its doctrines are most accordant with, and sustained by, the truths of the Bible and by sound philosophy.

Although not a minister of the gospel, he is permitted to officiate every Sunday morning in the Presbyterian church at Carrollton.

Regarding the intelligence of the people, as well as religion, essential to the maintenance and prosperity of free institutions, he was among the foremost of those who sought to promote the interests of education in our midst. He accordingly united with the late Samuel J. Peters, Joshua Baldwin, Leonard Mathews, Dr. Picton, and other high-toned and patriotic men in the great educational reform which was introduced here in 1841, and which secured for the inhabitants of this city and State, and ultimately (as the light of example spread) for the inhabitants of the whole Mississippi Valley, the advantages of a course of popular education, which united all the best traits of the New England and Prussian systems. To the promotion of this cause, Mr. Maybin, "in season and out of season," devoted all the energies of a benevolent heart and of an acute and powerful intellect.

He was, for nine consecutive years, chairman of the Committee on Teachers for the Schools of the Second Municipality,—a difficult, delicate and responsible trust, in the discharge of which (however attached to his own religious opinions) he endeavored not to be influenced by any theological bias. Whether the applicant for a place were a Catholic, a Protestant or an Israelite, it mattered not to this truly liberal man, provided he or she (as the case might be) possessed the necessary qualifications for teaching. On the latter point, he was inflexible.

During the same period, he also acted as a member of the different committees for visiting the schools in the same municipality.

After a high-school for boys was established in the second municipality, he did not regard the system complete till a similar institution was introduced for the benefit of the other sex. The paternity, so to speak, of the Young Ladies' High-School, in this city, it is believed, is to be attributed to Mr. Maybin, who, for the space of five years, watched over its interests and progress with enlightened and ceaseless vigilance.

Mr. Maybin, if not the founder of the Houses of Refuge in this city, was one of the first of our philanthropic citizens who took effectual steps for their establishment and organization; and, with a view to the reformation of the juvenile inmates, the commissioners procured the erection of and rented different buildings for the two sexes.

Mr. Maybin was appointed by the Council of the Second Municipality a commissioner of those houses for eight consecutive years; and, during the nine years last past, he has, every Sunday afternoon, instructed the inmates of the Girl's House of Refuge, in the Holy Scriptures.

In 1837, Governor Edward White offered to appoint him one of the Judges of the Supreme Court of the State, but he declined.

In the year 1841, his friends requested him to apply for the appointment of District Judge of the United States for the District of Louisiana, which application would probably have been successful. He declined this also.

For the space of twenty years, commencing from 1841, and extending down to the secession of the State from the Federal Union, he was in the habit, as opportunity offered, of giving oral religious instructions on Sunday afternoons to colored people, in the Lecture Room of the First Presbyterian Church.

When the question of secession was agitated, Mr. Maybin was opposed to the measure. He delivered his first public speech against it in the theatre on Poydras street, and other public speeches in opposition to it at different places, and wrote three articles on the subject, which were published in the *Picayune* with his name attached.

He did not discuss the constitutionality of secession, admitting that there were great authorities in its favor, but he denied its expediency, considering it a bold and dangerous remedy, and recommended the coöperation of the several slave States for the adoption of such measures as would most fully protect their interests and rights.

But, when the State of Louisiana adopted its ordinance of Secession, on the 26th day of January, 1861, Mr. Maybin could not unite with men, who, for a quarter of a century, had assailed our institutions in violation of the Constitution of the United States, who were strangers to him, and for whom he had no sympathy; and he determined to unite with his fellow-citizens, with whom he had resided forty years, to whom he was attached by strong associations, and with whom he was identified by pecuniary interest. He accordingly laid aside the abstract question of the propriety of secession, and heartily united with his fellow-citizens in favor of the Confederate cause.

He was a member of a company of one hundred men, too aged to perform military duty, but who were organized to maintain order and preserve peace in the city, in imitation of a corps of citizens formed for the same purpose during the invasion of Louisiana by the British in 1814 and 1815; which company of one hundred men were called

ORLEANS COTTON PRESS.

"The Fossils," and, during the whole year of 1861, paraded the streets with their double-barreled shot guns, and were called, by Mr. Maybin, "Old Fogies."

Governor Moore appointed him Chaplain in the Louisiana Militia, which office he accepted, in order to be with the sick, wounded and dying soldiers, and administer to them those comforts and consolations which humanity and religion prescribe. He, however, had no opportunity to perform the duties of the office, as the city was soon afterwards captured.

Mr. Maybin has nearly lost the sight of his eyes, but his intellectual vision is bright as ever. He is still professionally consulted, but, in preparing law documents, employs an amanuensis. He may be seen, nearly every day of the week, at the Sun Mutual Insurance Company's office, whose law concerns are committed to his management, in which, however, he is ably and faithfully assisted by Henry J. Leovy, Esq., of this city.

No citizen of the living generation, in New Orleans, has devoted himself, for half a century, with more singleness of purpose, with a clearer and more comprehensive intelligence, or more sustained perseverance, to the great interests of law, religion and the education of the people, than the venerable citizen, to whose active and able career we have, in these brief remarks, only done partial justice.

JAMES I. DAY, ESQ.

This distinguished gentleman, descended from one of the oldest families of New England, was born at New London, Conn., in 1812. No incidents connected with his childhood and early education have come to our knowledge, but his career as a man of business is well understood. In 1827, at the age of fifteen years, he became connected with a hardware establishment in New York city, in the capacity of a clerk. Five years afterwards, viz: in the Fall of 1832, he came to New Orleans, and connected himself in the same way with a mercantile concern of like character, the old and respectable firm of Whiting & Slark, of which firm he became a partner in the year 1837, and in which he continued, under the respective firms of Whiting & Slark; Slark, Day, Stauffer & Co.; and Slark, Day & Stauffer, until the year 1853, when he retired and removed to Connecticut, his health having been considerably impaired by his long and close application to business.

In 1836 Mr. Day formed a matrimonial connection with Miss Armitage, of Baltimore, sister of Mrs. Robert Slark, of this city, an alliance which contributed greatly to his domestic felicity.

Upon the death of Mr. Benjamin Story, in consideration of his financial abilities and influence, he was elected to supply his place as President of the Bank of Louisiana, which position, however, he resigned in favor of Mr. Wm. W. Montgomery, his own avocations not permitting him to give as much attention to the Bank as he thought necessary.

After taking up his residence in Connecticut, he became partner in the house of Bruff, Brother & Seaver, in New York, who, at the commencement of the war, were doing the largest hardware business in that city, and that almost entirely with the South, and which, in consequence of the war, became utterly ruined, involving him (being the capitalist in the concern), in very large losses.

Mr. Day was for many years President of the New York, Providence & Boston Railroad Company, and of several other Corporations in Connecticut and New York.

In consequence of his sympathies with the South in the early part of the war, he was threatened with arrest and imprisonment, and other hostile demonstrations. An order was at one time issued in New York for the seizure of his papers and effects, and only deferred through personal influence of Republican friends. The pressure on him was so great that he at length felt compelled to leave the country for a time. He accordingly went to Europe, where he spent about a year, till matters were quieted at home. He then returned to New York, where he remained until the close of the war, which stripped him of all his property.

In 1865 he returned to the Crescent City, where he associated himself with his son-in-law, C. H. Slocomb, Esq., and where he remained until his election recently to the office of President of the Sun Mutual Insurance Company.

During his long residence in New Orleans, he has been associated with most of the public enterprises of the day, always acknowledging the obligations which every successful man of business owes to the community in which he lives, and consequently co-operating with a cheerful spirit with all patriotic men, and contributing substantial aid to every meritorious object that claimed his attention. A Northern man, trained in Southern principles—the principles of the Federal Constitution—he loved with ardor the land of his birth, but has always adhered to his political faith with inflexible firmness. Exposed to the vicissitudes of fortune, he has never succumbed to them, but with every reverse that has befallen him has reasserted his independence, and addressing himself with renewed energy to the task of triumphing over difficulties and achieving the success which, for the most part, crowns the labors of courageous men.

THOMAS SLOO, ESQ.

This venerable gentleman, now in the eighty-third year of his age, but with intellect unimpaired, and a cheerfulness of temper which promises a prolongation of his active and useful life, was born in Washington, Mason County, Kentucky, April 5th, 1790. At sixteen years of age, he removed from his native State to Cincinnati, Ohio, and the first position in which we find him, is that of Assistant to General Findlay, Receiver of Public Moneys at Cincinnati, and which he appears to have occupied till the year 1820, when he removed to Illinois, and devoted himself to agriculture.

The interest which he took in public affairs led to his election several times to the Legislature of that enterprising and prosperous State. On one occasion he was nominated as the Whig candidate for Governor, when he canvassed the entire State, in opposition to the celebrated Ninian Edwards.

In 1828 Mr. Sloo removed to New Orleans, and established himself as a Commission Merchant, maintaining a high reputation for gentlemanly demeanor, honor and integrity. For several years he occupied the responsible post of City Treasurer.

Upon the organization of the City Schools, about the year 1840, the deep interest he had always taken in the cause of popular education, led to his appointment as one of their Directors, in connection with Leonard Mathews, Esq., Hon. Joshua Baldwin (then Recorder of the Second Municipality), Dr. Picton and J. A. Maybin, Esq.—all men of great respectability and among the leading citizens of New Orleans, at a period when it was the custom of the city to appoint only such men to stations of trust and honor.

From the time of the incorporation of the Sun Mutual Insurance Company of New Orleans, he has filled, with marked ability, the office of President of that flourishing institution; but, in consequence of advancing years, has recently retired from its arduous labors. He still takes a lively interest in its affairs, is provided with a seat at its office, which he frequents daily, and retains for life, through the courtesy and liberality of the company, his annual salary.

Trained in the old school of politeness, no gentleman is more remarkable for the urbanity of his manners, the equanimity of his temper and the eminent purity of his character; none is ever more ready to find some apology for any one whom he may hear accused of wrong. So scrupulous is he as to injuring the virtue of others, that he was never heard to speak ill of any one, or repeat a rumor to his injury. In his friendships he is as reliable as he is slow and deliberate in forming them.

In politics Mr. Sloo used to belong to the Old Line Whigs, when that party was in the ascendency, and his memory still lingers with fondness over its history. In religion he is a quiet, steadfast devotee of Episcopacy. In opinions and practice he is a conservative, holding the golden mean that lies between objectionable extremes.

The City Prisons.—These edifices are built of brick, and plastered to imitate granite, they are three stories in height, occupying one hundred and twenty three feet on Orleans and St. Ann streets, by one hundred and thirty-eight feet nine inches between them. They are two in number, and divided by a passage way that is closed to the public. The principal building has its main entrance from Orleans street, through a circular vestibule, closed by strong iron doors. The lower story contains the offices and apartments of the jailor. The second story is divided into large halls for such prisoners as require to be less strictly guarded. The plan of the third story is similar. The whole is surmounted by a belvidere, with an alarm bell. The cost is estimated at $200,000.

MRS. MARY S. WHITAKER.

This well known poet, essayist and novelist, is a daughter of Rev. Prof. Samuel Furman, one of the most eminent, eloquent and learned divines of South Carolina, and granddaughter of Rev. Richard Furman, D. D., of Charleston, S. C., *clarum et venerabile nomen*, connected with the annals of the American Revolution, and the early history of South Carolina, of whose Constitution, such as it was before the commencement of the late war, he was one of the original framers. So powerful was the influence exerted by this celebrated divine in spreading, among the masses of the people, the flame of liberty and independence, during the revolutionary era, that Lord Cornwallis set a price upon his head. He was greatly beloved by all classes and denominations of people while he lived, and his funeral, upon the interment of his remains, was the largest ever seen in Charleston, except that of the late John C. Calhoun.

On the mother's side, Mrs. W. is of Scottish lineage, of the family of Scrymgeour, famous in Scottish history, and including among its celebrated names, those of Montook and Dundee, immortalized by their heroism, and by the pens of Sir Walter Scott and the late lamented Aytoun.

She received her earliest instructions under the domestic roof, from her now venerable father, always a ripe scholar, an acute logician, and imbued not less with the love of letters than philosophy. She early exhibited a sensitive genius, and displayed much poetic power, devoted herself assiduously to the study of history on an extended scale, and of English classics, particularly the poets of Great Britain. To an amount of learning, rarely attained by the women of America, she unites a cultivated taste and a high order of intellect. Probably there is no English prose writer, of either sex, who has attained to greater vigor and purity of style. She particularly excels in the delineation of scenery and character. Her Poems, published in 1850, elicited the highest praise from William Cullen Bryant and other American critics. In Europe, her poetical effusions attracted attention, and the celebrated Thomas Campbell, at a literary reunion at the house of the late Robert Chambers, on hearing one of her pieces recited, clapped his hands, exclaiming: "That belongs to the school of Pope and Campbell, which is the best of all schools, and I claim this young lady as my spiritual daughter."

While in Scotland with her parents, she married John Miller, Advocate, of Edinburgh, brother of the present Member of Parliament for Leith and the adjacent boroughs. Mr. Miller was at that time Assessor for Leith, and, subsequently, her Britannic Majesty's Attorney-General for the British West Indies. This distinguished official died at Nassau, New Providence, three months after their marriage.

Mrs. Whitaker is still actively engaged in writing, and, if her life is spared, will, in all probability, be better known to the public hereafter than she now is; although, by her voluminous communications to the press, and her published pieces, prose and poetical, she has already acquired the reputation of being one of the most finished and elegant authors of this century.

She is wife of Prof. D. K. Whitaker, of this city.

NEW TEMPLE SINAI.

ALFRED HENNEN, ESQ.

This truly estimable and learned jurist, who has recently passed off the stage of life, at the advanced age of eighty-five years, is deserving of the highest tribute of respect that can be paid to his memory by the living generation. His name is a connecting link between two centuries, of which the eighteenth claimed his boyhood, and the nineteenth his youth, manhood and old age. Around both epochs his numerous virtues have shed an undying charm. Louisiana will never forget one who was a denizen of her territory five years before she became a State, and who, through all the mutations of politics, was an unflinching advocate of her sovereignty and her honor. New Orleans, with whose interests his own were identified, from the time it was a village till it became the great and flourishing city it now is, where he acquired solid and enduring fame and an ample fortune, in his capacity of an able advocate and a learned counsellor, has equal cause to remember the venerable sage, who, by his wisdom, energy and lofty example, has shed lustre on her history.

This distinguished personage was born in Maryland, A. D. 1786. He pursued his collegiate course of studies at Yale College, where he graduated with distinction in the twentieth year of his age. Piously trained by excellent parents, the religious element of his nature was fully developed at the early age of sixteen years, when he became, by open profession, a member of the Presbyterian Church, to which he was ardently attached and of which he was a Ruling Elder for nearly half a century, having been raised to that influential position by regular ordination in the year 1828, according to the forms of that church. "His name," says Dr. Palmer, in the eloquent discourse of that distinguished divine, delivered on the occasion of his death, "heads the list of the original twenty-four, who, in the month of November, 1823, were organized, according to our ecclesiastical canons, into the First Presbyterian Church of New Orleans."

In his youth he was inclined to adopt the ministry as his profession, but subsequently shrank from its lofty responsibilities, and, on his graduation, determined on the study of the law, which he commenced and prosecuted for a couple of years at New Haven under the direction of Judge Chauncey.

To the noble profession he adopted he was always passionately devoted, especially to the Department of the Civil Law, emphatically the law of Louisiana, the fountain, as well as crown, of the Common Law of England. It would be invidious to compare him with other great civil law lawyers with whom the New Orleans bar has been graced from time immemorial. Suffice it to say, that he was among the most prominent of its expounders and among the most successful of its practitioners. To great legal lore he added a taste for literature, which served to elevate the tone of his profession. He had no mean acquaintance with the Oriental tongues, especially the Hebrew. To great dignity of manners he added a grace and affability that were truly attractive; and to very decided views a spirit of conciliation, that secured respect and prompted affection. Few individuals who have adorned the municipal, ecclesiastical, and legal annals of the Crescent City, have passed off the stage with a nobler and more stainless record than the late venerable Alfred Hennen.

For about twenty years he was an able and efficient Director of the old Bank of Louisiana, during its days of prosperity.

JAMES FRERET, ESQ.

James Freret, Esq., descended, on the mother's side, from the Chevalier D'Arensbourg, of Swedish stock, and, on the paternal, from the Frerets, of England, belongs to one of the oldest families in Louisiana. His maternal ancestor, the Chevalier D'Arensbourg, emigrated to this country in the early part of the last century, and was invested with the government of the "German coast." According to Gayarré, about 1721, three years after the foundation of the city. His name appears in the roster of the garrison, as Captain, in 1740.

His paternal grandfather, James Freret, emigrated from England some time previous to 1790. It is worthy of mention that he started the first cotton press ever used in this city, (a hand-power press,) on Royal street, in the first decade of the present century. His example was shortly after followed by his brother-in-law, V. Rillieux, who also had a hydraulic hide press.

The subject of this notice was born at New Orleans, April 26, 1838. He commenced his studies as an architect, the profession for which he had an early predilection, in 1856, at the age of eighteen years, remaining for a few months in the sash factory of Mr. George Purves, then in the office of that architect, who was then erecting the First Presbyterian Church. One year afterwards, he entered the office of W. A. Freret, Esq., one of our most highly esteemed architects, where he remained till the month of June, 1860, during which he drew the plans for the Touro Alms House, unfortunately consumed by fire before the edifice was completed; the celebrated Moresque Building, corner of Camp and Poydras streets, three iron buildings on Canal street, &c., &c.

In June, 1860, Mr. Freret visited Europe with a view to perfect himself in his profession, where, for the space of thirteen months, he prosecuted with diligence the course of studies prescribed by *L'Ecole des Beaux Arts*. He then travelled in Italy, Switzerland, France and England, sketching notable buildings.

In August, 1862, he returned home through the blockade at Charleston, S. C., entered the engineer service of the Confederate States Army; was disabled at Port Hudson; began business again after the war; completed the Moresque Buildings; designed the first Fair buildings, the Louisiana Savings Bank; the four-story building at the corner of Common and Magazine streets, the new office (shortly to be built) for the New Orleans Gas Light Company; also, the new Spring Hill College, the extension of the Convent of Visitation, and the new front of the Cathedral, at Mobile, Ala.

Mr. Freret is highly esteemed by his brother architects, and his fellow citizens, for his skill in his profession, and for the honor and integrity which have always marked his career in life.

REV. JOSEPH P. B. WILMER, D.D., BISHOP OF THE EPISCOPAL CHURCH OF LOUISIANA.

This learned and eloquent prelate is of a Maryland family, well-known in the annals of that State. He removed in early childhood to Virginia. He was educated at Kenyon College, Ohio, from which he received his first degree. His ministerial life passed in Virginia, where he married into the Skipwith family, and where he lived in charge of a parish, until he accepted a call to St. Mark's Church in Philadelphia. He received his Degree of Doctor of Divinity from Union College, Schenectady, N. Y. He resigned his parish in Philadelphia, at the commencement of hostilities between the North and South, believing that the course pursued by the former towards the latter was not only unconstitutional but unchristian, and feeling that he could not conscientiously invoke the blessing of Heaven on the success of a cause essentially unjust. On thus severing his connection with the North, and with a people to whom he was greatly attached, and who regarded him with love and veneration, and deeply regretting the step which, from a sacred regard to principle and a deep sense of duty, he felt himself compelled to adopt, he returned to his estate in Virginia and remained in retirement with his family till the close of the war. He was, soon after, elected to the Episcopate of Louisiana, and removed to this city.

Bishop Wilmer is about five feet eight inches in height, compactly built, with strongly knit and well-proportioned limbs, blue eyes, broad forehead, fair complexion, open countenance, plants himself firmly on his feet, gesticulates but little, and has a clear, rich and singing voice suited to an orator, and reaching, without difficulty, the remotest parts of a large church. His head is silvered over with the snows of nearly three score years, but his aspect in the pulpit, when animated by his subject, is that of a man of forty or forty-five at the utmost. His manner is rather calm and dignified than impassioned; but he immediately arrests attention by the strong and generous thoughts that spring from his heart, and by the order and convincing force of his arguments. No scholar is a greater master of pure, vigorous, flexible and elegant English. No divine of the Church of England, or of any other church, is more liberal and tolerant in his opinions, nor more free from cant. He makes no compromise, however, with vice, folly or egotism, which he regards proper subjects of rebuke or censure.

He is a fine conversationalist, and the attentive listener knows not which to admire most, the breadth of his intellect, the extent of his information, or the goodness of his heart. The interests of Christianity and of the church are uppermost in his mind, and those who are honored by his friendship never fail to be impressed by the loftiness of his motives, and the extent of his charity. His object, in his interviews with others, seems to be to render the obligations of truth more imperative, and the Christian virtues more attractive than they were before. He has a decided antipathy to political preachers, political sermons, and political prayers, regarding them fruitful sources of the skepticism that prevails in this country at this time.

When the illustrious General Lee, at the close of the late war, doubted as to the expediency of accepting the invitation he had received to take charge of Lexington (afterwards Washington) College, he visited Dr. Wilmer to consult with him on the subject of his duty in this matter. At first Dr. Wilmer endeavored to dissuade the General from accepting so humble a post, adding that the Presidency of the Virginia University would be more suitable for him. The people of Virginia, and of the whole South, would be proud, he said, to see him placed at the head of their time-honored University.

General Lee, thanking the Doctor for his flattering proposal and promised aid in consummating it, promptly but decidedly declined, saying that Providence seemed to have clearly opened the way to his acceptance of the Lexington College, where he thought there would be a sphere of usefulness which would task his powers to the utmost.

His friend was deeply affected by his arguments, yielded to the modesty of this truly great man, acquiesced in his judgment, and embraced him with a degree of warmth which honest sympathy alone could inspire. "Now," said the latter, "I listen to you with pleasure."

The two friends, it is said, then discussed, *in extenso*, the great questions of education, and General Lee proceeded to organize and establish the Washington College, and to place it on a footing which has made it one of the most celebrated and valuable educational institutions in the country. A fairer illustration of the spirit of true Christianity cannot be furnished than was exhibited by those two eminent men on this occasion.

Dr. Wilmer, for the space of two years, was a Chaplain in the American Navy, during which engagement he visited various centres of civilization, among others thrice visited England. Few Americans have enjoyed finer opportunities for observation, and an extensive knowledge of mankind. He has four children—a daughter and three sons. One of his sons is a practitioner at law in the City of Baltimore.

MAJ. JOHN H. NEW.

Maj. New within a few years has succeeded in placing himself in the front rank of his profession.

He is a native of Louisville, Ky.

He commenced the study of the law in the University of Mississippi. He afterwards graduated with high honors in Harvard College, Mass.

He first went to practice at Baton Rouge, where he soon made himself known for his intellect and legal lore.

In 1861 when the South resorted to arms, Maj. New served in Gen. Hays' brigade as Adjutant Genral and distinguished himself for his ability, ready knowledge and efficiency, in the discharge of his duties.

After the war Maj. New settled in New Orleans and devoted his attention to the practice of his profession. He has since visited the principal cities of Europe.

As a lawyer he is noted for the quickness of his perception. In an examination he fathoms the inmost thoughts of witnesses. Although generally dispassionate, he is an excellent speaker.

CHARLES FITZENREITER.

INTERIOR VIEW OF B. T. WALSHE'S

Well known Shirt, Mens' Furnishing Goods and Boy's and Childrens' Clothing Establishment,

NO. 110 CANAL, NEAR ST. CHARLES STREET,

NEW ORLEANS.

REV. HENRY SAMUEL JACOBS.

Minister of the Hebrew Congregation, "Dispersed of Judah," was born at Kingston, Jamaica, in the British West Indies, on the 22d day of March, 1827. Exhibiting a decided inclination for the ministry from his youth, he early qualified himself for the sacred calling, beginning his theological studies under the Rev. Moses N. Nathan, who was subsequently the first minister of the Hebrew Congregation in this city, to which Mr. Jacobs is now attached. After officiating for three years as lay reader, he was, in his twenty-first year, placed in charge of the small congregation, "Habitation of Peace," at Spanish Town and Jamaica, till he was called to fill the important office of minister in the Kingston Congregation, "Gates of Righteousness."

His health having become impaired by too studious and sedentary a life, and feeling an irrepressible yearning to make the United States his home, he left his native island on the 3d of January, 1854, and reached New York the following week. His reputation as a zealous, devout, and indefatigable minister of his faith had preceded him, and this, together with the demand for English preachers (which has since assumed the largest proportions) led to his receiving more than one call, terminating in his acceptance of that of the Portuguese Hebrew Congregation of Richmond, Va., the duties of which he assumed about a fortnight later. Here he labored successfully for nearly four years, when the pulpit of the Congregation, "Shearith Israel," of Charleston, S. C., then one of the largest and most influential in the Union, having become vacant, was tendered to him in the most flattering terms; but loath to leave his Richmond flock, he eventually consented to change his field of labor, only on the urgent advice of his numerous friends, who believed that his efforts in the holy cause would be more valuable in the wider ministrations to which he was so earnestly invited.

In this position he continued successful in his clerical charge, gaining many friends and winning golden opinions from all sorts of men—but "grim-visaged war" had overtaken the land—the battle of Secessionville had been fought—the "swamp-angel" had commenced shelling the chief city of South Carolina, and its streets were deserted of their many familiar faces. The Synagogue was "under fire," and the congregation had dispersed.

In this emergency, the Board of Trustees suggested to Mr. Jacobs to move to Columbia, where a large part of his flock had taken refuge, and he accordingly proceeded thither and organized public worship. This state of affairs continued till February 17th, 1865, when the Union Army, under General Sherman, reduced that beautiful inland city, the capital of the State, to a heap of ruins.

Sharing in the general calamity Mr. Jacobs lost all his earthly possessions, and escaped from his burning homestead with but the clothing on his back, finding temporary shelter with his family under the roof of a friend in the suburbs of the city, till opportunity offered of moving to Augusta, Ga., the nearest point of refuge and safety. For about a year he continued there still ministering in his holy avocation.

Peace, meanwhile, had been restored; but it was destined that he should not resume his clerical charge at Charleston; for the Synagogue there had been so injured by the shelling of the city that it could not be used in its then condition; whilst the few members of the congregation who remained were too impoverished either to repair it or provide the necessaries to continue public worship. Hence he had to resign the office he held there notwithstanding the attachment he felt to his Charleston flock.

Receiving several calls at this time he elected to accept the one coming from this city, which he now fills as minister of the Hebrew Congregation, "Dispersed of Judah."

Mr. Jacobs belongs to the conservative party of his denomination, which, whilst recognizing the necessity for some legitimate concessions to the scientific progress and inquiring spirit of our times, and the social condition of the country in which we live, yet respects the pious usages of antiquity, and holds firmly and uncompromisingly to the fundamental principles of Judaism, thus taking the intermediate position between Radical Reform and ultra-Orthodoxy.

Having been educated as a teacher, he has given much thought and labor to the cause of education. In his eighteenth year he was placed in charge of a Public School in his native country, and subsequently elected principal of the consolidated Hebrew schools. He was also engaged in the same duties in Richmond, Va., Columbia, S. C., and Augusta, Ga. In this city, at the establishment of "The Hebrew Education Society," he was its first President and afterwards became Superintendent,—a post which he has only recently relinquished. His interest in education has been most pronounced, and is his marked characteristic, and, it is expected, will continue to be exercised for the general welfare of the community.

None of our ministers, of any denomination, are more distinguished for learning, eloquence, and urbanity of manners, than the Rev. Mr. Jacobs; and none exerts a more decided and high-toned influence in the various circles of society in which he moves.

MARKETS.

The markets are a prominent feature in a description of New Orleans. They are numerous, and dispersed, to suit the convenience of the citizens. The prices of many articles they offer are very fluctuating. Not dearer, however, on an average, than in New York. Stall-fatted meats are not so usual here as at the North, preference being given to the grass-fed. The mutton has no equal in America. Poultry and fish are fine; and vegetables, except potatoes, are abundant, and speak well for the soil that produced them. Fruit, from the West Indies and our own West, is not only plenty but of the best kind. The regulations are excellent, and are strictly enforced by officers appointed for that purpose. The greatest market day is Sunday, during the morning. The traveler, who leaves the city without visiting one of the popular markets on Sunday morning, has suffered a rare treat to escape him.

ALEXANDER HAY, ESQ.

ALEXANDER HAY, Esq., President of the St. Andrews Society of New Orleans, was born on the 26th of February, 1832, in Stranraer, a small seaport town in Wigtonshire, Scotland, near the seat of the Earl of Stair, of "the Massacre of Glencoe" notoriety. Mr. Hay was educated at the old University of Glasgow, and, at the age of twenty-two, after an apprenticeship of three years, took the management of the large Tannery of Messrs. Thomas Pitling & Co., of Port Glasgow, which position he filled for eight years, until compelled by ill health to relinquish it.

From the time of his leaving the tan-yard till his departure to the United States, he traveled over the larger portion of Europe in pursuit of health, but seeking that blessing in vain. His physician then advised him to take passage on a sailing vessel and try a warmer climate. Complying with this recommendation, he set sail for the port of New Orleans, and by the time of his arrival here in June, 1863, after a long voyage, found his health completely restored. It was not in his nature to remain inactive. His old occupation among hides and leather had great attractions for him, and he thought there was a good opening here in that line of business. He was first employed as a clerk merely, but, in the course of a year from the time of his arrival, was able to set up business on his own account, when he established (taking into partnership a native of New Orleans) the firm of Hay & Mehle (50 Commerce and 120 St. Peters streets), one of the largest houses, if not the largest, in the trade of Hides and Wool in the city of New Orleans, and which has been exceedingly successful.

Mr. Hay furnishes an instance, not uncommon among his countrymen, in which the character of the industrious, persevering tradesman, is fully blended with that of the scholar and the gentleman. It is to the union of such characteristic traits (and which are worthy of all imitation where they are attainable) that he is largely indebted for his prosperity and success.

Mr. Hay was married in Bannockburn to a lady of that memorable village, Miss Miller, by whom he has two children alive, a son and a daughter. He had the misfortune to lose two fine boys in 1867.

In November, 1869, he was first elected President of the St. Andrews Society, and has had the unusual distinction conferred upon him of being annually reelected the President of that most honorable and beneficent association ever since.

He is Agent for the Anchor Line of Trans-Atlantic Steamships, running twice a week between New York and Glasgow. This Company has a fleet of thirty-six steamers afloat, and seven more on the stocks. The career of the founder of this Line is somewhat remarkable, and affords evidence that colossal fortunes are often made in the Old World as well as the New. Forty years ago, three little Scotch boys started life together, owning first a sailing smack only; gradually rising in the gradation of tonnage and rig, until they had served in schooners, brigs, barques, ships, and were conversant with every detail in connection with those different types of vessels. These little Scotch boys rapidly rose to be the world-wide known firm of Handyside & Henderson of Glasgow, the owners of the Anchor Line, a fleet that cost $150,000,000.

REV. GEORGE H. DEERE.

This highly esteemed pastor of the Unitarian Church in this city was born at Oswego, N. Y., September 4th, 1827. He was the son of an artist who entertained very liberal notions on the subject of Religion, took great pains in the personal training of his son. Owing to a defect in his eye-sight which became apparent in his infancy, his education was necessarily domestic.

The mother of young Deere was a Methodist, and as mothers are apt to exercise a controlling influence on the minds of their children, and do much towards shaping their character and opinions, it is not surprising that, shut out measurably from the world by his misfortune, and consequently addicted much to meditation and reflection, the youth should have adopted the maternal creed. In 1843, however, "a change came over the spirit of his dream," and at Brooklyn, N. Y., to which city he had removed, and where liberal views of theology had obtained a lodgment, he became an Universalist, the paternal recollections and influences now prevailing over the maternal.

Inclination and circumstances pointed him to the church as the department best fitted for him. He, accordingly, devoted himself to the study of theology, first under the tuition of Rev. Dr. Sawyer, now Packard Professor of Theology at Tuft's College, Boston, and, afterwards, under that of Rev. Dr. Thayer, of Brooklyn, N. Y., now editor of the *Universalist Quarterly*, and, in due time, became a licentiate, and ultimately an ordained minister of the gospel.

After a short ministry at Danbury, Conn., and Warren, Mass., he was settled as pastor at Brattleboro, Vt., where he remained seven years. Removing to Melrose, Mass., in September, 1860, and finding the climate of the New England sea coast prejudicial to the health of his wife, he accepted a call, at the close of a year, to a pastorate at Shelburne Falls, Mass., which continued six years. In October, 1867, he accepted an invitation to the charge of a parish at La Crosse, Wis., whence, after a ministry of four years, in October, 1871, he removed to New Orleans. The parishes which he has hitherto served have been in fellowship with the Universalist branch of the Liberal Christian Church; and he has, thus far, been very acceptable as well as useful in his ministrations. The society over which he now presides, and which was very large under the ministry of the late Rev. Dr. Clapp, (but which declined after the war,) has taken a new start, and seems likely, under its new auspices to recover much of its former strength and influence.

Mr. Deere, like Dr. Clapp, is an extemporaneous preacher, and never writes a discourse before its delivery. His mind is clear, orderly, and didactic, and his manner serious and impressive without rhetorical display. His conversational powers are considerable, and whenever he appears in social circles with his intellectual and accomplished wife, he throws a certain charm over them.

THE STORY BUILDING.

COLONEL ISAAC G. SEYMOUR.

In no other city in the United States, perhaps we might say in no other city in the world, have there been so many journalist soldiers as in New Orleans. Peter K. Wagner, so long editor of the Louisiana "Courier," and the recognized champion of the Democratic party of the State, was a lieutenant in the army with which Jackson defended New Orleans. John C. Larue of the "Delta," subsequently of the "Crescent," who was, in his day, among the ablest as an editor, as a jurist, and as a politician, served as a volunteer in the ranks of General Taylor's army, on the Rio Grande. General William Walker, the celebrated filibustero, who made his name famous, as a desperate fighter in Nicaragua, was a colleague of Larue on the "Crescent." Alexander Hays, the most capable practical newspaper man we have ever had in New Orleans, who was one of the founders of the "Delta," and one of those who established the "Crescent," sought dangerous adventures, during the Mexican war, as an amateur, under his friends, Captains Fairchild and Kerr, types from New Orleans, who held commissions in the Louisiana cavalry. George Wilkins Kendall of the "Picayune," was one of the Texan band who undertook the main expedition, for the invasion of Mexico, the misfortunes of which are the themes of a melancholy history written by him, and, during the Mexican war with the United States, while corresponding with his paper, he was on the staff of General Worth, sharing the dangers and hardships of that enterprising and gallant officer. F. A. Lumsden, the associate of Kendall on the "Picayune," was, during the early period of that war, attached to the Texas Rangers, and was with them when they rendered themselves famous in the attack upon Monterey. In the civil war we had, in the Confederate army, J. O. Nixon, proprietor of the "Crescent," as Lieutenant-Colonel of the First Louisiana Cavalry; Israel Gibbons, an attaché of the "Crescent," who served as a private, in the Nineteenth Louisiana, until physical disabilities incapacitated him for service in the line, and he was appointed quarter-master, with the rank of major; Lieutenant Wright of the "Bee," an officer of the Thirtieth Louisiana, killed in battle; Joseph Hanlon, of the "True Delta," who from captain rose to the command of the Sixth Louisiana, three of its colonels having been killed instantly, upon different battle-fields; Daniel Scully of the "Delta," and "True Delta," who, as correspondent of the "Picayune," saw service on the staff of General Joe Lane, the "Marion of the Mexican war," and, in the late war, was senior line officer of the Second Louisiana Batallion of Heavy Artillery; and Major William J. Seymour, son of the subject of this notice, and associate editor of the "Bulletin," who was Aid-de-Camp to General Duncan, during his defence of Fort Jackson, against Farragut's fleet, and, subsequently, until the close of the war, was on duty, as chief of staff, with the indomitable brigade of Louisianians, commanded by General Henry T. Hays.

Isaac G. Seymour, of whom we are writing, as one of those who dropped the pen, and buckled on the sabre or shouldered the musket, at the call of duty, was a man whose life and services deserve more than a passing notice. His family was a branch of that Connecticut stock of Seymours who have been so eminent for virtues and for talents, and, as publicists, have been so conspicuous for the courage and force with which they have maintained and constantly adhered to the great principles of constitutional liberty. He was born in Savannah, Georgia, in October, 1804. He graduated, creditably, at Yale College, and, soon after, established himself, as an advocate, at Macon, Ga. His practice gave early promise of an ample income, but he found the profession distasteful and abandoned it for journalism, when he became editor of the Macon "Messenger," which, while he was connected with it, was regarded as the organ of the whig party of the State. Civic honors came upon him too. For several successive terms, embracing a period of six years, he was chosen mayor, by his fellow citizens of Macon.

His advent, as a soldier, was made in the war with the Seminole Indians in Florida, in 1836, when he raised a company of Georgia Volunteers. He was favorably noticed by General Clinch and by General Scott, under both of whom, successively, he served. General Scott, particularly, seems to have been impressed with the martial aptitude and conduct of the captain, for the General repeatedly offered his influence to procure a commission for him in the regular army, which was declined because of the inertia and monotony of military life in time of peace. The Mexican war, however, which commenced in May, 1846, brought him to the "tented field" again. He organized a battallion of infantry in his native State, and was selected for its colonel. Shortly after the capture of Vera Cruz he reported for duty to his former commander-in-chief, General Scott. Cerro Gordo fought and won, La Hoya abandoned, Puebla fell, and a few months after our forces made their way into the City of Mexico. General Scott showed his appreciation of Colonel Seymour's ability, judgment and courage, by confiding to him the command of the town and castle of Perote, one of the most important posts on the line of communication from the capital to the American base at the Gulf. In command of that post he remained until the close of the war, in the summer of 1848, when he returned to Georgia, where his battallion was mustered out of service, and again he returned to private life.

In the autumn of that year he removed to New Orleans, to make it his permanent residence, and immediately purchased the "Bulletin" newspaper from Mr. William L. Hodge. Under Mr. Hodge the "Bulletin" had been a zealous propagandist of those extreme measures which were forced upon the whig party, by Northern and Eastern cupidity, and which compelled the abandonment of the National organization of that party by so many Southerners. Colonel Seymour brought the paper back to what it had been, under the control of William Casey Jones, son-in-law of Thomas H. Benton, and the immediate predecessor of Mr. Hodge. Thus Colonel Seymour made it the acceptable representative of the ideas and interests of the agricultural, as well as the mercantile communities of the State, and speedily it became a journal respected by, and popular with, all classes.

Associated all his life with a party tinged more or less,

according to place and occasion, with ideas antagonistic to the sovereignty of the States; circumspect in all things and especially in politics, and slow, therefore, to venture upon experiments in public affairs, it can well be imagined that he thought long and thought deeply upon the election of a sectional man to the presidency, and upon all those issues which resulted in our civil war. His judgment was that the election of Mr. Lincoln left no honorable recourse to his native South but secession, and, if invaded, resistance. That judgment formed, thenceforth, with pen and with sword he maintained the cause of the Confederate States.

In 1861, when hostilities began, he was nearly fifty-seven years of age. He had reached a time of life when most men long for retirement and ease, but with him as with the illustrious Lee, duty was paramount. His reputation as a soldier induced the line officers of the Sixth Louisiana Regiment of Infantry to tender to him, unanimously, the command of the battalion, and it was instantly accepted. With his regiment, he was at the first battle of Manassas, and, during the retreat of General Joe Johnston upon Richmond, to him was assigned the honor of commanding the rear guard. He was with the heroic Jackson throughout that splendid campaign, in the Valley of Virginia, against Banks, Fremont, Shields and Milroy. He was engaged in the attacks upon McClelland's right, before Richmond, on the 26th and 27th June, 1862, and was instantly killed, on the last mentioned day, at the battle of Gaines Mill being the 2d days fight in the battles before Richmond—having been pierced by two minnie balls.

The reader will readily infer the esteem in which this admirable representative of Southern character was held. With professional talents as a journalist he had discreetness and a remarkably sound judgment. He was not more remarkable for these qualities than for the firmness and vigor with which he guarded the columns of his paper against wrong, or misrepresentation, and against every unseemliness that might give offense to the most fastidious of well-bred people. As a soldier he was loved by his rank and file, as well as by his subordinate officers.

His latest command, composed of men of invincible bravery, demanded a high standard of courage in their leader. They regarded him as up to that standard, and loved and respected him accordingly. When not in active service, abounding animal spirits often made them mischievous and sometimes disorderly, but he never failed to enforce strict discipline when the good of the service demanded it. And that discipline was submitted to, without complaint. He demonstrated that volunteers, though prone to turbulence, as they often are, may be made equal to the best of soldiers when they see in their commander an officer without partialities, who never allows his men to be imposed upon, and who follows the advice of Luttrell of Arran to his son: "When perils are to be encountered never say go, always say come."

In no case was the conduct of General Butler more offensive to the people of New Orleans than when he suppressed the publication of the "Bulletin," confiscated the materials of the office, and turned them over to a pair of adventurers who had followed him. The paper was, at the time, conducted by Maj. Wm. J. Seymour, a pardoned prisoner awaiting exchange, and Mr. J. C. Dinnies, the commercial editor.

Both these gentlemen, Mr. Dinnies well advanced in years, were sent to Fort Jackson, where the latter was subjected to severe treatment for many months, and where the former remained a close prisoner until he was exchanged. It is imputed to General Butler, and not without reasonable grounds for belief, that his object was to secure to his followers to whom he gave the "Bulletin" office, the profits of a contract which the paper had as city printer.

Subjoined is an extract from an editorial notice of the death of Colonel Seymour, in the "Bulletin," written by Mr. Dinnies, which extract was quoted by General Butler, as justifying his proceedings. It simply did justice to the character and the fame of Isaac G. Seymour, and we reproduce it to aid us in illustrating the nobility of his nature:

"Others who have done their duty to their country as nobly, disinterestedly and bravely, were impelled by the ardour of youth and the stimulus of ambition, as well as by the dictates of patriotism. But with him, who had outlived the fires of youth, and was superior to mere aspirations for fame, the motive that carried him to the field was simply DUTY. It was DUTY that led him to accept the command of his regiment. It was DUTY that governed him in camp, in giving his men those lessons in the soldiers' science, which fitted them to fulfill the various requirements of the service with intelligence and efficiency. It was DUTY that kept him at his post, under all discouragements. It was DUTY that inspired him in his intrepid charge at Port Republic. It was DUTY that placed him in the front of danger at the battle of the Chickahominy; and, in fine, it was on the altar of DUTY that he offered up his life."

CARROLLTON, a distance of six miles by the railroad, is an exceedingly pleasant resort. The line, for nearly a third of the way, passes through the suburbs of the city, and is dotted on either side with beautiful residences—the remainder passes through pleasant pastures, and delightful woodlands. The road, like the country, is perfectly level shelled and kept in the finest condition. At the end of the route is situated the village; which is principally composed of tastefully built cottages, constructed in every variety of architecture that suited the individual fancy of the owner. Opposite the railroad depot, is one of the handsomest and most extensive public gardens, that is to be found in the vicinity of New Orleans. Here the genial and warm hearted Daniel Hickok presides with that ease and air of hospitality that have made him so popular and so widely known. He delights in showing the rare flowers of his beautiful garden to the many strangers who visit him and it is always his aim to please those who resort to the Carrolton Gardens for recreation and amusement.

AT the commencement of the holydays, the city begins to put on a gay aspect. Visitors from all parts of the habitable globe, come here, either on business or pleasure. A general round of balls, masquerades, soirees and parties begin, and are continued without intermission during the season. Theatres and operas with their stars and prima donnas, circuses and menageries, bell-ringers and serenaders, are in full success.

BANK OF AMERICA.

INCORPORATED 1857.

Capital, $507,800.

Officers:

[illegible] FORTIER, President,
J. E. PASCAL, Cashier.

Directors:

Ant. Fortier,
C. J. Leeds,
J. J. Fernandez,
J. I. Adams,
J. Scherck,
D. Bouligny,
W. B. Schmidt,
D. Fatjo,
F. W. Tilton,
M. Puig,
Ant. Giraud,
Gus. Miltenberger,
A. C. Hutchinson.

Corner of Canal Street and Exchange Alley.

This well-known and excellent Banking Institution located in the fine building fronting on Canal street, and of which an engraving is given above, the rear of the premises (which belong to the Bank) being occupied by [illegible] wholesale wine and liquor store of Messrs. Cavaroc & Son. The Bank of America was established in 1857, with a capital of half a million of dollars and was originally located in one of the Pontalba Buildings on the corner of St. Peter and Old Levee streets, and where the People's Bank now stands. Mr. W. G. Hewes, an old and highly-esteemed merchant of New Orleans, was its first President. Mr. Amilcar Fortier, the present very able and popular President of the Bank, receiving the appointment of cashier. Upon the death of Mr. Hewes in 186[illegible], the Presidency of the Bank was successively held by Messrs. Wm. Whann and Charles Cavaroc, when, upon the resignation of the last-named gentleman in 1866, the office was unanimously tendered to the present incumbent. Mr. J. E. Pascal, the present Cashier of the bank of America, is also a native Louisianian, and is held in very high esteem by all those who have been in contact with him either officially or personally.

MAYOR JOHN T. MONROE.

THE capture of New Orleans in April 1862, by Farragut and Butler, brought the name of Mayor Monroe before the country, and the people, both of the United States and the then Confederate States. Nor was this prominency confined to the belligerent powers. It pervaded all British journalism, and even made its way into Parliament. Mayor Monroe's refusal to surrender the city, although under the guns of the Federal fleet, his subsequent refusal to lower the Confederate flag floating from the City Hall after the enemy was in full possession, resulted in his deposition from the Mayoralty (when near the expiration of his term) by General Butler, and his incarceration in Fort St. Philip, and afterward in Fort Pickens. Refusing to take the new oath of allegiance imposed by the Federal Government he endured, until the summer of the succeeding year, all the rigors of prison life, consigned at one time to solitary confinement and doomed at another time to wear ball and chain. Regarded at last as one possessed of a spirit untameable by any process known to jailors, he was released on condition that he should immediately go within the lines of the Confederates. This he did, going first to Mobile and from thence to Richmond, where he was received by Mr. Davis with unusual cordiality and finally fixing his residence in the former city, where he was when captured by General Canby. Returning to New Orleans after the close of the war, Mr. Monroe was arrested and kept under surveillance for several months. No reason was assigned by the Federal Provost Marshal for his extraordinary proceeding. Shortly after the reorganization of Louisiana under what is commonly known as the Johnsonian policy, Mr. Monroe was re-elected Mayor of New Orleans. He took his seat in March 1866, and was deposed by General Sheridan under the Reconstruction Act of Congress, the pretext being complicity in the celebrated riot of the 30th of July of the same year.

The second deposition of Mayor Monroe took place in March 1867, after much *ex parte* testimony taken against him at the instance of General Sheridan. This act was followed by the appointment of a Radical Mayor, and an Americo-African Common Council, the genesis of the humiliation and misrule which has since befallen Louisiana. In April following, Mr. Monroe visited Washington and and was kindly and sympathetically received by President Johnson and Attorney-General Stanbury. Nor did he leave the capital until his restoration was clearly intimated and the removal of General Sheridan made certain. There can be no doubt that the deposed Mayor would again have been seated but for the second batch of Reconstruction measures which overthrew the opinion of the Attorney-General defining and limiting the provisions of the first Act.

John T. Monroe, a blood relation of President Monroe, was born in Dinwiddie County, Va., and was carried to Missouri when quite young. His father, Daniel Monroe, represented at an early period the latter State in Congress. Coming to New Orleans before his majority, the future Mayor learned the business of a stevedore, which made him familiar with the men who form and control what is popularly known as the "masses." Over the working classes he possessed a power which was not broken at any time. He was of the people and with the people, and they looked upon him as their representative and champion. They made him an Assistant-Alderman and the lower Board seated him as its President. He served as Assistant Recorder and was twice elected Mayor. His mind was eminently practical, his integrity unquestionable, and his proverbial fearlessness, the sequence of the practicability and integrity of character. He knew men so well that it was difficult to impose upon him, and he discharged his duties with a conscientiousness which made him disregard clamor or criticism. Mr. Monroe removed to Savannah, Ga., and died there in February 1871, when about forty-eight years of age. The rigors of imprisonment and of official vicissitudes told severely upon him. He looked old while yet in his prime of years. He had ascended the Masonic ladder to its topmost round, and hence was buried in Savannah with distinguished Masonic honors. The year succeeding his death his remains were brought to New Orleans, where they were deposited in the family tomb by his Masonic brethren beside the body of his favorite son. When this son lay upon his deathbed, the father was a prisoner in Fort St. Philip. General Butler sent word that if the Mayor would take the new oath of allegiance he might come to the city and see his dying child. The offer was promptly and firmly declined, and father and son never met in life. Of such Roman mettle was the subject of this brief biographical sketch.

DOUGLAS SQUARE.—This is bounded by Washington, St. George, Second and Freret streets, and was inclosed in 1864. It is notable for an irregular and luxuriant growth of indigenous and tropical trees, shrubs, flowers and grasses, and for its numerous birds of bright plumage.

HON. J. S. WHITAKER.

This prominent jurist and lawyer was born at New Bedford, Mass., March 8, 1817. While he was yet a child, his father, Rev. Jonathan Whitaker, removed with his family to South Carolina, where he united the duties of a clergyman with those of an instructor of youth. A graduate of old Harvard, a ripe scholar, and enthusiastically devoted to the training of the youthful mind, he presided over the education of his son and fitted him, at an early age, for entrance into college. Judge Whitaker, however became, without the advantages of a college course, the architect of his own fortunes, and few of our own citizens can claim to have been better educated.

He pursued the study of law at Charleston S. C., in the office of James L. Petigru Esq. one of the most eminent members of the legal profession in South Carolina, and having in 1838 successfully passed the ordeal of an examination before the Judges of the Supreme Court, received a license to practice in the Courts of law of that State as soon as he should attain the age of 21 years, which he had not then quite reached. In the mean time, and for a considerable period after he came of age, he devoted himself to the occupation of a teacher of youth, taking charge, in the first instance, of "the South Carolina School" at Charleston, a richly endowed institution and one of much note, but which was subsequently superceded by the establishment of the "Charleston High School," a classical institution, organized by the celebrated Mitchel King, a native of Scotland, on the plan of the Edinburgh High Schools. Mr. H. M. Burns, a fine scholar and teacher of long experience, was appointed to the first, and the subject of this notice to the second place in this school, being Latin teacher. He held this position, a highly respectable and important one in such a city as Charleston, for a couple of years.

Anxious now to enter on the profession of his choice, and the Charleston bar being crowded to repletion, with candidates for its honors and emoluments, he, in 1840, resigned his position and came to New Orleans, and became a student in the office of the late Alfred Hansen, one of the oldest and most esteemed of our Civil Law Lawyers.

Mr. John A. Shaw was then establishing the public school system in this city, and, among the first teachers of the new organization, we find the name of J. S. Whitaker enrolled. In the year 1843 he was invited to take the position of English Professor in Mandeville College, in the Parish of St. Tammany, and subsequently became President of the Institution. Martin G. Penn, Judge of the 8th Judicial District Court, found him vegetating in this position, and advised him to return to the profession he had seemingly abandoned. On the 22nd of May, 1845, he was admitted, by the Supreme Court, to the practice of the law in this State, Judge Martin being then Chief-Justice.

With few clients and little to encourage him, he was by good fortune elected Attorney of the then Third Municipality of New Orleans, and, after a time, entered into partnership with the late John C. Larue, an able Judge, an acute advocate, well-versed in every branch of the law. This partnership continued for some years, and was a successful one. On the death of his partner, Mr. Whitaker remained for many months, laboring in his profession, single handed; but eventually took as a partner, a former student in his office, J. Q. A. Fellows, Esq., who remained with him till his appointment in 1862, to the position of Judge of the 2nd District Court of New Orleans. Mr. Whitaker was the first Judge appointed by the military Governor, General Shepley, after the occupation of the city. While filling this position, he received from the Governor, a commission as Associate Justice of the Supreme Court, but declined the honor, being unwilling to accept such position under Judge Peabody, then Judge of the U. S. Provisional Court, and holding at the same time, a commission as Chief Judge of the Supreme Court.

In 1864, Judge Whitaker resigned the office he held, and was subsequently appointed Chief Justice of the Supreme Court, by Governor Hahn, but was not confirmed by the Senate.

From the middle of April to July, 1864, he was employed by the then proprietors of the "Times" newspaper to write the leading editorials of that paper. The State Convention was then in session, and these articles had, it is said, a salutary influence upon their deliberations.

We find Judge Whittaker, about this time, again actively engaged in his profession, taking little part in politics, but known to be Republican in his principles, and a supporter of the administration.

The Degree of Master of Arts, recently conferred on him by Dartmouth College, (founded by his Grandfather) evinces the consideration which is entertained for his scholarship. We may add that no gentleman has taken a deeper interest in the cause of popular education than Judge Whitaker. He was, for several years, one of the most active as well as the most popular Directors of the Public Schools in this city.

During the late war, Judge W. was an outspoken Union man, though on all occasions affording such assistance as was in his power, to the citizens of his adopted state. He was, in 1864, solicited by many influential citizens, to become candidate for the office of Governor of the State, but declined.

It is said, by his friends, and intimates, that his talents are eminently judicial, and he is held in high repute as a counsellor and advocate. Many important cases are intrusted to his management. The habits of industry, which he acquired in youth, still adhere to him in mature life. He is very social and hospitable, and, when he entertains his friends, displays all the qualities of the urbane host, and abandon and buoyancy of the learned jurist enjoying a holiday.

His passion for gardening, flowers and trees, planted, trimmed and cultivated with his own hands, is evinced in the spacious and Eden-like grounds that encompass his fine residence on Carondelet street, the interior of which exhibits, in a rich and costly library, his taste for letters, and in all its domestic accompaniments and appointments his fondness for comfort and elegance.

MORESQUE BUILDING,

Corner of Camp and Poydras Streets, New Orleans.

THE SAINT LOUIS HOTEL.

Thirty-seven years ago, the spot where now stands the Saint Louis was selected for the purpose of building a hotel, on a scale commensurate with the growing importance of New Orleans. At that time the only hotels in the city were the Stranger's Hotel, kept by Marty, and the Orleans Hotel, kept by the beautiful Mrs. Page, both houses being still used for the same purpose on Chartres street. The space now occupied by the St. Louis Hotel and the surrounding structures, was, thirty-seven years ago, a conglomeration of stores, shops, and private dwellings. On the side fronting St. Louis street, where the rotunda now stands, was the residence and pharmacy of Mr. Germain Ducatel, flanked by the residences and offices of Dr. Fabre Fonvergne, a collecting agent and broker; Antoine Abat, the well-known capitalist and banker; Leroy, an individual so named because he sold the then celebrated patent medicine known as Leroy's specific; a barber's saloon, and a cooper's shop. An importer of foreign goods named Belanger, occupied the corner of Royal and St. Louis streets, while at the corner of Chartres and St. Louis streets stood Hewlett's Exchange, consisting of a coffee house and auction mart, with billiard tables and a "cock pit" in the rear. On the opposite of Chartres street were the original ice house (La Glacière), now located on Bienville street, and the residence of Judah Touro. On Royal street, going towards Toulouse, were the well-known stores of Larue and Seignouret. On the northeast corner of Royal and St. Louis stood the drug store of Grand Champs, now kept by Dr. DeCastelnau, which enjoys the distinction of being the oldest establishment of the kind in the city, having preserved its well-earned reputation for over sixty years. Diagonally across the street was, above, the residence of Mr. Le Carpentier, the grandfather of Paul Morphy, the great chess player, and underneath was the dwelling of Mr. Brumage. Over the way, at the northwest corner, stood the fashionable jewelry store of Hyde & Goodrich, which still maintains its place in the front rank under the title of A. B. Griswold, on the corner of Canal and Royal streets. Among the well known citizens residing around the hotel were D. Ambrosio, Lucien Carrière, Mioton and Girod, the first Mayor of New Orleans, and the founder of the Girod Asylum, who kept an importer's store on the northwest corner of St. Louis and Chartres streets. The Improvement Bank, by whom the old St. Louis Hotel was built, was presided over by Judge Jean François Canonge, and numbered the late Pierre Soulé among its directors. The edifice was commenced by Mr. Depouilly, a distinguished architect still living; in 1835, and at about the same time the stately building in the rear of the hotel on Toulouse street, subsequently occupied for many years by the Citizen's Bank, was also erected by the Improvement Bank for its own use. The total cost of the hotel, and the annexed buildings, was nearly a million and a half of dollars. It was at first contemplated to take up the entire block, but the commercial crisis of 1837 interfered with the plan, and in 1841 the whole structure, which was even more stately than the present one, was accidentally destroyed by fire. The present edifice soon rose from the ashes of its predecessor, and under the skillful management of the well known James Hewlett, the St. Louis Hotel became the most celebrated house of entertainment in the South. One of the most pleasing reminiscences of the palmy days of the St. Louis Hotel is the annual series of "Bals de Société," or Subscription Balls, that took place every Winter in its magnificent ball room, then fronting St. Louis street. Nowhere else could a better idea of Creole beauty and elegance be realized so well as in those delightful gatherings, in which none but the representatives of the most refined circles of our city were invited to participate, although a generous welcome was also given to visitors from the other States, and to distinguished foreigners. Some of the most pleasing recollections of former days are identified with the gay scenes of which the St. Louis ball room was the theatre between twenty and thirty years ago. Particularly vivid among the survivors of that period is the remembrance of a magnificent "Bal Travesti" given in the Winter of 1842—'43, and above all of the splendid entertainment gotten up the same Winter in honor of Henry Clay's visit, by his New Orleans friends and admirers. The subscription price was one hundred dollars, and there were two hundred subscribers—the ball and supper costing twenty thousand dollars, an enormous sum for that period. Over six hundred ladies and gentlemen sat down to a feast of regal magnificence in the spacious dining hall of the hotel where the finest orchestra of the French Opera discoursed sweet music, and a most felicitous and graceful tribute was paid by the "old man eloquent" to the ladies of New Orleans, "beautiful, accomplished, and patriotic." This was the only time the Demosthenes of the American Senate ever spoke in public in Louisiana. Mr. Mioton, the present able and popular manager of the St. Louis Hotel, has just inaugurated a series of subscription balls, under the patronage and direction of the ladies of this city, which, judging from the success with which the first one was attended cannot fail to revive the pristine terpsichorean glories of the house. The Convention of 1843 to form a new State Constitution, and which embraced almost every man of talent and influence in Louisiana, such as John R. Grymes, Soulé, Roselius, Mazureau, Roman, Downs, Conrad, Marigny, Brent, Eustis, and other distinguished men was held in the old St. Louis ball room.

The St. Louis Exchange, under the management of the universally popular Alvarez, and his genial assistant, Santini, was, for a long period, the favorite resort of all the leading politicians, planters, and merchants of the city and State. From twelve o'clock, meridian, till three in the afternoon the splendid rotunda was occupied by the auctioneers whose resounding appeals in the English, French, and Spanish languages made it a modern counterpart of the Tower of Babel. This rotunda, with its beautiful frescoes (now used as a restaurant, attached to the hotel) served the purposes of a Chamber of Commerce, Board of Brokers, and Cotton Exchange. Meetings for political, charitable, or patriotic purposes were frequently held there, as were also the Conventions of the Old Whig and Democratic parties.

More than a year ago, Mr. E. F. Mioton, aided by a few other enterprising and public spirited citizens of the Second and Third Districts of New Orleans, succeeded, after much labor and trouble, in organizing a joint stock company for the purpose of purchasing, renovating, and re-opening of the St. Louis Hotel on a scale consummate with the present wants of the community. Of the association Mr. Mioton was made the President, and Messrs. A. Chaffraix, Charles Cavaroc, M. Puig, Charles Lafitte, and A. Rochereau, were elected directors. The remodelling and improvements of the building were made by Mr. A. Sassi, architect, under the supervision of Mr. L. L. Pilié, late City Surveyor. A magnificent verandah, new in pattern, elegant and unique in design and consisting of a series of arches supported by a colonade of Corinthian pilasters ornamented in the highest style of art now surrounds the building on every side, with the exception of the grand entrance on St. Louis street, where the fine marble peryistile is covered with a terrace or balcony, above which a superb illuminated clock has been placed. The entire verandah is lighted at night by a great number of beautifully ornamented lamps, and the whole structure now presents a most beautiful and imposing appearance. Elaborate as the improvement has been in the outside, equal labor and skill has been brought into requisition inside to render the hotel one of the most commodious and comfortable in the world. There are 237 sleeping rooms besides the offices, parlors, drawing and reception rooms, dining halls and parlor suits on the first floor, affording ample accommodation for five or six hundred guests. The papering, carpeting, and furnishing of these rooms and parlors is of the best modern style and pattern. The hotel is kept on the European and American style combined, there being a restaurant where meals are furnished to the guests of the hotel as well as to the public generally, at fixed prices, and a magnificent dining room for the exclusive use of the boarders who prefer to live in the American style. This dining room, which is brilliantly lighted by eleven splendid chandeliers, is also used as a ball room in connection with the spacious and magnificently furnished parlor on Royal street. The hotel kitchen is 40 feet by 60, is probably the largest and best appointed in America; the ranges, cooking, and roasting apparatus, ovens, etc., being of the best and most modern patterns, and the arrangements for ventilation, and the removal of every offensive smell being altogether perfect. On the Chartres street side are numerous parlors, reception rooms, a nursery, dining room, a gentlemen's reading and smoking room, with a small bar and lunch room attached. There are thirty bath rooms in the main building, and it is contemplated to convert the old Bank building, on Toulouse street, into a Roman *aquarium*, or swimming bath.

The hotel is divided by iron sliding doors into three distinct fire-proof compartments, and the iron tanks on the top of the building contain 50,000 gallons of water, so that in case of a fire, the means of putting it out would be instantaneous. One of the most pleasing features of the St. Louis is the fact that owing to the great space covered by the building, the bed rooms are either on the first or second floor, thereby saving the fatigue and inconvenience of going up a great many flights of steps.

The hotel is now under the management of Mr. E. F. Mioton, the energetic President of the St. Louis Hotel Association, aided by able and courteous assistants; and since he took charge of the house it has become a favorite and fashionable resort for the planters and their families, as well as for that already large and daily enlarging class of persons who prefer the comfort of a well kept hotel to the trouble and expense of house-keeping.

REV. WILLIAM T. LEACOCK, D. D

This eminent divine was born at Barbadoes, A. D. 1800, commencing life with the day dawn of the present eventful century. He went to England in the year 1818, and received his education at the renowned University of Oxford. He was ordained in 1824, by the Right Rev. Dr. Howley, Lord Bishop of London. In 1825, he went to Jamaica, where, for the space of ten years, he labored as a popular and successful clergyman of the Protestant Episcopal Church. In 1835, in consequence of the state of his health, which had been effected by the unpropitious climate of the West Indies, he removed to the state of Kentucky in this country, and subsequently became Rector of Williamsport Church in Tennessee, in the diocese of the Reverend Bishop Otey. He thence removed to Natchez, Mississippi, and, in 1852, became Rector of Christ Church in this city, over which, in that capacity, he has since presided. He is assisted by the very estimable, Rev. Campbell Fair.

The family of Dr. Leacok, consists of his wife and three children, two daughters and one son, Rev. William Leacok, of the Diocese of California. He lost one son by yellow fever.

The Rector of Christ Church is physically of large proportions and unusual height, reaching probably to fully six feet. His aspect is venerable and commanding, his manner fatherly, affectionate and guileless, his style logical, terse and suggestive. His sermons contain a happy combination of the intellectual and the pathetic, appealing, in adequate proportions, both to the head and to the heart. He is a man of large experience and shining virtues, whose influence is deeply felt in the circles in which he moves. As a clergyman, his principles are both liberal and evangelical.

ANNUNCIATION SQUARE.—This is situated on the four squares bounded by Annunciation, Orange, Chippewa and Race streets. It is protected by a substantial iron fence, and has been otherwise partially improved. St. Michael's Church (Catholic) overlooks the square from the east. Fronting upon the square are several elegant residences surrounded by choice varied and luxuriant shrubbery. At at cost of a few thousand dollars the square itself might be converted into a miniature forest if desirable.

B. M. TURNBULL.

LANE'S COTTON MILLS.

REV. THEODORE CLAPP.

Mr. Clapp was a native of the State of Massachusetts. He pursued his classical course at Yale College, and completed his theological studies at Andover Seminary—an institution preeminently evangelical. Such was the type of his own theology, when, at an early age, he came into the Valley of the Mississippi, and commenced his clerical career under the auspices of the Presbytery of that State. Thence, upon the death of the Rev. Dr. Larned, he came to this city, accepting a call from the First Presbyterian Church to become its pastor.

It appears that in the year 1830, or thereabouts, an entire revolution took place in the views he entertained on religious doctrines and discipline. These views assumed a particular shape, but no particular name. It was understood that he had become a liberal thinker on subjects of infinite scope and moment, and, had he not, at the same time, possessed a logical mind, enriched with varied learning, his renunciation of one creed and adoption of another, would have been a matter of comparatively little consequence to the public, or to the great and most respectable Presbyterian body politic, with which he was associated. It was because he was "a master in Israel"—a controlling mind in the church, that a radical change in his opinions produced a profound sensation, which culminated in a serious rupture of that church, and finally led to the exclusion of Mr. Clapp, and about one half of the congregation, composing his special friends and adherents, from its sacred precints and associations.

At the very moment when the excluded dissentients from orthodoxy were "without a local habitation and even a name," the late Judah Touro, Esq., an affluent and liberal minded Israelite, who had purchased, singularly enough at sheriff's sale, the church which then stood at the corner of St. Charles and Gravier streets, gave the use of it for an unlimited period, or, which was the same thing, for ninety-nine years, to Mr. Clapp and his congregation, for a permanent place of worship.

It was a large and commodious edifice; and the popularity and eloquence of Mr. Clapp were such, that it was soon filled with hearers, even to overflowing. Mr. Clapp was in the habit of renting out the pews himself, and the proceeds, thence arising, constituted his income, which was not only adequate but large, even for a great and opulent city. He had the entire control of the society and its affairs, like a monarch in and over his own domain, and it was known, for a considerable time, only as Mr. Clapp's Society and Mr. Clapp's Church. Of the hundreds of individuals who reached New Orleans on Saturday evenings, coming from various States scattered along the banks of the great Father of Waters, the majority, on Sunday morning, would seek out and attend Mr. Clapp's church. Many would inquire, but nobody could inform them, with certainty, what were the doctrines inculcated in Clapp's church. The truth is, he dwelt more on precepts and facts than doctrines, and, when he handled the latter, (which he seldom did) wished to have the whole field of theological speculation open before him, in order to select "here a little and there a little, line upon line and precept upon precept," as was suggested by his particular subject, the special occasion, or the character of his audience, composed, it might be, of men of all creeds, for the time being.

The divine authority of Revelation, of Jesus, man's relation to God, the universal Father, to the human race, individually and socially considered, to life with its fleeting hours, to eternity with its countless ages, to duty in its multiplied forms and extensive relations, these were his favorite themes, on which he dwelt with abounding power and touching fervor, now arresting attention by the force of his logic, anon opening the fountain of tears by his touching appeals, drawing his illustrations from the inspired volume, from the book of Nature, from human history, from the works of the poets and philosophers, and, more especially, from the course of events in his own day, of which he was an acute observer, and always an independent, outspoken critic.

In 1833, the legislature chartered Mr. Clapp's church, under the name of "the First Congregational Unitarian church in the city and parish of New Orleans." The corporation was to exist for twenty years, and had twenty corporators, viz: Samuel McCutchen; Jacob Baldwin; James McReynolds; Richard Davidson; Henry Babcock; Peter Laidlaw; John D. Bein; Stephen Henderson; Charles Lee; P. S. Newton; Wm. C. Bowers; Henry Carleton; James H. Leverich; Wm. G. Hewes; Isaac G. Preston; Benj. Story; Henry Lockett; J. W. Lee; Joshua Baldwin; Abijah Fisk. The act was approved February 20, 1833.

In 1851, the church building which the society had occupied twenty years, through the liberality of Mr. Touro, without cost, was burned in the conflagration which, at the same time, reduced to ashes the stately and magnificent St. Charles hotel, which stood in close proximity to it. Mr. Touro again came forward and gave Mr. Clapp another church, which he had purchased, and which was originally built for the Baptists. It was also situated on St. Charles street, a little below the present edifice, and served for the temporary accommodation of the society till a larger and more commodious church could be built. Mr. Clapp officiated in it four or five years.

In 1853, the congregation resolved to build a church edifice, and to organize a society. A charter was drawn up for the purpose, but was never signed, adopted, or approved, by the District Attorney, or recorded as the law requires.

Samuel Bell, Henry D. Richardson, John D. Bien, H. S. Buckner, J. J. Day, A. M. Holbrook, Samuel Stewart, Isaac Bridge, John Leeds, Christian Roselius, Henry Renshaw, Lewis Soalles and Thomas A. Adams, were named as members in this inchoate charter. It purports to bear date March 17th, 1853. The title to the property bears date March 29th, 1853.

The church referred to, which is one of the most elegant edifices of the kind in the city, was finished in 1855. There was no dedication. Mr. Clapp was opposed to it. He would never consent to have the society called by the name of any particular denomination. As indicative of the nature of the organization, it was styled "Congregational or Independent." The edifice was called "the Church of the Messiah."

Mr. Clapp officiated only a few months in the new edifice, in consequence of failing health; but his congregation, greatly attached to him, on his retiring and removing to Louisville, Kentucky, were in the habit of contributing liberally to his support up to the time of his death, which occurred in 1867. On that occasion, the Rev. Dr. Elliott, of St. Louis, Missouri, then on a visit here, delivered an appropriate and eloquent discourse, which was listened to with profound sensibility, by a thronged audience, composed of persons of all denominations, who hold the memory of the deceased in the highest esteem and even veneration.

THE OPERA HOUSE.

Although its population was scarcely equal to fifty thousand inhabitants, during the greater part of that period, New Orleans enjoys the distinction of being the only city upon this continent which has supported, for more than half a century, a regular Opera Company.

There were two French theatres, one in St. Peter street, and another in St. Philip street, near Royal, which were in operation from 1808 to 1811. At the latter period, Mr. John Davis, a French emigré from St. Domingo, built the Orleans theatre, on the square, now partly occupied by the First District Court, near the Catholic Cathedral, and the adjoining court buildings, and engaged in Paris the first regular Opera Company that ever came into this country. The enterprise proved a highly successful one, and upon the death of Mr. John Davis the management of the theatre devolved upon his son, Mr. Pierre Davis, (now residing in France), by whom it was most ably conducted during a period of over twenty-five years. It was under his management that those twin stars of the Parisian theatrical world, Mmes. Fanny Elssler and Damoreau, were first seen and heard in this city, and that the great master-pieces of Rossini, Meyerbeer, Auber, Donizetti, Herold, Mozart, Spontini and Mehul became familiar as household words to the highly-refined audiences which crowded the small but elegant and comfortable Opera house, which, after the one originally erected by Mr. John Davis, had been burnt down, was rebuilt the next year.

Mr. Varney, the author of "Le Chant des Girondiers," and afterwards leader of "Des Bouffes Parisiens," the late Eugene Prevost, (whose sketch may be found in another part of this book), Mr. John, and since the war Mons. E. Calabresi, have successively wielded the *baton* of leader of the orchestra.

In 1859, Mr. Chas. Boudousquié, having some years before succeeded Mr. Davis as manager of the Orleans theatre, the building was bought at the judicial sale of the estate of John McDonough by Mr. Parlange, who failed to agree with Mr. Boudousquié as to the lease of the theatre, whereupon a new company was formed, and the present splendid edifice on Bourbon street was built by Messrs. Gallier & Esterbrook, architects for the Opera House Association.

It was upon the boards of this theatre that the charming Adelina Patti made her *debut* in Meyerbeer's "Pardon de Ploermel," on which occasion the writer of this sketch remembers with pardonable pride and pleasure that he was among the few theatrical critics of the day who at once recognized and proclaimed her transcendent merits as a vocalist and actress. There, too, the dying notes of another great Italian artist, Madame Frezzolini, were heard just upon the eve of the great civil war, which, shortly after, led to the temporary suspension of all theatrical enterprises in New Orleans.

On the return of peace, a French strolling company, under Mr. Marcelin Alhaiza, proving highly successful, a number of subscribers furnished him at the close of the season with the means of engaging a complete dramatic and operatic company. The result was most unfortunate, Mr. Marcelin Alhaiza having died on the eve of his company's departure from France, and the latter being shipwrecked and lost on the steamer in which they had taken passage from New York to this port.

Mr. Paul Alhaiza, the brother of the deceased manager, collected a few artists who had remained here, and engaged some of the members of another strolling company whose performances at the old Orleans theatre had been brought to a close in 1867, by the burning of that edifice. In 1868, he attempted, in partnership with Mr. Calabresi, to revive the opera, but the attempt proving unsuccessful, a new Opera House Association was formed, composed of leading capitalists and merchants of this city, by whom the opera house was purchased, and liberal provision was made for the engagement of a first-class opera company. Mr. E. Calabresi, was by them appointed manager and leader, at a very high salary, but although he succeeded in engaging two or three singers, of talent and reputation, such as Michot, Castelmary and Dumestre, most of the other artists brought over by him proved lamentably deficient, and after two seasons the members of the Opera House Association found themselves in debt after having expended the whole of their capital, and were therefore compelled to go into liquidation.

This happened at the close of the season of 1871-2, when Mr. Placide Canonge—a distinguished creole journalist and playwright, who had already given evidence of his tact and good taste in the selection of a dramatic company for the old Orleans theatre, obtained quite late in the summer a lease of the Opera House for the winter of 1872-3. The dramatic company brought over by M. Canonge has proved eminently successful, Mmes. Miller, Beauvais, Protal and Goelte, and M. M. Molina, Ariste, Deschamps, Schaub, and Scipiore, the leading comic and dramatic actors, having proved very acceptable to the public.

A strong effort is now being made by some of our leading citizens to form another Opera House Association, with the view of enabling Mr. Canonge to engage an Opera Company mostly of the past reputation of our lyrical stage—a task for which no one is better qualified than he is, and in which we most heartily wish him to succeed, as he can not fail to do if he is supported as he deserves to be by the "solid men" of his native city.

RESIDENCE OF C. H. SLOCOMB, ESQ.,

Corner of Esplanade and St. Claude Sts., New Orleans.

DAVID BIDWELL.

In the theatrical world no name is more familiar or better known than that of Mr. D. Bidwell. Recognized throughout the country as one of the most enterprising and successful managers of public entertainments of the present day, he has achieved this reputation in a comparatively short space of time. Embarking in life at an early age he was thrown upon his own resources and forced to carve out his own future. That his career in life so far has been eminently successful, is fully established by his present influential and wealthy position. Mr. Bidwell was born in the town of Stuyvesant, Columbia Co., N. Y., in the year 1821. He was educated at the Kinderhook Seminary, and, after leaving school, joined his father, Alex. Bidwell, who was at that time commander of a steamer on the Hudson River. After a term of service as clerk upon his father's boats, he became the proprietor of the Empire House, just in the rear of the Astor House, a place famous in the days of the Presidential Campaign of 1844, the year in which the noted Empire Club was organized and located at this place. In 1846, Mr. Bidwell came to New Orleans and engaged in business with his brother, Mr. H. Bidwell, as ship chandlers, under the style of H. Bidwell & Co. In 1852 the partnership was dissolved, when Mr. David Bidwell became the proprietor of the Phœnix House. In 1853 Mr. Bidwell took charge of the property now known as the "Academy of Music," and acted as agent for the proprietor in renting it to combination theatrical companies until 1856, when, in partnership with Spaulding & Rogers, he became the proprietor and manager of this theatre, and has continued to control and direct it until the present time, when he is the sole proprietor.

Mr. Bidwell's theatrical associations have not been confined exclusively to New Orleans. In 1867 he organized and took charge of the American Champion Circus Company and gave a series of performances in Europe, which created a great *furore* in the amusement circles of Paris. In connection with Dr. Spaulding, Mr. Bidwell also built the Olympic Theatre, in St. Louis, in 1867-8, and in 1869, with the same partners, he became interested in the New Memphis Theatre and the Mobile Theatre. Besides the present management of the "Academy of Music," Mr. Bidwell is the sole owner of the author's playwright of the Black Crook for a large portion of the country, and with one of the largest traveling combination companies ever organized, is making the tour of the United States, giving representations of this gorgeous spectacle. One secret of Mr. Bidwell's success is his thorough knowledge of the people of New Orleans and the peculiarities of their tastes, acquired by a long residence in their midst. Knowing their fancy he has always exerted himself to the utmost to please and gratify them. Money, time and labor have all been freely used to give eclat to every entertainment prepared by Mr. Bidwell for the citizens of New Orleans. That his efforts in this particular have been abundantly successful, is evidenced by the fact that he stands in the front rank of his profession, and is deemed the most successful theatrical manager in the country. Whilst catering to the amusement-loving portion of the people, Mr. Bidwell is not unmindful of the general interests and welfare of the entire city. His contributions for public works and improvements, for railroads and other enterprises, are liberal and numerous. Having accumulated a fortune here, thoroughly identified with every interest of the city, it is quite natural and proper that he should feel a deep concern for the future prosperity of the Crescent City and contribute, all in his power, to aid in the good work of developing its wonderful resources. In this respect he plays the part of a valuable and useful citizen, and as such commands the respect of the community of which he has been so exemplary member.

JAMES BARRY PRICE,

Was born in Pittsylvania County, Va., January 19th, 1819. His ancestors were prominent in the Revolution, and from them were directly descended the late distinguished soldiers and citizens, Generals Sterling and Thos. L. Price of Missouri. Among his not distant collateral relations were the late Admiral Barry. Mr. Price emigrated with his parents to Middle Tennessee at an early age. Few men during the last thirty years have been more prominent in the politics and business interests of that State than his father, Col. M. A. Price; while on his mother's side he is connected with the Sanders, Caruthers, Cabal, Donelson and Gentry families, than which none have been more conspicuous in the public affairs of Tennessee during the last two generations. Mr. Price has enjoyed all the advantages of wealth, education and travel, visiting all Europe, Egypt, Nubia, Arabia, Palestine, and the remote East as the *compagnon de voyage* of the late Lucius C. Duncan of New Orleans, and the distinguished and Hon. Edwin H. Ewing of Tennessee. His travels in America are probably more extended than those of any man in the States. He married and settled in St. Mary Parish in 1853, since which time he has been extensively engaged in agriculture, commerce and transportation. In transportation of the mails by steamboat and stage coach he had been more extensively engaged than any man in the South. He was one of the few bold enterprising spirits who established the Great Overland Mail Line of Stages connecting St. Louis and Memphis with San Diego and San Francisco, which practically demonstrated the feasibility of the existing and projected lines of travel and mail carriage across the Continent. Mr. Price has not confined himself to any specialty, but has taken a leading part in many enterprises with a large measure of success. During the war he and his partners, F. P. Lanyer and G. H. Giddings, controlled nearly all the stage transportation in the Trans-Mississippi Department, through which means incalculable service was rendered to the people and soldiers, thousands of whom were transported to and from their homes gratuitously. Mr. Price more than once was offered high military rank, by reason of greater usefulness in the Civil Service of the Confederacy he was kept employed therein, and throughout the war he enjoyed the confidence of the Confederate rulers to the fullest extent. Mr. Price is accredited, by many familiar with his record, as having contributed as much material aid to the Confederacy as any other man in the South, though he was originally opposed to Secession. At the close of the war he at once went to work to aid in restoring the prostrate interests of Louisiana, especially in his own section, as the local papers abundantly testify. In 1866, in connection with those well known merchants, T. D. Hine of St. Mary, and G. Tupper of Charleston, S. C., he established the commercial firm in New Orleans of Price, Hine & Tupper. In 1867 he, Gen. Hersey of Maine, Robert Hare, and T. M. Simmons, and others of New Orleans, organized the Louisiana Petroleum and Mining Company of Calcasieu Parish, of which Mr. Price was elected President. In 1868 he induced his kinsman, Gen. T. L. Price, and Chas. P. Chouteau of Missouri, to lease and work the Avery Salt Mine, the firm of Price, Hine & Tupper being agents of the same. In 1867 he was appointed by Gov. Wells Special Commissioner to the Paris Exposition, and he doubtless deserves a considerable share of credit for the distinction which Louisiana there enjoyed. These things are all mentioned here to indicate that the subject of this sketch is one of that active, bold, enterprising, and intelligent class of men who are required to revivify Louisiana, and whose acts would all be vitalizing and beneficial, while those of mere politicians only tend—as we know by sad experience—to impoverish, to enervate, and to destroy. In June, 1872, the above facts and traits of character seem to have impressed the public mind to such an extent that those representative of public opinion, most of the delegates of the Democratic and Reform Conventions from the Third Congressional District of this State, paid him the remarkable compliment of inviting him to stand as an independent candidate to represent the District, saying, in their letter of invitation, substantially that his character for wisdom and integrity was all the declaration of principle required. His frank and manly letter of acceptance elicited the most complimentary notice of the Press, one of which held the following language—"No man is better acquainted with the wants and necessities of Louisiana, or more capable of relieving the same and promoting her welfare. He is much loved by his old servants, and is highly esteemed by his numerous employes. He is a good citizen, a thorough gentleman, a kind neighbor, and a true friend. A golden future awaits him," etc., etc.

From parental influence, liberal education, a large-hearted and broad-minded nature, with much travel and mixing with men, both in the old and new worlds, he is expanded in his feelings, liberal in his views, and thoroughly Cosmopolitan in his tastes. He is free alike from bigotry and sectionalism, and religion, education and morals find in him a hearty promoter.

In physique he is one of the best specimens of the Anglo-Saxon race, while a total abstinence throughout life, from beer, wine, spirits, and tobacco, and from any form of dissipation or gambling, has secured to him the multiplied blessings which flow from a good constitution and perfect health.

L. E. REYNOLDS, ESQ.

None of our architects is better known, few or none are more highly esteemed, than Mr. Reynolds. A passion for drawing, a fondness for handling tools, and a readiness in the use of them, marked his childhood, and seemed to indicate the special and important purpose to which his subsequent life was devoted. The training and experience through which he passed from the humbler labors of a carpenter, till, in maturer life, he adopted the nobler and more exacting profession of an architect, contributed to the gradual, but certain, development of powers essential to excellence in the Art of Design.

L. E. Reynolds was born at Norwich, Chenango County, in the State of New York, on the 29th of February, 1816. At an early age he went to Cincinnati, then rapidly rising into importance among the cities of the West, regarding it, as he did, a favorable locality for the commencement of his labors. The carpenter's trade first engaged his attention; but with the practical part of it, into which he was soon inducted, he united the study of architecture as a science—a study which he prosecuted with unceasing diligence, until figure, form, harmony and proportion became familiar ideas with him.

With a view to finish his education in the line of life he had adopted, he placed himself under the direction of distinguished architects in Louisville, and subsequently in New York, with whom he remained several years, diligently pursuing a prescribed course of study, and uniting the theory with the practice of the Art of Design as he had opportunity. He spent from ten to fifteen years in this way, building and designing buildings, before he considered himself competent to enter on the duties of a professional architect.

Having now become proficient as a draughtsman, and being inspired with a great love of his profession, as well for purposes of emolument as fame, he determined to teach its principles to others as a public lecturer. In this capacity, as well as that of an architect actively engaged in his profession, he visited New York, Philadelphia, Baltimore, St. Louis, Washington and New Orleans, and hundreds of young men in these cities, after the labors of the day were over, gathering around him, received their first instructions in building, architecture and civil engineering. He taught them a new system of prospective, reconstructed and improved many problems in carpentry and in cylindrical and conic sections. He invented five original methods of Hand-Railing, including all that have been of any practical use since the days of Peter Nicholson, and published a treatise on the subject accompanied with plates. The work is highly commended by skilled architects on both sides of the Atlantic, for the originality of its views and the beauty of its geometrical figures.

Mr. Reynolds paid his first visit to New Orleans in 1833, and came permanently to reside here ten years afterwards, viz: in 1843. Since that time he has pursued his profession with exemplary diligence and signal success. The monuments of his skill as an architect are scattered all around us. Many of the fine buildings that adorn the Third District were designed by Mr. Reynolds; and he

MUTUAL NATIONAL BANK OF NEW ORLEANS.

OFFICERS.

Paul Fourchy,
President.

Albert Baldwin,
Vice President.

Joseph Mitchel,
Cashier.

DIRECTORS.

P. Maspero,
John D. Cobb,
Adolph Meyer,
Ernest Miltenberger,
John T. Hardie,
Charles Lafitte,
Paul Poursine,

CAPITAL STOCK PAID IN, $500,000.

DEPOSITS

Six Months After Organization,

OVER $1,000,000.

Dividends for First Six Months Operations.

June 30, 1872.

6 1-2 Per Cent to the Stockholders.

3 1-2 Per Cent to all Depositors,

NO. 106 CANAL STREET.

ABOUT a year ago, Mr. Paul Fourchy conceived the idea of applying the *mutual* principle on which most insurance companies are now conducted to banking operations, and having matured a plan which was highly approved by many of our most intelligent business men, he organized under the Act of Congress of 1864 the Mutual National Bank of New Orleans, which commenced operations on the 1st of January 1872, with a capital of five hundred thousand dollars, and of which he was appropriately made the President. The annexed semi-annual statement of the operations of the bank during the first half year of its official existence demonstrates that the idea upon which it is based is an eminently practical one, and that it has been most judiciously and successfully carried out. The distinctive feature of the new system is contained in Article Ninth of the Charter of Mutual National Bank, which provides that "the depositors shall receive on the average amount of their cash balances for the preceding six months, and the stockholders shall receive on the amount of their stock a contingent semi annual interest equal to the net profits of the bank for the preceding six months, after deducting from said net profits the following items:—1st. the reserve of one-tenth required by the 33d Section of the National Currency Act approved June 3, 1864; 2d, a regular semi-annual dividend of 5 per cent. for the stockholders on the amount of their stock." It is further declared in the said Charter that "depositors receive a contingent interest, not as partners, but as a just and proper remuneration for their patronage." This contingent interest is distributed by adding up the daily cash balances of each depositor for six months and dividing the grand total by (180) the quotient showing the average balance, and the proportional interest to which each one is entitled.

Mr. Joseph Mitchel, the Cashier of the Mutual National Bank of New Orleans, is a gentleman of large experience in business, having long been connected as a partner with the Anglo-Spanish Banking House of Drake & Co., in Havana, and having on his removal here in 1846 held responsible and confidential positions with Messrs. Barelli & Co. and O. B. Graham, of this city. With his qualifications as a bank officer, Mr. Mitchel combines the advantage of being an excellent French and Spanish scholar, writing and speaking both languages with the same fluency and elegance as he does his own.

has, certainly among his brother architects, largely contributed to the beauty and permanent improvements of the city. The houses he has designed are models of elegance and high finish in their way. Among them we may mention Mr. Lafayette Folger's, corner of St. Charles and First streets; Dr. Campbell's, corner of St. Charles and Julia streets; Mr. Hale's corner of De Lord and Camp streets; the Canal Bank on Camp street; the Story Buildings, corner of Camp and Common streets; Mr. W. M. Perkins', corner of Jackson and Coliseum streets; St. James' Hotel on Magazine street; Crescent Mutual Insurance Building, Camp street; Mr. H. S. Buckner's house, corner of Coliseum and Jackson streets; the Factor's Row on Carondelet street; Row of Stores opposite St. James' Hotel; Mr. S. H. Kennedy's house, corner of First and Camp streets; Mr. Andrew Smith's house, corner of St. Charles street and Tivoli Circle; Jackson & Manson's extensive stores on New Levee streets, and many more fine and substantial buildings in the city than we have space or time to enumerate, and which testify to his genius and tasteful skill in execution.

By strict attention to order and system in his business arrangements, Mr. Reynolds has found considerable time for study, reading, writing and even publishing. He has one of the best, if not the very best, professional library in the city, and is thoroughly conversant with the architectural lore it contains. In his "Mysteries of Masonry," recently published by the Messrs. Lippincott of Philadelphia, he has treated a curious and transcendental subject in a clear and philosophical manner. A large edition of the work has commanded a ready sale, and elicited favorable criticisms both in the United States and in England. He is now engaged on a work of still higher pretensions, entitled "The Science and Philosophy of Creation," which, when it appears from the press, will be likely to produce a sensation in literary and philosophical circles.

MRS. MYRA CLARK GAINES.

This remarkable lady, whose name is the common property of every part of the American Union, literally the heroine of a romance in real life; more familiar with the doctrines which regulates the succession of real estates than many of the learned civilians who frequent our courts of justice; an eloquent and able champion of her own rights in any and every forum where she has ever been permitted to appear in person; better acquainted with the great men who for the third part of a century have figured at the Bar, on the Bench, in the Senate Chamber, and other high and envied places in America, than most of her masculine cotemporaries; bold, intrepid, undaunted, indomitable and successful in the pursuit of an object which deservedly occupied her whole mind and heart, was born at New Orleans in the year 1806, of the present century, of which she herself is one of those shining marks which green-eyed envy is said to love.

Her father, David Clark, Esq., an Irishman by birth and a large capitalist, by his enterprise contributed greatly to the advancement of the Crescent City, then in its infancy, and was successfully employed in 1803 by Mr. Jefferson to negotiate the purchase of the great territory of Louisiana, and its cession to the United States by Napoleon, the Emperor of France. Her mother, Zulime, née Carrière, of French extraction, is said to have been endowed with the charms of a magical beauty, which rendered her, in her day, very celebrated.

We have not time to recapitulate the interesting events which checker the history of Mrs. Gaines. Suffice it to say, that she has been twice married, first to Mr. Wm. W. Whitney by whom she had several children, of whom two only survive, a son and daughter, both of whom are married and have children. The second marriage took place with Major General Gaines, of the United States Army, a gentleman and soldier, and whose well-known devotion to her amounted almost to idolatry.

Mrs. Gaines must have passed her climacteric, which has not, however, deprived her, as yet, of the coveted glory of youth which have rolled imperceptibly over her head, have scattered their roses while they have concealed their thorns. Her hair still retains its golden hue; her face is fair and unwrinkled by the cares of half a century, while her symmetrical form is as erect, her eye as lively and benignant, her laugh as ringing, and her step quick, light and buoyant as ever!

An ubiquitous person wherever she is, be it New Orleans, New York, Philadelphia, Washington, or Boston, her *petite figure* may be seen almost any day of the week, and at all hours of the day, moving rapidly along their great thoroughfares,—the very beau-ideal of nerve, enterprise, gracefulness, gaiety and good humor. Who would suppose, from her nonchalant air and smiling aspect, that the expectations of a millionaire fluttered around her heart strings?

But so it was! The highest judicial tribunal in the United States, after a controversy prosecuted, with zeal and enthusiasm, during a space of thirty years and upwards, has confirmed her *status* as entitling her to the largest estate that has ever fallen to the lot of any American female. Between her and the possession and fruition of her queenly wealth there still lie many difficulties, and those of no small magnitude.

She is aware that the glittering rewards that beckon her in the distance, and to which she is entitled, can only be reached at the expense of thousands of individuals, who have long been in the quiet and undisturbed possession of her property, and who can only be ousted from it by regular process of law.

What a world of litigation lies before her! Most women, endowed with sensibility, would shrink appalled from the prospect. But Mrs. Gaines is no ordinary woman, and with a heart overflowing with benevolence, retains a keen sense of the wrongs she has suffered from the willfulness, the mistakes or ignorance of others, and is upheld by a lively sense of the right and justice of her cause, and of the duty that devolves on her to prosecute it to the best of her ability. It is known that she is liberal and ready to make many sacrifices, provided she can be substantially righted. She has, accordingly, for the sake of humanity, and for the sake of peace, proposed to compromise with her debtors, whether individuals or corporate bodies, for refraction of her vast estates. Admitting that she has an unquestionable right to all that the courts have decided to be her property, however large the amount may be, if with a view to relieve those who are in possession of her rights, she is willing to surrender a considerable portion of her legal claims. Who can withhold from her the praise of nobleness and generosity!

It adds largely to the merit of Mrs. Gaines, that the prospect of untold wealth, which lies before her, has never roused within her those feelings of arrogance and pride which are often the accompaniments of large expectations. In her intercourse with society, her manners are simple, frank and genial, devoid of the slightest approach to assumption. She despises none because they are poor, but is ever disposed to aid them as she has opportunity; she respects none because they are rich, regarding wealth a blessing or a curse as it is employed to good or evil ends. No religious devotee seems more intensely conscious of the leadings of Providence, and no Christian entertains a profounder reverence for the Creator, whom, in her conversations with friends, she always styles, with evident affection and trust, her "Heavenly Father."

We cannot refrain from concluding our brief sketch of this distinguished woman, by quoting the significant opinion expressed by the Supreme Court of the United States on the subject of the Gaines' controversy:

"When, hereafter, some distinguished American lawyer shall retire from his practice, to write the history of his country's jurisprudence, this case will be registered by him as the most remarkable in the records of the courts."

JOSEPH ADOLPHUS ROZIER, ESQ.

ANY account of distinguished members of the New Orleans bar, and of prominent citizens, would be signally deficient, which omitted a proper notice of this gentleman.

Mr. Rozier, as we are informed, is of French extraction, and was born at St. Genevieve, Missouri, December 31st, 1817. After completing his classical course at St. Mary's College, Mo., he commenced the study of law at Kaskaskia, Ills., under the direction of Judge Nathaniel Pope, then District Judge of the United States; and, subsequently, under that of John Scott, Esq., a distinguished member of the St. Genevieve bar. It was doubtless fortunate for the future reputation of Mr. Rozier, that the gentlemen who presided over his legal education, were men of a high order of intellect, and well versed in their profession. It is always beneficial to young men of ingenuous temper and honorable ambition, to have influential examples constantly before their eyes when engaged in the prosecution of their studies; and such was the case with the subject of this notice. But his success, in after life, was more attributable to his own energy and his ardent devotion to the noble profession he had adopted, than even to the force of brilliant examples.

When he had completed his preparation for the bar, Mr. Rozier presented himself to the bench of judges for examination, and having successfully passed through that ordeal received his diploma.

It is an era in the career of the young advocate in our wide-spread country, when the question of an advantageous location for practice is first raised, and its solution is often attended with difficulties. Missouri was then, comparatively speaking, a young State, and its cities, now populous, were then small. He commenced the practice at home where his information and habits for business were duly appreciated; but, animated by the spirit of adventure, or seeing a wider scope for the exercise of his abilities in New Orleans, he removed to this place, and having, as a necessary step, first mastered the doctrines and problems of the civil law, (which is itself a science,) and been examined as to his proficiency, commenced practice in this community in the year 1840. Here he has since resided, occupying a position among the prominent members of his profession, greatly respected for the virtues which have adorned his career in the various relations of life—domestic, social, civil and religious. His practice has been lucrative, and his income adequate to all the requirements of taste and elegance. His habits are literary, his disposition social, and his acquaintance with men and events, in past times and present, large. He always prepares himself thoroughly in his cases, comes to trial fully armed with authorities, never loses sight of the interests of his clients, never trifles with grave topics, and uniformly speaks with fluency, dignity, grace and effect.

A trait, which eminently distinguishes Mr. Rozier, is decision of character—an invincible adherence to his principles. This was manifested, in a remarkable degree, during our late troubles. Though a member of the State Convention that resolved to resort to secession as a remedy for Federal grievances, he voted against the measure and refused to sign the ordinance of secession, being one of the only seven of the whole body comprising the Convention who pursued this course. In this instance, as in all cases, he was doubtless influenced by his convictions, being governed by a sense of what he regarded right. His Roman firmness and conscientiousness displayed on this occasion, have been much admired and even praised by those who, to this day, differ from him in political opinion.

The ability of Mr. Rozier, and his earnest devotion to the interests of the Federal Union, attracted the attention of President Lincoln who, regarding him the proper person for the place, appointed him District Attorney of the United States for Louisiana. Mr. Rozier possessing a remarkable share of that modesty which is always characteristic of minds of a certain elevation, could not be tempted either by the distinction or emoluments attending the office to accept it. He accordingly declined the appointment.

Unobtrusive in his manners, affable in his intercourse, *sans peur et sans reproche*, Mr. Rozier would be regarded a model man in any community.

Mr. Rozier is, at present and has been for several years, President of the Law Association, composed of the most distinguished members of the profession in this city.

JOCKEY CLUB RACE COURSE.

D. K. WHITAKER, ESQ.

THE following embraces some of the principal events, and all that are important to be known in the life of this gentleman. He was born at Sharon, County of Norfolk, and State of Massachusetts, on the 10th day of April, A. D., 1801, being the second son and child in a family of ten children, of Rev. Jonathan and Mrs. Mary Whitaker, his father being minister of the Congregational Church and Society of that town. He received his education, preparatory to entering Cambridge College, first at home, from his father (a son of Harvard of the class of 1798; next at Bradford academy, on the Merrimac River—place of nativity of his mother); subsequently at Derby academy, Hingham, then under the direction of his uncle, Rev. Daniel Kimball, also a graduate of Harvard College, and for some time its Latin Tutor, after whom he received his baptismal name); and, finally, at Andrew Phillips' academy. Upon leaving the last named institution, where he spent three years, he delivered, at the anniversary exhibition, by appointment of the principal, the Latin Salutatory Oration, the first time such an honor had ever been conferred on any pupil of that seminary.

At sixteen years of age he entered Cambridge College, where he received the degree of Bachelor of Arts in 1820, and that of Master in 1823. His favorite studies, in college, were the Latin and Greek Languages, Moral and Intellectual Philosophy, Politics, Logic, Rhetoric, and the Belles Lettres, in all which he is said to have excelled. In 1819 he obtained a Boylston Gold Medal for a dissertation on "The Literary Character of Dr. Samuel Johnson," for which all the undergraduates of the four classes, as well as resident graduates, were at liberty to contend; and, in 1820, a Bowdoin Gold Medal for Oratory, open for competition to undergraduates and the graduate class. John Quincy Adams and Daniel Webster were among the judges who awarded the latter prize.

Inheriting a partiality for the clerical profession both from his paternal and maternal ancestors, he, shortly after leaving the university, placed himself under the theological tuition of the Rev. Dr. Richmond, an eminent clergyman of Dorchester (in the environs of Boston), and upon the completion of his studies, having been pronounced morally and intellectually fitted for the sacred office, received, from the Bridgewater Association of Divines, a license to preach the Gospel.

About this time he suffered severely from the condition of his health, which had been frail from his childhood. He had had alarming attacks of illness while prosecuting his studies both at Andover and Cambridge, which led to his temporary abandonment of them; and, upon his recovery on this occasion, his family physician and friends recommended, as indispensable to the complete establishment of his health, his temporary, if not permanent, removal to a Southern and more genial climate. His parents consenting this course was adopted; and towards the close of the year 1823, he, in company with his venerable father who had recently dissolved his pastoral connection with his church and his congregation in New Bedford, Massachusetts, (previously presided over by the celebrated Dr. Samuel West, and subsequently by the equally celebrated Dr. Orville Dewey), left that place for the South. He had previously elaborately prepared a few discourses with a view to make a favorable impression on any audience he might be called on to address, and some of which he soon had occasion to deliver to large audiences in New York City, in Philadelphia, Penn.; in Washington, D. C.; Baltimore, Md.; Richmond and Petersburg, Va.; Raleigh and Fayetteville, N. C.; Cheraw, Camden and Charleston, S. C., and Savannah, Milledgeville and Augusta, Ga. These discourses were said to be very eloquent and effective, and, as a youthful preacher, he started on his career with no inconsiderable reputation. While in Charleston, S. C., he was invited by the Rev. Dr. Gilman to supply his pulpit during the Summer months on the occasion of his exit North, and the congregation of that eminent divine and scholar paid him the compliment of publishing two of his sermons. At the beautiful town of Augusta he succeeded in organizing a society, of which he was invited to take the charge, and, for his accommodation, a neat and commodious church edifice was erected. There he continued to officiate for nearly a year, when his health, in consequence of his constant and novel labors, was completely broken down. He now, as a measure of duty and prudence, determined to abandon the ministry altogether.

Removing to South Carolina where his parents and family had now arrived and settled themselves, he remained with them till his health was recuperated. He shortly afterwards married a lady residing in St. Paul's Parish, Colleton District, of that State, widow of an eminent physician and planter, and devoted himself for about ten years to the culture of the great staples of the South—rice and cotton. The daily exercise his new avocation required him to take in the open air, proved highly beneficial to his health, while the associations he formed with educated planters, presented to him an entirely new and favorable phase of Southern society. Having been invited to become a member of the State Agricultural Society of South Carolina, he delivered by appointment before that body, an anniversary discourse on "The claims of Agriculture to be regarded as a distinct Science," which was published by the society and republished in "the Southern Agriculturist," edited by Dr. Bachman, our great Southern Naturalist. The subject of making the science of agriculture a distinct branch of education for Southern young gentlemen was much discussed about that time, and the plan of making it a part of the college curriculum was actually adopted by the States of South Carolina and Georgia.

The quiet and monotonous pursuits of a country life were not, however, altogether adapted to the peculiar tastes of the subject of this notice. He desired to be an active participator in more exciting scenes. He had determined, for the reasons already assigned, not to resume the ministerial profession, but the law had its attractions, and, as his health was now established, he had ample time and opportunities for the purpose, he resolved to enter upon its study; and placing himself under the direction of James L. Petigru, Esq., the leading lawyer of South Carolina, he prepared himself for the bar, in due time passed a successful examination before the judges of the Supreme Court, and was admitted to practice in the Courts of Law and Equity in South Carolina. He had scarcely opened a law office in Charleston when he was solicited by the Hon. John Lyde Wilson, ex-Governor of the State, and an eminent practitioner at the Charleston bar, to enter into co-partnership with him. Governor Wilson placed in his hands the trial of several important causes, both in the lower and higher courts, in which he was successful.

In 1832, he was appointed Chairman of the Committee of the citizens of St. Paul's Parish (consisting chiefly of planters,) to draft a series of resolutions on the subject of Nullification, which were unanimously adopted. Those resolutions he supported in a speech which was published in the Charleston *Mercury*. He spoke occasionally at public meetings, and, in the midst of the crisis, delivered, by invitation, the Fourth of July Oration before the "'76 Association" of Charleston, availing himself of the occasion to express the views he entertained on the important questions of the day.

He was a member of "the Literary and Philosophical Society of South Carolina," of which the Hon. Joel R. Poinsett was, at that time, President, composed of the most distinguished scholars of all professions in Charleston, a city second to none other in America for its high literary tone. On one occasion he had the honor to be appointed the anniversary orator of this association, and selected for his subject, "The Habits, Customs, Genius, and Languages of the Indian Tribes of North America."

Under the auspices of this learned body, in the year 1835, he issued proposals for the publication of a Southern monthly magazine at Charleston, S. C. The proposition was received very favorably throughout the whole South. After the demise of the old Southern Review, brilliantly edited, first by the Messrs. Elliott (father and son), and subsequently by the celebrated Hugh S. Legare; some such medium for communicating to the Southern public the opinions of distinguished Southern writers on literary topics was deemed highly desirable. This work, under the editorial conduct of Mr. Whitaker, was for some years well sustained by himself and the same corps of writers.

A work of a graver character than the monthly journal just referred to, was now demanded by the necessities of the times, in which the prominent interests of the country, political as well as literary, should be fully and elaborately discussed, with a view to the creation of a sound public sentiment, at the instance, once more, and upon the recommendation of "The Literary and Philosophical Society of South Carolina," Mr. Whitaker issued proposals, in 1840, for the publication of the "*Southern Quarterly Review*." It was thought best, this time, to transfer the place of publication from Charleston to New Orleans, as likely to command a more extensive circulation throughout the whole South and Southwest. By the energy of Mr. Whitaker, a subscription list amounting to $16,000 was procured, and the publication was commenced in this city in January of the following year.

Its contributors were numerous, embracing the ablest writers and scholars in the Southern States. After conducting it for a series of years with marked ability Mr. Whitaker sold the *Review* to a company of gentlemen, who were aware of the difficulties in which he was involved by the heavy outlay he had incurred at the beginning of the enterprise and afterwards. The proceeds enabled him to meet honorably all the liabilities occasioned by the publication of the work, which then passed into the hands of other able editors who continued it for twenty-one years from the date of its announcement up to the time of the breaking out of the late war. It was very influential, and continued to maintain a reputation fully equal to that of any quarterly published either in the United States or in Great Britain.

Having had the mis-fortune to lose his wife, Mr. Whitaker, in 1848, formed a matrimonial alliance with Mrs. M. S. Miller, of the High Hills of Santee, South Carolina, widow of the Hon. John Miller, advocate of Edinburgh, Scotland, and subsequently Queen's Attorney General for the British West Indies, a lady equally celebrated for her personal and literary accomplishments, and by whom he has had six children, a son and four daughters, of whom only two daughters survive, having lost their son, a promising child of five years on a visit of a year spent in the bleak latitude of Canada. Of two sons by his former wife, one survives, who now resides on his own homestead near Greenville, S. C.

During the administration of Mr. Buchanan, Mr. Whitaker held an official position under the United States Government, until the secession of South Carolina, when he removed to Richmond, where through the kind instrumentality of the Hon. Alexander H. Stephens, he obtained a post first in the General Post-office Department of the Confederate Government, and subsequently in the War Office. He left Richmond on the day of its evacuation by the Confederate troops, came to New Orleans early in January, 1866, was for a year and a half, associate editor of the New Orleans *Times*, and has since been engaged in various literary avocations.

The writer of this sketch, who is intimately acquainted with Mr. Whitaker's literary character and entire career, feels fully authorized to say in conclusion, that, as a writer, he is distinguished by a style critically correct, and in argumentative powers is rarely surpassed. A total absence of affectation assists in establishing the cogency of his reasoning and the logical accuracy of his deductions. Few care to measure swords with him in a fairly conducted argument. His blows fall with persevering force, and, even when diffuse, as he sometimes is, he seldom fails in establishing any point for which he contends.

A sketch of Mr. Whitaker was written many years since by Edgar A. Poe, and published in a periodical edited by that great American poet, in which he makes the following assertion: "Mr. Whitaker is one of the best essayists in North America, and stands in the foremost rank of elegant writers." His habits are those of a man devoted to letters, and the want of a publishing house at the South, and his own modesty, though operating against his celebrity, have not been sufficient impediments to seriously cloud his well earned reputation.

GEN. P. G. T. BEAUREGARD.

E. J. HART & CO.

Wholesale Dealers, Importers and Commission Merchants,

IN

GROCERIES AND DRUGS,

Nos. 73, 75 & 77 TCHOUPITOULAS ST.

E. J. HART,
B. B. HART

New Orleans, La.

CHURCH OF ST. JOHN THE BAPTIST.

THIS noble edifice, built in the Renaissance style of architecture, measures, on the outside, 172 feet in length by 75 in width. Its ceiling, groined and arched, is fifty-five feet in height from the floors, and the groins supported by columns. The pews, 180 in number, are made of black walnut with mahogany trimmings. The Organ Gallery is of elliptic shape. The impressions made on the mind of the beholder on entering this sacred edifice are those of simple grandeur, accuracy of proportion and beauty of finish. The senses are charmed, the tastes gratified, the sensibility touched, and the imagination exalted. All the surroudings are calculated to awaken emotions at once august and tender—in a word—to lift the soul from earth to heaven. Over the alter of St Joseph, (in fresco) you see a representation of one of the earliest and most touching incidents in Christian History, the Flight of the Savior of Mankind into Egypt, a picture, and, over the Virgin Mary's altar, another picture of the Assumption of the Blessed Virgin.

All the decorations of the Church were in the beautiful Renaissance style, but they are not yet completed. An organ is being built, in that style by Henry Eben, Esq., of New York city, the fourth of the kind built in the United States, and the most powerful ever introduced into this city. Altars are being built for the Church at Cork, Ireland, of pure white Italian marble, the shafts of the columns and pilasters of Irish Green and Gold marble. A statue of St. John, is to be on one side of the altar, and one of St. Patrick on the other, the altar itself to be surmounted by the Angel of Hope holding a Chalice. The sanctuary floor will be in Mosaic, with different light-colored Irish marble, and the floor of the Transept and Sanctuary steps, of Italian marble. The estimated cost of St. John's Church, when completed, is set down at $200,000. The grand structure reflects infinite credit on the skill of Thomas Mulligan, Esq., the architect, as well as from the indefatigable zeal and enterprise of Father Moynahan, (who prosecuted the arduous labor to its completion with the spirit of another Solomon), and upon the citizens of all classes and creeds, who contributed to its erection with unbounded liberality.

The dedication of this church took place on the 9th of January 1872, under the auspices of his Grace, the Most Rev. Arch-Bishop Perché, (all the Catholic clergy attending) with the imposing magnificence that belongs to the ceremonials of the Roman Catholic church on such occasions, and in the presence of a vast concourse of citizens. The well known poet-priest and orator, Father Ryan, of Mobile, officiated on the occasion, and rendered it more memorable by his eloquence.

THE NEW ORLEANS MUTUAL INSURANCE CO.

THE New Orleans Insurance Company was incorporated in 1835, a fact which confers upon it the distinction of being the oldest Insurance Company in New Orleans, and the oldest but one in the United States. Its first officers were M. M. P. De Buys and Thos. Urquhardt, Mr. A. Saint Martin succeeding the latter as President in 1845, in which year Mr. Jules Tuyes took Mr. Saint Martin's place as Secretary. On the retirement of Mr. St. Martin in 1851, Mr. Jules Tuyes was promoted to the Presidency of this company—a position still filled by him with credit and ability. In 1859, the mutual system being much in vogue, the stockholders of the company reorganized it in accordance with that system and under its present title of the New Orleans Mutual Insurance Company, its capital being then $500,000, and its assets amounting to $750,000. The New Orleans Mutual Insurance Company is justly looked upon as one of the safest and best managed public institutions of this city. It is distinguished from the other companies by a feature which originated with Mr. Tuyes, and has proved generally acceptable as well as eminently successful. Instead of being merged together, the dividends earned in each of the three departments (Fire, Marine and River,) are paid out to each insurer in proportion to the premiums he has paid in the particular department in which the profit was made thereby securing to him *in practice* the lowest rate of insurance attainable under the mutual system, as he receives the full share of the profits realized in the department to which his insurance belongs without being called upon to make, from his earned dividends, any deficiency that might occur in another department. Mr. J. W. Hincks, the present efficient Secretary of the New Orleans Mutual Insurance Company, was for more than twenty years Deputy Collector of the Port of New Orleans. Like Mr. Tuyes, he is a native of this city, where he has always stood deservedly high.

THE FERRIES.

THE Third District Ferry plies every half hour from the head of Elysian Fields Street, Left Bank, and Olivier Street, Algiers, from 5 A. M. to 8 P. M., and is owned and conducted by Jose Carreras, Esq.

Morgan's Railroad Ferry plies between the head of St. Anne Street and the landing in front of his depot in Algiers. The arrivals and departures of his boats are regulated to correspond with the time of the passengers and freight trains to and from Algiers. Cars from Brashear over the Morgan road are crossed to the Left Bank and sent east over the New Orleans, Mobile & Texas Road without change or breaking bulk, the gauge of the former having been lately changed, to correspond with the entire line from New Orleans to New York.

The Second District Ferry plies every half hour between St. Anne Street and Bouny Street, Algiers, from 4½ A. M. until 8½ P. M. under the direction of Messrs. Dram and Hanley.

Canal Street Ferry plies from the head of Canal Street to Villere Street, Right Bank, two, three or four times each hour, from 4½ A. M. to 9 P. M., and each half hour during the night. This ferry employs two boats, the "Louisa," with capacity for 25 carriages or vehicles, with ample accommodations for passengers. The cabins and decks of the boats and the ferry passages and platforms are kept in scrupulous order and the officers are noted for vicinity. The Tug propeller, Little Jerry, performs the night service for foot passengers and at times alternates with the Louisa. In warm summer, by invitation of the liberal proprietors, the boats are thronged with citizens who remain on board for hours enjoying the breezes of the river, making several trips for a single fare.

The Ferry is owned and conducted by Capt. John Kouns and Capt. Wm. T. Boswell, under the firm of John Kouns & Co.

The Fourth District Ferry plies between the head of Jackson Street and the village of Gretna, making twelve or fifteen trips per day, between 5 A. M. and 7 or 8 P. M.

The Sixth District (or Bobb's) Ferry plies from the head of Louisiana Avenue, Sixth District, to Bobb's Mills from dawn until dark.

THE ACADEMY OF MUSIC.

Although the Academy of Music is of more recent establishment than its competitors, it can boast of being the oldest building after the St. Charles' Theatre, devoted to theatrical entertainments. It was constructed in 1853 by George C. Lawrason, Esq., of this city, for its present lessee and manager, Mr. D. Bidwell, and opened the same year as an amphitheatre, with a portable stage, by the renowned circus man, Dan Rice. Its character as an amphitheatre was retained until the next year, 1854, when the "Varieties Theatre"—where Mr. and Mrs. Dion Boucicault were then to perform—was destroyed by fire for the first time. The opportunity of supplying the deficiency was seized upon by Mr. Bidwell, who immediately transformed the amphitheatre into a regular theatre. Mr. John Calder, who had been the treasurer of the Varieties, opened the institution with the unemployed members of the Varieties company, and the "Pelican Theatre," was thus inaugurated. From this time until the year 1856 the Pelican Theatre was rented by Mr. Bidwell to combination companies, until that gentleman was joined by Messrs. Spaulding and Rogers in the proprietorship and management of the theatre, and it assumed its present popular name, "The Academy of Music." The attractions to the Academy were increased by the addition of a museum, in which was gathered a large collection of natural and other curiosities. In 1866 Mr. Rogers' connection with the firm ceased, and Dr. Spaulding, in 1870, leaving Mr. Bidwell, the original manager, sole proprietor. Every year the Academy, under its intelligent and energetic administration, has received new improvements which make it now one of the most complete of modern theatres. The museum has been discontinued, and the space allotted to that department, in the front portion of the building, has been converted into neat and elegant reception and dressing rooms for the use of ladies and children, who so liberally patronize the Academy. The seasons at the Academy commence earlier and end later than at any of our other theatres, and its administration presents besides several important and noteworthy features, an elaborate steam apparatus supplies the auditorium with hot or cold air, according to the season, and ample provision is made for a copious supply of water in case of fire; an admirable arrangement exists about its stage, consisting of the entire absence of scenery, except that which is needed for the evening's performance. All surplus scenery is carefully stored away in an adjoining fire-proof room, to which it is easily shifted by means of a simple contrivance. This is an excellent arrangement (which, we believe is not adopted by any other theatre in this country,) not only as an additional precaution against fire but because of the facilities it affords in the stage operations. The Academy is the original matinée theatre in New Orleans, and the success and popularity resulting from these noon performances have led the other theatres to follow Mr. Bidwell's example. The Academy was also the first theatre in New Orleans to be provided with the patent iron settees now so generally popular in the North. To say that the Academy is one of the coziest and most elegant places of amusement in the country is but to confess the public opinion. The uninitiated would be surprised, in fact, at the first glance to conceive that its seating capacity is nearly 1,800, and that very few theatres in the country have achieved the pecuniary success which has attended its management—the clear profits of one season, since the war, being estimated at a figure approximating sixty thousand dollars. During the career of this theatre most of the distinguished actors, actresses, and combination companies, varying from negro minstrelsy and the burlesque to the most refined comedy, and the lightest order of the drama, have appeared on its boards, and entitled it a patronage rivaling the most successful enterprises of its kind. In Mr. Jake Kittredge, who has been connected with the Academy in the capacity of Treasurer, for many years Mr. Bidwell has found a valuable assistant in the management of his theatre. Combining, as he does, strict business qualifications, and a peculiar tact to make himself the favorite of the patrons and the employées of the institution, his services have been as invaluable as his popularity is extensive.

THE MORESQUE BUILDING.

This magnificent iron edifice, which occupies an entire square at the corner of Camp and Poydras streets, was commenced by J. C. Barelli, Esq., in the Winter of 1859—1860. It was originally to have contained six stores, and a ball room 68 feet by 147. One-half of the building was roofed, when its further progress was interrupted by the war, during which all the copper was stolen, and the timbers of the unstated ball room rotted. About $249,000 had then been expended on it.

Subsequently, the building was purchased by John Gasche, Esq., for $160,000, who received an offer equivalent to about $37,000 per year for it, to be converted into a hotel. He refused taking the risk of the additional cost, about $200,000, including furniture, and expended about $110,000 in putting it in its present condition.

The building covers a small square of 150 feet on each side, between Poydras, Camp, North, and St. Mary streets. It is three stories and an attic in height. The four fronts are of iron in the Moorish style, or style of the Alhambra, and were executed at Holly Springs, (Miss.,) by Messrs. Jones, McElvain & Co. This foundry was used for an ordnance foundry in the early part of the war, but was afterwards destroyed.

SHAKESPEARE CLUB.

THE claim of the Shakespeare Club for public favor is based on its usefulness to the community, and hence deserves the attention of all who have an interest in its welfare.

Members of the Louisiana Histrionic and Crescent Dramatic Associations are requested to meet on Sunday, March 17, 1867, at 10 o'clock, a.m., at No. 26 Commercial Place (up stairs), for the purpose of consolidating and forming a permanent organization. By request of MANY FRIENDS.

The above notice, published by G. H. Braughn, Esq., who had at various times been President of the Association mentioned, brought together at the place indicated, Messrs. Braughn, T. O'Neil, Mark O'Rourke, F. G. Chamberlain and Peter Hart, and the Shakespeare Club was created.

Profiting by their ante-bellum experience, the club resolved that their theatrical entertainments should be private, and the expenses borne by its members. Meetings were frequently held thereafter, and to the rolls were, from time to time, added the names of some of the most prominent young men of this city.

On the 8th of May, 1867, the club, which then numbered about fifty members, adopted a constitution and by-laws, and was thoroughly organized by the election of the following officers:—Geo. H. Braughn, President; Dr. J. K. Walker, Vice-President; Walter H. Rogers, Secretary; J. G. Campbell, Treasurer; and T. O'Neil, Stage Manager; nearly every one of whom is still a member of the club, and Mr. Braughn has, from year to year, been re-elected as its President.

On the 25th of May, 1867, the club gave its first performance at the National Theatre. The play was "The Wife; or, A Tale of Mantua."

On the 24th June following, the second entertainment was given with "Love's Sacrifice" and "To Paris and Back for £5." On the 23d of the same month the third entertainment, "Money" and the "Loan of a Lover," occurred, and the fourth, "Hamlet," on the 19th August following. This last performance was given at the Opera House to unquestionably the largest and finest audience that ever filled that Theatre. On the 25th August, "The Wife" was repeated, for the relief of the yellow fever sufferers of New Iberia, which netted nearly two thousand dollars. On the 10th of September the last performance of the season was given at the old Varieties Theatre, producing "The Rivals." Since that time the club have produced "Lady of Lyons," "Marble Heart," "Dead Heart," "Richelieu" and "Ingomar."

During its existence the club has encountered many difficulties, which have been overcome by dint of intelligence and perseverance, its affairs have been carefully and judiciously administered, until it numbers two hundred members, comprising many of our most influential and respectable citizens, has a handsome sum in its treasury, and is in every way in a flourishing condition.

The social feature of the club, diminutive at first, has grown into splendid proportions; so much so that vaster quarters have been selected for the accommodation of its members. The Tilton Mansion, at the corner of Canal and Dryades streets, the new home of the club, and represented by the above engraving, has been entirely repaired and refitted in a sumptuous style and provided with all the accessories of a modern club-house, which make it now the finest in New Orleans.

The club is literary, social and dramatic, the latter feature being participated in only voluntarily by the "active members," the others being termed "passive" members. It possesses a complete miscellaneous and dramatic library, keeps all the prominent magazines and periodicals, and presents many other pleasant club-life features.

HON. DUNCAN F. KENNER.

This gentleman, whose name was so familiar to the people of Louisiana before the late war, as a Sugar Planter and leading turfman, was born in New Orleans in the early part of the present century. The best portions of his life have been devoted to agricultural pursuits and the cognate matter of rearing and improving the thorough-bred horse. Few persons of the present day have been more successful in either pursuit. As a planter he was active, energetic and devotedly attached to his vocation, for he was a strong believer in the good old maxim, that

> "He, who by the plough would thrive,
> Himself must either hold or drive."

As a turfman, his career was brilliant, as all who recollect the glories of the old Metarie, Eclipse, Louisiana and Bingaman course, will testify. In the days of the glories of the American turf, Mr. Kenner's name ever ranked among the first.

Like many planters, he devoted much of his time to reading and to study. The taste and habits of his collegiate education was not allowed to rust from neglect. He possessed one of the finest private libraries in the State, and devoted hours, each day, to literary pursuits. A man of enterprise and progress, he never hesitated to adopt the most scientific methods of perfecting the development of the cane and manufacture of sugar.

It is not to be supposed that a gentleman of his fortune and attainments should not have been frequently called upon by his fellow-citizens to take an active part in the political affairs of his native State. He first took his seat in the House of Representatives of the State Legislature in 1836, and continued, almost without intermission, a member of the House, or State Senate, from that time till 1860. He was elected to the State Constitutional Convention called, in 1844, to remodel the Constitution of 1812, and again, in 1852, when he was elected to a Convention called to amend the Constitution. Over this Convention, which embraced among its members many of the ablest jurists and leading politicians of that day, Mr. Kenner presided, having been elected its President by a most flattering majority.

In 1860, Mr. Kenner was a candidate for what is known as the Secession Convention, and, for the first time in twenty-four years, was defeated by his old constituents of Ascension Parish, the people of Ascension having strong Union sentiments, and Mr. Kenner equally decided Secession proclivities. After the adoption by the Convention of the Secession Resolutions, Mr. Kenner was elected by the Convention as one of the six Representatives to the Congress called at Montgomery, Alabama, to frame a Confederate Constitution and Government. He continued a member of the Confederate Congress ,from its first formation to the final disruption of that Government and the surrender of General Lee. Probably the best estimate of the appreciation in which Mr. Kenner was held by his colleagues is found in the fact, that, after one year's service in the Provisional Congress, he was appointed Chairman of the Committee on Ways and Means of the House of Representatives, the most important Committee of that body, whose Chairman is the acknowledged leader of the House. This position was not attained by the power of speech nor by the graces of oratory, for to these Mr. Kenner never pretended (though no member, when he rose to address it, ever commanded the more undivided attention of the House), but to the exhibition in the Committee Room, where the real business of legislation is usually done, of practical good common sense, and a thorough knowledge of the adaptation of the means to the ends to be accomplished.

In 1863 and '64, Mr. Kenner became convinced that the great difficulty in the way of the recognition of the Independence of the Confederate States by the European powers was *the institution of Slavery*, and that, without such recognition, the question of Confederate Independence was probably destined to defeat, in fact, that the institution of slavery had to be given up, or the hopes of Confederate Independence would, more than probably, be lost forever.

Under this conviction he urged upon the Richmond Government to assume, in the face of the world, the obligation to abolish slavery in the event of the success of the Independence of the Confederate States. Though the views entertained by him were assented to, more or less, by many of the leaders at Richmond, it was thought that the public sentiment of the Southern States was not ripe for so bold a movement at that time. These views, however, were strengthened by the progress of events, and, in October or November 1864 Mr. Davis determined to adopt the policy of Emancipation as an extreme means to secure recognition by England and France, and, as he then thought, the consequent Independence of the Confederate States.

A trusty and confidential agent, fully possessed of the wishes of the Richmond Government, and, at the same time, a discreet and judicious person was required to go to Europe and communicate this change of policy on the subject of slavery to the Emperor Napoleon and to Lord Palmerston, the then recognized controllers of the French and English foreign policy. Mr. Kenner was selected by Mr. Davis and the Richmond Cabinet as that agent. To pass through the Federal lines, which were then being gradually drawn closer and closer around Richmond, was no easy or altogether safe trip for a Confederate Congressman. Provided with the proper credentials and documents, all in cypher, concealed on his person, Mr. Kenner accepted the mission with all its chances of discovery, imprisonment, and, probably, death, and left Richmond to go *via* New York, in December 1864. He arrived in New York in some three weeks from the time of his departure from Richmond, walking nearly across Maryland, hid for days, occasionally, in farm houses, where the owners avowed themselves as "Southern sympathizers;" he often made narrow escapes of detection, under an assumed name and for an assumed purpose. He arrived in England in January or February 1865. Steps were immediately taken to bring to the notice of Louis Napoleon and Lord Palmerston the intentions and purposes of the Richmond Government. How unsuccessful the effort was need not now be dilated on. The constant advance of the Federal armies on to Richmond, and the evident weakening of the Confederate defences, destroyed all possibility of foreign recognition.

Immediately on Mr. Kenner's return to Louisiana, after the war, he was elected to the State Senate by his old constituents. He served in this capacity in the sessions of 1866 and 1867; and, since the adoption of the Reconstruction measures of 1868, he has confined his attention to his private affairs, and returned to his former occupation of cultivating the sugar cane, which, we learn, he is doing on a very extensive scale, being, with one exception, probably, more largely interested in that cultivation than any person in this State.

FATHER CORNELIUS MOYNAHAN.

Father Cornelius Moynahan emigrated to the United States at the same time, and in the same ship, with his distinguished brother, Father J. Moynahan; and so similar has been the career of these two brothers, the influence they have exerted in Catholic circles, the energy they have displayed in building churches, founding schools and convents, the ecclesiastical offices they have filled, and the esteem in which they have been held by all classes among us, that they have acquired in this community, the title to be regarded and to be called, *par nobile fratrum*.

Father C. Moynahan received his classical education in Ireland, finished his theological course in the Diocese of New Orleans, and was invested with the functions and dignity of the priesthood by the Most Reverend Archbishop Blanc, in the year 1848. The sphere of his operations lay in the Third District of New Orleans, which, at the time of his investiture, was without any proper ecclesiastical organization for the Roman Catholics. He was accordingly commissioned by the Archbishop of the Diocese, to build a church for the English speaking population of that district, and first erected a framed edifice for the purpose; but the congregation increased so rapidly under his administration, that a more commodious and substantial building for its accommodation became necessary, and the result was, the erection of what is now St. Peter's Church,—a fine brick edifice of sufficient dimensions to meet the requirements of that portion of the metropolis. The frame church, first erected, was converted into a Parochial School, largely attended by the children of that and the neighboring parishes, the department of female instruction being presided over by the Sisters of the Holy Cross, and the male department by lay teachers.

No naturalized citizen has ever identified himself more entirely with our national institutions than Father C. Moynahan,—none is more universally respected and beloved; none more influential in social, theological, and educational circles; none a more decided champion of Roman Catholic schools to be placed exclusively under Roman Catholic influences. His pulpit eloquence is classical, pathetic, earnest, persuasive and impressive, deeply imbued with what the French call *onction*, and the Latins *suaviter in modo*. The latter trait is conspicuous in his general intercourse with society, whether lay or clerical. Like his older brother, he has been raised to the dignity of Canon, and is one of the Counsellors of his Grace, the Archbishop.

PROFESSOR EUGENE PRÉVOST.

Mr. Eugene Prévost, the distinguished musical composer, professor and orchestra leader, was for ten years a pupil of the Paris "Conservatoire de Musique," where he obtained in 1829 two prizes for composition, and in 1831 received the unanimous vote of the jury (composed of the most eminent musicians of that period) for the "Grand Prix de Rome," the highest honor bestowed by the Conservatory of Music. In 1835 Mr. Prévost's first opera, *Cosimo*, was produced at the "Opera Comique," where it was performed for more than two hundred nights in succession, and at once gave him a reputation as one of the most promising musical writers of the day. This charming opera *bouffe*, which still retains its place upon the stage, was followed in quick succession by "Les Pontons de Cadiz," one act, and "Le Bon Garçon," both of which were also performed at the Opera Comique with great success, the latter especially, as well as "L'Illustre Gaspard," another comic opera produced upon the same boards in 1837. The next year Mr. Prévost came to New Orleans, having been engaged by Mr. P. Davis as leader of the orchestra of the French Opera—a post he has filled almost uninterruptedly for over twenty years with immense credit to himself and great benefit to the management, the artists, and the musical amateurs of New Orleans. During that period Mr. Prévost composed "La Esmeralda," a four act opera; "La Chaste Susanne," four acts; "Alice et Clair," three acts; "Jonas," an oratorio in three parts; "L'Orléanaise," a patriotic overture; several cantatas with full orchestral and choral accompaniments; a "Solemn Mass," a "Te Deum," dedicated to the Queen of Spain, and for which the author received the grand cross of Charles the Third; a "Requiem Mass," and other compositions too numerous to mention, all of which were performed here with great success. In 1862 Mr. Prévost returned to Europe, where, after filling for two seasons the post of leader of the orchestra in several first-class theatres, he was engaged by the celebrated composer, Offenbach, as leader of his theatre, "Les Bouffes Parisiens," which position he subsequently relinquished for the leadership of the grand concerts of the "Champs Elysées," in Paris. Since his return to New Orleans, Mr. Eugene Prévost has devoted himself almost exclusively to teaching, and the eagerness with which his lessons are sought after is the best evidence of the excellence of his method, and of the gratifying results he has obtained. It may safely be asserted that to no single individual in our community more deeply indebted for the excellent musical taste and the general cultivation of that most fascinating of the fine arts than to Mr. Eugene Prévost. Should Mr. Placide Canonge succeed in engaging an operatic company for the season of 1872–3, it is gratifying to know that the orchestra will be under the experienced leadership of the learned and accomplished musician whose career we have briefly sketched, and whose pre-eminent claims to the distinction are universally acknowledged by all competent judges.

Since the foregoing sketch was written, Mr. Prévost has died. His illness was brief and his demise was as unexpected, as it was sincerely regretted.

Merchants' Mutual Insurance Co.

104 CANAL STREET.

INCORPORATED 1854.

THIS is the oldest and undoubtedly one of the strongest, if not the first in point of capital and resources, of all the Insurance companies of New Orleans. It was founded in 1832, with Mathew Morgan as President and Mr. Relf as Secretary. Mr. Morgan having transferred his business to New York, Mr. Dupuy was elected in his place, and upon the death of the latter, Mr. John Pemberton, who had been acting for some years as Secretary, was called to the Presidency of the Company, an office which he held until his death in 1868. Mr. Pemberton was a kind-hearted, genial and well-educated gentleman, and under his management the Merchants' Mutual Insurance Co. acquired great popularity and influence. Of his successor, Mr. Paul Fourchy, we have already spoken in no exaggerated terms of praise, and the present highly flourishing condition of the company, as exhibited in its annual statement, as well as the large dividends paid during the past years to its patrons are the best evidence that could be produced of the faithful and able manner in which the affairs of the Company are now conducted. Whilst giving full credit to Mr. Fourchy and the Board of Directors presided over by him for the success of the Mutual Insurance Co., the services of its young and popular Secretary, Mr. G. W. Nott, should not be overlooked. Mr. Nott is the grandson of W. Nott, Esq., one of the merchant princes of New Orleans half a century ago, and on his mother's side of the late distinguished Judge Jean Francois Canonge, whose eminence as a jurist was only equalled by his accomplishments as a wit and a man of the world. Of these ancestors Mr. G. W. Nott is no unworthy scion, and his friends have every reason to anticipate for him a bright career.

CAPITAL STOCK,

$1,000,000.

Average Premiums Paid In,

$1,000,000.

Last Dividend, May, 1872,

30 PER CENT CASH.

OFFICERS:

PAUL FOURCHY, *President.*

G. W. NOTT, *Secretary.*

DIRECTORS:

PIERRE MASPERO,	DAVID MCCOARD,
J. M. ALLEN,	P. S. WILTZ,
D. A. CHAFFRAIX,	M. PUIG,
S. Z. RELF,	J. J. FERNANDEZ,
L. F. GENTREZ,	CHARLES LA FITTE.

DR. DANIEL WARREN BRICKELL,

Was born in Columbia, S. C., in 1824. His ancestry, of mixed Irish, French and English blood, were among the earlier settlers of the State, and his maternal grandfather, Daniel Faush, was the founder of the first newspaper in Columbia, which became the official organ, when that town was made the Capitol of South Carolina.

Dr. Brickell received a careful classical education at the best schools, and graduated as a physician in the University of Pennsylvania in 1847.

In the fall of the same year he was passed second, in a list of some forty applicants, before the Naval Examining Board at Philadelphia, and received his Commission as an Assistant Surgeon in the U. S. Navy. His orders, however, assigned him to duty at the Naval Station of Pensacola, in the place of active service afloat, which he strongly desired, and throwing up his Commission, he began his career as a practising physician in the City of New Orleans, in January, 1848.

The reputation which he soon acquired as a thoughtful, earnest, and indefatigable student, gave him early admittance to the Charity Hospital, as one of its attending physicians, and in the winter of 1859 he established a private class, and begun his distinguished career as a teacher of medicine.

The success of himself and colleagues was immediate and marked, and in 1856 he, together with Drs. Fenner, Choppin, Beard, A. & F. Penniston, J. M. Picton and Howard Smith, organized the NEW ORLEANS SCHOOL OF MEDICINE, which opened with a class of 76 students. In 1860 the class aggregated 270, with the promise of larger numbers thereafter. These hopes were disappointed by the war; but at its close in 1865, the college was re-opened, and at the death of Dr. Fenner in 1866, Dr. Brickell was chosen the Dean of the school he had helped to found, and of which he always was one of the chief ornaments and supports.

The Chair of Obstetrics and Diseases of Women, which he so long and brilliantly filled, gave him a steadily increasing reputation in the South and West, and at his resignation from it, in 1870, he occupied the foremost rank as a Gynaecologist in his state and section.

For many years Dr. Brickell was connected with the *N. O. Medical News and Hospital Gazette*, and with the *Southern Journal of Medicine*, as editor-in-chief, and exhibited, during a long career and in an eminent degree, all the high qualifications of a successful journalist.

As a citizen Dr. Brickell's deep interest in and capacity for public affairs, have won him the largest esteem and confidence of his fellow townsmen, who have more than once called him to their head in cases of the most trying and delicate nature. And in every relation of life, his lofty character, his earnest manhood, his spotless integrity, his strong love of justice, his truthfulness, fidelity and generous temper have ensured him the regard and friendship of all classes.

In stature Dr. Brickell is tall and spare; of a delicate frame, and nervous temperament; but capable of unusual energy and endurance. His features are classically regular, almost stern in their faultless outline, but luminous with an active and overflowing sensibility. A high-bred self-repose, a marked dignity of manner, mingled with much grace and sweetness, and his surpassing tact, have given him a sure passport to general and continued favor. Nor is it overpraise to add that nature has adorned him, in a conspicuous degree, with those rare accomplishments of mind and heart which go to make up the enviable *ensemble* of a successful and beloved physician.

Dr. Brickell has been twice married and has a large family.

PATRICK IRWIN, ESQ.

THIS opulent and public-spirited citizen was born in the county of Cork, Ireland, in the year 1810. In 1829 he emigrated to the United States. In 1832 he came to New Orleans, with the progress and prosperity of which he has since been largely identified. In 1853, he was elected an Alderman of the city, and, in 1854, appointed to fill a vacancy created in the Louisiana Legislature by the death of Hon. Preston W. Farrar.

In 1840, Mr. Irwin built, at his own expense, the Dryades Street Market, in a part of the city which was then little better than a wilderness, but which has since become one of its most populous thoroughfares. This market alone would be an enduring monument of his wealth, enterprise and municipal ambition, had he conferred no other benefits on the city; but he has added many to the list, which will cause his name often to be repeated with esteem and gratitude.

In 1850, he established two lines of omnibuses, one on Rampart, the other on Carondelet street, which were kept up for the space of from twelve to fifteen years, and were not only a great comfort and convenience to our citizens in this warm climate, but the source of a princely income. When city railroads superseded the omnibus, he invested capital in them, and became one of their largest stockholders. As an evidence of his abundant means, when the city, a few years since, proposed to dispose of its entire interest in the markets, he offered to purchase it, at a cost of two millions, two hundred thousand dollars, but the offer was declined. No capitalist, in New Orleans, enjoys more unlimited credit.

Without making any pretensions to religion, Mr. Irwin has always, in fact, been one of the most ardent friends and supporters of the Roman Catholic Church in the Crescent City, and one of the most liberal contributors to its progress. Had it not been for his efficient aid, it is not perhaps too much to say, that the elegant church of St. John the Baptist, the Parochial School House, the Convent, and other edifices connected with the church, which occupy an entire square on Dryades Street, would never have been built.

Mr. Irwin had not only been a purchaser, to a large extent, of real estate in the city, but has built many stores and houses on Tchoupitoulas, Natchez and Dryades streets, (near the Market,) and is now erecting a building on Gravier street, (next to Lum's Carriage Ware Room,) all of which edifices have added to the beauty and wealth of the city and the convenience of the inhabitants.

In 1870, he was elected President of the Hibernia Bank, which situation he still occupies with the reputation of a skillful financier and an energetic executive officer. The confidence reposed in him is such that he has recently also been elected President of the Hibernia Insurance Company.

ACHILLE CHIAPELLA.

Mr. Achille Chiapella, President of the Union Insurance Company, is of Italian descent, his grandfather, Geronimo Chiapella, having come here from Genoa towards the middle of the last century. Of his two sons, Celestin and Stephen Chiapella, the former, after realizing a handsome fortune on his fine Sugar estate in the Parish of Plaquemine, went to live in France, where he purchased in the vicinity of Bordeaux, the celebrated vineyard of "Haut Brion, La Mission," better known to every Louisiana gourmet of the *Ante Bellum* period, as the place where was produced the superb "C C" claret, so called because every bottle came here labeled with the initials of the proprietor. Stephen Chiapella, the father of the subject of this sketch, preferring the life of a sailor, took command of a merchant ship plying between New Orleans and Europe, where his son, Achille Chiapella, received his education. Returning here, after completing his studies, Mr. Chiapella embraced the Notarial profession, in which he was very successful, and which he relinquished to assume the Presidency of the Union Insurance Company, which office he still continues to fill with much credit to himself and great advantage of the shareholders of that well managed corporation. Besides the above positions Mr. Chiapella was twice elected to the City Council at a period when that body was composed of many of our best and most intelligent citizens, and in which his knowledge of business, strict integrity and a thorough acquaintance with the wants of the city enabled him to render valuable service to the community.

He was one of the originators of the Opelousas Railroad and acted for a short period as its President. He was also the founder and presiding officer of the first Oddfellow's lodge established below Canal street.

Mr. Chiapella is yet in the full vigor of manhood, having been born in 1813. In addition to his laborious duties as President of the Union Insurance Company, he also fills the position of Director of our most important Banking Institution—the Citizen's Bank.

Affable in his manners, and generous in his hospitality, he is a gentleman of cultivated taste, a lover of the Fine Arts, and a liberal patron of artists and musicians. When the Opera Company was formed, Mr. Chiapella was selected as one of the Directors, and was retained in that position until 1871, when he declined a reelection.

If the Union Insurance Company owes much to its accomplished President, the latter has been fortunate in securing the services of its intelligent and popular Secretary, Mr. J. M. Crawford, a son of the late John Crawford, formerly Her B. Majesty's Consul in New Orleans, where he left a large circle of attached friends, and gave unlimited satisfaction to the mercantile community.

PROF. G. COLLIGNON.

Mr. Gustave Collignon, was born in Rennes, Brittany, in 1818, and entered the "Conservatoire de Musique"—the most celebrated musical school in the world—in 1824. His teachers were: Zimmerman for the piano, and Barbereau for harmony and composition; the last named professor, (whose daughter M. Collignon afterwards married,) being the author of the best and most complete treatise on musical composition ever published. In 1837, Mr. Collignon left the Conservatoire after receiving the first prize in his class, and in 1848, he was induced by Mr. Davis, then manager of the French Opera, to come to New Orleans, where he soon became known as an accomplished musical instructor, and when he established in [illegible] the Classical Musical Society, which has been lately revived, and of which M. Collignon is still the leader, and the moving spirit.

In addition to his numerous professional engagements, M. Collignon is the Musical Director and Organist of the Church of the Immaculate Conception on Baronne street, where many ladies and gentlemen, constituting the *élite* of our musical amateurs may be heard every Sunday. One of the greatest attractions of those religious concerts, it is proper to add, is the magnificent voice, faultless style and impressive singing of Madame Comes, M. Collignon's daughter and pupil—a young lady who possesses a soprano voice, ranging with ease from the lower B flat to E flat above the line, and whose musical attainments are worthy of the splendid vocal gifts bestowed upon her.

Having lived in New Orleans for nearly a quarter of a century, M. Collignon justly considers himself a Louisianian. As a gentleman and as an artist, there is no one who stands higher, or who enjoys a larger share of the esteem of the community

CLAY STATUE AND CRESCENT HALL.

The corner stone of the above statue was laid by the Clay Statue Association of New Orleans on the 12th of April, 1856.

The inauguration, which called out one of the grandest and largest public gatherings that ever took place in New Orleans, was on the 12th of April, 1860. On that occasion, Col. J. B. Walton acted as Grand Marshal and Col. J. O. Nixon as First Assistant Marshal.

J. Q. A. Fellows appeard at the head of the Masons as Grand Master.

Gerard Stith, now of the "Picayune" office, was Mayor of the city at that time.

Joel T. Hart, of Kentuky, the artist who gave form and proportions to the Clay Statue, was present at the inauguration.

Wm. H. Hunt, Esq., was orator of the day.

He said, that in 1852, a number of public spirited citizens determined to erect a bronze statue of Henry Clay. They entrusted the work of making the statue to Joel T. Hart, of Kentucky.

"We are here to-day to dedicate this statue, the statue of Henry Clay."

"Behold, his life-like image stands before you. No royal robes adorn his person; no crown, no sceptre, no badges of ancestral glory. No sword is by his side to tell of battles fought and won; no baton to indicate the pomp and power of authority.

"A plain man in the simple garments of a citizen; his image challenges not our admiration through the adventitious aids of rank, or the tinsel ornaments of military glory. But he stands before us as we knew him, as we loved and honored him, the embodiment of the genius, of the wisdom, of the eloquence, of the courage, of the public virtue, of self-sacrifice, of the patriotism which filled the measure of his country's glory, and made his name and his fame immortal."

"A circle of fifty feet in diameter, surmounted with an iron railing, and a flight of hexagon shape granite steps, each one smaller than the one on which it rests, forms the foundation on which the pedestal and statue rest. The pedestal, like the firm foundation, is of granite, fitting emblem of the lasting fame of the subject of the lasting figure which stands upon its top.

"The statue itself is a perfect likeness of the illustrious statesman. Its height is about fifteen feet. This, with the height of the foundation circle, steps and pedestal, makes it stand some forty feet high, an ornament to our grand and beautiful thoroughfare, Canal street."

CRESCENT HALL.

This building was originally erected by Cornelius Paulding, Esq., about the year 1826. In 1858 it was purchased by Mrs. Cora A. Slocomb, and remodeled into a hotel, known as the "Merchants." In 1865, Col. A. W. Merriam transformed it into a Billiard Hall.

HUGH McCLOSKEY, ESQ.

Since the publication of this work was begun the people of New Orleans have lost one of their noblest citizens, Hugh McCloskey, who died in his residence, on St. Charles Street, on the 28th January last, in the fifty-eighth year of his age.

Mr. McCloskey was a native of Dungiven, in the county Derry, Ireland, the same village in which the distinguished Irish patriot and exile, John Mitchell, was born. Mr. McCloskey's father was a shoemaker, who, in Dungiven and the country about, was universally known as "Honest George McCloskey," a title bestowed upon him, by his neighbors, because of a just, good and blameless life.

Hugh had a good English education, which was finished at the Royal College at Belfast. His father's means being insufficient to send him to that institution, while yet a stripling, he earned enough himself, by teaching in his native place, to accomplish that object, and, late in life, when he appeared as a public writer to expose and denounce the political wrongs the people of his city and State were suffering, his terse and effective compositions, betrayed the culture of his early years.

When but little over age his eyes turned to America, as the eyes of so many had before and so many have since, as the Mecca of the poor, the industrious and the enterprising. He landed in one of the northern cities, whence, failing to find employment, he wended his way to the South and arrived in New Orleans, on Christmas day, 1838. A stranger, without a friend or acquaintance, in his new home, his purse light, unable to find a situation for which his education fitted him, he was constrained to seek any employment that he could get, rather than incur debt. He was wont, when prosperous and influential, to refer back to this period of his life, with a pride, which was commendable. Although of a slender frame and a by no means vigorous constitution, he worked as a laborer, laying gas pipes, in the streets of the city, and, month after month he toiled, with blistered hands, rather than eat the bread of dependence.

After a while he fell into a small ready-made clothing business, on the Levee, but did not succeed. Then he became an employe of Mr. Stevenson, who kept a soda and meal establishment, at the corner of Exchange Alley and Custom House streets, noted for the purity and excellence of the beverages. To that business Mr. McCloskey succeeded, and, thenceforth, was invariably a prosperous man, never relinquishing the trafic in which fortune first favored him.

Modest and unobtrusive, it was not until the year the civil war closed that public attention was drawn to the merits of this valuable citizen. His manly bearing, during the war, in maintaining his opinions, as a supporter of the Confederate cause, and his generous benevolences to the unfortunate, during that distressing period, impressed his fellow citizens with a high respect for his character and attracted the affectionate regard of good people in every rank of society. Upon the re-organization of the State government that year, he was, by a large majority, elected a delegate to represent the Third Ward, in the House of Representatives of the General Assembly. That Legislature of 1865-66, was distinguished in the annals of Louisiana for the high order of its average ability, for the moral elevation by which its deliberations were guided, and by the dignity with which its proceedings were conducted. Take it, in every aspect, no law-making body superior to it, has ever been assembled in any part of the Union and its equal has been rarely seen. It is not a small compliment to say that in that assemblage, Hugh McCloskey exercised no inconsiderable influence. He was an active member of several important committees, and he showed that with the private excellences which made him so estimable, he had talents and aptitudes for political affairs, which rendered him a most useful public servant.

Now the calls upon him to give his attention to matters, more or less public in their nature, became frequent. He assisted in organizing a company, which is permanently established, to secure, by importation, a constant and sufficient supply of ice for the city, and was one of the first directors. At a critical time with the Canal and Claiborne streets Railroad Company, he was chosen a director, and was largely instrumental in saving the corporation from bankruptcy and ruin. He was among those who initiated the project of the Hibernia Bank, a very successful institution, of which he became a Director and Vice-President. The last useful scheme of this sort, in which he was a pioneer, was the Hibernia Insurance Company, of which he was the first President. His services, in every one of these associations, were gratuitous. He sought none of these distinctions in business life, nor did he accept them as a money monger, for, personally, he adhered to the law of the middle ages, which forbade the lending of money on interest. Nor could he be prevailed upon, whatever the temptation of gain, to connect himself with any of those legislative schemes and monopolies, which have so multiplied since the General Assembly of 1865 and 1866, for public plunder, although repeatedly solicited and urged to do so. He would touch nothing that was adverse to the interests of the people.

So much in regard to him as a business man, a legislator, and a projector. We now come to his personal characteristics. He led no campaign, he made no notable speech, he wrote no book, he discovered no new principle in science or in art, nevertheless he is worthy of high eulogium, for he was one of the most exemplary and valuable citizens we have ever known, possessing moral traits which are very rarely found united in any one man.

He accumulated a handsome fortune, in a calling commonly thought belittling, which he had the sterling sense to stick to after he became affluent. Engaged in trade, during the greater part of his manhood, and successful in it, he was never known to utter an untruth or practice a deception. Profoundly and practically religious few knew it, since the dawn of day was his favorite hour for attending mass, the hour when the lowly and the unostentatious, in the Catholic church, usually attend divine service. He was never known to turn away the distressed or the unfortunate with an empty hand or a cold look. In his own poverty and hardships he did not forget the duties of charity. As he prospered he became generous, and as he grew affluent his benevolences were munificent. The severe struggles of his youth did not harden his heart, nor did his advanced years bring with them avarice.

His life was sacrificed in the performance of a public duty, voluntarily undertaken, at the instance of his fellow citizens. As one of the great committee sent to Washington, to procure from the Federal authorities a redress of political grievances, he remained in the North several weeks, laboring in the cause with his accustomed zeal and enthusiasm, and in the extreme rigor of the weather, during December and January, he contracted a disorder, which resulted in his death, soon after his return. Whatever he was enlisted in, whether to advance the interests of a friend, to perfect some project of public utility, to aid a charity or to promote good government, his noble mind was absorbed in the matter until success attended his efforts, or until success was obviously impossible. And all this with the most perfect disinterestedness, entirely void of political ambition or design of pecuniary advantage.

No wonder that his funeral was a demonstration almost unequaled in its kind, in New Orleans. Hundreds of his good deeds that had been hidden, came to light when he was no more in this world. The beneficiaries and other inmates of most of the charitable institutions in the city, participated in the obituary ceremonies, and a great multitude surrounded his late dwelling, attesting, in every becoming way, the respect and veneration in which the memory of the good man and public-spirited citizen was held by all classes, by all nationalities, by all creeds.

Algiers is the great work-shop of New Orleans, for the building and repairing of vessels. It has its dry docks, and other facilities for the most extensive operations. In business times, it presents a scene of activity that is seldom observed in any other part of these regions, and reminds one of the bustling and enterprise of the North.

THE FORT ST. PHILIP CANAL.

The Mississippi river has three principal outlet channels. They are the pass l'Outre, N.E., S.E., South, and West passes. Of these passes, the Southwest, is most used by vessels of the deepest draught, and this channel has been for two years past kept at a depth of 19½ feet by dredge boats, built and worked at the expense of the Federal Government. One vessel drawing 22 feet has entered the channel during the past season (1872). The navigation is, however, deemed precarious, and demands a more permanent outlet. Soundings at the mouth of the navigable channels of the Mississippi, run back for a century and a half, and show a bar of from one to two thousand feet across, with depth of from eleven to thirteen feet on the bars. It is the regimen of the river essential to regulations of its current. This depth on the bar continues though the bar itself advances annually into the gulf—the bar and outlet being over twelve miles lower down than it was a century and a half ago, while the water above the bar is from 40 to 50 feet deep. With this perpetual tendency to obstruction, the suspension of the dredge for even a short period allows the channel to fill, so that there has been at one time a number of ships loaded with cotton and other merchandise stranded on these bars, to the great detriment of the city and shipping interest. These obstacles long since led to scientific discussions, as to the best means of relieving navigation. Experiments and estimates were made for concentrating the current by wing dams, and caissons, lightering vessels, by canals and dredging. About the year 1832, Mr. Buisson, a civil engineer in the service of Louisiana, proposed to flank the passes by a ship canal leading from the river at a point about 27 miles above its mouth, into a deep water harbor in the gulf, a distance of seven miles. The studies and estimates of Mr. Buisson were adopted by the Legislature of Louisiana and Congress was asked to cause an examination of the practicability and cost of the work. A report was made by the topographical Bureau in 1837, expressing his opinion that the canal could be built at a cost of $10,000,000. This was an impossible sum at that period, and the prospect fell. About the year 1858-59, Mr. Montagu, a civil engineer, renewed the proposals, fortified by a re-survey and estimates, and proposed the formation of a joint stock company to construct the work and conduct the trade, for a compensation to be collected from tolls on the commercial tonnage. This plan, favored by the Insurances offices and the Chamber of Commerce, was prevented by the war, but was renewed in an application to Congress for a survey, and appropriations to construct the canal as a national ship canal, open in free passage to all vessels. The aggregate endowments mentioned were confirmed by a survey, made by the Federal government in 1871-72, with an estimate of cost at $6,000,000. A bill has been printed for this object at the present session of Congress. All the Western cities favor this work, and the National Board of Trade at its New York session, unanimously recommended its construction.

The permanent deepening of this outlet has assumed

P. F. HERWIG, ESQ.,

DEPUTY COLLECTOR.

OFFICE OF THE

LOUISIANA STATE LOTTERY COMPANY,

Corner of St. Charles and Union Streets,

NEW ORLEANS.

new importance, since the immense increase in the production of corn in the States so distant from the sea board. From the western verge of this cereal area, it now costs from fifty-five to sixty cents to place a bushel in the markets of Europe. This leaves so small a balance to the credit of the cultivator, that corn is not worth in Iowa more than twenty cents a bushel. In some cases it has come to be used in the place of fuel. This cost of transportation is increased by the great quantity of corn sent forward just before and just after the ice blockade, it being greatly in excess of the motion stock. At this point the Mississippi affords a way always open and always adequate to this immense commerce. It thus becomes a regulator of freight on other waters. Now, as the rate of freight is always proportioned to the capacity of the ocean-vessel, it is plain that with a depth of thirty-five feet, proposed to be given by the outlet, canal vessels of such burden could be put in the bulk grain trade, as would carry from 90 to 100,000 bushels. The reduction of freight resulting from this enlargement of vehicles, would extend the cereal productions much further west, and add a value to the material domain much greater than the cost of the work, necessary to effect it.

As a general proposition; the outlet to 850,000 square miles, occupied by little less that 20,000,000 of people, and producing $2,000,000 annually, should be opened without regard to cost. It may be remarked that it is the only obstruction to the principal navigable waters of the Mississippi, which remain to be provided for by the government. The Des Moines Rapids, the Falls of the Ohio and the Muscle Shoals of the Tennessee, being all completed or under construction.

The outlet canal completed, this noble river will be thrown open to commerce from its mouth, along its whole navigable courses, free from natural obstacles or tolls. In this result the whole Union is interested.

NAPOLEON JOSEPH PERCHÉ,

ARCH-BISHOP OF NEW ORLEANS.

ONE of the most disastrous draw-backs of biographical literature is, that the individuals, who most prominently figure in it, are precisely those who have done the least good or the most harm to humanity. The world's real benefactors have a peculiar secret in which they wrap themselves, just as if they were ashamed even of the treachery of effects in betraying them as their cause. To this modest but truly illustrious class of men, the subject of this sketch belongs, and, in our succinct notice of his beneficent career, we here assert, unhesitatingly, that he occupies in it no secondary place.

Napoleon Joseph Perché was born of pious and honorable parents at Angers, the capitol of the Department of Maerie-et-Soire, formerly called Anjou, on the 10th of January, in the year 1806. He was educated in the same city and in colleges of the vicinity; was ordained priest in 1829; came to the United States in 1837; was four years in the Missions of Kentucky; came to New Orleans in January, 1842; remained as Chaplain to the Nuns of the Ursuline Convent till 1870, when he was appointed Coadjutor to Arch-bishop Odin *cum jure successionis;* was consecrated on the 1st of May of the same year; at the death of Arch-bishop Odin, succeeded him, and received the *pallium* from his Holiness, Pius IX., in December, 1870.

Arch-bishop Perché is largely identified with the history of religion and religious institutions, both in France and America, during the present century. The developments of his powerful intellect appeared at a very early period of his life. He read the French language with facility at four years of age. At fifteen, he studied philosophy with enthusiasm. At eighteen, he was promoted to a Professorship of it, and wore its mantle with grace and dignity. He is equally distinguished as a divine and a canonist. In the former august character, he writes French unction with intellectual vigor in the highest degree.

We do not know for which to admire this great man most, the paternity which he displays in the sphere of parochial and diocesan duty, or the championship he exhibits in the conduct of theological arguments. The characteristic traits of his genius are amenity and force.

He thinks for a whole community, and his affections are as diffusive as his thoughts. He understands the power exerted, in a free country, by the press as well as the pulpit, and has, for many years, been at the head of a catholic press in this city (which is his own property), and which has exerted immense influence. He is a charming conversationalist, always bringing wit, learning, good humor, knowledge of the world, and a varied experience to embellish his discourse.

Though a Frenchman by nativity, he is thoroughly identified with America and her institutions, and has attained to the mastery of a pure, forcible and elegant English style, which places him in the front rank of American writers. Nothing can be more finished than the Archiepiscopal letters which he, from time to time, communicates, when the condition of the Church requires it, to the numerous parishes in his diocese, and which, by all liberal and discriminating men outside of the Catholic church, as well as within its circles, are nearly equally admired, not only for their literary execution, but for the genial and apostolic tone which pervades them.

In looking through the annals of this time-honored Church for representative men, we find that there is one individual whom Arch-bishop Perché strongly resembles—we allude to Leo Tenth, who, to the manner and refinement of a polished gentleman, added the impressive carriage of a dignified ecclesiastic, equally cognizant of the affairs of the world and of the Church. We believe his Grace is on terms of excellent understanding with Pius Ninth, the Catholic Head of Christendom, whom he visited at Rome during his recent troubles, and that there is no dignitary of the Church, in the United States, in whom his Holiness places more entire confidence for upholding its integrity, maintaining its unsullied honor, and securing its triumphs over its enemies, than Arch-bishop Perché.

JOHN DAVIDSON, ESQ.

JOHN DAVIDSON, the subject of this memoir, was the eldest son of James Davidson, of Dundee, Scotland, at which place John was born, on the 13th of December, 1816. His father emigrated to this country, in the year 1818, and settled at Monticello, in the State of New York. After an unsatisfactory trial of farming, he determined to embark in the slate business, in the city of New York; and for that purpose, made his home anew in that wonderful centre of industry, wealth and enterprise. It was there, amid the excitements and energy of the most rapidly developing emporium of the world, that the childhood and youth of our subject was passed. It was there, under those influences, that his character, which was afterward so distinguished by earnestness, energy, and practical judgment, was formed.

He received a good grammar-school education, and, at an early age, became connected with his father in business. It was not long before his intelligence, strict reliability and indefatigable industry made him complete master of that business, and placed upon his young shoulders the responsibility of its management.

At the age of twenty-two years, when most young men are commencing life, he left New York, and came to our sister city, Mobile, a complete business man. Mr. John Lyall, whose death has been so recently recorded, and who was so universally respected in this community, was then actively engaged here in the importation of slates. He was an intimate and old friend of the Davidson family, and had formed for young Davidson a strong friendship, which, as it was founded on respect for his real sterling merit, lasted through his entire life.

Mr. Davidson visited this city soon after he reached Mobile, and, in fulfilment of a promise made years before, called to see Mr. Lyall, and laid before him the plans and purposes of his opening career in the sunny South. The result was the immediate formation of a partnership between them, and thus commenced the history of a commercial firm whose standing and credit has never been surpassed in this busy mart of commerce. None of our old merchants will need an introduction to the firm of Lyall & Davidson. The story of their success and rapid growth in wealth, is inter-woven with the commercial history of the State. They were engaged, from 1839, when the partnership was formed, in the importation of slates from the quarries of Wales, and supplied, to a large extent, the whole southern market, and, indeed, the whole country bordering upon the Mississippi river, until 1850, when John Lyall retired from the firm with handsome capital, which he embarked in sugar planting on Bayou Lafourche. He was succeeded by James C. Davidson, a younger, and only, brother of John Davidson, and the style of the firm was then changed to J. & J. C. Davidson. From 1850 to the commencement of the war in 1861, the career of the new firm was one of unparalleled success in that line of business—yielding immense profits and rapidly enriching both partners. Their importations amounted to over two-thirds of the entire importations to the United States. This business was conducted and developed by their good judgment and clear business sense. By well-directed movements and combinations, coupled with perfect mercantile reliability, they succeeded in bringing to New Orleans almost the entire control of this most valuable trade; thereby not only enriching themselves, and adding largely to the prosperity of the state, but at the same time setting an example, in the imitation of which by our people the material prosperity of Louisiana may yet be greatly enhanced.

The practical character of Mr. Davidson led him to make the safest investments of his capital, and, when the recent war commenced, it found him the owner of an immense amount of real property in and around New Orleans. He also had a large planting interest in the adjoining parish of St. Bernard. He suffered severely from the war. His property was taken possession of by the federal forces and large assessments laid upon him by the commanding officers of the Union army on account of his known sympathies with the confederate cause. He lost a large negro property, and was compelled to abandon his business during the occupancy of the city by the federal forces; but, such was the good sense displayed by the investment of his means, that, at the close of the war, he was still a man of large wealth.

So soon as he could make his arrangements to recommence business, his brother having retired, he formed a partnership with his nephew, Col. James D. Hill, a gallant and highly distinguished young officer of the confederate army, and the business of the firm was resumed under the style of J. Davidson & Hill. On the third day of January, 1872, his life, which had been a singularly useful and happy one, was brought to a sudden close by one of the most shocking calamities that ever startled this community. He was driving, in his buggy, upon the streets of New Orleans in the forenoon of the day, when he was most unexpectedly overtaken by a dummy-engine, drawing freight cars through the city, and, in attempting to escape from the perilous situation in which he was placed, jumped from the buggy and fell. He was struck by some portion of the train and so severely injured that death quickly ensued.

He was a member of the Presbyterian church. By a strange coincidence, one year from the day of his funeral services were conducted by Rev. Dr. Palmer, a like solemn duty was performed by the same divine over the remains of Mr. Lyall, who had died while visiting his old partner's homestead and family in the city of New Orleans.

His strongly marked qualities, both of head and heart, had made a deep impression upon the people of this city, and the news of his death was received everywhere, and by all classes, with unfeigned sorrow. The death of such a man at such a time, was indeed a public calamity. He not only possessed large means, but was full of enterprise, and, up to the last day of his life, was earnestly engaged in pushing forward every project which promised relief to our suffering people. There was nothing little or contracted about him. His views, upon all subjects of public interest, were broad and enlightened, and he never refused to embark his means freely in reasonable ventures for the

LAKE PROTECTION LEVEE.

restoration of our lost prosperity. He gave his time and counsel, without stint, upon all important public committees, and although for years before his death an invalid, yet he never failed to appear with punctuality at the council board of our various public institutions with which he was connected. But the supreme virtue of his character, to those who knew him best, was the loveliness of his private life. At home, he was the centre of happiness in a family circle of more than ordinary attractiveness. He was always cheerful, and, though by nature painfully sensitive, he bore all the vexations incident to such an active life as his was, with a quiet patience and gentleness which diffused around him a spirit of contentment. Such a man was John Davidson, and our country would be happier far if there were more such characters to delineate.

H. C. CASTELLANOS.

This eloquent criminal lawyer was born in New Orleans on the 12th of December, 1827.

He was educated at Georgetown College (D. C.) and at St. Mary's, Baltimore, where he graduated with the degree of Bachelor of Arts, in 1847.

In 1848 he was admitted to the bar of New Orleans, and belonged to the first class of graduates in the University of Louisiana, his classmates being George Eustis, D. C. Labatt, Peniston and others.

At the age of twenty-four, he was elected delegate to the Constitutional Convention of 1852.

He was Editor of the "Louisiana Courier," of the "New Orleans Delta" and the founder of the "Attakapas Register.

As a criminal lawyer it is conceded that he has not a superior in the State.

JAMES McCONNELL.

This accomplished lawyer and worthy gentleman, is a native of Louisiana. He was educated at Washington College, Penn., and is a graduate of the Law Department of the University of Louisiana, having begun the practice of the law in this city in 1852.

During the late war he served as a Lieutenant in the First Regiment Louisiana Heavy Artillery.

He also served in the Legislatures of 1866 and '67.

Devoted entirely to the practice of his profession, in which he has attained success, he eschews politics and is quite popular.

Mr. McConnell is a vigorous speaker. The character of his argument is more of the solid and sensible than of the sensational and can be relied on usually. He has a noble heart located in the right place.

The education of youth is of the utmost importance to a country—especially to one like this, that should be governed by the intelligence of its citizens. The portals to learning should be thrown wide open, equally to all—for upon knowledge is based the beautiful temple of liberty. Tear away this foundation and the fair edifice must fall.

GEN. ALBERT G. BLANCHARD.

General Blanchard, a distinguished Civil Engineer of this city, graduated at the West Point Military Academy, in the year 1829, in the 3d United States Infantry. In 1832, he married Miss Susan T. Thompson, from whom descended two children, a son, the Rev. H. Blanchard, of Lowell, and Mrs. S. B. Elder, one of our most popular Southern poets, known as "Hermine."

He married, a second time, Mademoiselle Herminie Benoist la Salle, from whom descended fifteen children, some of whom are living.

General Blanchard left the Army in 1840, and engaged in commerce until 1846, during which time he was an efficient Director of the Public Schools of New Orleans.

In 1846, he entered the Army as Captain of the 2nd Regiment of Louisiana Volunteers and went to Mexico. On the disbanding of General Smith's Brigade, he raised a company, called the Phœnix Company of Louisiana, served as the representative of Louisiana at the storming of Monterey and was complimented in General Orders, and subsequently at the siege of Vera Cruz, where the company was mustered out, their time having expired. He was then appointed Captain of Voltigeurs, which post he declined, but accepted that of Major of the 12th United States Infantry, in which capacity he served till the close of the war.

Returning to civil life, he became a teacher in the Public Schools, and was elected District Surveyor of Municipality No. 2, and Surveyor, on the death of G. T. Dunbar, Esq., who had previously occupied that position. He was subsequently, elected Deputy Surveyor of the City of New Orleans, and filled the place until the year 1854.

He is a Fellow, and was one of the original founders of the New Orleans Academy of Sciences.

From 1854, to 1861, he was Secretary and Manager of the Carrollton Railroad Company.

In 1861, on the occurrence of the late war was elected Colonel of the 1st Confederate Regiment from Louisiana, and went to Virginia. In September 1861, he was promoted to the office of Brigadier General, served through the war in Virginia, Louisiana, South Carolina and North Carolina, being in the last great battle of the war at Bentonsville, North Carolina.

Since then, he has been directly engaged in engineering on the Opelousas Railroad and the City Railroads, and in the City Surveyor's Department as Deputy Surveyor.

None of our citizens has led a life of more activity and usefulness than General Blanchard. Equally noted in military and civil life, he will never fail to be mentioned as one who has done the State good service, and his works and the shining record of them, are of a character to resist the corroding influence of Time. Of unobtrusive manners, his sole ambition seems to have been to perform all the duties devolving on him as the head of a family, a private citizen, and a member of the Commonwealth, constantly employed in the Public Service. His habits of temperance have preserved his health and strength, and, though past the prime of life, he is ready for any enterprise, and capable of any.

PROFESSOR GREGORIO CURTO.

Professor Gregorio Curto is, we believe, the oldest teacher of musical composition and singing now living in New Orleans, where he arrived in 1820, and where he has resided uninterruptedly ever since. Mr. Curto is a native of Spain, but received his musical education in Paris, where he was admitted at a very early age into the celebrated Singing School of Choron, and had for his fellow pupils Dupray, Mompou, Scudo, Marié, Rosina Stoltz, and a host of other musical and artistic celebrities. In one of his most charming *feuilletons*, published about fifteen years ago, Scudo relates a visit paid by Choron to the Minister of the Household (under whose superintendence all artistic and operatic matters were then placed), in company with three of his favorite pupils, his object being to give to that official a practical demonstration of the efficiency and success of his method of teaching. The Duke De Larochefoucauld, the then Minister, was a man of taste and artistic accomplishments, and so well pleased was he with the performances of Choron's pupils that he forthwith granted a liberal appropriation for the support of the school. Young Curto was one of the scholars who figured upon the occasion, Dupray and Scudo completing the trio. Before he had completed his fourteenth year, Mr. Curto received the appointment of organist of the Cathedral of Soissons, which he relinquished one year later to resume the study of musical composition with his old teacher, Choron, acting at the same time as "Maitre de Chapelle" at the church of the "Sorbonne," then a favorite place of worship for the Parisian *beau monde*. In 1830, Mr. Curto made a highly successful *debut* at the Italian Opera in Rossini's "Gazza Ladra," and shortly after was engaged as *primo basso cantante* by Mr. Davis, then manager of the Orleans Theatre. In this capacity Mr. Curto remained here for two seasons, performing with great success in "La Dame Blanche," "L'Italiana in Algieri," "Anna Bolina," the "Huguenots," and also acting occasionally in Racine and Corneille's classical pieces, in connection with the distinguished *tragedienne*, Madame Clozel, whom he subsequently married. In 1835, Mr. Curto left the stage to devote himself entirely to teaching and musical composition. Of his very great success as a teacher of vocal music no better proof is needed than the fact that two of his pupils, Mlle. Minnie Hauck and Mme. Fleury Urban have already achieved a European reputation, and that another one, Mme. Durand Hitchcock, bids fair to obtain very soon a no less enviable position as a lyrical artist. As a composer, Mr. Curto has written many operas and oratorios, several of which have been performed with great success in this country and in Europe. Among the latter may be cited "Le nouvel Ermite," three acts, performed in 1852; "Amour et Folie," three acts (1853); "Sardanapale," two acts and three tableaux (1848); "L'Héritière," two acts; "La Mort de Jeanne D'Arc," two acts; "Le Lepreux," a dramatic scene, the words by Placide Canonge, and "La Mort d'Abel," oratorio, composed in 1866. We would exceed the limits of this sketch were we to enumerate Mr. Curto's church music, in which we find three Stabats, one intended exclusively for female voices, over fifty Masses, ten of which have been published, and more than two hundred motets, solos, duetts, trios, quintettes, etc. His Stabat No. 1 was lately performed with great success at the church of St. Eustache in Paris, and his grand Mass of the Immaculate Conception, with full orchestra, was repeated three times in the same church. Professor Curto is the organist of St. Anne's Church, on St. Philip street, and still devotes a portion of his time to a select class of pupils who have prevailed upon him to give them the benefit of his invaluable services as a teacher of vocal music. As a master of this art, Mr. Curto occupies a very high rank in this country, and as far as this city is concerned, there is no one, with the single exception of Mr. Eugene Prévost, who can dispute the palm with him as a professor and composer.

NAPIER BARTLETT, ESQ.

Mr. Napier Bartlett for many years connected with the press of this city, and now the proprietor of the *Claiborne Advocate*, may be said to have inherited the editorial. His father, Myron Bartlett, established, fifty years ago, the Macon *Telegraph*, at the present day one of the most prosperous in Georgia, and his uncle, Cosam Emir Bartlett, is spoken of in "Sparks' Fifty Years' Recollections" as the leader of his party in that State.

Mr. Napier Bartlett graduated at Andover, Mass., in 1854, and had for his fellow students Edwin L. Jewell, Tobias Gibson, and many other Southern youth, who have since obtained honorable preeminence. His first essay as an editor, was in connection with a paper then published by a literary society, and to the management of which he was elected by his classmates.

After being admitted to the bar in Georgia, and graduating in the Law Department of the University of Louisiana, Mr. Bartlett published the *Atlanta Confederacy*, two years before the name was applied to the seceded States, and was, for a short time, connected with the *Atlanta Intelligencer*.

Having fixed his abode in New Orleans a short time before the war, he contributed to the *Crescent* a number of stories and sketches, and upon the breaking out of hostilities a number of letters from camp, which were extensively copied. He went out as a volunteer in the Washington Artillery, a batallion made up of the best young men of the city, and remained with it until the close of the war. A reminiscence of army life in Virginia still remains in a story which was written on the straw of a soldier's tent, under the name of "Clarimonde."

Since the war Mr. Bartlett has been successively connected with the *Southern Star*, *Crescent*, *Bulletin*, and New Orleans *Times*. Besides the work before mentioned he is the author of stories of the "Crescent City," the entire edition of which was almost entirely sold the first week of its publication. A more extended work of a somewhat similar character will shortly appear from his pen.

LOUISIANA COTTON MANUFACTORY.

The Louisiana Cotton Manufacturing Company was formed in 1869. The mill is near the Barracks, about three miles from Canal street, fronting (216 feet) on the Levee, the premises comprising about six acres on which the company propose to build houses for one hundred and fifty operatives. The capital of the company is $250,000 and over $100,000 is paid up. The mill runs about sixty looms and 3360 spindles. The fine machinery is from the works of Curtis, Parr, & Morley, Manchester, England. The operatives are all white, being chiefly creoles from Third District, who have proved to be excellent in industry and fidelity, and of more than average aptitude in learning difficult processes. At fair remuneration the supply exceeds the demand, and the poorer white people in the lower portion of the city are partial to the new industry that is here opened to them.

Although the products of this mill are comparatively small, the experiment has proved that cotton can be successfully spun and woven near to the place of production, thus avoiding compression, freights, duties, interest, commission, and risks by sea and land. The fabrics of this mill are in demand in this city, and have already gained favorable notice in Western trade centres. The Company readily sell all they make at paying rates, and for cash. The affairs of the Company are controlled and regulated by W. T. Hepp, L. Folger, F. Gueydan, M. A. de Lizardi, and J. C. Denis, who constitute the Board of Directors. The officers of the Company are: J. C. Denis, President; George Perrilliat, Secretary and H. V. Meigs, Superintendent.

For want of sufficient capital the operations of the Factory have been somewhat limited—but a reorganization of the Company with ample funds is contemplated.

DR. WILLIAM NEWTON MERCER,

Who now resides on Canal street, in this city, at the advanced age of eighty-one, is one of the most venerated and beloved of our citizens. His name has long been regarded as the epitome of benevolence, kind-heartedness, of genial hospitality, and refined learning and manners.

With these qualities he combines excellent judgment and good knowledge of men—a well-trained intellect, large information, and admirable powers of administration.

To this rare combination, Dr. Mercer owes his great success, and the accumulation of the large fortune which he now enjoys, and from which he derives the means of his highest enjoyment in life, that of relieving the wants and alleviating the distresses of the unfortunate, and promoting meritorious enterprises of Religion, Benevolence and Education.

Dr. Mercer was born in Cecil County, Maryland. He received a good education, and attended the course of lectures at the University at Pennsylvania, when Dr. Rush was principal professor at that institution. Graduating with distinction, he received the commission of Assistant-Surgeon in the regular army, about the beginning of the war with England, in 1812.

In this position Dr. Mercer served with great credit. The only action of the war in which he took active part was at the disastrous fight, or rather race, at Bladensburg, when the raw militia which had been hastily gathered for the defence of the National Capitol was so quickly put to flight by the Peninsular veterans, under General Ross. The only fighting done on that occasion was by Captain Barney, of Baltimore, with a small force of sailors and marines, and a few pieces of artillery. This little detachment held the British army at bay for some time, and only yielded their position when overrun by an overwhelming force, and their gallant commander was shot down at his post. Dr. Mercer was attached to that command, and bravely and faithfully performed his duty.

After the close of the war, Dr. Mercer remained in the army, and came, with a portion of it to this city, as a Post-Surgeon. This was in 1816. After remaining here for a short time, he was transferred to Natchez, Mississippi, where he resided for some years. At this time Natchez was a very important town—and its society was of a very distinguished character. The rapidly-increasing wealth of the cotton planters, and the attractive prospects of this commanding position in the south-west, had drawn thither a number of men from the old States of marked characteristics.

Then was laid the foundation of what was well known throughout the country as the Adams County Aristocracy. It was in this society Dr. Mercer obtained admission, through his gentlemanly bearing, refined and dignified deportment, and his many admirable and genial habits. He soon became a great favorite with all persons, especially with the ladies, who were always won by his graceful gallantry and playful wit. Among the gentlemen, the Doctor was regarded as first, on this account with some slight jealousy. This, and his freedom from the vices and dissipations, then quite prevalent in that section, led them to regard him as more of a beau and ladies' man, than was compatible with the manly qualities of the age. But this idea proved a delusion, the doctor's courage and power of will, were quite as conspicuous, when occasion demanded their exercise, as were his courtly ease and amiability of manners and deportment.

These virile virtues were not displayed in physical combats, or in deeds of violence, and indistinctiveness so common in the south-west, but in the higher forms of an immovable firmness in every duty, a tenacity in the maintenance of his convictions, and rights, and fearless intrepidity in the defences and relief of the oppressed and the unfortunate.

A striking example of this was related to the writer, by the late Robert Walker, who was for many years a distinguished citizen of Natchez. It happened that a large and brilliant company had assembled at one of the fashionable summer resorts in East Mississippi. A number of Natchez families were included in this company. One day there was an alarm, a cry of distress, a call for a doctor. Dr. Mercer, who happened to be in attendance, repaired to the spot, and there found a crowd, surrounding a negro boy, a slave of one of the families sojourning at the resort; the boy was in an agony of fright and pain, and the spectators were all in wild panic what to do. The poor boy had been badly bitten by that most poisonous of snakes, the copperhead moccasin. Gently waving aside the helpless crowd, Dr. Mercer quickly examined the wound, drew from his pockets his surgical instruments, scarified it, and then applying his lips to it, sucked out the poison. The boy recovered, never experiencing any effect from the poison.

For a gentleman of such fastidious refinement and elegance as to incur the suspicion of effeminacy from his ruder and more boisterous contemporaries, this action of Dr. Mercer was justly regarded by the fair sex as one of the highest manifestations of real courage, such as is prompted by the triumph of true benevolence and philantrophy over the love of self—of an utter insensibility to danger in discharge of duty to suffering humanity.

These, and like incidents in Dr. Mercer's career, at Natchez, quickly dissipated the erroneous impressions in regard to his true character. It was discovered that whilst the most benevolent and most amiable of men, he was also, one of the finest, most positive and consistent.

An amusing illustration was given of this, when, during one of those spasmodic efforts, which used to characterize the legislation of the Southern States, a severe militia law was passed in Mississippi.

This law required frequent parades, provided for a thorough organization of the citizens into battallions and companies, who should elect their own officers, and that said officers should call out their companies, whenever they deemed it necessary, and should subject them to a thorough drill.

Under this law one of the companies, composed of the wealthy and aristocratic citizens of Natchez, thought it a happy practical joke to elect, as their captain, the courtly and elegant ex-surgeon of the army; Dr. Mercer had resigned his commission in the army sometime before. Great was their surprise when they were assured by the doctor of his high appreciation of the honor conferred on him. And they were still more surprised when the doctor, buckling on his sword, and donning his epaulets, entered upon the duties of his command, and with such vigor and earnestness, that they quickly discovered that the joke had been turned on the engineers. There never was so unhappy a militia as that of Dr. Mercer's became, under his command. The frequency and severity of the drilling to which he subjected them, the pertinacity with which he marched them in the hot sun, and through the streets of Natchez, the vigor with which the fines were imposed and collected, and the general severity of his discipline produced so profound a disgust with themselves and the law, which their commander had so faithfully carried out, that petitions were got up and dispatched to Jackson for the immediate repeal of the law.

Dr. Mercer pursued his practice for some years in Natchez with great success. Marrying into one of the oldest families of the State, he found himself charged with the responsibility of administering a large cotton plantation. It was in the execution of this trust that the admirable administrative abilities of Dr. Mercer were displayed. His good sense, clear and practical views of financial management, and promptitude and firmness in all his transactions, rendered him one of the most successful planters in the South.

By a firm adherence to certain simple rules of management, and apparently without an effort, the estate of his wife was rapidly increased in value and productiveness. And, when her lamented decease occurred, a large fortune had been accumulated, mainly through the judicious management of Dr. Mercer.

The death of his wife clouded the remainder of Dr. Mercer's life—and some years afterwards the loss of his only daughter, just entering womanhood, and adorned with all amiable and attractive qualities of her sex, completed the cycle of his domestic calamities, and condemned him to long years of sorrowing and melancholy.

Even now, in his extreme age, the afflictions give a painfully perceptible tinge of melancholy and of conscious bereavement to the expression of his noble countenance, showing that his thoughts and memory have never been relieved of the heavy burden of grief, which fell upon him so many years ago.

Shortly after the death of his wife, Dr. Mercer removed to this city, and has resided here continually for nearly thirty years. Erecting an elegant residence on Canal street, and investing largely in this city, he has led the life of a retired gentleman, dispensing a most elegant hospitality, and enjoying himself in acts of charity of the most liberal and generous character.

The characteristic of Dr. Mercer's contributions to the relief and aid of humanity, has been the modesty with which they have been dispensed. A shrinking from all notoriety or ostentation, a desire "to do good by stealth," has been his chief ambition in life. His charity has been directed by the suggestion and emanations of his own mind and heart, rather than from concession to the demands or solicitations of others. It would not be appropriate here during the life of this modest old gentleman to refer to the various incidents of his life illustrative of this quality of his benevolence. But there is one of those which has already gained a place in history to which we may be excused, for referring. It relates to that affecting incident in the life of Henry Clay, when that great man, having served his country for more than a quarter of a century, returned to his home to find that his financial affairs, having been so long neglected, had fallen into a condition verging on bankruptcy. A note for a large sum held by the bank in Lexington was rapidly approaching maturity. It was impossible to meet this and his other liabilities.

If it were not renewed, but pressed for payment, it would involve the sale of his homestead. This was a very distressing circumstance for the great statesman. It may be imagined with what chagrin and distress the proud man proceeded to the bank on the day when the debt became due, to solicit its extension, to do that which, to Henry Clay, was one of the hardest of all sacrifices and struggles, to solicit a favor from men whom he looked down upon as his inferiors in all the claims and attributes of greatness and illustrious public service.

Imagine the surprise, the relief and the joy of the old gentleman, when, on applying at the bank for the renewal of his note, he was informed that it had been paid, and the cancelled instalment was handed to him.

It is said that the proud old man burst into tears at this announcement, and exclaiming, "Well, I must have some true friends after all," retired to his home, and his own reflections. No inquiry, however, could elicit the information as to the generous friend who had rendered him this great and timely aid, and thus smoothed and brightened the declining years of the great Kentuckian. We imagine, however, that his sagacity and knowledge of the character and of the affection so long manifested for him by his old friend with whom he had passed so many agreeable days in New Orleans, did not permit Mr. Clay to doubt who was that friend in need.

It was the timely intervention of Dr. Mercer, and his friend, Mr. Duncan, of Natchez, who had saved the great Kentuckian from the mortification and anxiety that threatened to darken his latter days, in his retirement from the active scenes of public life in which he had played so distinguished a part.

As we have said, we do not intend to repeat the many other instances of generous liberality and beneficence of this venerable gentleman. It would require a volume to narrate them all.

It was, however, especially during our civil war, that the sterling qualities, and courageous devotion to friends, to principle and duty, of Dr. Mercer were most conspicuously displayed. The doctor had earnestly opposed the secession movement. He was a warm, sincere and out-spoken Unionist. Unable to resist the impulse of the people to secession and civil war—but alway predicting its ultimate failure—he determined when war came upon us to share its calamities and burdens with his fellow citizens.

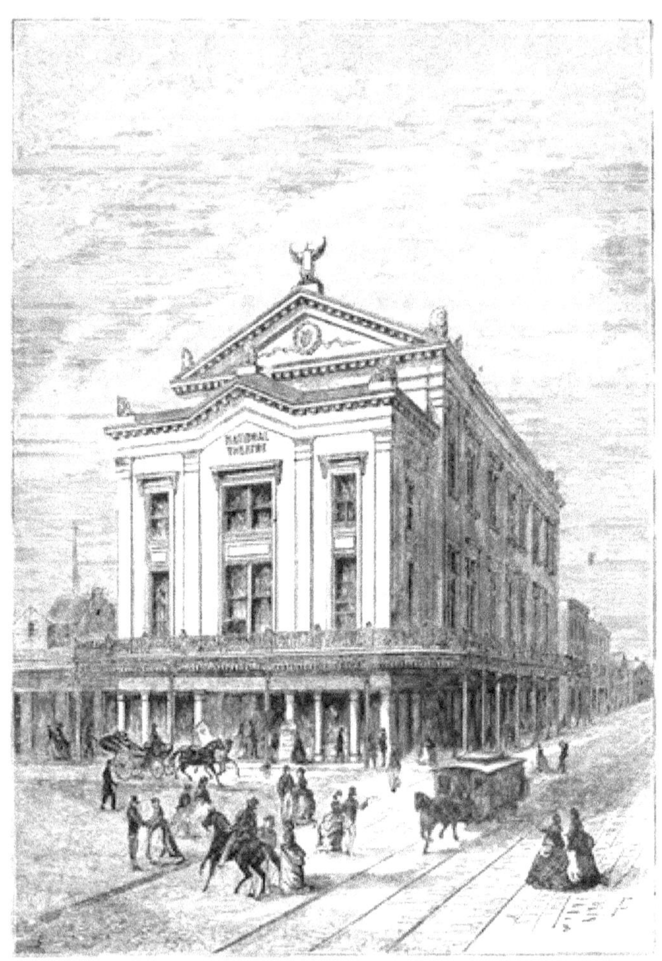

NATIONAL THEATRE,

Corner of Baronne and Perdido Streets, New Orleans.

As president of the most solid banks of the city, he favored the aid and support of the authorities, who were engaged in the defence of the State from invasion. To that object, he contributed largely from his private means. On the approach of the Federal army and fleet to the city, he recommended to the directory of the banks of which he was president, to pay its large specie deposit of over two millions of dollars to the depositors. This proposition was objected to by the State authorities, as hostile to the credit of the Confederacy.

It was determined by them that the specie of the banks should be removed into the Confederacy to place it beyond the reach of the invader. This measure or mandate was most reluctantly yielded to by the president and directors of the bank of Louisiana, and the whole two millions of gold which had long lain in the vaults, were now transferred into the interior, where, after many abortive attempts to procure its release, and to guard it from seizure and expropriation, the whole amount finally disappeared in that charm, which had swollowed up so many more millions of the wealth of the South.

When Butler occupied the city, and commenced his career of bullying and persecution of the people, he threatened vengeance against the bank president for snatching from him this valuable spoil. They were all ordered before him, to answer for their conduct.

When they appeared—they were all citizens of the highest repute and wealth—Butler favored them with some of his choicest democratic oratory, and with unbounded denunciation, as a set of bank robbers, who had betrayed their faith to their depositors and note-holders, and had thus perpetrated a double treason to their country and to the people who had entrusted them with their hard earnings. After a long harrangue, full of abuse and bitterness, he asked them what excuse they could give for their conduct. Several of the presidents offered various pleas; they had been coerced in the matter; they had always opposed this transfer, and they had already set on foot measures to have their specie returned. It was very perceptible that the worthy gentlemen were not a little alarmed by the threatening tone and manner of Butler. Dr. Mercer alone, remained unmoved, and maintained a dignified silence under the fierce oratorical blast of the unblushing demagogue. At last Butler turned to him and asked: "What have you, Dr. Mercer, a Union man, to say in justification of your conduct in this matter?"

"Nothing," replied the bland and brave old gentleman; "but to bear my share of the responsibility and penalty for the act."

Not a word was said of his own earnest opposition to the measure; no promise or pledge of reparation, no expression of regret or repentance, though of all present he might justly and honestly have availed himself of such pleas. It was not the time now, it would have been incompatible with true manhood, thus to separate himself from his associates in peril and misfortune. And so the doctor, not only maintained his self-respect, but managed to secure the confidence and admiration of Butler, who made vigorous efforts to win the confidence and regard of the brave but always courteous and dignified old gentleman.

It was due to this feeling of Butler toward Dr. Mercer, that the latter was enabled frequently to intervene in favor of his fellow citizens, who were subjected to the violent treatment of that officer, during the whole period of Butler's command in this city. Dr. Mercer was almost incessantly engaged in these acts of interposition and remonstrance against the hard orders and acts of the Federal General.

Finally, however, Butler became dissatisfied with the doctor. Of all our rich men, he alone refused to take the oath, which Butler required of all citizens, on the penalty of confiscation of all their property. If this oath were not taken by a certain day, the non-jurors were commanded to hand over the schedules of their property.

When that day arrived, Dr. Mercer walked to the office of the Provost Marshall, and duly delivered to him a complete list of all his large estate, retaining, as he stated, two thousand dollars in gold, for his necessities, which, however, he agreed to report to General Butler.

This adroit demagogue could not resist the opportunity for a display of his zeal for the Union, and his love of equal rights, and accordingly, he had published his letter refusing the doctor permission to retain this small sum referred to, stating that he, of all others, from his high position and great influence, over his fellow citizens, should set the example of a prompt renewal of his allegiance to this government.

It does not appear, however, that Butler intended anything more than to make a display before the people, for he never disturbed the doctor in the possession and enjoyment of this small remnant of his princely estate.

An incident, growing out of this event, may be here related as illustrative of the quiet humor and sharp repartee of Dr. Mercer. Shortly after the publication of the correspondence between Dr. Mercer and General Butler, the Dr. was taking his customary promenade on Canal street, when a hearty and robust young man, a native of the city, whose friends had been not a little mortified, that he should be absent from the scenes in which nearly all the able-bodied young men of the city were then playing their parts, saluting the doctor, inquired, jocosely, whether he had any of those two thousand gold dollars left.

"Oh! yes," quickly responded the doctor, "I have a small sum left, which I keep for a special purpose."

"May I inquire what that purpose is?"

"It is," whispered the doctor, looking around as if he intended to guard against Federal detectives, "to buy you a fine Confederate uniform."

Immovable in his purpose, the doctor remained in the city throughout the whole war, without taking the oath, or, as it was styled, renewing his allegiance.

But our sketch has extended beyond the limits we had prescribed, we must bring it to a close.

After the war, with a single interruption of a short visit to the North, Dr. Mercer has remained in New Orleans, a calm and philosophic, but not uninterested observer of passing events and characters; a great reader, not only of the current literature of the day, but of the works of the great English and French authors, and the dispenser of the most cordial and sumptuous hospitality.

By every class of the people he is looked up to with the most profound veneration, love and respect, as the model of the Southern gentleman, patriot, philanthropist and Christian, as, indeed, the single survivor of a generation, whose standard of virtue, of dignity, of refinement and honor, was far higher than that which has succeeded it.

NEW ORLEANS CHAMBER OF COMMERCE.

This institution was founded and incorporated February 26th, 1830. The charter was renewed for an additional term of twenty years, on the 25th of April, 1853. Its earlier labors were very useful, and the decisions of its committees of arbitration were published, and were of analogous authority in the business transactions of the merchants. Suspended by what the resolutions of reorganization calls "fortuitous circumstances," the members on the 17th of February, 1864, and renewed their organization, by the election of Charles Briggs, Esq., as President, and of A. C. Waugh, Esq., Secretary and Treasurer. From that time it has continued in active usefulness. Its membership has steadily increased, although not so great as the population and interests of the city would justify. In the midst of the political contest which has raged for the past six or seven years, the Chamber of Commerce has devoted itself by pressing good measures of legislation, and preventing others tending, in its opinion, to injuries, or retard the commercial interests of the city.

Among the most prominent of the measures advocated by the Chamber, may be mentioned the limitation of State debt by constitutional amendment. Advocacy of a railroad system, with an investigation into their progress, or cause of their delayed completion. Application for Federal aid in improving the Mississippi from its mouths to its outlet canal, levee reparation, and postal appropriations for establishing postal connections with foreign countries. Also for such amendment of our commercial treaties as will give greater intercourse with the States on the continent and Island, south of the United States. An amendment and explanation of the law of lien on property, and endorsement of a system of Industrial education in the South and for the South. Such are some of the measures which have been commended, and enforced upon public adoption by the many active and able merchants of New Orleans. To enumerate them would occupy too much space, and to designate any of them as especially effective would be invidious. It is proper to be said that for the patriotism, integrity and wisdom of its action, as well as in the confidence of their fellow citizens, the Chamber of New Orleans has a most respectable record. The present membership number more than two hundred, and its officers are Joseph H. Oglesby, President; J. M. Sandidge, Vice President; C. E. Slayback, Second Vice President; W. M. Burwell, Secretary and Treasurer. The Chamber holds its sessions on the 1st Monday of each month, in the hall over the Louisiana National Bank.

TWELFTH NIGHT REVELLERS.

FIRST FESTIVAL, 1871.

In the latter part of the year 1870, it was resolved by certain genial enterprising spirits in this city, to re-establish the ancient and honorable Festival of the 12th Night, so memorable in history.

It was found that these annual celebrations not only contributed to the public enjoyment, but, by giving the city a reputation for gorgeous public festivities, had the effect of drawing here that vast pleasure-seeking element, which is yearly becoming larger, and whose presence always acts as an impulse to every description of local business.

Accordingly, on the evening of the 6th of January, 1871, the initial pageant of the 12th Night Revelers made its appearance upon the streets.

Public curiosity had been greatly excited, and all the thoroughfares which were known to be included in the line of march, presented the spectacle of one dense mass of spectators.

The entire central district of the city, indeed, was one brilliant scene of life and gaiety. The whole population was in the streets, and, with the bright and balmy night, the gay throngs and the flashing lights, the *tout ensemble* was one which belongs only to New Orleans among American cities. When it was found that the pageant was to represent the familiar characters whom Mother Goose has made immortal, the delight of the spectators can be better imagined than described, and, as the costly, fantastic procession filed slowly by, each new tableau was greeted with shouts of enthusiastic recognition from the innumerable throng.

The pageant was headed by a grotesque and gorgeous figure with the title of the Lord of Misrule, who was followed in regular order by the characters who have been handed down to us in the old nursery rhymes of that mysterious poet Mother Goose.

We can not, perhaps, give a clearer idea of the nature of the procession and the elements which entered into its composition than by quoting the following clever verses which were written by a prominent member of the New Orleans press, one of the most versatile, piquant and brilliant of our writers, and on which the formation of the affair was based.

We will only premise that the representations were all gotten up in the most expensive and artistic style, and were aided by every accessory of color and illumination which it is possible to employ in such cases.

The poem itself is complete and perfect in construction, and although on the most familiar of subjects, is full of harmony, and will be read with pleasure by every one whose memories carry them back to the loving care of a mother and the innocent joys of childhood.

MOTHER GOOSE'S TEA PARTY.

I

Hink! minx! hink! my eyelids wink;
Marry I'll have a feast;
Since all were out at my last rout
Is many a year at last.

THOMAS O'CONNOR,

CHIEF OF FIRE DEPARTMENT

Accommodation Bank of Louisiana,

MASONIC HALL.

E. B. BENTON, PRESIDENT. R. H. WOOD, CASHIER.

INCORPORATED 1868.

CAPITAL, $200,000.

THIS BANK ALLOWS LIBERAL INTEREST ON DEPOSITS,

And advances MONEY in sums to suit on every species of Personal Property, Warehouse Receipts, Stocks, Bonds, Warrants, Gold, Silver, Diamonds, Furniture, Pianos, Merchandise, and Valuables of every description. Has large Warehouse and Store-rooms attached to the Bank.

The prating fools of modern schools
Would have me sound asleep :
'Tis time to call my children all
And give the world a peep.

So take the broom, sweep up the room
And then the table spread ;
We'll have one night as gay and bright
As any that have fled.

II

Wake Little Bo-peep, now fast asleep,
And rouse up Heart's good Queen ;
Bid Robin Hood from out the wood,
With his men in Lincoln green.

Bold Valentine, and Jack so fine,
Who cracked the Giant's pates,
To come with Spratt, who eat no fat,
And his wife who licked the plates.

Tell Jack and Gill, upon the hill,
And Humpty on the wall,
With Old King Cole, that good old soul,
They must obey the call.

III

We'll have a feast, where Beauty's Beast
Shall sup with Silver Hair,
Red Riding Hood and Orson good,
And Cinderella fair.

The children, too, who in the shoe,
Were all so poorly fed,
With Jenny Wren, and the little men,
Whose bullets were made of lead.

The summons sound till it shakes the ground,
So Fee-Faw-Fum may hear,
And Ogres come with Piper Tom,
To share our merry cheer.

IV

Quick, Saddle My Cock, hunt up the flock,
With a hop, step, jump away ;
Gather them all, both great and small,
Before the dawn of day.

There's Parson Rook, with solemn look,
Must bring young Johnny Grace.
Jack Horner too, with Buckle-my-Shoe,
Shall also have a place.

Nor maid forlorn, nor Crumple Horn,
Must either be passed by ;
Both girls and boys shall make a noise,
And sup on Blackbird Pie.

V

The fiddling Cat shall feed the Rat,
That quarrelled with the Frog ;
The Market Pig shall dance a Jig,
With Mother Hubbard's dog.

And Puss in Boots, in best of suits,
Shall pay Miss Muffet court ;
While Beanstone Jack rolls on his back,
With laughing at the sport.

Old Wondrous-Wise, with blinded eyes,
Shall mash Kriss-Kringle's corn ;
And Little Boy Blue, a hullabaloo,
Shall waken with his horn.

VI

Come out, come out, with song and shout,
Obey the grandame's call ;
To her bright eyes and golden skies,
We owe allegiance all.

The gems she wears distill no tears,
Her flowrets bloom for aye ;
Her castle walls and fairy halls,
Shall never pass away.

Like us who, back o'er life's dull track,
Our glance at Lapland throw ;
To hours of youth, to love and truth,
We never more may know.

SECOND ANNUAL FESTIVAL, 1872.

The second Festival of these unknown Revelers was a splendid effort. With a more perfected organization, and with increased expenditure, they came to the front, determined to out-do their former effort and realize the brilliant expectations which their many admirers had founded upon the inaugural ceremony of their order.

They could scarcely have chosen a better theme than

THE TIDE OF ENGLISH HUMOR.

In all the realm of literature there is no richer field than this; and our Revelers certainly culled its very fairest flowers as they wandered. Headed by Don Quixote (a pardonable theft from other lands) the pageant showed Humor, Its Gods, Its Fathers, Its Fountain, and Its Tide, in a splendid and harmonious sequence.

Shakespeare, Rare Ben Johnson, Gray, Swift, Sterne, Goldsmith, Burns, Scott, Irving, Dickens and Bret Harte!

These were figures which followed in the Tide of Humor; each one set in a group of his own choicest creations, and clustered with them on their respective pedestals rivaling in chiaroscuro splendor the majestic sculptures of Praxiteles himself.

In all the appointments of artistic elegance this display was considered as being yet unequalled. It was a daring flight into the realm of art, this attempt at marbleizing Humor, but the Revelers assuredly achieved a brilliant success.

The closing ceremonies, were, as on their first occasion, similar to those observed by the Mistick Krewe. There were two magnificent tableaux, representing

FIRST.

HUMOR'S PANTHEON.

"Above the smoke and stir of this dim spot which men call earth."

SECOND.

THE APOTHEOSIS OF HUMOR.

"The mob of gentlemen who wrote with ease."

After the falling of the curtain on the closing tableau the usual ball commenced in which the fashionable company joined, finding no less delight therein by reason of their ignorance of their Hosts.

THIRD ANNUAL FESTIVAL, 1878.

This year the Revelers carried their representations into a still more elevated field of literature speaking with reference to utility and intrinsic dignity. In doing so they paid a merited tribute to the greatest genius ever produced by Louisiana—

JOHN JAMES AUDUBON.

"That cheerful one who knoweth all,
"The songs of all the winged choristers,
And in one sequence of melodious sound,
Pours out their music."

It was a specially happy conceit of theirs that, while they reproduced the birds of Audubon with the most astonishing fidelity, and while each individual figure was perfectly true in plumage, proportions and coloring, to the original which it was intended to represent, yet these were grouped in tableaux which were in most instances deliciously humorous in their meaning.

It was a curious and an artistic accomplishment, and, in that sense the 12th Night Revelers exceeded any similar effort of theirs.

This magnificent pageant was composed of seventeen immense cars or floats, fifteen of which bore groups of from five to ten figures. They were brilliantly illuminated with lanterns, transparencies and calcium lights, which, together with the gaudy coloring of the birds themselves, and the continuous blaze from the houses along their route, combined to make, not only one of the largest, but one of the most magnificent and imposing displays ever known in the history of our Carnivals.

There was also a novel idea shown in the management of the tableau. Instead of having a multiplicity of representations, the figures of the entire pageant were grouped in one colossal picture.

In the centre, on a raised pedestal was the immense statuary, composed of

AUDUBON AND HIS TWO COMPANIONS,

and round about him were the numerous birds which had followed him in the procession.

There were water, and marsh, and rocks, and sand, and trees and undergrowth, in which the birds were disposed appropriately; thus making one grand tableau in which more than a hundred different contrasting figures were collected. The coup d'œil was inexpressibly striking, and when the curtain fell it was some time before the immense throng of spectators ceased their plaudits.

Thus, in a resumé of the past pageants which have made our city so famous over the whole continent, we cannot assert that anything in the past has exceeded this latest effort of the Revelers, all things considered.

It was in every sense a magnificent spectacle and it has proved that the Mistick Krewe have at last foemen worthy of their steel.

This chapter in the history of Revelry brings us up to the present day, when, if we may believe the mysterious hints which have been rife for weeks past, both Rex of the Carnival, and the Mistick Brotherhood of Comus intend to surpass all former displays.

THE BULK GRAIN TRADE.

THIS is comparatively a new commerce in the United States. It originated in Buffalo, upon the idea of applying the band and buckets employed by Oliver Evans in carrying grain and flour in a common flouring mill, and was adapted on a much larger scale as a means of handling cargoes.

Formerly, corn was received at New Orleans in the ear, shelled and sacked for sale. Wheat was exported in considerable quantities before the war, and, on some occasions, grain in quantity was shipped to Europe by sail, and sometimes received in such condition that it had to be dug out of the hole with the spade. The plantation demand for corn at New Orleans, which, even now, reaches 4 to 5,000,000 bushels per annum, was sufficient to consume the surplus by the then West, which, until within the past twenty years, converted its surplus corn into cattle, hogs, horses and whisky. The vast growth of the West from foreign emigration, and the opening of canal and lake outlets to the East, has given a consequence to the grain trade which was not originally contemplated.

In the year 1868, L. J. Higby, Esq., having been for some years engaged in the Lake grain trade at Milwaukie, came to the conclusion that the Mississippi was the natural route for western grain to the ocean. Perhaps one of his strongest reasons for the opinion was that the ice blockade usually closed up from 20 to 30,000,000 bushels of grain, and subjected the grower and dealer to shrinkage, interest and insurance, or to the exaction of the Eastern Railroads.

He accordingly prospected this channel, and was the first person that put money into it as a practical proposition. In this enterprise it was necessary to provide for two transfers.

St. Louis had built a Grain Elevator, but like the canoe of Robinson Crusoe, it was so far from the water, that it might have rotted down before it could be put to any use. This Elevator was, in the year 1860, and at the instance of Mr. Higby, brought into close connection by rail with the cars and shipping.

It was, however, in 1868 that pioneer of the bulk grain trade removed to New Orleans, purchased the ground, and erected the present Elevator, an illustration of which appears on another page of this work. He thus describes the installation and prosecution of the work in a letter to the Missouri "Democrat."

"After twelve days consultation in my own mind, I concluded to help New Orleans to a Grain Elevator—and make her the first grain mart in America. Consequently I brought my youngest son here, bought a block of land, built a wharf 275 feet long and 200 feet into the water, bought a steamboat, hauled her alongside, and made a boarding-house for ourselves and men, took off our coats on the first of June, and built an Elevator which is now, (25th December, 1868) able to hold and handle 120,000 bushels of grain in 24 hours. The building is 250 feet long, 100 feet wide, and 130 feet high, and will hold, when completed, 750,000 bushels of grain. The tower and Marine Elevator at the edge of the wharf is 102 feet high. The Marine Elevator is connected with the main elevator by a conveyor 33 feet high, and run-

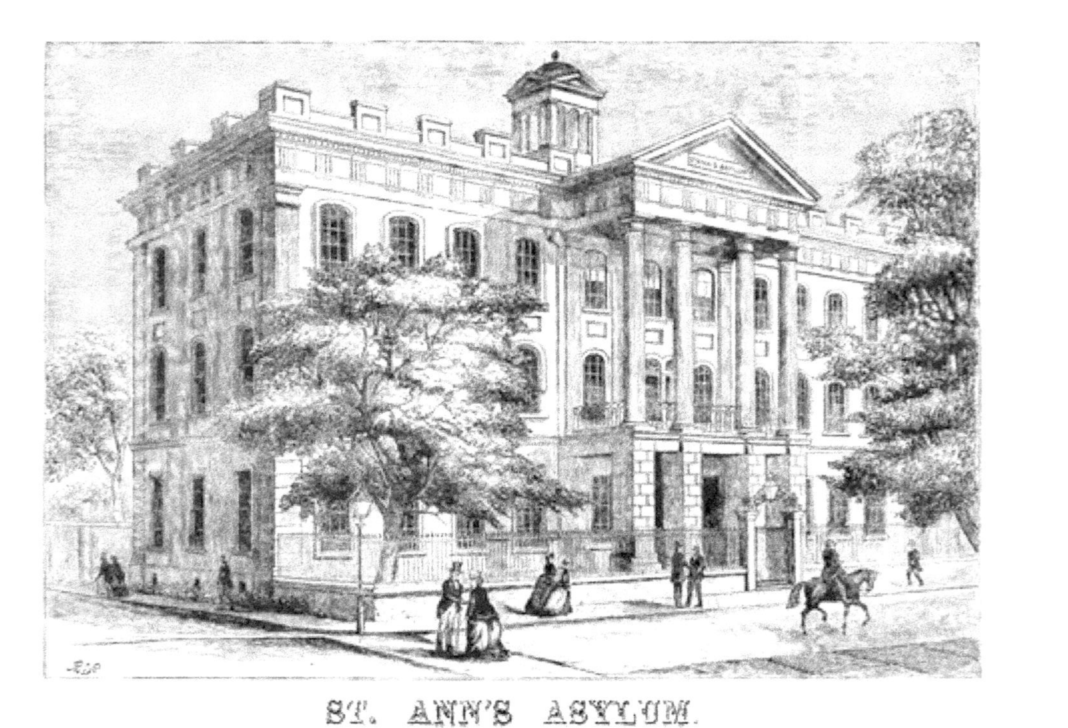

ST. ANN'S ASYLUM.

ning over the wharf and street. It is the only conveyor of the kind in America. The wharf Elevator can take grain out of a vessel at the highest or lowest water—there being a variation of 15 feet in the extreme stages. The wharf storage building is 200 by 275 feet, capable of storing 65,000 barrels of flour which can be loaded by machinery at the rate of 1,000 barrels per hour. The whole machinery is run by an engine of 500 horse power."

The enterprise of moving bulk grain by way of New Orleans was ridiculed by those who had not examined the subject, and especially by the Chicago Press. The "Times" said it would be as natural for Chicago to undertake the commerce of cotton, rice and sugar, as for New Orleans to control the grain of those high latitudes.

The St. Louis "Democrat," one of the earliest and staunchest advocates of the river grain trade, came to the rescue of New Orleans, and vindicated "De Bow's Review," from the imputation of having advocated an absurd proposition in maintaining the feasibility of the enterprise.

There was another imaginary impediment. All the Eastern interests maintained that grain could not be moved through the latitude of Louisiana without injury. Essays were written on the effects of humidity, and the temperature of the gulf stream was deemed fatal to a grain cargo.

This imputation was refuted by undoubted experiment. Grain was received by barges, transferred in elevator, sent by steam to England in the summer months, and was sold at a higher rate than other grain of its class, then in market. Some years later it having been assumed by some writer that grain must be dried at New Orleans before it could be exported safely, the indefatigable Mr. Higby published an account of sales of grain, sold abroad at a satisfactory profit; and produced proof that grain had been kept in his elevator 167 days in the summer time—and was sent sound into the English market. Since that it is admitted that the Mississippi and gulf is a sound route for sound grain; and western crops are fearlessly forwarded by this route.

There is in the opinion of the writer but one obstacle in the way of perfect success. The cotton crop comes to market at the same time with the western grain; the first commodity being worth ten times as much as the last, can afford to pay higher rates—the shipment of grain then arriving at New Orleans may find Orleans freights too high for profit—uncertainty embarrasses the foreign purchaser. By the time the cotton crop is off hand, the lakes and canals are open, and grain resumes its direct route to the East. If a line of grain propellers were established in close connection with the river craft to prorate with them and sign through bills between Liverpool and St. Louis, the shipment would be direct and continuous; the purchaser could tell what his grain would cost laid down at Liverpool, and we should have a steady business at least from October to May.

THE BARGE LINES.

In treating of the grain trade it would be improper to omit the influence resulting from the establishment of the river tow-boats and barges. This enterprise was started in 1866, and was the first to inaugurate the bulk grain trade. When we consider that the grain crop of the United States is estimated at 2,500,000 bushels, and that it is grown chiefly on land west of the Mississippi, that a great part of this vast and increasing trade is frozen up for six months in the year, that the Mississippi is a sound and adequate route for the exportation of this crop at all seasons—the complete and independent organization of this trade is inevitable. We can not leave the subject without announcing that Chicago herself has modified her incredulity as far as to accept the agency of New Orleans in exporting her grain surplus, and as a relief against the exactions of Eastern lines. The Illinois Central Railroad now delivers grain to barges at Cairo, and prorates for delivery at New Orleans. Efforts have been made to induce this company to emulate the example of the Baltimore and Philadelphia Railroad—and build barges, and even ocean steamers, to conduct the corn commerce with Europe.

NEW ORLEANS AND SPANISH AMERICA.

The slightest reflection will show that it is the especial office and duty of the port of New Orleans to conduct the exchange trade between the valley of the Mississippi and the Rocky Mountain states, and the cis and citra-tropical countries lying south of the United States. The physical reasons are obvious on the map. The commercial causes are just as decisive. Trade and travel now move in right lines both over land and ocean. New Orleans is a deep water port on the direct line between the populations of which it is the outlet and of those who desire intercourse with them, in the sale of tropical and other products, and the purchase of food and manufactures. Trade lines drawn between these reciprocal and compensating consumers concentrate for collection and distribution at New Orleans. It is at once a depot and entrepot of all these exchangeable commodities. It is the natural point at which many of these Spanish American States will receive their European goods, immigrants and mails. The differential tariff alone prevents this, but this removed, the stock and selection of goods by the jobbers of New Orleans, supplied by the merchants and manufacturers of the Union, will present such an assortment as will command the custom of smaller cities in the South, and of the whole retail trade on the coast and in the interior. These obstacles will be removed by the rapid growth of the United States, and the mutual promotion of interest on the part of itself and of its neighbors. The trade lines between St. Louis, Chicago and Cincinnati, and Rio Janeiro and Valparaiso, taken as extreme southern points, pass through and are concentrated at New Orleans. The whole of the western coast of South America connects at Panama with a line of steamers from New Orleans. Central America, Mexico and Cuba will likewise conduct their trade with the cities named through New Orleans.

There is an especial reason why the postal and passenger routes between these great interests should be conducted from New Orleans as a postal centre. The mail service between the United States and Brazil, Central America and Mexico, is conducted by steamer by New York. These routes are respectively about 3500, 2700 and

2000 miles. They are all subjected to insurances along the whole coast of the Atlantic States. When it is remembered that from each of the principal cities of the Union to New Orleans the government has a double daily postal service already paid for, it will be seen that a steam postal service to the ports named could be organized with great economy of time, distance and rate of insurance. The cities of the interior could conduct their intercourse with the foreign countries named directly with New Orleans, thus saving the cost of an extra journey to and from New York as a point of departure. The travel and trade between the countries named and the United States would be conducted inland, over our own railroads and rivers, instead of coastwise and outside, over an ocean route affording no such incidental advantages. It is useless to encumber these pages with an estimate of the value of trade or the number of passengers to be calculated on by a perfect organization of these enterprises. Such statistics change constantly, but the natural advantages are permanent, and sooner or later they will be realized, either by public appropriation or private enterprise. The trade of New Orleans in sugar and coffee is very heavy and is increasing annually. We require, however, our freights to Brazil upon which to base a regular system of coffee imports. Coffee is brought from Rio principally by vessels which take cotton, corn, or tobacco to New York or Liverpool. The coffee import should be based upon a direct exchange of commodities between New Orleans and Brazil.

MESSRS. A. B. GRISWOLD & CO.

This firm, of whose establishment we give a fine interior view, is the oldest and largest house in their line of business in the South. And, in fact, there are probably not more than one or two firms in New Orleans that can carry the record of a continuous business under different styles so far back as these gentlemen.

In the year 1815, in the then central portion of the city, at the corner of St. Louis and Chartres Streets, the business was established by Mr. Hyde, who was shortly after joined by Mr. Goodrich, composing the firm of Hyde and Goodrich. This name, by many years of honest industry, enterprise, and fair dealing, was made familiar as a household word throughout the whole South. When the weight of years compelled the founders of this house to cease from their labors, their sons assumed control and continued its affairs with the same system of honesty and liberal dealing, and with a still greater share of pecuniary success, commensurate with the growth in wealth and prosperity of the city. They weathered successfully all the financial storms of the last half century, preserving intact, through every disaster, the mercantile credit and honor of the house. As the tide of trade in New Orleans set more and more towards the American portion of the city, the firm removed their place of business to No. 15 Chartres Street, which was henceforth connected with their name, and extensively known through the Southwest for more than twenty years. It was while in Chartres Street, in the year 1847, that the head of the present house, Mr. A. B. Griswold, became connected with the firm: first as a clerk, then as a partner, and has, during this long period of over a quarter of a century, been identified with it under its different styles of Hyde and Goodrich; Thomas, Griswold and Co., and A. B. Griswold and Co. In 1853, for the third time in their history, the firm made a change of location, and removed to their present admirable position at the corner of Canal and Royal Streets, into one of a number of stores just built by Judah Touro, and the completed row of which now forms one of the handsomest ornaments of Canal Street.

Here, for twenty years more, they have successfully prosecuted their business and preserved the ancient reputation of the house, as well as maintained its commercial credit on a solid and substantial basis. Having their own office and resident agent in New York, and with foreign connections in England, France and Germany, they have facilities for the conduct of their business not excelled in the United States, and can always furnish to their customers at short notice, by direct orders, what their own large stock fails to supply. They are also agents for two of the most substantial manufacturing firms in the country, viz: "The Howard Watch and Clock Co." and the "Gorham Manufacturing Company," the largest manufacturers of Sterling Silver Ware in the world. The advantages offered to their retail customers by these agencies are a very large and well assorted stock to select from, and at the schedule prices of the companies.

The Howard Watch and Clock Company manufacture the most reliable American watch in the market, as well as the finest counting-house clocks, regulators, watchman detector clocks and electric clocks. They make no inferior or low-priced goods, as is the case with so many other American makers, and any purchaser of a genuine Howard watch can depend upon its being an accurate timepiece.

The Gorham Manufacturing Company is universally known in this country, (and their fame is now also European,) for the originality of their designs in silver and plated ware, the exquisite beauty and finish of all their work, and that combination of elegance and taste with economy in fabrication, (effected by machinery) which enables them to furnish a choice and beautiful article of silverware at a price no greater than for ordinary goods. Messrs. A. B. Griswold and Co., notwithstanding the age of their firm, are by no means old fogies, but are fully alive to the exigencies of the times, and realize the fact that those who would do a successful business now, must do it on the basis of "quick sales and small profits." They guarantee their goods in every respect, and offer in all cases a first-class article at the lowest market price. With a record behind them of some *fifty-eight* years of honorable dealing, we think our readers, both citizens and strangers, cannot transact their business in New Orleans more safely and satisfactorily with any firm in that line, than with Messrs. A. B. Griswold and Co.

THE MECHANICS' AND TRADERS' BANK, is situated on Camp street, occupying only an ordinary house, compared to some others, and requires no particular description. Capital $2,000,000.

CHARITY HOSPITAL.

WILLIAM HENRY HOLCOMBE, M.D.

THIS very popular physician and distinguished author was born at Lynchburg, Va., May 29th, 1825. He pursued his academical course at Washington College, Lexington, Va., the institution now known as Washington Lee University, and his medical studies under the direction of his own father, a physician of skill and large experience in that State; and graduated April, 1847, at the University of Pennsylvania, the *alma mater* of a large portion of our most distinguished American physicians.

On receiving his diploma, the Western country, rapidly increasing in population, attracted his attention, and regarding Ohio a favorable theatre for his future operations, he removed thither, establishing himself at Cincinnati, its most flourishing city, where he practiced his profession and prosecuted it successfully for several years.

It was his good fortune, in this famed city of the West, to meet with the accomplished Miss Rebecca Palmer, to whom he subsequently, in the year 1852, became united in marriage, and who, by her steadfast affection and many virtues, has contributed largely to his domestic felicity. None, who are well acquainted with this fortunate couple, can deny that real marriages are made in heaven, and consummated on earth for its adornment. Three children, the result of this union, were removed from the endearments of their fond parents by the mysterious hand of Providence, almost in their infancy; but one flower still remains to cheer them on life's pathway—the object of their most devoted affections, as well as proud anticipations, and who seems every way worthy to elicit both.

While earnestly engaged in the practice of his profession at Cincinnati, a disease spread far and wide through the Western country, reaching to our Southern population, which produced the greatest alarm and consternation—the Asiatic cholera. He had been trained in the strictest school of the allopathists, as much so as Paul was in that of the Pharisees, and, to his great surprise, discovered that this terrible disease yielded, in most instances, to the treatment of the nearly universally proscribed homœopathists. With prejudices, almost invincible, ranged on the side of the old, orthodox, regular school of medicine in which he had been educated, he asked himself, in theological parlance (for which he had a kind of reverence): "Can any good thing come out of Nazareth? Is empiricism at length entitled to carry off the laurels from the regular practitioner? Is this wonderfully successful practice really empirical?" And the answer of a monitor was heard within his breast: "Come and see!" The prescriptions of the innovators were very simple. No harm could result from a resort to their infinitesimals, and he would try them. No novitiate must be passed through, no diploma obtained from their schools, to authorize him to do this. Nature, to him, was as open a book, and as complete a possession, as to them. He tried the homœopathic remedies. He succeeded admirably; he became a homœopathist. He still sustains the doctrines and practice of the new school by authorities quite satisfactory to himself and his patients, doctrines going beyond Hahnneman, back to the days of Lucretius, who was the real promulgator of the system.

In 1864, Dr. Holcombe removed from Natchez, Miss., where he lived many years, to New Orleans. He has always devoted himself assiduously to his profession, and has a large practice, besides being a voluminous writer. His first works were, "The Scientific Basis of Homœopathy," published in 1852; "Yellow Fever and its Homœopathic Treatment," appeared in 1856. His brochures, "What is Homœopathy?" and "How I became a Homœopathist," were exceedingly popular, and ran through many editions, besides being reprinted in England and translated into the French language. He was, for many years, co-Editor of the *North American Journal of Homœopathy*, the leading publication of that school of medicine, and has contributed many articles to its pages. As a member of the American Institute of Homœopathy, he has furnished that body with some elaborate and instructive papers. He has, several times, been offered professorships in medical colleges, but preference for Southern climate and practice has prevented him from accepting them.

In the department of authorship, Dr. Holcombe has given to the public four admirably written volumes, illustrative of the Swedenborgian philosophy of mind and matter, bearing the following titles, viz.: "Our Children in Heaven," published in 1867; "The Sexes, Here and Hereafter," 1868; "In Both Worlds," 1869; "The Other Life," 1870. To those fond of the transcendental ideas of the great Swedish sage, these works are very attractive. They have passed through many editions in the United States. Three of them have been reprinted in England, and two of them translated into German.

Dr. Holcombe has published two volumes of Poems; one in 1860, which first brought him favorably into notice as a votary of the Muse; the second, entitled "Southern Voices," published in 1872, has endeared him to many Southern hearts by the tender and profound emotions and reminiscences it has embodied in song. Another, on Southern topics, we understand, is shortly to follow, which will identify him still more with the land of his birth and the history of recent events. His pen is constantly employed in the cause of Medicine, Theology and Belles Letters, and much more than he has hitherto produced may be expected from so ready, copious and versatile a writer, if his life is spared. The amount of literary matter he has given to the world within the last decade, and that too of a high order of excellence, is truly surprising, when the engrossing demands of an exacting profession are taken into account, and can only be explained by supposing that he invariably pursues a certain method, and devotes more time to intellectual effort and less to relaxation and repose than is customary with most scholars.

THE Iron Foundry of Messrs. Leeds & Co. produces every variety of machinery, that steamboats and manufactories require for extensive operations. It has been established many years, at the corner of Foucher and Delord streets, and occupies nearly a whole square. The business-like and prompt system practiced by the conductors, is known to all who require their aid upon the Mississippi.

THE KNIGHTS OF MOMUS.

THIS is a new organization, having made its initial appearance on New Year's eve, last.

When it became known towards the end of the year 1872 that another organization was in process of being formed, and that the night of December 31st would witness its first appearance, the curiosity which has always attended such affairs was at once aroused.

In a community where the spectacular appetite is so strong, and yet so epicurean, and where such gorgeous and elaborate efforts have already been successfully made, it was certainly no slight undertaking in the Knights of Momus to enter the arena, and promise an event worthy of addition to the memories of past pageants, and of comparison with those which are to follow.

Yet all this was confidently promised, and, as a consequence, New Orleans turned out in force, and the known route of he procession was, at an early hour, lined with expectant crowds.

Need we say to any true lover of traditions that no happier selection of a subject could have been made than that which distinguished this event? In that dim age which the masters of romance and poetry have peopled with grand figures, and to the beautifying of which the immortal Scott has lent his genius, are to be found the most majestic subjects of pageantry. The stark old days of Richard Cœur de Leon and of Godfrey de Bouillon, and the countless other personages who animate our legends and our songs, make a rich field from which to cull the very fairest flowers of pageantry, and in this field our knights have roamed with unhindered feet, and culled a lavish wealth of beauties for our enjoyment.

The sireless deity of raillery, who, in the dim old days of mirth, make gods the victims of his ridicule, and but hardly spared the matchless Aphrodite, daughter of the Foam, descends through the generous shadows of the centuries with a kindlier spirit, with a touch whose magic only beautifies, and the grim old motto "*dum vivimus vivamus*" takes a better significance through the interpretation which his latter-day votaries have given it, and gives us the right to welcome his advent with every sincerity and pleasure.

THE PROCESSION

Was of the gorgeous fashion peculiar to our festival pageants, and represented the principle figures in the grand tableau of the "Talisman."

First came

MOMUS—1873.

On either side of him ride his attendant knights, and so, with all appropriate surroundings, the pageant of Momus comes into full view, hemmed in by the rippling sea of eager faces, and shimmering in the radiance of a thousand lights.

Then came the English Division headed by Devereux, the Lord of Gilsland, bearing the standard of the Plantagenets. The Hermit of Engaddi and the Earl of Salisbury follow.

Here is Blondel, the faithful troubadour, whom Richard loved, and who, in the dark days when wily John turned traitor, and friends forgot their benefactor, showed that the devotion of the minstrel was a sweeter thing than the boastful friendship of the warrior. He holds the lyre which many a time soothed the fierce king's wayward heart, and near him sit Edith and Calista, Maids of Honor to the Queen.

Upon the throne reclines

RICHARD CŒUR DE LEON

beneath a royal canopy, on which blaze the leopards and the crown of England. He never greatly loved the glory of the court, nor the sweet favors of ladies' hands and eyes, and yet the

ROYAL BERENGARIA

who stands beside him now, was the loveliest woman of her day. The mellow sun of fair Navarre never shown on a statelier crest, nor did the lovelights ever dwell in deeper blue eyes.

The French Division was composed of a cavalcade of knights and priests, noblemen and pages, in the midst of whom sits upon a dais

PHILIP OF FRANCE,

robed and crowned, magnificently attired in armor silken draped. On his right stands that famous prelate,

THE ARCHBISHOP OF TYRE,

who in the days of handsome men, was noted for his splendid beauty, and in a court where magnificence of dress was the rule, was distinguished by his matchless costume.

On the left the

EARL OF CHAMPAIGNE,

dressed in a complete armor.

The Austrian Division was headed by

LEOPOLD OF AUSTRIA,

who, tall and strong and handsome, fair of face and hair, and brave as the lion whose effigy he wore, was yet an awkward and ungainly man, save when the grandiose carousals infused his stalwarth frame and the fierce light of battle in his eye burnt only on his prey.

Conrad of Montserrat stood by him here as he used to stand in war, and about him were the knights and pages and jesters of the Ducal household.

Here comes the gigantic Wallenrode, of Hungary, with visor drawn and the lion of his house upon his shield.

And then, after the splendid christian cortege had passed, it was only fitting that our friends of Momus should give us some pictures of the nation against whom the crusade was directed. So it happened that the fourth platform was preceded by horsemen of another race from those who had gone before. Here were the representatives of that nation which, in those wild days, had drawn its myriads around the shrines and sepulchres of Palestine and made the hot sands of Syria sodden with the Christian's blood.

Tramping down the streets of an American city, between rows of stately modern edifices came the dusky battalions of the Saracens representatives of the race who could not be conquered, and who fought with blind savagery for things they only prized because the hated Christian de-

THE ONLY HOME COMPANY.

LOUISIANA EQUITABLE LIFE INSURANCE CO.,

ORGANIZED MAY, 1868.

JAMES H. LOW, PRESIDENT. W. C. ROBINS, MANAGER OF AGENCIES. W. HENDERSON, SECRETARY.

Corner CARONDELET AND GRAVIER STREETS,

New Orleans.

DIRECTORS.

CHARLES CAVAROC,	GEO. A. FOSDICK,	JOHN I. ADAMS,	JAMES I. DAY,	B. T. WALSHE,	C. E. GIRARDEY,
C. H. SLOCOMB,	EDWARD RIGNEY,	A. THOMSON,	D. K. PENN,	WM. CREVY,	JOSEPH ELLISON,
DAVID WALLACE,	E. J. HART,	SAM'L M. TODD,	I. D. BRIGGS,	J. W. STONE,	WM. HENDERSON.
W. B. SCHMIDT,	JOHN HENDERSON,	S. CAMBON,	A. H. FAIRCHILD,	F. A. TYLER,	

MEDICAL EXAMINERS.

DR. B. H. MOSS, DR. HENRY SMITH, DR. SAM CHOPPIN, DR. J. H. LEWIS, DR. J. DICKSON BRUNS.

sired it. Their swarthy faces and the barbaric splendor of their trappings recalled the vanished centuries and re-peopled the arid plains of Acre with Paynim and Crusader.

To complete the picture here comes the dais of

SALADIN.

About his royal couch the semi-savage creatures of his household group themselves, the hideous deformed eunuch and voluptuous Odalisque making vivid contrasts with their matchless ugliness and beauty. And in the midst was Saladin himself, the splendid barbarian who divided with the lion-hearted king the crowns of history; in whom Richard owned his equal in prowess as in generosity.

It was a splendid pageant, and did fair justice to the gorgeous epoch from which its figures have been drawn. Our brethren of Momus have cast no flimsy gage into the lists, and they of Comus and Revelers must take heed of their laurels, for henceforth they will be more hardly won.

The usual Ball and Tableau at the Opera House completed the affair, and as a matter of course, the tableaux were a reproduction of the procession.

TABLEAU FIRST.

The Defiance.

King Richard trampling the Austrian Banner,
at St. George's Mount.

TABLEAU SECOND.

The Council of the Crusade.

Richard's Reconciliation with Leopold.

TABLEAU THIRD.

The Victory.

Defeat of Conrade of Montferrat by Sir Kenneth
of the Leopard.

TABLEAU FOURTH.

Honoring the Victor.

"High place to thee in the Royal Court;
High place in battle line:
Where Beauty sees the brave resort,
The honored meed be thine."

FINAL.

A Happy New Year.

The Ball was such as they have always been on similar occasions. The most select company of our city was present, and ignorance as to who were the hosts had no power to lessen the enjoyment.

Thus terminated their first entertainment. The ability and energy displayed by our Knights of Momus, their happy choice of subject, and the felicitous manner in which their ideal has been realized, gave us good reason to welcome them in the present and anticipate their reappearance in the future with every expectation of pleasure.

HON. JOHN McENERY.

This distinguished civilian and gallant soldier was born at Petersburg, Va., March 31st, 1833, the fifth child of Col. Henry O'Neal McEnery, a native of Limerick, Ireland. In early life his father emigrated from the old country to Virginia, where he formed a matrimonial alliance with Miss Caroline H. Douglas of James River, by whom he had eight children, only three of whom survive. He had a decided genius for military affairs, which soon developed itself in the chivalrous state of his adoption, where he held the rank of Colonel of the Virginia militia for several years. In the year 1834, he removed to Monroe, Louisiana, became a planter, and, at the same time, filled, with reputation to himself and advantage to the community, the position of Register of the Land Office for a period of eight years. His superior knowledge of land matters contributed largely to the settlement of North Louisiana by emigrants from other states, enabling him to furnish them with valuable information as to localities for settlement, &c. A practical man of business, distinguished for his intellectual activity and knowledge of public affairs, few individuals, in that section of the state, exerted a more wide-spread influence than Colonel McEnery.

His son, the subject of this notice, received the rudiments of his education in the common schools of Monroe. In 1848, at the age of fifteen, he went to Hanover College, South Hanover, Indiana, and remained there till the fall of the year 1849. He then returned home, wrote for his father in the Land Office, and continued to prosecute his studies, and extend his information by assiduous and varied reading. In 1850, he entered the law office of Isaiah Garrett, Esq., of Monroe, La., a prominent and able lawyer read with him till 1852, attended the lectures of the Law University of New Orleans during the sessions of 1852 and 1853, and graduated in due course. He immediately went into partnership with his brother, (J. D. McEnery, Esq., recently deceased) at Monroe, where he obtained a very fair practice in a short time.

In 1856, Governor McEnery married Miss Mary Thomson, daughter of the late Dr. Thomson, of Caldwell Parish, by whom he has had eight children, four of whom only are living. In 1857, he was, without solicitation, appointed Register of the Land Office at Monroe, La., a lucrative and responsible office, (previously held by his father,) and to the administration of which he gave general satisfaction. He occupied this important post till the year 1861, when Mr Buchanan removed him from it in consequence of his advocacy of Mr. Douglas's election to the Presidency, and his championship, on the stump, throughout the state, of the claims of that distinguished senator to the first office in the gift of the people. Had Mr. Douglas succeeded in that canvass, little doubt is now entertained by any party that the secession of the Southern states would never have taken place, or, if it had, that the war, inaugurated by Mr. Lincoln, would never have occurred.

He now resumed the practice of the law, but, immediately upon the commencement of the war, waged by the Federal executive, by and with the consent of his cabinet, and the military aid supplied by the governors of seven Northern states, he entered the Confederate army as captain of a company of infantry, was soon promoted to a majority, and, subsequently, to the grade of lieutenant-colonel, commanding the 4th Louisiana Battalion. He served, with gallantry and distinction, in the campaign of 1861, in West Virginia, in Kanawa, under General Floyd—was ordered to Richmond, and, in the winter of 1862, was sent with his battalion to Savannah, Ga.,—that place, as well as Charleston, S. C., being then threatened. In front of Savannah, he held the advanced posts. General Lee then commanded there. He has now in his possession a friendly note, (which he highly prizes) under the hand of that illustrious personage, complimenting him for his dispositions, entrenchments, &c.

In 1862, he was ordered to Charleston, and participated with his command in the celebrated battle of Secessionville, on James Island, June 16th, 1862. His battalion arrived at the fort in time to save the day, and, consequently, to save the City of Charleston. The Southern troops were driven out of the fort. The battalion under his command recovered it, and drove back the enemy, who were ten times their number. He was complimented in the General Orders, and the citizens of Charleston, always alive to feats of chivalry and bold daring, showered honors on him and his command.

Governor McEnery also figured in the battles of Jackson, Miss., of Chicamauga, of Dalton, Resaca, &c., &c., and was wounded twice, which disabled him for nearly a year.

At the conclusion of the war, he resumed the practice of the law, in which he was successful. In 1866, he was elected a member of the popular branch of the state legislature, and served till 1867, when he was disfranchised by the so-called 14th Constitutional Amendment of the Reconstruction committee of the Federal Congress. He now devoted himself, with renewed and increased energy, to his chosen profession; and the law, in his case, as with many statesmen, proved for him the stepping-stone to political eminence. Probably his firm adherence to principle, and the gallantry he had so often displayed on the battle-fields of the Southern Confederacy, were in a still higher degree, elements of his popularity with the high-toned and true-hearted masses of his fellow citizens. Suffice it to say, that, in June, 1871, he was nominated, almost with acclamation, by the Democratic convention, and, in July, by the Democratic and Reform parties, and, in August, by the Democratic and Liberal party, for the office of governor of Louisiana, then reduced to the lowest stage of political degradation by Federal speculators and spendthrifts. The state, in consequence of the nearly universal apathy that prevailed among its friends after the war, and its total indifference to politics, had, without due reflection—without "looking before and after"—surrendered all its great interests, State and Federal, into the hands of a set of desperate sharpers and adventurers, y'clept "carpet-baggers," who flocked hither in large numbers, after the Southern cause was lost, in order to share the spoils of an ill-gotten victory; and who, by seizing on the reins of government, and using their power only to enrich themselves, have reduced this once opulent state and flourishing city to the very brink of bankruptcy and ruin. In the year 1871, the friends of civil liberty and state rights made a bold and united effort to throw off the incubus of this disgraceful and pernicious misgovernment. Governor McEnery advanced gallantly into the breach, as the trusted file-leader of the large party which advocated reform in state and municipal affairs, and the restoration of the original principles of the Federal constitution, and, with heavy odds against him, will, we trust, come off victor in the contest as he did in the famed battle of Secessionville, during the late war. Louisiana has again unfurled the state rights banner to the breeze, and other states, North as well as South, who were once independent, look to the result of her present political controversy with "the powers that be" with intense and trembling interest, knowing that their own fate will, in all probability, be involved in that of down-trodden Louisiana, if she does not, at an early date, extricate herself from the dangers which now threaten her very existence as an independent member of the Federal union.

Governor McEnery unites a naturally strong and vigorous intellect with great sweetness of temper and extraordinary firmness and singleness of purpose. He is a man of action, and, having once adopted a plan that meets the approval of his judgment, suffers nothing to divert him from its accomplishment, and is subject to none of those outside influences which have degraded the American character in this age of political corruption. A thorough conviction of his honesty, of his steadfast adherence to principle under all circumstances, of the transparency and simplicity of his character, and his lion-like courage, has made him, wherever he is known, a universal favorite. No individual, in the midst of times of high party excitement, was ever more remarkable for the equanimity of his temper, nor for the self-possession and cool deliberation with which he addresses himself to the discussion of subjects and the adoption of measures. The style of his proclamations and public speeches, is equally marked by strength and terseness, while it exhibits no vicious fondness for rhetorical ornament. He is certainly an impressive speaker. In social life, he is rather reticent than loquacious, and never obtrudes his opinions unasked.

Governor McEnery is a conservative politician, opposed to everything like proscription. He is a friend to immigration from all lands and all sections that can supply the state with good citizens, and is disposed to do equal justice to all parties and all classes of men among us.

THE ORLEANS COTTON PRESS.

This vast establishment fronts on the Mississippi, running back on Roffignac and New Levee streets. The ground occupied is six hundred and thirty-two by three hundred and eight feet, and is nearly covered by the buildings. The whole was built according to designs made by Charles F. Zimpel, begun in 1833, and completed in 1835, at a cost, including the site, of $753,558. The front on the river, although having no pretensions to architectural effect, is still, from its location and extent, quite impressive. This press can store twenty-five thousand bales of cotton; and compresses on an average, one hundred and fifty thousand bales per annum; but its capacity is much greater.

CHRISTIAN ROSELIUS, ESQ.

ST. CHARLES THEATRE.

HON. HORATIO N. OGDEN.

THIS eloquent and accomplished advocate was born in Adams County, Mississippi, August 1st, 1840. He is the son of Hon. Abner Nash Ogden, formerly Judge of the Supreme Court of Louisiana, and great-grandson, in the maternal line, of Abner Nash, a distinguished lawyer of North Carolina, and during the revolutionary era, Governor of that State, who died in Philadelphia while a member of the first American Congress. He is descended from the New Jersey branch of the Ogden family, of which Governor Aaron Ogden and Colonel Mathias Ogden, of General Washington's staff, were illustrious members, his great-grandfather, in the paternal line, having been a Presbyterian minister, and brother of Col. M. Ogden, just named. He is directly descended from John Ogden, who was knighted by King Charles Second on account of services rendered to his ill-fated father.

The subject of this sketch enjoyed all the advantages of a grammar-school education, and graduated at Oakland College, Miss., in the year 1858. As a student he was remarkable for a high ambition, and for his facility in the acquisition of knowledge. He was particularly fond of intellectual philosophy, moral science, rhetoric and oratory, and excelled as a graceful and impressive speaker in all the college exercises, whether at the public exhibitions, or the debates of the literary society of which he was a member. In manliness of character and vigor of intellect, he was recognized by both Faculty and students, as occupying the front rank, and as possessing accomplishments which would fit him for eminence at the bar, which was then understood to be the profession of his choice.

He pursued his legal studies under the direction of his eminent father, and graduated in the Law School of New Orleans in the class of 1860, at the age of nineteen years, on which occasion he delivered the Valedictory Address. To the ability and accuracy of Professor Roselius, he has always attributed, in a large measure, his subsequent success as a lawyer.

He had scarcely entered on the practice of his profession when the war commenced, in which, like every true Southerner, capable of bearing arms, he took an active part. He entered the Confederate service as a Lieutenant of Artillery, and was stationed near the city until its capture in 1862. He assisted in erecting the first batteries upon Walnut Hill at Vicksburg, and took part in the defence of that place, until it was surrendered by Pemberton in July, 1863. After the fall of Vicksburg, he was detached from the Western Army, and placed on ordnance duty by the Secretary of War.

On the conclusion of hostilities, he surrendered with the Army of General Joseph E. Johnson, and remained at Hillsboro, North Carolina, for at least six months, where he taught school in order to secure the means of returning home with his family, consisting of his wife and two children, and who were at that time with him.

In December, 1871, he was appointed a member of the Committee of Fifty by Judge Lea, took an active part in the proceedings of the Committee, and finally introduced the Resolution which called the great meeting of citizens on the 17th February 1872, from which sprang the Reform party. As chairman of the Sub-Committee of ten he proposed the address read upon that occasion, and afterwards gave shape to the policy of the new party in the address of the Provisional Central Committee which was written by him as chairman of the Sub-Committee on Address. His great aim, in this movement, was to form a basis of reconciliation of the two races in Louisiana, and expel corruptionists, of every complexion, from offices of the State.

He was nominated for the office of Attorney General first by the Conference Committees of the Democratic and Reform parties. The result of that conference having been accepted by the Reformers, but rejected by the Democrats, he was subsequently nominated by the Democrats, and declined the nomination. He was afterwards nominated by a Conference Committee of Democrats and Reformers, which nomination he accepted.

The canvass commenced at a barbecue at Monroe, Louisiana, when he was present, and, in a speech, severely condemned the idea of affiliating with Governor Warmouth for any purpose. He was bitterly opposed to that alliance and fought hard against the fusion which finally took place in August, while he was absent from the State. By that fusion his name was retained on the ticket, on the demand of the Democratic party. He was finally induced to make the canvass for this new ticket upon the ground that his opinions had been overruled by the masses of his own people, and that, to make further resistance, might contribute strength to the Republican ticket nominated at Baton Rouge. When the struggle came, the result was, that he was elected, by a large majority, to the office of Attorney General. He will continue to hold and exercise the duties of the office, if the will of the people, fairly expressed at the polls, prevails. In the present anomalous condition of affairs in this commonwealth, encumbered as it is with two Legislatures, two Governors and two sets of State officials, each claiming to exercise the supreme power, and the party in the minority being sustained by Federal authority, regardless of the popular will, it is difficult to see what, under the circumstances, save anarchy and misrule, will be the result. It seems probable, at present, that the American experiment of the self-government of independent states has, as was long since predicted by the monarchists of the old world, proved a decided failure.

Mr. Ogden is already a prominent member of the New Orleans bar. This position he has attained mainly by his ready and fascinating eloquence, a rare accomplishment. To this he adds as much legal lore as could be expected to be acquired by one who has been so short a time at the bar. His practice is good, and on the increase, and we anticipate for him in the future, both in the walks of his profession and in the stormy field of politics, and the higher one of statesmanship, a career of usefulness and honor.

On the subject of religion, he adheres to the faith of his ancestors, and is a decided Presbyterian,—being an active and exemplary member of Rev. Mr. Markham's church in this city. In his manners, he is gentle and courteous to all, possessing those characteristics which not only render him a valuable and influential citizen, but a favorite of the people.

COL. DANIEL EDWARDS.

THIS eminent manufacturer and distinguished citizen was born at Liverpool, England, August 6th 1814. He arrived in New Orleans, which was to be his future home and the scene of his useful labors, on the 27th day of May 1837; went to Texas for a couple of years with a view to business engagements in that thriving State, but returned to the Crescent City in the month of May 1837. He became from this time forth, identified, as an engineer, with the Sugar interest not only of Louisiana, but of the entire South. His first contract, in this capacity, was to take off the crop of Judge Porter, of Attakappas. From that period until the year 1848, he entered into engagements for putting up Sugar Mills and engines, &c., throughout the entire State, as well as in Florida and Texas.

He first commenced business in New Orleans in 1848, and, in 1853, built a large establishment for carrying it on, on New Levee and Front streets. That location, becoming very valuable, he disposed of it to J. M. Lewis, Esq., and, in 1869, built the edifice now occupied by his firm, (Daniel and James D. Edwards,) having purchased the ground in 1866, it being a portion of the "Batture Property."

We extract the following interesting account of this firm from the New Orleans *Merchant's Semi-Annual Advertiser*:

"The firm was established in 1848, on Tchoupitoulas street, and, in 1850, was removed to a larger building on the then new Levee street, which runs through to Tchoupitoulas street, on the property of the late John McDonough. The business so rapidly increased, that, in the year 1853, Mr. Edwards erected new shops on the opposite or Levee street."

"J. D. Edwards, the junior member of the firm, is a son of the founder of the same. Their specialty consists of the manufacture of copper trains for the making of sugar and molasses. They also make all articles of copper, brass, and sheet iron work of good quality. "A. S. Cameron's Special Steam Pump," is also sold by them as agents. It is a pump peculiarly fitted for feeding boilers aboard of ship, or supplying mills, sugar houses refineries and rail roads. "Woodward's Patent Steam Pump," is another valuable article for which they are agents, and for which the utility of the machine and the reputation of this firm, have established a very large demand. It is particularly adapted for pumping cane juice and other plantation liquids. "Dreyfus' Patent Self-oilers," for locomotives and marine and stationary engines, is a convenient appliance for which they are also agents. They are also agents for lump lumbago, a patent lubricator, unequalled for economy in use; also, graphite axle-grease, the cheapest and best in the southern market. They also sell the American Steam Gauge Company's Vacuum Steam Gauges, and all other manufactures required for use in this market.

"The above mentioned works have achieved a great Southern reputation. They are located in Delta street, fronting the Mississippi river, one square above Canal street. These buildings cover an acre of ground, all of brick, and two stories in height. One of the largest buildings is 110x137½ feet. They employ thisty workmen.

"This is the largest and best conducted establishment of the kind in the Southern States. Their sugar trains are great improvements upon the former system of sugar and molasses manufacture. They are labor saving machines, conduce to the cleanliness and purity of the article produced, and by them a better yield from the same amount of cane, can be had than by the old unimproved process. The great extent to which the cultivation is being extended to the Southern States, promises a large sale for this sugar train. Its favorable reception and well-known value, throughout the sugar producing country, will make it hard to be pushed out by competing machines.

"While recently in New Orleans, we were shown samples of sugar made by these trains. It is of much better quality than the common product. It secured the first premium at the Louisiana State Fair, and was made by McCall & Bro., of the Parish of Ascension. We also saw samples of sugar made by P. J. Kennedy, of the Parish of Jefferson, which took the second premium against a number of aspiring competitors.

"The style, finish and durability of their machinery is a full guarantee to planters that it will do all the work its manufacturers say it will, and do it effectually, economically, cleanly and rapidly. These sugar trains are the products of long experience and knowledge of the wants of Planters. They know fully the wants of the sugar house, and, connected with this machine, is everything necessary and required. These trains are manufactured and placed in position on the plantations under the formal supervision of this responsible firm. Hence planters can rely that their purchasers will meet their demands fully. They have had such great experience, that planters can consult them to advantage for the location of their works,

POYDRAS ASYLUM.

and they are able to furnish plans and specifications for all changes in sugar houses, mills, engines, vacuum pans, centrifugals for drying sugar, etc. The cheapness and durability of the trains furnished by the firm of D. & J. D Edwards, have stimulated the cultivation of sugar in some places. No planter should be without one. They are made of a size, and cost, to suit the individual wants of purchasers, and have, in a multitude of instances, given practical proofs of their superiority to all other trains. Planters throughout the South should avail themselves of the facilities offered them by this firm, for making cheap and good products from cane. They guarantee to do their work as good and as cheap as any, and we have no hesitancy in saying, that their long experience of the practical wants of the sugar house enables them to give their trains more complete adaptation to the requirements of plantations. We are glad to note the prosperity of this active and reliable firm. It has only to become known to quadruple its sales.

"Their machinery consist of one fan blower, six lathes, two gas pipe machines for cutting pipes and thread, two drill presses, two bolt cutting machines, one power press for punching washers, etc., one large planer, and two emery polish machines.

"They are also agents for all kinds of wrought and galvanized iron pipes and fittings for steam, water and gas; also, steam and gas-fitters' tools, force pumps, brass work for steam and water, water-guages, ratchets, wrenches, wire brushes, jacks, screw pulley blocks, and many other valuable articles."

* * * * * * *

"Such manufacturing firms have a great work to perform. They have it in their power to develop a new industry, to furnish remunerative employment to thousands of people, to bring under cultivation thousands of now idle acres, and to be the indirect agents of adding to the individual and the national wealth."

Col. Edwards, in 1869, purchased property adjoining the establishment above described, on which he is now erecting an elegant three story brick building, on the corner of Gravier, Front and Delta streets. He commenced business with a small capital. He has now the largest Copper and Brass establishment, east or west of the mountains.

It is doubtless more to the interests of planters who wish to have proper engines and machines for their sugar operations, to have them made on the spot, where they can examine the style of workmanship and strength of material, than to order them from distant points, such as Cincinnati, or other Western cities, inasmuch, as in the latter case they cannot judge of their fitness to meet their requirements, until they receive them. We have had an opportunity to visit the extensive establishment of Col. Edwards in this city, and from a careful examination of all its appointments, feel authorised to advise all those who wish to equip their plantations with the best kind of engines and machinery for the manufacture of sugar in all its processes, to visit the same and examine and judge for themselves, before they go elsewhere, and to employ their highly skillful and approved engineers in supervising the erection of mills on their plantations, which they do on the most reasonable and accommodating terms. They will be as surprised and pleased as we were to see what a large stock of material suited to the wants of sugar manufacturers, they have on hand; also, all necessary equipments for steamboats, steamships, locomotives, railroads, distilleries and breweries, which they sell at New York prices.

Col. Edwards has occupied various conspicuous and influential stations besides that of an engineer. In 1856, he was appointed Aid-de-Camp to Governor Jos. Walker, and to each consecutive Governor until the breaking out of the late war. At a later period, he was appointed one of the Administrators of the University of Louisiana, was elected member of the Mechanics' Society in 1856, and served two years in the capacity of both its President and Treasurer. He was instrumental in carrying a bill through the Legislature for the erection of the edifice belonging to that Society after its first building had been destroyed by fire. In June 1872 he was elected President of the Polytechnic Institute and holds that distinguished position at this time. He is, in a word, one of the most enterprising, prosperous and public-spirited of our citizens, and his influence is deeply and beneficially felt in the various walks of life and society.

THOMAS MULLIGAN ESQ.

Mr. Mulligan was born in the town of Raphoe, and County of Donegal, in the North of Ireland. In 1836, he emigrated to America, settling in Mobile, (Ala.) in the month of October of that year, where he remained nine years. He afterwards spent two years in Montgomery, and one in Lowndes County in that State. In June, 1847, he removed to New Orleans, and has resided here ever since.

As a modest, unobtrusive, skilful artisan, Mr. Mulligan has acquired a reputation which entitles him to consideration and notice in this work. He is chiefly known as a master builder, having put up some of the finest buildings in the city. Among these are St. Alphonso's Parochial School, on St. Andrew street; the Academy of the Holy Cross, in the Third District, corner of Love and Congress streets; St. Vincent's Infant Orphan Asylum, corner of Magazine and Race streets; St. Elizabeth's Orphan Asylum, on Napoleon avenue; St. Mary's Dominican Convent, and the magnificent Church of St. John the Baptist, on Dryades street, and two Parochial School-houses, in St. Theresa's Parish, on Erato street. Of all these handsome edifices he drew the plans, with the exception of the Church of St. John the Baptist, which was designed by the distinguished architet, Albert Diettel, Esq.

No master builder among us is more constantly occupied than Mr. Mulligan—none is more energetic, none exhibits a sounder judgment or a finer taste in building. This is evinced by the above-named ecclesiastical and educational edifices, and others not here enumerated, all of which are highly ornamental to the city.

We add, with pleasure, that among our adopted fellow citizens, none are more highly esteemed for their quiet, unostentatious virtues than Mr. Mulligan.

ROBERT M. LUSHER, ESQ.

THE former State Superintendent of Public Education for Louisiana, (from December, 1865, to July, 1868), and lately re-elected to that important post, was born at Charleston, S. C., and was the youngest son of parents who were in easy circumstances, and both of them members of the Scotch Presbyterian Church. His rudimentary education was received in private schools at Charleston, up to the age of thirteen years. His health having been impaired by close application to study, he engaged, for a couple of years, in the active duties of a clerk in the bookstore of S. Babcock & Co.

In 1837, he was induced to visit Washington city, where he pursued the study of Architecture, under the guidance and counsel of his uncle, Mr. Robert Mills, the able and well known author of "Statistics of South Carolina," and other works, who had been State Engineer of South Carolina in 1827-8, and subsequently the Architect of the Washington Monument in Baltimore, and who, in 1837, was the Government Architect at Washington, where he designed and was supervising the erection of the Patent Office, Treasury Office and General Post Office buildings. His nephew's duty was to draw from the Architect's sketches or outlines, the working and other detailed diagrams for contractors and mechanics, which gave him ample opportunities for acquiring a practical acquaintance with the art which Vitruvius enthusiastically terms, the *Mater omnium artium et Scientiarum.*

Young Lusher, however, influenced by the brilliant conversation of Alexander Dimitry, then in his prime, and other scholars of distinction frequenting his uncle's dwelling, ardently desired greater scholastic advancement, and therefore, with his mother's consent entered the famous College of the Jesuit Fathers, at Georgetown, D. C., where he remained during the years 1841 and 1842, studying with unflagging zeal, and rising rapidly through the various grades, under the guidance of enlightened instructors. Rev. Dr. Ryder, an eloquent divine, was then President, and Fathers Fenwick, Jenkins, Ward and Curley, the chief Professors; and Hon. Thomas J. Semmes, (now of New Orleans), Brigadier General W. S. Walker, Hon. Hugh Caperton, of Georgetown, D. C., Judge Adonis Petit, of Iberville, La., and other Louisiana gentlemen, were alumni of the College.

After completing his scholastic education, Mr. Lusher remained in Washington city until July, 1842, aiding his uncle in drawing plans, enjoying the privileges of the Congressional Library, listening to debates in Congress, and occasionally writing for the Washington *Globe* and *Intelligencer.*

In July, 1842, he removed to Louisiana, in company with Professor Alexander Dimitry's family (Mrs. Dimitry being his cousin), and domiciliated in the Parish of St. Charles (25 miles above New Orleans), where he was engaged chiefly as assistant teacher in Professor Dimitry's Collegiate Academy, but devoted his leisure moments to the study of Sir William Blackstone, Domat, and the Civil Code of Louisiana, preparatory to a regular course of law.

In 1846, Professor Dimitry having been appointed Superintendent of the Third District schools, Mr. Lusher removed to New Orleans, where he continued teaching private classes and writing for the New Orleans journals. In 1847, during the sickness of the veteran editor, Peter K. Wagner, he was invited to edit the English columns of the Louisiana Courier, continuing in this service till April, 1848, when he was requested by an estimable friend, N. R. Jennings, Esq., to assume the post of Deputy Clerk of the United States District Court for Louisiana. Soon after he was appointed by Hon. T. H. McCaleb (United States Judge) a Commissioner of the United States for taking testimony, inquiring into offences on the high seas, assessing damages in Admiralty cases, etc., and continued in the discharge of the duties of these offices until the final closing of the court in 1861 (the date of the secession of Louisiana). With what degree of satisfaction to the bar and the court the functions were performed the practitioners of that period can testify. During his official career in this court he counselled thousands of foreign born citizens as to the steps needed for their admission as citizens, and the obligations imposed thereby.

His study of the law was meanwhile continued in the Law Department of the University of Louisiana under the able and courteous direction of Professors McCaleb, R. Hunt, Roselius, Hennen, Johnson, Monroe, and Mayes. He was admitted in 1856 to practice in the State District Courts and the Supreme Court. Official attention to the U. S. Courts, however, allowed only an occasional exercise of his profession.

From 1854 to 1862, during which time Mr. Lusher was a director of the public schools of the First District, he devoted every possible moment of leisure to a personal inspection of the schools, inciting the pupils of the intermediate schools to a more careful study and application of English grammar, and encouraging the teachers in their efforts to develop the thinking faculty in all the branches. The subsequent examination of candidates for the high schools, particularly after the system of written examinations was introduced by Superintendent W. O. Rogers, showed clearly the improving effects of such a method.

As Chairman for five years of the Committee on the High School for Boys, Mr. Lusher counselled and upheld the principal and assistants in the discharge of their duties, and in a general expansion of the curriculum of the school, supervised the examinations of candidates, and, occasionally, in the absence of the principal, assumed the direction of the school. The energetic Samuel H. Torrey, and the accomplished and faithful Robert McNair and W. McGregor, were Principals of the High School during this period, with John H. McNair in the Chair of Mathematics, and Prof. Marc Roux in the French Department. He aided, also, in the general improvement of the High School for Girls.

As Chairman, for six years, of the Committee on Teachers (examinations were then protracted and rigid), he warmly encouraged the graduates of the High and Normal Schools in their aspirations for employment, but rigidly observed, in his recommendations to the Board, the just policy of

PARISH PRISONS.

promoting capable and experienced teachers already in the schools before electing others to positions. He also introduced the method of attaching Normal graduates or senior pupils as supernumeraries to the respective Public Schools, thus enabling the principals of such schools to fill a vacancy in the teaching corps without delay.

Teachers in those days in New Orleans were selected with careful reference to their moral qualifications and teaching faculties, as well as to their scholastic proficiency, and removals were rare, and, indeed, never made without dispassionate investigation. The political status of an applicant was not even inquired into.

As Chairman of the Executive Committee of the Normal School, opened in 1857, in the First District, and recognized in 1860 as the State Normal School, Mr. Lusher was untiring in his efforts to rear an institution for the methodical training of teachers for the Public Schools of the city and State, and was ably seconded in this design by W. O. Rogers, Esq., then Superintendent of the First District School, and by teachers of approved experience and capacity, such as Mrs. A. B. Pangard, Mrs. K. Shaw, Mrs. A. V. Wengle, and Miss Jane Benedict, under whose enlightened instruction three or more classes of competent, energetic young teachers were (ere June, 1862, when the school was suspended by the war) graduated with honor and distinction. Most of these young ladies had received a fair scholastic education in the High Schools of the city, or other institutions of similar grade, and, with the greater maturity of judgment and firmer hold of knowledge and teaching experience, acquired by two years professional teaching in the Normal School, they found no difficulty in securing employment in the Public Schools, and in rising, from year to year, through the various assistants' grades. Several of them are still employed in teaching as principals in the Public Schools, or in flourishing private schools in the city and elsewhere.

In association with his intimate friend, N. R. Jennings, Esq., to whose liberal hospitality and enlightened discrimination the larger pupils of the Public Schools, and the citizens, generally, were indebted during a series of years for instruction and brilliant courses of lectures in Lyceum Hall, by such notable men of science as the astronomer, Prof. Mitchell; the profound and versatile naturalist, Agassiz; the erudite and eloquent mathematician, Prof. Gould, of Boston; the famous eclectic Egyptian archæologist, Gliddon; the learned Grecian archæologist and linguist, Koeppens, and others. Mr. Lusher labored to build up the Lyceum Library on a firm basis, and to expand the usefulness of the Society. At his instance the privileges of life-membership in the Library were extended, on liberal terms, to all the children of the city, and to all adults who were disposed to aid in creating an accumulating fund for the support and enlargement of the Library. Prior to this action on his part, none but contributing pupils of the First District Schools were admitted to life-membership in the Library.

Mr. Lusher was also, for several years, Vice-President of the First District School Board, and often acted as President during the necessary absence of Dr. W. B. Lindsay.

During the existence of the Confederacy, Mr. Lusher was domiciled chiefly in Columbia, S. C., and Shreveport, La., exercising important trusts in connection with the Confederate Courts and the Treasury Department. He had joined the Volunteer Company of "Louisiana Guards" in New Orleans, but was called out of service by Mr. Memminger, who was then Secretary of the Treasury.

In the Fall of 1865, the war having closed, Mr. Lusher, in association with Mr. W. O. Rogers, opened the first session of his Commercial and Classical Academy in the basement of Trinity Church, corner of Jackson and Coliseum streets. The patronage extended to this school was, and has continued to be, of a very gratifying character.

The City Superintendency of the Public Schools was offered, about this time, to Mr. Lusher by Glendy Burke, Esq., then President of the Board of Directors of the City Schools, but he declined it, suggesting, 1st. That Prof. Alexander Dimitry, who had been the first organizer of Public Schools in rural Louisiana, as State Superintendent in 1847, be invited to New Orleans to assume the City Superintendency; or, 2d. That W. O. Rogers, an experienced and excellent administrator, be appointed to the post, which he had already worthily filled. Mr. Rogers was subsequently elected to the Superintendency of the City Schools, and so remained until April, 1870, when the new Public School Law deprived the city of his valuable services. In 1865 Mr. Lusher was elected State Superintendent of Public Education, and the Reports submitted, in 1866 and 1867, to the Legislature, and the Digest of School Laws, compiled in the latter year by Mr. Lusher, now embodied in the public records of the State, eloquently testify to the ability and unflagging zeal with which he labored for the promotion of general education.

On November 21st, 1867, Mr. Lusher was removed from office by General Mower, on the pretext of being an "impediment to reconstruction." (On what evidence has never been ascertained.) General Mower's order having been suspended by the President, and he himself superseded by General Hancock, the latter rescinded the order of removal and restored the Superintendent and other State officers to their positions.

In April, 1868, while Mr. Lusher was still acting as Superintendent, the Rev. Barnas Sears, D. D., General Agent of the Peabody Education Fund, visited New Orleans, and, after conferring with him, requested him to act as Agent for Louisiana. Mr. Lusher having then suggested that he would probably soon have to vacate the office of Superintendent (a successor having been elected under the Constitution of 1868), Dr. Sears expressed the desire that he would accept the trust personally, or independently of his tenure of the State Superintendency. This was done, and Mr. Lusher has ever since been exercising the Agency (without salary) in conformity to Dr. Sears' instructions. It is well known to the people of the State that to his zealous and disinterested labors as Agent, have been due, in a great measure, the existence and prosperity of several elementary schools in rural Louisiana, in which upwards of three thousand children have received free instruction, as well as of various Normal Departments in existing Colleges and Institutes, including the "Straight University" in this city, and the New Orleans Normal School, and its nobly named successor, the "Peabody Normal Seminary," in which nearly three hundred young persons have been reared without charge, and trained professionally for the exercise of the teacher's vocation.

In November, 1872, Mr. Lusher was again elected by the people Superintendent of Public Education, the position he now fills.

In September, 1851, Mr. Lusher had been united with Miss Augusta C. Salomon, eldest daughter of our old fellow-citizen, E. Salomon, Esq. Of the six children born of this marriage, but one—the last—now survives, a boy in his twelfth year. Two daughters, reared to the ages of eleven and eight respectively, died in the Confederacy in May, 1862. The other children all died in their infancy.

In conclusion, we may say that Mr. Lusher has done good service to the Commonwealth. From youth to manhood, of which he is now nearing his prime, he has been more devoted to the public interests than to his own advancement. No individual in Louisiana, probably no citizen of the United States, has been more deeply devoted to the cause of education, in an age when knowledge constitutes the basis and crowning glory of free institutions, and none has brought higher intelligence, greater ardor, more incorruptible fidelity, and more untiring labors to the cause. In this respect—it is probably not saying too much to add—that Americans, when enumerating their benefactors, will place him, side by side, with their Manns and other eminent educators and patrons of education. He has manifested a spirit of self sacrifice, and an indifference to pecuniary emoluments, when great ends were to be achieved, worthy of all praise, and he will doubtless receive his reward in the confidence entertained for his merits by an appreciative people. To sum up his passport to general favor in a word—no individual among us, endowed with his high qualifications, is more noted for that absence of assumption, and consideration for the claims of others, which impart an unequaled lustre to the highest attainments.

The Protestant Cemetery.—This burial place fronts on St. Paul street, and occupies about two city squares. The inscriptions do not date back beyond 1810. It is a spot, however, where the northern and eastern traveller will often recognize familiar names of those who have found graves far from endeared friends and connections. There is little of the display here that is observed in other grounds. Tombs that, apparently, were commenced with a resolution to show honor to the departed, have been left without a stone to record the memory of the neglected tenant.

In one of the side walls, is a tombstone of plain white marble, with only the words: "My Husband!" engraven upon it. In this vault were deposited the remains of a distinguished tragedian, who fell a victim to the yellow fever some years since in this city. It is a delicate souvenir that bespeaks the true feeling and affections of a desolate widow. On another is the emphatic inscription, "*Poor Caroline.*"

MR. S. N. MOODY.

Is an Englishman by birth, from the great cotton consuming and manufacturing city of Manchester, so intimately linked in interest with our own cotton-shipping port. It is not strange, then, that he should emigrate direct to New Orleans. In 1848 he arrived here, having barely attained the age of majority.

His father, George Moody, was a flourishing manufacturer of stuffs, merinos, &c., with large houses in Manchester, Bradford, and London. He received the advantages of a good early education in the best schools in Manchester, and went through a collegiate course under the Rev. Isaac Bell, at Heawood Hall, Alderley. But the crash of 1842 carried his father down with it, leaving him penniless, with a large family, and the boy resolved to at once relinquish his studies and "paddle his own canoe."

It was a year or two before the great railway-stock mania of 1845–6, that about a dozen gentlemen conceived the idea of establishing a Stock Exchange in Manchester. This was done, and the institution was started in a small room, about twelve by sixteen feet, with only a lad as office boy, among whose duties it was to furnish the press with reports. That lad was Moody, and that was his first employment.

In the rapid growth of railway excitement, and the gigantic strides of speculation, Moody's position soon grew into the responsible one of Secretary of the Stock Exchange, which, with a rapidity equaled only on Wall street, and almost as if it were by a magical spell, had now swelled into the proportions of an immense building with members numbered by hundreds.

Moody next secured a still more desirable position in the house of George Carr & Co., one of the oldest of the Stock and Share Brokers of Manchester. Of this firm Mr. Moody shortly became the head, and subsequently he became its successor. This was before he was twenty years of age. He continued in this business until the dread railway panic of 1846–7, which again beggared him, with, however, the consciousness of paying to every one twenty shillings on the pound.

Staggered, humiliated, crest-fallen, but not dishonored, a ray of hope beamed upon him in an offer from an uncle to try his fortune in the New World. This he willingly embraced, and, landing in his adopted city with his last shilling in his pocket, he commenced the world anew, at the bottom round of the ladder, as a clerk at thirty dollars per month, in the Gentlemen's Furnishing Goods business. At that time he did not know linen from cotton, and had never sold a dollar's worth of goods in his life. His uniform courtesy, however, shrewd business capacity, and indomitable perseverance, coupled with the encouragement of assured success in a new sphere of action in a new world, secured his advancement and soon gained him a place amongst our merchants. Entering into business for himself, he sprang out of the ordinary channels of business routine, made the manufacture of shirts a specialty, and by a novel and liberal system of advertising, by winning premiums for his goods at all the first Southern State Fairs and at the European Expositions, and by other new and attractive features in his business, he soon attained the front rank as a merchant and realized a handsome fortune.

In 1851 Mr. Moody married his accomplished wife, and he has now a family of two sons and a daughter. During the war he took a lively interest in the welfare of the South, was aide-de-camp to General Lakeman, and under the administration of Gov. Allen with the rank of Lieut.-Colonel.

THE SLAUGHTER HOUSES.

About four miles below Canal street, immediately above the dividing line of the parishes of Orleans and St. Bernard, and about two hundred yards below the United States Barracks, stands the aggregation of buildings of which a partial view is herewith exhibited. This is the spot where the law prescribes that all animals intended for our markets must be slaughtered, under the supervision of officials appointed, some by the State and others by the "Crescent City Live Stock Landing and Slaughter House Company."

The arrangements for carrying out the objects contemplated by the law creating the Slaughter Houses are very complete. There are two wharves for landing the stock, with pens for receiving them upon the Levee. Immediately adjoining the wharves, and also upon the Levee, is a building containing a pumping apparatus worked by steam and capable of supplying 150,000 gallons of water daily to the entire establishment. Fronting the public road, a row of one-story buildings contains the telegraph, the company's offices and also the private offices of Messrs. C. Mehle & Co., Inbau, Aycock & Co., and L. B. Collins, live stock dealers.

In the rear of these offices at 200 feet from the public road, there are twelve large covered cattle pens, 67 by 15 feet each, where the live stock are first placed for inspection and sold to the various stock dealers who are always in attendance. Adjoining these are the main pens for cattle, twenty-eight in number, and each one having the dimensions of 75 feet by 17, and also eighteen hog pens for sheep and other cattle. After these you come to the large hog and sheep slaughter house, 265 by 80 feet which is constantly supplied with hot and cold water, pulleys, etc. On the right hand as you look toward the river, is another immense building containing twenty-two divisions 32 by 25 feet for slaughtering beeves and calves, each division having in its rear two large pens 60 by 10 feet for receiving the cattle previous to slaughtering. Fronting the above building from which they are separated by a broad paved alley for carts are twenty-two stables for the horses of the butchers, and next to these, nearer to the river, are covered vats for salting and curing the hides. Some fifty feet in the rear of the whole is another steam engine, and a little further back of this stands the Blood Fertilizer Manufactory, occupying a space of 200 feet square, lodging houses for the employees etc. The outhouses are all new and in perfect order, and in another part of the grounds there is an apparatus for curing hides by acids in two hours, and Esteban's large sheep-skin tannery. The other buildings are rented by the company to various parties, who are principally coffee-house and tavern keepers. The charges for slaughtering are as follows:

Beeves	$1 00 per head.
Calves	50 "
Hogs	50 "
Sheep	50 "

The average number of cattle slaughtered daily is about 700 during the summer, and from 800 to 1,000 in the winter. With the present arrangements there is ample accommodation for the slaughter of 1,500 head of cattle daily, and these facilities can be increased to any extent, the

company owning 240 acres of land. All the buildings, pens and slaughter houses are lighted by Barbarin's apparatus, at the charge of the company.

The Slaughter House company was incorporated in the summer of 1869, and at its inception met with much opposition from the butchers and live stock dealers, but a compromise having been effected on the 15th March 1871, between the contending parties, a new Board was elected, composed almost entirely of stock dealers and butchers, under whose administration the present location of the Slaughter House was purchased from the Butcher's Association and the operations transferred from the right bank to this side of the river. The officers of the company for the present year (elected March 15, 1872,) are as follows:

President	C. Cavaroc.
Secretary	J. N. Augustin.
Superintendent	John Delhonde.

Directors: L. E. Lemarié, C. De Ruyter, P. Sarthon, L. Rock, E. F. Mioton, C. A. Weed, J. Donaldson, J. N. Asegno.

THE CITY PARK.

Between the old and new canals fronting for about one mile, on the Metairie Road lies the property bequeathed to the city for a Public Park by the late John McDonough. Being about half a mile in depth it contains an area of about half of a square mile. The Park is crossed in one direction by the Orleans Canal, and in another by the bed of the Metaire Bayou, recently dried by drainage. In front the Park is high and it was not overflowed by the flood of 1871, when the city was submerged from the swamp up to Rampart street and when 20,000 inhabitants for several days could only move from their houses by means of boats and rafts. In the rear the once marshy land has been rendered solid and dry in consequence of the opening of the Orleans canal and Taylor's canal but the thick undergrowth of palmetto weeds and grass still obstruct passages by any but hunters.

The Park is abundantly supplied with enormous Live Oak shade trees some of which measure twenty feet in circumference and spread their massive branches fifty feet in all directions from their gigantic trunks. These will be retained for ornament and shelter when the city government begins to make improvements. No attempts have yet been made to lay out or adorn the Park although the donor has been dead more than twenty years. The extension of the city in the direction of the Lake will in a few years render the adornment and protection of the Park more important. When the time arrives the productive soil of the Park will give a quick response to the labor of those who may plant it with trees, flowers and shrubbery.

Annunciation Square, in the First District, is the largest, and, consequently, may some day become the most elegant in the city. Orange and Race streets are on its front and rear—and facing are some very tasteful private residences—the handsomest of which is that of Mr. E. J. Hart.

THE NEW ORLEANS ST. ANDREW'S SOCIETY.

The commendable friendship which Scotchmen entertain for each other, when worthy of their respect, and the pride and fondness with which they recall the valor and glory of their Fatherland, and the fame of their distinguished men, acquired in war, letters or civil life, are proverbial all the world over. It is with a view to cement, vitalize and perpetuate sentiments so honorable to them as men and patriots, that in several cities of the American Union to which they have emigrated from the Old World, they have formed themselves into associations bearing the above characteristics and time-honored titles. Another and leading object of the society is the encouragement and promotion (not by words only of sympathy, which they do not withhold, but by positive acts,) of the greatest of the virtues, charity. The objects of the association are succinctly stated in the preamble to its constitution as follows:

"Whereas, A number of the citizens of New Orleans, Scotchmen by birth, desirous of cultivating the friendship and promoting the welfare of each other and of assisting their countrymen in sickness and distress, have banded themselves together for these philanthropic and charitable purposes, they cordially and earnestly invite all respectable Scotchmen, residing in New Orleans and suburbs, to join them in the above good works; that, by their cordiality and good-will to each other, they may show to the world that the countrymen of Wallace, Burns and Scott still love their country."

The New Orleans St. Andrew's Society was incorporated March 11, A. D. 1837, and reorganized October 27, 1865. During the late war its meetings were suspended. The officers of the society consist of a President, Vice-President, Secretary, Treasurer and nine Directors, chosen by a majority of the members present, by ballot, at the meeting immediately preceding St. Andrew's Day. Any native of Scotland, or person of Scotch descent, who has attained the age of eighteen years, and bears a good moral character, may be admitted a member of the society; and the society may, at any time, confer honorary membership on any person of whatever nation he may be, whenever they may deem it proper. Application for membership is to be addressed in writing to the President and members of the society, inclosing the initiation fee of $5. At the next regular meeting, a committee of three reports on the qualification of the applicant, and if the report be favorable he is elected by a two-thirds ballot. In case of rejection, the initiation fee is returned. By Article 13th of the Constitution, every member is required to contribute and pay to the funds of the society $1 each month into the hands of the Treasurer.

St. Andrew's Day and the anniversaries of the birth of Robert Burns and Sir Walter Scott are usually celebrated by the society with appropriate ceremonies and festivities.

The present officers of the society are Alexander Hay, Esq., President; Duncan Sinclair, Esq., Vice-President; Alexander McIntosh, Esq., Treasurer; and W. R. Russell, Esq., Secretary.

P. J. KENNEDY.

The best among practical philanthropists are those who teach by their example, and the most useful of all the lessons taught by such is that which inculcates the spirit of industry, and holds up to the view of honest labor the reward to be hoped for by those who toil with well directed energy. Such examples are benefactions, whose usefulness extends as far as they are known, and to make them widely known is one of the pleasing duties which fall to the public press. It is therefore very gratifying to us to present to our readers a sketch of the biography of one who has been the maker of his own fortune, and whose wealth and honors have been honestly and nobly won and worn.

Mr. Kennedy was born Sept. 23, 1827, in Palmerstown, county Dublin, Ireland, and when twenty years of age he sailed for America. The vessel which bore him towards the land of hope was wrecked on the banks of Newfoundland, and returned to Ireland for repairs. She sailed again for America and reached New York March 31st, 1848, after the double voyage which lasted four months and twenty-one days. When the boy Kennedy landed he had but a single sovereign in his purse, but he had what was better than money, health, stalwart strength, abiding hope, habits of industry and frugality, courage, a warm heart, and a high character. He needed all these for the career which began with the perils and trials of the sea, led through many hardships and disappointments. Failing to find work in New York he went to Bloomsburg, Pennsylvania, where he worked in an iron foundry three years, for thirty dollars wages a month. We next find him on a farm in Ohio, where he labored for his board and fifteen dollars a month. He was next employed as foreman on an Indiana railroad at fifty dollars a month, but after saving eighty dollars from his scanty salary he loaned it to a contractor, who ran away with his little treasure, and the wages due to some hundreds of other Irishmen. For one whose whole wealth lay in his head and hands, this was a very serious pull back, but it was not enough to daunt Mr. Kennedy, whom we next find employed in Louisiana as a landscape gardener, and that beautiful State has been chiefly his home since 1853.

He soon won the confidence and good will of several enterprising gentlemen, who found him to be not only temperate, honorable and industrious, but endowed with singular native intelligence and administrative skill. He undertook a contract on the North Louisiana railroad, the successful completion of which may be regarded as the corner stone of the handsome fortune which he has since built up.

He next constructed the Diamond Head Levee in Louisiana, a work in which his remarkable skill in constructive engineering, and his splendid managing talent, won the applause of scientific men. He now began to be designated as the "Prince" of Levee contractors; a soubriquet well deserved, and eminently fitting for one who did so much to dignify labor and ennoble mechanical enterprise. Many other contracts for building levees followed, and wherever a levee was needed Kennedy was generally offered the task of building it, because it became well known that his work was reasonable in cost, as well as substantial, and in every way trustworthy. He has thus planned, superintended, or constructed much of the greater part of all the new levees along the banks of the lower Mississippi, during the past sixteen years. These humble earthworks make but little show in the eyes of the traveler, but when their vast extent for hundreds of miles along the river, and their vital importance to a wide and wealthy domain are considered, they loom up to dimensions of true grandeur.

During the war Kennedy lived in Vicksburg, and during the noted and eventful seige of that city, he greatly assisted the inhabitants by constructing vaults and caves, in which women, children and servants found protection from the rain of balls and bombshells, which fell upon their streets and buildings. Many of these catacombs for the living were constructed by Kennedy at his own expense, and their arched entrances, wide rooms, diverging passages and long alleys, extending deep into the hills, still bear testimony of his benevolence and skill. By this and many other well-timed charities to the distressed and famished inhabitants of Vicksburg, he gained their gratitude and a lasting place in their remembrance.

After the war he resumed the construction of new levees, and the repair of such as had become dilapidated by neglect. His more recent works sustain and enlarge his reputation as a contractor. He has kept many thousands of laborers and mechanics constantly employed, and as he pays liberal wages punctually, and looks well to their convenience and comfort, he can readily command the best that the labor market affords.

He has shown excellent judgment in the investment of his ample gains. In Louisiana he owns two extensive cotton plantations, and a sugar plantation of about thirty-four hundred acres, upon which he has expended $350,000. It is on the right bank of the river, about seven miles from

W. P. HARPER.

CIVIL SHERIFF.

LOUISIANA JOCKEY CLUB.

THIS Club was chartered May 15 1871, for the purpose of establishing a race course for the advancement of racing and improving the breed of horses, and the erection or the purchase and equipment of a club house for the social enjoyment of the members. The stock of the Association is $100,000 in 1,000 shares, which may be increased to $250-000. By agreement with the Fair Grounds Association, the club has the exclusive use of the race course, for four weeks before and during each Spring and Fall meeting, for the period of twenty years, upon condition of erecting upon the grounds a Public Stand of the value of $20,000, which is to revert to the Association at the end of the period of the lease, without incumbrance. The Club has, accordingly erected the splendid stand noticed in the account of the Fair Grounds.

The Club bought the property adjoining the Fair Grounds, which was once the residence of Mr. Luling, for $90,000. It has a front of 300 feet on Esplanade street, by 2,500 deep, with an area of nearly 30 acres, situated on the Metairie Ridge and exempt from overflow. The grounds are well arranged and thickly set with choice shrubbery. The family mansion has been converted into a club house. It is a substantial and handsome three story brick edifice, with a gallery extending entirely around it at each story. The lofty, wide and airy rooms are employed for Reception and Dining rooms, Parlors, Library, Reading and Billiard rooms, Restaurants, &c, all very handsomely and liberally furnished, most of the oaken furniture being elaborately carved by hand. The other buildings on the premises are in keeping with the main house, consisting of bowling alley, Pavillion, Kitchen and ten costly stables, with ample room for a hundred horses.

The flower garden contains an extensive collection of indigenous and exotic plants and flowers comprising all the rarer varieties to be found in the temperate zone or within the tropics. The adjoining Park has a great number of forest trees of every kind, and orchards of orange, peach and apple trees, and grapevines, all bearing plentifully in their proper seasons. In the centre of the Park is a lake of pure fresh water surrounding a small island.

Thus the members of the club have the benefits of a princely private establishment, adorned with all that taste or comfort could suggest or wealth command. This they obtained already prepared, and at a cost less by many thousands than its real value, which can be little if any short of $100,000. The club is under judicious, energetic and liberal administration, and its perfect prosperity and progress, give high hopes of its future career.

New Orleans. He planted, in 1872, a thousand acres of corn, using three hundred mules and horses, and employing a battalion of field laborers. The numerous dwellings and buildings give the place the appearance of a large village. Mr. Kennedy here dispenses a generous hospitality, wholly in keeping with his large-hearted benevolence and genial good nature. He is also extensively engaged in stock raising, on a large and beautiful farm in Sangammon county, in the State of Illinois, where he exhibits some of the finest cattle, horses, mules, sheep and swine in North America. He has a charming residence in St. Louis, where he is often obliged to go upon business.

In 1870, urged by love of his native land, he purchased Dunboyne Castle, in county Meath, Ireland, for which he paid three hundred (300,000) thousand dollars in gold, as clean as was ever won by faithful work and honorable enterprise. There he spends a portion of each summer when business permits, surrounded by chosen friends from America, and the gentry of the neighboring estates. Though his life has been one of laborious industry, he wears the honors of wealth and social position, with natural grace and easy dignity. He impresses all who meet him with the extent of his information, the force of his intellect, the generosity of his disposition, and the broad and noble manliness of his views and feelings. The guest feels that he is entertained by an uncommon man, and one who needs no title to stamp him as one of nature's own lords and gentlemen.

The catalogue of Mr. Kennedy's charities cannot be written. Of late years his income has been large, and freely shared with the unfortunate. He has endowed many charitable institutions, contributed largely for the relief of widows and orphans, and proved a benefactor to many men in distress. He has been a patron of talent and the arts, a friend of learning, an encourager of struggling industry, and a lover of every species of honorable enterprise.

As an Irishman, he is a true and devoted friend to his countrymen, who have become residents or citizens in America, and has freely employed his time and money for their benefit. Under his auspices, and by his aid, many emigrants have gone out to enrich the country by their labor, and to make homes for themselves and their children. This had been a double benefaction, first to the emigrants, and then to the people among whom they have gone to dwell. It is thus that the misfortunes of Ireland, and the abuses under which her people groan, have been the cause of good to the land so beautifully called by an Irish orator, "the home of the emigrant and the asylum of the exile."

The shell road affords an agreeable ride to lake Pontchartrain, a distance of six miles. The highway runs on the margin of the canal, and is not excelled by any road in the United States. It is the great resort for every species of pleasure vehicle that the city furnishes; and here may be seen, on an afternoon, all grades of society, from the gay sportsman, mounted on his fast trotter, to the sober citizen, who sallies forth on his ambling pony, all of whom appear to realize an equal share of enjoyment. Half way on this road, between the city and the lake, is the highly celebrated Metarie race track.

THE BATTLE GROUND,

(Formerly known as "the Plains of Chalmette,") the very naming of which causes the bosom of an American to swell with patriotic pride, lies five miles below the city. It may be approached by the Barracks Railroad, or by a good highway along the levee, the new Convent and United States Barracks being within full view. But first it may be necessary to look briefly at the historical facts which give celebrity to the spot.

Early in December, 1814, the British approached New Orleans, about 8,000 strong, by the way of the lakes Borgne and Pontchartrain. Their passage into the lake was opposed by a squadron of gun-boats under Lieut. Jones. After a spirited conflict, in which the killed (500) and the wounded of the enemy exceeding the whole American force, he was compelled to surrender to superior numbers.

On the 21st of December four thousand militia arrived from Kentucky and Tennessee, under General Jackson. On the 22d, the enemy having previously landed, took a position near the Mississippi, eight miles below the city. On the evening of the 23d, the Americans made a furious attack upon their camp, and threw them into disorder, with five hundred of their men killed. The enemy rallied; and General Jackson withdrew his troops, and fortified a strong position six miles below the city, supported by batteries on the west side of the river. Here he was unsuccessfully assailed on the 28th of December and 1st of January, the enemy losing two hundred to three hundred men. In the mean time both armies received reinforcements.

The decisive battle was fought on the 8th of January, 1815. The American right was on the river, running in a right angle to the wood. A redoubt was raised (which is still visible) strengthened by bales of cotton along the whole line. The enemy were about a half mile lower down, on a parallel line, their head quarters resting on the river, near three large oaks which still mark the spot. The scene is distinct, and this is *the battle ground.*

The British commenced the assault at daylight. As they approached the works, sixty deep, many were killed by grape shot; but, when they came within musket range, a destructive stream of fire burst forth from the American lines. Our troops were placed in two ranks, the rear loading while the front fired, thus pouring an incessant peal—which, from Kentucky and Tennessee riflemen, was deadly. While leading on the troops of the enemy, General Pakenham, the chief in command, was killed; General Gibbs, the second in command, was wounded mortally; and General Keene severely. Without officers to direct them, the troops halted, fell back, and soon fled in confusion to their camp. In a little over an hour, two thousand out of eight thousand veterans lay dead upon the field, while the Americans had but seven killed and six wounded—a disproportion unparalled in the history of warfare. General Lambert, upon whom the command then devolved, after one more unsuccessful attempt to assault, availed himself of a truce of twenty-four hours to bury the dead, made good his retreat—which Gen. Jackson felt no disposition to molest, as he was resolved to hazard none of his advantages.

MAYOR GERARD STITH.

Among the prominent and public-spirited citizens of New Orleans, Mr. Stith is well entitled to a place. Though not a native of Louisiana, he has been a time-honored resident, and filled several places of responsibility and distinction in the city and State. In 1851, he was chosen a City Councilman, and discharged the duties of Alderman with great ability, and highly to the satisfaction of our citizens. The talents and sound judgment displayed by him in that post led to his election, in 1856, to the office of Recorder of the First District, in the discharge of the duties of which he exhibited a high degree of judicial capacity, and unbending firmness, tempered with humanity. The next and highest honor which it was in the power of the city to confer was his election, in 1858, to the office of Mayor, in the administration of whose affairs he brought into play a wise circumspection, a liberal spirit of improvement, promptitude of action, and executive ability of a high order, traits which entitle him to be regarded one of the best and most efficient Mayors New Orleans ever had.

His administrative abilities, manifested in these departments of the public service, were equally exhibited by him as head of one of the most extensive printing establishments in this city—we mean the *Picayune* office, over whose mechanical operations he still presides with consummate skill.

It will be understood from this statement that Mr. Stith commenced life as a practical printer, and to this circumstance, above others, he owes the distinctions he afterwards attained. The Press, to minds of an inquisitive turn and earnest purpose, often supplies better means of instruction in the belles-lettres and the various arts than the university, and the accomplished principal of a printing office, who has been thoroughly inducted into its mysteries, is well entitled to graduate with the diploma of Artium Magister—Master, at least, of one of the noblest arts known to civilization.

The Hon. Mr. Stith is exceedingly well descended, coming from the line of Virginia Cavaliers. His father was Griffin Stith; his mother, Mary Dent Alexander; both tracing their ancestry back to the earliest settlers of the Old Dominion—to such names as Bolling, Meade, Fitzhugh and Randolph, celebrated in Virginia annals. Born in 1821, he has now just passed his fiftieth year, the period from youth to maturity, having been devoted almost exclusively to the public interests of the city and State of his adoption. No resident of the Crescent City has, during that period, pursued a more honorable and consistent course, and none is more esteemed for the virtues that have adorned his private or illustrated his public career.

HON. EMILE LA SERE.

But few of those who might casually meet the subject of this sketch on the street would realize the fact that he has very nearly reached the period allotted by the Psalmist to the age of man. The bright eye, the quick, active step, and the almost youthful buoyancy of temper and movement which are characteristic of Mr. La Sère are but the outward indications of the indomitable activity and energy of the man. Mr. La Sère was born in 1802, of French parents, whose ancestry may be traced to one of the most illustrious families of Béarn (the Montesquiou Fezensac) and received his school education in New Orleans, whence he was sent to complete his *curriculum* at the Transylvania University, where among other boys destined to future eminence he numbered Jefferson Davis as one of his college mates. Returning to New Orleans, Mr. La Sère commenced life as a clerk in the well-known commission house of Wil Bogart & Co., but his ardent temper soon impelled him to take an active part in politics, in which he became conspicuous as a zealous adherent to Andrew Jackson and the Democratic Party of Louisiana, a line from which he has never swerved to this day, being at the very moment we are writing the President of the Democratic State Central Committee of Louisiana. During Mr. Tyler's administration, Mr. La Sère was nominated to fill a vacancy in the First Congressional District of Louisiana, and was subsequently three times re-elected to the same position, which he filled with great satisfaction to his constituents of all parties by his strict and unremitting attention to their interests and the pertinacity and success with which he urged every measure beneficial to the State at large. In 1849, having received the appointment of State Printer (he was then proprietor of the *Louisiana Courier*) Mr. La Sère declined to run for another term, and became the President and Chief Manager of the Democratic State Central Committee. A few years later he accepted the Presidency of the La Tehuantepec Company an enterprise in which he is still largely interested and for which he lately obtained a new grant from the Mexican Government. When the war broke out, Mr. La Sère, although long past the prime of life, volunteered as a private in the Tenth La-Regiment,

CATHEDRAL AND COURT HOUSES.

THE CATHEDRAL AND COURT HOUSES front on Jackson Square—which is bounded by St. Ann street on the North, St. Peter street on the South, Chartres street on the West, and the Levee, open to the river, on the East. The splendid rows of the Pontalba Buildings, with their lofty gables and broad verandahs, overlook the square from the upper and lower sides. A massive paling of iron, set in a low wall of granite, encloses one of the most interesting and peculiar of public squares, which is European in character, and reminds the foreigner of the gardens attached to palaces in the old world. Flowers in great variety bloom here in the open air at all seasons, and there is no month in the year when the rose, the indigenous and favorite flower of Louisiana, is not found here in profusion in all stages of development. The walks are bordered with orange trees, which show their golden wealth throughout the Autumn and Winter; the glossy green leaves of the magnolia reflect the sun back upon its vast snowy and grove-like bowers; the clustering bananas hang in luxuriant bunches under their canopy of gigantic leaves; and birds of rich plumage and choice notes, unmolested by their familiar human companions, mingle their music with the voices of children, the tread of passengers, the panting of steamers, the rattle of cars and carriages, and the solemn echoes of the cathedral clock marking the hours of joy or care for young and old.

The most interesting and conspicuous object in the Square is the colossal equestrian statue of Andrew Jackson, standing in the centre on ground slightly elevated, enclosed in an iron fence, and based on an enormous block of granite containing about thirty cubic yards. The statue represents the grim warrior in the full dress uniform of 1815, in the act of raising his military chapeau in salute, his ponderous sword hanging from his belt, his left hand griped firmly to the reins of his horse. The latter is represented in the act of rearing, and stands balanced upon his hind feet. It is a spirited copy from life, and so well has the artist succeeded in this minor part of his great study, that one almost looks to see the bronze counterfeit spring from his granite footing.

where he was at once elected to the position of Quartermaster and took part in every one of the battles in which that gallant regiment was engaged until his transfer to the more responsible position of Chief Quartermaster of the Trans-Mississippi Department under General Dick Taylor. Although he has repeatedly filled offices of high trust, Mr. La Sere, to his honor be it said, is still a poor man, having lost all his property by the confiscation of the Federal authorities in New Orleans. There is no man in Louisiana who has made more sacrifices to the cause of the South, or whose character for integrity and patriotism stands higher at this day than the veteran Democrat who still presides over the councils of his party.

L. J. HIGBY,

Was born in Otsego County, N. Y., on the 20th of April 1812. He lived and worked on his father's farm until the age of nineteen, when he taught school and studied medicine, paying his own expenses by tending as clerk in a drug store. His employer, Dr. Pomeroy, struck with the energy and business capacity of the young man, proposed that he should take his stock and capital invested in the Drug business, and go west for a location. He accordingly drove a buggy 1200 miles west to Milwaukee. He thinks this was the first wheel carriage that was ever driven between Chicago and Milwaukee, for the road lay through an open prairie, and across unbridged streams. It required the traveller should keep the Lake in sight. There was then in 1836, three thousand whites and six thousand Indians on the site of the present city, now claiming nearly 100,000 population, and to be the second grain-shipping port in the West. For ten years Mr. Higby followed the business of general merchandize, and was then engaged subsequently in the sale, storage and shipment of grain, until 1868. During this period he built a bridge pier 1700 feet into Lake Michigan, and four grain elevators; and in one year, (1867) handled 10,000,000 bushels of grain in and out the elevator. In 1860 it occurred to his mind that the Mississippi river was the natural outlet of the grain grown in the northwest, and intended for an eastern or foreign market. He had already invested money in the first elevator in St. Louis, but the consummation of his purposes was suspended by the war. In the year 1868, Mr. Higby committed himself, like Columbus, to the new enterprise. He sold his elevators and other real estate in Milwaukee and started for the South.

An examination of the grain business in St. Louis convinced him that there must be another transfer at New Orleans, and he at once departed for this city to prospect for the agency necessary here. His observations convinced him that all grains shipped from the west to Liverpool, *via* New Orleans, had an advantage of fifteen cents per bushel over any other route; that it was open during the six months that the water routes of the North were closed, and that these advantages made New Orleans, in his own words: "*The great Grain Mart of America.*" After canvassing the city for subscriptions towards the erection of an elevator, he decided to undertake the work almost without pecuniary aid from others. He promptly purchased the ground on which the New Orleans grain elevator stands, and commenced himself the personal superintendency of constructing that work. There was a further impediment to be removed. The elevator at St. Louis was an isolated building. The grain received by the river or railroad, had to be carted to and from the elevator. He spent some months in St. Louis, and secured connection between the Railroads, the elevator and the river. At the same time the experiment of the steam tow barges was initiated and soon demonstrated its capacity to convey western produce in the safest, soundest and most economical manner. The arrangements for the transportation and transfer of grain cargoes in bulk, were completed by the erection at New Orleans of one of the largest and best built elevators in the United States. The plans thus perfected by this judicious merchant, were executed so far as they may depend on the organization of agencies adequate to their consummation. There were some obstacles which have been obviated. It was charged that grain could not be received and exported in good order from N. O. Mr. Higby has proven and published that this charge is unfounded. He has forwarded grain in bulk at all seasons of the year, and at a profit over other routes, without the slightest complaint of its condition when received in New York or Liverpool. The grain dealer no longer fears this route or this market, and a very large increase in our receipts and exports has been realized. There is still some difficulty in securing sufficient tonnage for exportation of all the grain that comes to our city. But with the immense increase of ocean steam tonnage within the last year this obstacle must soon be removed, and the trade in bulk grain between the illimitable west and the world will find its best market at New Orleans and its best outlet by the Mississippi. The perception and organization of this immense trade is due chiefly to the energy and sagacity of a single individual. He had staked fortune health and commercial reputation upon success.

At an age and with a fortune that would admonish most men to withdraw from the toil of business to the comfort of an independent and happy home, he has undertaken a large enterprise, in a southern climate, and among a strange people. It must gratify every member of this community, for which he has attempted and achieved so much, to know that he has fair prospects of complete success. The history of Mr. Higby illustrates some truths.

First, it shows the tendency of northern capital to seek the attractive resources of the south. Second, that intelligence, industry and integrity constitute in themselves, a capital that ensures honor and success. Third, that all such men are welcomed by the southern people, and recognized at once as benefactors and friends. Mr. Higby at the same time built a residence in this city, and removed his family here.

A favorite place of resort for pleasure-seekers in the Summer season is the magnificent garden of Col. Dan Hickok, at Carrollton. It is about six miles from Canal street, and can be reached either by the Baronne street cars, or by the shell road up St. Charles street.

PROF. C. G. FORSHEY.

THIS distinguished scholar and man of science is a Huguenot by descent, and a Virginian by nativity. His father was an Alleghanian mountaineer, and his grandfather a Revolutionary soldier and officer, who bequeathed a rich inheritance to his son in his sword and an untarnished reputation. Caleb, the fifth among eight sons, in a family of thirteen children, worked on his father's farm until he was seventeen years of age, when from the books he read at the winter schools, he began to be inspired with the love of learning. The seed, thus sown, fell into good ground, and, in due time, produced a plentiful harvest. He had naturally a fine constitution, which he inherited from a long line of "stalwart ancestors," and his physical education, so much neglected in times past in the training of youths intended for public life, had been admirably promoted by his farming operations. Thus he possessed a sound mind in a sound body, while his habits of persevering industry, exemplary temperance and superiority to the temptations to which many promising Americans, in their early years, fall victims, enabled him, manfully and successfully to struggle in those great combats of life which soon put to the severest test the strength of his principles and the measure of his virtue.

The instincts of such a youth and the passion for mental culture, and intellectual improvement of the highest type, which he early exhibited, led him to be dissatisfied with the superficial and very incomplete education which could be obtained, in the years of his minority, at the common schools of the country, and which were open, to pupils of all classes of the Caucasian race, only during one half of the year. He seems to have thoroughly imbibed the opinions of Pope on this important subject:

> "A little learning is a dangerous thing,
> Drink deep or taste not the Pierian Spring—
> Where shallow drafts intoxicate the brain,
> But drinking deeper sobers us again."

We cannot refrain here from introducing a pointed extract from the testimony which Prof. Forshey, gave in relation to himself, when questioned, as to the antecedents of his history, by the Reconstruction Committee.

It is *Multum in Parvo*, and having been already published, is public property, of which we feel at liberty to avail ourselves. Nor can we avoid adding, that the whole of Prof. Forshey's testimony, on that occasion, displayed a courage, a manliness, and an adherance to principle, which startled his questioners from their propriety, and produced as profound a sensation throughout the country as the celebrated and intrepid testimony given by the Hon. Alex. H. Stephens before the same Committee:

In that remarkable testimony, Prof. Forshey said:

"My ancestry, all Virginian, descended from a Huguenot immigrant of the earliest date. My rearing was chiefly in Ohio, whither my father removed in my fifth year. My collegiate education was at Kenyon College, Ohio, whence I was appointed a cadet to West Point in the Class of 1833. I resigned in 1836, before graduation, and have spent my life of manhood as a civil engineer and student of science in Mississippi and Louisiana, and, the last thirteen years in Texas."

All this is very modestly told. He speaks of being a "student of science," and yet no individual in America is probably better entitled to be regarded as a master of science—at least of Physical science—than Prof. Forshey. We must add a word or two about his entering Kenyon College, and the steps which circumstances compelled him to pursue, for admission to its classic halls. He determined, as we have intimated, to obtain a thorough education. His father, from his unlimited means, was unable to gratify his aspirations in this particular, and so he determined to educate himself, i. e. to employ those means for obtaining a superior education which "God and Nature had put into his hands;" in other words, to employ his physical powers to secure for himself the triumphs of intellect. His father encouraged him, as well as his other talented sons, in all the struggles they made for their own improvement; but perhaps nothing contributed so much to stimulate his ambition, as the knowledge that a college founded by the distinguished Bishop Philander Chase, actually existed in his own neighborhood, only sixty miles from his father's homestead. Removing to this neighborhood he diligently applied himself to the preparatory studies, and learned with so much rapidity that, at the end of two sessions, he was able to enter the Freshman class of the College, with whose Professors and students he, in the meantime, became well acquainted.

But his purse was soon exhausted, and, after entering college, he found himself destitute of the means of defraying the expenses of his education. In order to meet the emergency he resorted to school keeping, and, by studying at night and noon, was able to keep up with the studies prosecuted by his class while he was so occupied! This course separating him from the college and regular recitations, was at length found to be impracticable, and he abandoned it; he thenceforth earned his tuition money by teaching writing in the Grammar school, and his board by chopping cord wood for the college, a feat which he accomplished with great dexterity, devoting three hours each

RESIDENCE OF JOS. H. OGLESBY, ESQ.,

206 ST. CHARLES STREET.

NEW ORLEANS.

day to the purpose, during three years of his college course.

Early in 1833, through the instrumentality of General Cass, who was connected with his family by marriage, and of Senator Ewing, whose career of early struggles his own resembled, he was appointed to a cadetship at West Point, and thus, upon the foundation of a literary, he was enabled to raise the superstructure of a military education. As none but youths of great promise, and of the best families were then selected for these cadetships, and it required powerful influence to secure them, this appointment was justly regarded by the friends of young Forshey, a high distinction.

Here he prosecuted his studies with great ardor, maintaining the rank of ninth scholar in a class of one hundred and twenty young gentlemen.

After mature consideration, as he had now passed his majority, he determined to resign his post at West Point and enter into the business of Surveying and Civil Engineering. He had scarcely reached Natchez with this object when he was elected Professor of Mathematics and Civil Engineering in Jefferson College, in Washington, Miss., with a salary of $2,000 a year. The appointment was as unexpected as it was gratifying and honorable, and the income attached to it was regarded by him, in those days, as positive wealth. After remaining there two years, and perfecting himself in the theory of his profession, he, in connection with the other professors of the college, who left it in a body, resigned his chair, when being elected City Engineer and Surveyor of Natchez, "he resumed his transit, theodolite and compass." His attention was directed, from this date, to the solution of some great scientific problems connected with the Mississippi river, and the labors of fifteen years of the best portion of his life commenced in earnest, among the most prominent of which were his mapping the city and its environs, his discovery of "the law of abrasion, encroachment and rebound of the river," in front of, and above the city, and his establishment of the grades of the Natchez and Jackson Rail Road. On transferring his office to Vidalia, on the Louisiana side of the river, he was immediately appointed Surveyor of Concordia Parish, then extending some two hundred and fifty miles from the mouth of Red river to Arkansas, and entered on the great enterprise of reclaiming, by levees that magnificent empire of fertility and wealth from annual inundation. A controversy now arose in which the ablest engineers took part, in favor of outlets, and against the levee system adopted by Prof. Forshey, in which the latter was victorious, both before the public and the legislature, and the whole line of levees projected by him was successfully completed.

We next find him occupied as State Geologist of Louisiana, and his explorations in this department of science were as thorough as they were new and interesting. Having completed his labors, in which he was assisted by the distinguished Riddell, Carpenter, Hale and Trastour, he prepared diagrams and an elaborate report for the legislature, which unfortunately for the interest of science, were lost.

In 1842-3 he was appointed Commissioner by the Governor of Louisiana, to select half a million acres of land for seminary purposes. In accomplishing this object, "confident of the ultimate redemption of the great alluvion from inundation, he selected large tracts beneath the water, and had the satisfaction of seeing them reclaimed by the adoption of the levee system, afterwards completed."

The writer of this notice of Prof. Forshey, is indebted for many of his facts, and some of his very language to a valuable sketch of that gentleman, which appeared in 1868, in a Texas newspaper.

In 1843, Prof. Forshey married Miss Martha A. Williams, of Cincinnati, a lady distinguished for her personal, moral and mental accomplishments. His only child, a son, was a lieutenant of artillery, and bore his part in the late war. Mrs. Forshey died in the year 1850, in New Orleans, to which city Prof. Forshey had previously removed and where, as a scholar and a man of science he continued to be highly distinguished. In 1844, in connection with Prof. Riddell, he delivered the first course of popular scientific lectures ever presented to a New Orleans audience, with the exception of a few which had been previously delivered by Prof. Silliman. They were exceedingly popular and numerously attended. His geological diagrams exhibited at these lectures, were the highest specimens of art in their way. These lectures, delivered before the People's Lyceum, of which M. M. Cohen, Esq., a gentleman and lawyer of high literary culture, was President, led in the course of a few years, to the building of the elegant Public Lyceum and City Hall on St. Charles street, and he was the first who was honored with a lectureship in the marble hall which his influence had contributed largely to originate. His lectures on Geology in 1851, in that hall, were largely attended throughout the entire course, by fashionable and intellectual audiences, who were more interested in instructive entertainments of this kind, than they have ever since been. He was also one of the original founders of the Academy of Sciences, in this city, composed of distinguished men who have extended their enquiries into nearly every department of science and history and which takes rank with the most learned associations of the kind in America and Europe. His constant aim was to apply the great principles of science to useful and practical ends. Hence, to him we owe the existence of one of our railroads to the lake, and the scheme of a railroad to Berwick's Bay, Opelousas and Texas, which he brought into general notice by the labors of his ever ready and active pen, assisted in making the surveys for it, "was in the preliminary Directory, but declined the place of Chief Engineer" in consequence of other numerous and profitable engagements.

Prof. Forshey was a member of the celebrated Memphis Convention of 1845, of which Mr. Calhoun, of South Carolina, was President and a leading star. That great statesman upon examining his maps, endeavored to dissuade him at first from what he was pleased to designate his "world scheme" of a railroad along latitude 32° to the Pacific, a favorite plan of Prof. Forshey, and which had been fully endorsed by the citizens of Louisiana, from which section he was a delegate to the Convention, but which Mr.

Calhoun regarded as premature. He enjoyed, however, the singular satisfaction and high triumph of having it subsequently approved by Mr. Calhoun, and that eminently practical railroad projector, Col. Gadsden also of South Carolina. In the contest of rivalry which sprang up in 1853-4 between the New Orleans and Opelousas, and the Vicksburgh and Shreveport railroads, in respect to the route to be selected, Prof. Forshey, from his thorough and intimate acquaintance with the country, was led to advocate the latter as well as former, and designated nearly every mile of the road as now located.

The legislature of Louisiana, having had its attention earnestly directed to the management and control of the Mississippi river, addressed a series of questions to various influential and practical men on the subject, which resulted in the publication by Prof. Forshey of his celebrated "Physics of the Mississippi River," which elicited the applause of the savans of the day, and, attracting the attention of that great geologist, Sir Charles Lyell, led to his appointment as corresponding member of the Academy of Sciences, of France. It immediately became authority, and formed the basis of the subsequent Mississippi Delta survey by the Corps of United States Engineers under the direction of Col. Stephen H. Long, and Capt. A. A. Humphreys. Prof. Forshey was appointed by them to attend to the most difficult parts of this great work, Hydrometry and Physics, and was richly rewarded by the government for his indefatigable and invaluable labors. In the voluminous report of 1860, by General Humphreys (the present Chief Engineer of the United States Army), assisted by General Abbot of the same corps, (a large quarto volume of a thousand pages) the leading doctrines of his essay on "the Physics of the Mississippi," are demonstrated and confirmed; and acknowledgments made of the valuable services rendered by Prof. Forshey, which are expressed in the strongest and most flattering terms.

In 1855, Prof. Forshey was engaged in Texas, for a few months, in making surveys for the Galveston, Houston and Henderson Rail Road, having obtained permission for that purpose from the U. S. Government, in whose service he was then employed. Texas opening a wide field for enterprise, and the kind of labors with which he was most conversant, he determined to transfer them thenceforth to that great State. Five years elapsed before the railroad referred to was completed, and which now connects with the whole network of railroads throughout the State of Texas.

This great labor accomplished, Prof. Forshey next turned his attention to the organization of a military institute in Texas, which was endorsed by the State Legislature, and during the six years of its existence, proved a complete success. The pupils and the professors, at the expiration of that period, which brought them to the eve of the great war between the States, already accomplished in all military exercises, sprang to arms, and gallantly performed their devoirs in the unhappy controversy that ensued. Prof. (now Colonel) Forshey immediately repaired to the coast, and commenced fortifying it with the aid of the citizens of the country, and establishing guards, lookouts and signals, soon placed it in a state of complete defence. These works were fully approved by the Confederate authorities, and Col. Forshey assigned to duty as Major of Engineers, to construct works from Galveston to Arkansas. The first trophies were won by him and Major Yager in a running fight in April 1862, by the capture of the captain's gig and two six-oared launches, with arms, compass, binnacle and provisions.

When in June, 1862, General Hebert evacuated Galveston, leaving Col. J. J. Cook with three companies and three guns, Major Forshey asked permission to report to Col. Cook, and it was granted. Under orders of that officer, he, in a few days, casemated the guns and made bomb proofs for the men, so that on the arrival of the fleet to bombard and take possession of the city, the aspect of affairs was so formidable as to prevent an attack, so that the city was held till October, when, being quite evacuated, only a few shots from Sherman's guns giving a congé to the Island.

On the 2nd of September 1862, Major Forshey by permission of Gen. Hebert, went to Richmond, and laid before the Secretary of War, his plans for defending the coast of Texas. An order soon followed assigning General Magruder to the command of Texas. The interview which passed between Major Forshey and Gen. Magruder, on this occasion, was so indicative of the character of the two men, and the spirit that actuated them, that we cannot refrain from inserting it. A report having been spread that Galveston had fallen and that the coast of Texas was in the hands of the enemy, General Magruder, addressing Maj. Forshey, said: "Now what do you say as to defending your coast?" Major F. replied: "I say that you have to recapture Galveston, or you had better decline the command of Texas." "Yes, that is easily said, but how will you do it?" replied General Magruder. "First decide to do it, and then consider the method." "Will you Texans sustain and help me?" "The bolder your undertaking, the better they will fight for you." "And would you take some of your own medicine? Would you like to aid me?" "Nothing would please me so much. It would be a distinguished honor to succeed, and a burning disgrace to the State, to surrender the coast, after all our fortifying and show of pluck, without a contest to measure our manhood."

During General Magruder's command of the District, Major Forshey served on his staff with the rank of Lieut. Colonel of Engineers, and being intimately acquainted with localities was prepared to give that distinguished General the best advice, always counselling him never to surrender one inch of the soil of Texas, so long as the slightest hope remained of retaining it.

It is accorded, in history, to Col. Forshey, to have urged and planned the attack upon Galveston which resulted in its heroic recapture by General Magruder immediately after his arrival in Texas. Upon the conclusion of hostilities, Major Forshey accompanied Ex-President Burnet on his mission in behalf of Mr. Davis, and spent six months in the leading cities of the North, endeavoring to make arrangements for the resumption of his professional duties as

JAMES F. CASEY, ESQ.,

COLLECTOR OF THE PORT.

a Civil Engineer. Gen. Grant and Secretary Stanton refused to permit him to re-open the Texas Military Institute. He was summoned to testify before the Reconstruction Committee of Congress, and astonished that Committee, and surprised the whole country, as we have before said, by the boldness and independence of his replies to the questions propounded to him on the occasion.

He subsequently returned to his old home at Galveston, where he established himself as "Consulting Engineer and Agent for Engines, Machines, new Inventions, &c." He had lost none of the energy which had distinguished his earlier enterprises, and still devoted himself with unflagging zeal, to the best interests of the country.

We, in conclusion, quote *verbatim* the following extracts from a fine manuscript sketch of Prof. Forshey, for which we are indebted to the kindness of a friend, and which has never been published. It forms a proper close to this somewhat voluminous notice.

"In 1866-7, Prof. Forshey wrote a series of articles in De Bow's Review in favor of a complete abandonment of broad-guage and heavy locomotives, cars and rails on all railroads. In this and the steel rail, he led the movement in America, which has now become almost complete, only that the vast investment in this line delays the completion of the revolution.

"At the same time, he wrote and spoke, and moved legislation for charters for wooden railroads, so extensively adopted, since, for minor local uses and tap roads, when expensive roads are not available and cannot be afforded.

"The two great roads now so rapidly progressing in Texas, have their origin in the Professor's schemes, writings, and continual agitations. These are the Great Northern and International, the former to reach from the Gulf at Galveston, due North, to the 49th parallel; the latter to be the Texas link of 690 miles of the great International line from Cairo, the centre of the Mississippi Valley, South-west, to the Pacific at San Blas, passing Little Rock, Austin and San Antonio, and linking the centre of empire in the West to the nearest point on the Pacific.

"Prof. Forshey represented the Chamber of Commerce of Galveston, in the Commercial Convention of the South, for three consecutive years, 1868, 1869, and 1870, and by his persevering labors, succeeded in passing, at the meetings at New Orleans, Louisville, Cincinnati and St. Louis, resolutions for Congressional aid in improving all the harbors on the Gulf coast. The response has been successful for nearly every harbor applied for.

"With a reputation which ought to gratify and satisfy any man in the profession, Prof. Forshey had offers and calls from a distance to which he could not respond. But when, in the summer of 1871, he was recalled to the Levee and River management in Louisiana, he felt it a duty to return to the completion of his former labors. This work was placed on a basis which he believed promised success in the control of the river. For the eighteen months, last past, he has been engaged as Chief Engineer of the Louisiana Levee Company and Commissioner of Levees. His labors have been most incessant and laborious, covering some 1500 miles of Louisiana levees.

"The Professor at once resumed his labors in the Academy of Sciences, and takes the highest pleasure in its deliberations. His pen, always ready, has been frequently adding to its consultations. His appearance in the "American Association for the Advancement of Science," was creditable to his section, and his great paper on the "Reclamation of the Mississippi Delta," places that vast work before the American people as the grandest National enterprise of the times.

"Possessed of rare physical powers and exemption from all disease and physical frailty, he works with the vigor of a man of thirty, at three score years. The cares of a growing family and his official duties, however exacting, do not prevent him from engaging in the leading enterprises of Science, Improvement and Education." *Sic itur ad astra.*

E. W. HUNTINGTON.

There is in New Orleans a member of the bar who stands in bold relief from those of his profession. His name heads these lines.

Mr. Huntington was born in Augusta, Georgia, in 18[illegible]. His father Alfred Isham Huntington, who was a prominent merchant of Augusta, settled in New Orleans in 1849. His grandfather Gen. Ebenezer Huntington, of Norwich, Connecticut, was a distinguished officer in the Revolutionary army.

Mr. E. W. Huntington is a nephew of the late Geo. W. Huntington, who was of the firm of Payne, Huntington & Co. of this city.

The subject of this sketch graduated at Marietta college, Ohio, in 1850. He studied law in the office of Christian Roselius, Esq., New Orleans, and received his degree from the Law Department of the University of Louisiana, in 1852.

He was associated in the practice of law with Charles M. Emerson, Ex-Judge of the Third District Court for the parish of Orleans, and afterwards with Henry C. Miller.

He has never held or sought a public office. Devoted to his profession, he has zealously striven to attain an honorable position at the bar. He has a large and lucrative commercial practice, and has acquired a considerable estate.

He is fond of books and reads a good deal.

Mr. Huntington uses his time in a characteristic manner. There is no waste in it. Every moment is occupied. Every stroke of his pen counts. He studies his cases, matures his plans and executes them promptly. Nobody in New Orleans attends to his own business so thoroughly as Mr. Huntington. He has the virtue of letting other people do the same. He is talented, keen, discriminating and accurate—candid and open in the avowal of his opinions, kind and gentle to his friends, and is generally liked and esteemed.

THERE are but three daily English papers published in New Orleans: The "Picayune," "Times" and "Republican." The "Bee" is published in French, and the "Gazette" in German.

An advance in the art of silk-worm culture has been made by the discovery that the color of the raw silk in the cocoon can be very materially affected by the food of the worm, a brilliant red, green and yellow being secured at will in this way.

A writer in "Iron" states that malleable iron was well known and widely used 4000 years ago, and probably at a much earlier period. The manufacture of cast iron is more modern, but from certain passages in Aristotle it is believed to have been carried on as early as his time.

A French veterinarian anoints the inside of a horse's ears with a drop or two of *huile de cade* (an oily liquid obtained from the wood of *juniperus oxycedrus*), in order to save the animal from annoyance by flies. The oil need not be applied more than once a week, and it is perfectly harmless when thus employed.

The water supply of Boston is greatly diminished by incrustations on the inside of the pipes. Thus a three-inch pipe that has been laid ten years becomes reduced to two inches, and six-inch pipes to five and four inches.

[illegible] R. BAYLEY, Esq.

No individual is more worthy of mention for his public services, and his private virtues, than the distinguished Civil Engineer, whose name stands at the head of this article. It is a pleasing and proud task to trace the ancestry of such men, and a satisfaction to know that they have pursued an honorable career from generation to generation. Mr. Bayley is descended from one of the oldest families in the United States, whose history has been illustrated by their heroism and spirit of self-sacrifice. The family is of English extraction. John Bayley, its progenitor, emigrated from Chippenham, Wiltshire County, England, in 1635.

Jacob Bayley, his great-grandfather, served through the whole of the old French War, and was Captain in Fort William Henry on Lake George, at the time of its capture and the massacre of its garrison by Indians under Montcalm. He served, afterwards, through the whole of the war of the Revolution. He was Assistant Quarter Master General under Gates at the battle of Saratoga, and in most of the battles that were fought, down to the surrender of Cornwallis, at Yorktown, bore a distinguished part. See letters to Colonel (afterwards Brigadier General) Jacob Bayley, in "The Correspondence of Washington."

The subject of this notice was born November 28th, 1821, at Saratoga Springs, in the State of New York. He graduated at Rensselaer Polytechnic Institute, as Civil Engineer, belonging to the class of 1838. He was immediately afterwards employed as Assistant Engineer on the location and construction of the Auburn and Rochester Rail Road in the State of New York. He continued on said work over all parts of it (from Auburn to Rochester), for four years, until its final completion and opening for traffic. His prompt and continued employment, for such a length of time, on so important a work, directly on his graduation, is a proof of the confidence that was entertained at that early period, in his skill and enterprise—a confidence which has been fully justified by the whole of his subsequent history, and which has placed him in the front rank of the Civil Engineers of this country. These were the early days of railroad construction, when the use of solid iron rails was unknown. The old method of construction was with sub-sills, cross-ties, wooden stringers, and flat bar-rail on stringers.

Mr. Bayley was afterwards engaged on surveys for the State of New York—in the north-eastern part of it; next on surveys, and the location of a railroad from Saratoga Springs to Whitehall, New York, with James B. Sargent.

While so engaged, was tendered the position of Principal Assistant State Engineer of Louisiana, by the then State Engineer, (afterwards Governor) Paul O. Hebert, which situation he accepted and came to New Orleans in October 1846. The Engineer department of Louisiana, then consisted of the State Engineer and one Assistant Engineer. All public works and surveys were in charge of the State Engineer's Department. He remained in the service of the State with Hebert, and with his successors, Williams and Wooldridge, until June 1852, travelled from fifteen to twenty thousand miles per year, making surveys, examinations of rivers, bayous, etc., in all parts of the state, during the space of six years; became intimately acquainted and familiar with the geography and topography of the whole State, with every part of the Gulf coast to its northern boundary and the Mississippi State line to the Sabine River; studied the phenomena of the Mississippi, its floods, crevasses, levee system, outlets, etc., and became convinced by observation of facts, surveys and examinations, that the then universally accepted theory, that levees caused constant increase in the height of the Mississippi water line, and the filling up of the river bed, was erroneous.

He boldly attacked this theory in the columns of the State press,—wrote often and extensively on the subject, and, finally, by argument and data furnished, succeeded in having a bill passed by the State Legislature to close Bayou Plaquemine, the largest remaining outlet of the Mississippi river. An able and eloquent pamphlet, rich and thorough in the information it imparted, and written in a true and masterly style, was prepared by Mr. Bayley, at the request of the then state senators, which caused the passage of the bill to close said outlet, by two-thirds majority, and that too, against the arguments of the State Engineer, who advocated making additional outlets instead of closing them.

Mr. Bayley did not know till long after he had commenced a war upon the "outlet theorists," that that most accomplished Civil Engineer and fine scholar, Prof. C. G. Forshey, entertained the same views and had arrived at the same conclusions with himself; these were that levees can be *relied* on for protection of the Mississippi Valley from overflow, if properly located and well constructed, and constantly maintained and guarded;—that the elevation of the Mississippi high water line is not increased permanently by building levees and *closing* outlets; on the contrary, that their tendency is to *lower* the high water line ultimately, and to lessen the danger of overflows.

Mr. Bayley left the State service and took charge

JUDGE E. NORTH CULLOM.

of the surveys and location of the New Orleans, Opelousas and Great Western Rail Road in the summer of 1852. In the year 1856, he was elected Chief Engineer by the Board of Directors, and held the position until 1866. During the Military occupation of that Road from 1862 to 1866, the work of its construction was of course discontinued, but the organization of the Company was maintained.

In January, 1864, Mr. Bayley was unexpectedly, and without solicitation, tendered the City Surveyorship of New Orleans, and upon being urged to accept on the ground of subserving the public interests by I. N. Marks, Esq., and other prominent citizens, he complied with the request, and used his best efforts to conduct the affairs and business of the Surveyors' Department, economically, efficiently and honestly, until April 1866, when the New Orleans Opelousas and Great Western Railroad having been restored to the Railroad Company, he was unanimously elected by the Board of Directors, their General Superintendent and Chief Engineer, and accepted the position.

During Mr. Bayley's Chief Engineership of the New Orleans, Opelousas and Great Western Railroad, he made surveys and examinations for the extension of said road to Texas, and located the line to the Sabine river. He also surveyed and examined the whole country on two routes, to Shreveport.

Mr. Bayley was also the Land Commissioner of the New Orleans, Opelousas and Great Western Railrord Company, and had entire charge of all matters connected with the Land Grant business of said Company from 1856 to 1866.

Probably no one is so familiar with the whole country and its topography from New Orleans to Red river and Shreveport, as Mr. Bayley.

Under his Engineership, the N. O., and O. G. W. Railroad was graded nearly to Opelousas, and, but for the late war, would have been completed to Texas. The accumulation of interest on the bonded debt of the road during the war, and military occupation, prevented its completion. He remained General Superintendent and Chief Engineer of the road till its sale to Charles Morgan, Esq., in May 1869.

In June 1869, he accepted service with the New Orleans, Mobile and Texas Railroad Company, and took charge of the location and construction of said Railroad from New Orleans to Houston, Texas, (Mr. Van Block being Chief Engineer,) and, superintended the building of the railroad to Donaldsonville. On the 1st of May 1871, he was appointed Chief Engineer of the road, in place of Mr. Van Block, resigned. In September 1871, he was, without solicitation, elected General Superintendent, in addition to his office of Engineer.

Mr. Bayley is a member of "the American Society of Civil Engineers," and of the New Orleans Academy of Arts and Sciences.

None of his contemporaries is better entitled than Mr. Bayley, to the character assigned in ancient times to Fabricius, of whom it was said, "It would be easier to turn the sun from his course in the firmament than Fabricius from the path of Justice." The same may be said truthfully and without exaggeration of this distinguished public servant. In a venal and corrupt age, he has, throughout his whole career, vindicated his entire incorruptibility. He is a man of rare ability in his profession, whom office has always sought, and who has never sought office. Of a genial temper and affable manners, and a fulness of information attained by few, he is yet so modest and unostentatious as never to obtrude an opinion until it is solicited. Such is the breadth of his intellect, and his knowledge of human affairs, that there is no office, which this quiet civilian is not adequate to fill, and which he would not adorn. Better, far better to fill places of trust in this country, from the rank of the conservatives, than that of the destructives of the age!

Mr. Bayley has been twice married. His first wife was a Miss Coppell of New York, who was subsequently lost at sea by shipwreck, on her way to New Orleans in 1849. He has one son living by his first wife.

In January 1851, he married a daughter of Samuel E. Lawes, Esq., of Plaquemine, Iberville Parish, Louisiana. They have four children living, one son and three daughters.

Mr. Bayley's father, aged 81, and mother, aged 77, reside with their son. Mr. Bayley's oldest son, from early in 1861 until the termination of the war, served in the Washington Artillery, of New Orleans, and lost his right leg in the trenches at Petersburg, about one month before the capture of Richmond. He was in the Richmond Hospital at the fall of Richmond, and was taken to Point Lookout, and thence returned to New Orleans.

The Pontchartrain Railroad runs to the lake from which it derives its name, from the head of Elysian Fields street, a distance of five miles. It is a very pretty ride. This route communicates with all the steamboats, that traverse the lakes to the various villages and landings that surround it, which make this their starting point. From here, a passage is obtained to Biloxi, which, the reader will recollect, was the first spot settled by the French in this portion of the world; and, from that circumstance, will naturally excite the curiosity of the intelligent way-farer. At the termination of this railroad is a first rate hotel for the accommodation of visitors. Here is good bathing, fishing and shooting; and beneath the shades of the trees, the breeze from the water is delightfully refreshing.

Gretna, is nearly two miles up the river, and stands opposite Jefferson City. The whole distance is spotted with comfortable residences, principally inhabited by the owners of the adjoining grounds, and the walk from Algiers to this village is very gratifying to one partial to such exercise. The village has a rural appearance, is regularly laid out, and exhibits some neat residences. The forest approaches quite near; and, the idea that one may lose himself in the neighboring woods, gives to the place a touch of romance which only the denizens of a crowded city know how to appreciate.

CHARLES FITZENREITER.

THE Administrator of the Water Works and Public Buildings of the city of New Orleans is the youngest member of the Board, having just attained the age of thirty-two years. The duties devolving upon him are of an important and responsible nature, and in the short time he has had charge of this department of the city government, he has evinced great aptitude and acquired a knowledge of all the details of the office that promise to make him an efficient and popular officer. His administration so far has been highly satisfactory to the public and gratifying to his many friends. Mr. Fitzenreiter received only a common school education, acquiring a knowledge of the English, French and German languages, completing his studies in the 3d District High School of this city, then under the charge of Professors Rapier, Canonge and Lognet.

In 1856 he entered the service of the Tow Boat Association, and continued there employed until the commencement of the late war. Then as a Lieutenant of the 22d Louisiana Volunteers he enlisted in the Confederate service. Subsequently he joined Fenner's Battery as a private, and there served until the close of the war.

Upon the restoration of peace we find Mr. Fitzenreiter again renewing his connection with the Tow Boat Association, a position he filled until November, 1872, when, by a large and flattering majority of his fellow-citizens, he was elected Administrator of Water Works and Public Buildings, the office he now occupies.

In all the relations of life, Mr. Fitzenreiter is an exemplary young man. Polite and affable in manners, warm-hearted and generous nature, strictly honorable and correct in all his dealings, no young man in the city has a brighter future before him, and no one more friends to aid and encourage him on the road to usefulness and success.

CAPTAIN WILLIAM McCANN.

AMONG the faithful and efficient officers of the police of this city, no one occupies a higher place in the estimation of the community than Capt. McCann. A strict attention to, and a thorough discharge of, the difficult duties devolving upon him have secured for him a rapid promotion, and from a private in the ranks of the Metropolitan Police he has advanced through the various grades to the position of Captain of the 4th Precinct. Capt. McCann first joined the police force in 1869, then under Col. Thos. E. Adams as its chief. Previous to this time, and up to the capture of the city, most of Capt. McCann's life had been spent upon the "ocean wave." At an early age he became a sailor, and in his various voyages has seen every part of the world. In August, 1861, he enlisted in the Federal navy, under Commodore W. H. Morris, of the sloop of war Pensacola, which afterwards formed a part of Farragut's fleet of the West Gulf Squadron. After the capture of New Orleans, McCann resigned in August, 1862, and from that time to his enlistment in the police, conducted the draying business.

Capt. McCann was born in Tipperary County, Ireland, in 1837, and married a lady of this city in 1865. New Orleans is now his future home, and in all that may contribute to the advancement of the interests of the city, the preservation of its good name and peaceful character, none will be found more active, vigilant and devoted than the subject of this brief sketch, Capt. William McCann.

WILLIAM P. HARPER.

THIS gentleman was born in New Orleans, November 5th, 1835. His family were among the first American settlers of Louisiana, his father and mother being natives of this city. He claimed descent on the father's side from the old and distinguished family of Pennsylvania—his grandfather having been a contemporary of, and connected in business with, Daniel Clark, whose name through the Gaines' case has become so indissolubly connected with the city of New Orleans.

His father, Capt. H. S. Harper, will be remembered by many of our old citizens as chief of the police department, under the regime of Samuel J. Peters and Joshua Baldwin, and was conspicuous for the high order of his executive abilities, his great personal courage, and strict probity of character. On his mother's side the family were French, and, like many of our old families, were refugees from St. Domingo—driven to Louisiana by the revolution in that island.

Mr. Harper was reared in this city, and passed his collegiate course in Mississippi.

After attaining the years of manhood he adopted commercial life as most suited to his taste, and for many years occupied a responsible position in a large commercial house, where he enjoyed the confidence and respect of his employers, until the tocsin of war resounded throughout the land, and William P. Harper was among the first to raise the standard and press to the conflict, where he gained for himself a reputation for gallantry and courage that soon obtained for him an exalted position in the Confederate army. In 1861 he was most active in raising the Second Company of Crescent Rifles, which company left for Virginia in the celebrated 7th Louisiana Infantry Regiment, then commanded by Gen. Harry T. Hays. Soon after its arrival it was engaged in the famous battle of Manassas, and afterwards, as Hays' brigade, took prominent part in all the hard-fought battles of Northern Virginia. This brigade had the honor of being attached to the corps of Gen. Stonewall Jackson, and under his command participated in the celebrated Valley Campaign, the battles around Richmond, and all the movements of Lee's army, till the final surrender at Appomattox.

Mr. Harper was severely wounded at the battle of Sharpsburg, and left for dead on the field, where he fell into the hands of the enemy. His life was spared, however, it is to be hoped for the fulfillment of higher ends, for he soon recovered, and was exchanged, when he was recommended for promotion by Gen. Frank T. Nicholls of the Second Louisiana Brigade, and by order of Gen. Lee transferred to that command as Adjutant-General.

THE CITY HALL.

Again had he the misfortune to be wounded at the battle of Rappahannock, and was sent to Johnson's Island, where he was confined for one year; then again exchanged, though still suffering from his old wounds; but, nothing daunted, his indomitable courage prompted him to fight unto the bitter end, and he was ordered to his native State, Louisiana, where he served until the surrender; then, and not until then, did he sheathe his sword to resume the more peaceful avocations of life, in which sphere he promises to distinguish himself as eminently for his probity and honorable course, as did he for his bravery and gallantry on the field of battle—for foremost among the rising young men of this city stands the subject of this sketch, carrying another banner with "Success" engraved upon its folds.

At the close of the war Mr. Harper resumed commercial pursuits, and became cashier in the large factorage firm of Cummings, Brown & Co. In 1868 the Louisiana Equitable Life Insurance Company was organized, and he was elected secretary of that body, which position he continued to fill until the city election of November, 1872. The Fusion party nominated him candidate for the office of Civil Sheriff of the Parish of New Orleans. The nomination of Mr. Harper proved a very popular one, for he ran at the head of his ticket, and was elected by over 11,000 majority; he was also returned by the two boards, which were in conflict in that momentous period, and declared elected by all parties. His star was still in the ascendant, and carried him successfully through the political conflict that agitated his native State, as fiercely almost as the last civil war.

In June, 1872, Gov. Warmoth appointed him Adjutant-General of this State, in lieu of Gen. Longstreet. He, however resigned that position on securing the nomination of Civil Sheriff, a position which he now fills with dignity and credit to himself and satisfaction to his many friends and admirers who are watching his career with eager curiosity to discover what honors fortune yet has in store for this promising and hitherto successful young man.—*Nous Verrons.*

The impunity with which the ladies of New Orleans promenade our streets at night, unmolested by passers-by, and unsubjected to offensive looks or comments, argues either a confidence in the character of our people, or the respect entertained for them by the sterner sex. In many other cities of the Union no lady can venture out without jeopardizing her modesty, by being aggressively approached, rudely leered at, or insultingly criticised. In some localities escorts are indispensable as a safe guard against indignities.

But here it is a common subject of remark and observation that our ladies, often belated after night-fall, return home, unintimidated by their tardiness, or unapprehensive of any unpleasant rencontre. The fact may not be of such catholic application as to indicate the character of all Southern communities, but certain it is that, in this city, the tone of popular sentiment towards the fair sex is one of marked deference, and eloquently asserts the gallantry of our people towards those whose gentler natures and purer hearts would instinctively shrink from an unseemly obtrusiveness.

B. M. TURNBULL.

B. M. Turnbull was born on "Longwood Plantation," Pointe Coupee, La., 18th November, 1836, and removed to New Orleans in 1847.

He was educated at the University of Louisiana up to the age of seventeen years, when he entered the Counting-house of William Mure, Esqr., British Consul. Under this strict and accomplished merchant, who was one of the largest buyers of cotton in the South, he was taught the rudiments of the commission business. He was next employed in a large cotton factorage house, where he worked until 1856 in a clerical capacity, when he entered into the same business in copartnership with his brother, and, until the breaking out of the war, was successful in conducting the affairs of the firm. In 1860 he was first drawn into politics, in a manner which showed the status held among the young men of the city. The branch of the young Democracy supporting Breckenridge and Lane in opposition to the old, or rather Mr. Slidell and his co-workers, organized for the Presidential campaign. A club numbering some 2,000 members was formed, and Mr. Turnbull was chosen president, owing principally to the fact that he was no politician but a merchant who, for his years, had few rivals in commercial standing.

The canvass was very spirited, and much acrimony marked its commencement between the two factions.

He set about to reconcile and bring them together in a united front, in which, after great efforts, he triumphed to the satisfaction of his party.

After the election he was conspicuous in organizing companies for the Southern army. He left the city when captured by Gen. Butler, and was in the Confederate service until the end of the war, having spent twenty-one months in the military prison on Johnson's Island. He fared sadly in the results of the war. His property was confiscated and sold, and he returned from prison with only $200, which he had borrowed, and a large family to look after.

Mr. Turnbull has always been an ardent and consistent Democrat. He was run for the same office, Administrator of Commerce, in 1868, and though elected, was counted out under the Warmoth regime. In the recent city and State election he was one of the principal leaders in shaping the policy of the Young Democracy or "Last Ditchers." In the ordeal of the many Conventions and Committees which were held for nominating a city ticket, he was always chosen unanimously for the position which he now occupies.

He married the eldest daughter of Judge T. Wharton Collens in 1859, and though only 37 years of age has a family of nine children.

He makes a conservative officer, though elected at a time of violent political excitement and party emotions; having in view solely the interests of the great city which he represents as one of her administrators.

JAMES SPENCER KNAPP, D.D.S.

This gentleman, son of Dr. Colby Knapp and Lucinda Murray, of German descent on the father's side, and of Scottish on the mother's, was born at Guilford Centre, Chenango county, New York, December 4th, 1824. His great grandsire, Knapp, of German extraction, emigrated from England to the British-American Colonies anterior to the Revolution. His grandfather, Elihu Murray, held a captain's position in the American army, and did efficient service in our first great struggle with Great Britain. He is said to have borne a strong personal resemblance to General Washington. Lucinda Murray was a descendant, in the natural line, from a titled lady of France, whose maiden name was Julie De Cavalrie. The union of the elements of the German, Scotch and French genius in one individual makes a strong character, from which something good or great ought naturally be expected.

Dr. Knapp was the eleventh of a family of thirteen children, and passed his boyhood where he was born, obtaining a good plain English education. That it was a good one, we infer from the fact that, at the early age of seventeen years, he rose from the grade of pupil to that of a teacher, and was at the head of a large district school, six miles north of Binghampton, Broome county, New York, which he is said to have conducted with unusual success; and we may here remark, in confirmation of his attainments, that no State in the American Union has probably paid more attention to the interests of popular education, by legislative enactments and liberal appropriations, and none has been more scrupulous as to the qualifications of those who are to instruct the rising generation, than our sister State of New York—the State of James Fennimore Cooper and Washington Irving. On completing his first engagement as a teacher, and wishing to possess the advantages of a still more liberal education than he had yet received, he, in the spring of 1843, resumed the course of his studies in a preparatory institution of the highest class, —at the academy just named, and where he had an opportunity to acquire an amount of learning sufficient to fit him to perform respectably to himself, and advantageously to others, the duties of an American citizen.

When Dr. Knapp had completed his academic course, he returned once more to his honorable avocation of a teacher, and took charge of a large school at Holmesville, Chenango, Co., N. Y., his native county, where his abilities, as a teacher of youth, were well known and highly appreciated. One of his pupils in this school was the celebrated Anson Burlinghame, of Massachusetts, who has often since acknowledged his indebtedness to Dr. Knapp for being the first teacher who inspired him with the love of learning, and aided him in his struggles to ascend the steeps of science. The teacher and his pupil were nearly of the same age, and although their paths in life were widely different, yet the eminent reputation to which Mr. Burlinghame attained as a brilliant orator in the popular branch of Congress, and his world-wide fame as a diplomatist, attested by his successful mission in China, must always have been a source of gratification to the less aspiring teacher, who, in early life, had contributed to shape his intellect and train his mind to virtue and knowledge.

At Binghampton Academy, Dr. Knapp first became acquainted with his future wife, Miss Emily A. Scott, of Bainbridge, N. Y., his fellow-pupil in the same institution, and who, upon leaving it, continued to prosecute her studies, for four years, under the private tuition of the accomplished Misses White, of the same place, and nieces of the celebrated Irish author Gerald Griffin.

Dr. Knapp came to New Orleans in the fall of 1845-'6, before he had attained his majority. Having pursued a partial course of medicine with his father at home, he continued his studies in that branch of it, relating to dentistry, which he made a specialty, and entered upon its practice in this city. His confreres have accorded to him the possession of a high degree of ability in this department of medical inquiry and practice, so essential to the relief of human suffering and the preservation of health, and his professional labors have been crowned with remarkable success.

On the 21st of October, 1849, he married Miss Scott, and brought her to New Orleans, living most happily with her until her death on the 15th of February, 1871.

The large number of educated and accomplished men, engaged in the practice of dentistry in this thronged metropolis, suggested to Dr. Knapp, and other members of the profession, the importance and necessity of establishing in our midst a dental College for their mutual protection against sciolists and pretenders; but, more than this, their thorough conviction that dentistry was not a mere art but a science, requiring to be thoroughly taught.

The first movement that was made for the establishment of a dental college in this community, and, we believe, one of the first, if not the very first, that was made in any of our cities, took place in the year 1867, in which Dr. Knapp took a leading and prominent part. The college was soon organized with a full corps of able and accomplished professors, who undertook to deliver lectures on all those branches of medical inquiry which are directly or indirectly connected with the science of dentistry. A regular course of studies is required to be pursued, and a certain number of sessions, of four months during each year, to be attended, before young gentlemen are entitled to their degrees, when, after having been thoroughly instructed, they take their walk in society as the members of a skilled and learned profession, and entitled to the confidence of the community.

From the commencement of its organization, Dr. Knapp has held the high post of Dean of the Faculty, and filled the Chair of the Theory and Practice of Dentistry, distinctions to which he is well entitled by his learning, his merits and the deep interest he has taken in the institution. He is an excellent lecturer, clear, intelligible, forcible and fluent. He reads, analyzes and methodizes everything that has been published on the science of

RESIDENCE OF E. T. WALSHE, ESQ.,

BARONNE STREET, NEW ORLEANS.

dentistry in this speculative age, and comes to the lecture-room with a fulness of information indispensable to the proper elucidation of the subjects of which he treats. This tact and skill, as a practitioner, have been recognized by his professional brethren both North and South, and his title to occupy a place in their front rank been promptly and generously accorded. If the agriculturalist, who plants a seed where one never grew before, is justly entitled to be regarded as a public benefactor, surely the individual, who contributes to impart a new dignity to science, whether relating to the body or the mind, and to elevate an occupation to the rank of a profession, is entitled to distinguished consideration in the community he has benefitted.

Dr. Knapp was appointed President of the Southern Dental Associatiion, and held that post of distinction during the usual term of one year. He has held the same office in the New Orleans Dental Association, of which it is needless to say he is a prominent member. For many years he has been a Fellow of the New Orleans Academy of Sciences. He is also one of the Board of Managers of the Louisiana Polytechnic School, now in course of organization. Though an exceedingly modest man, none of our citizens has more completely won his way to popular favor by his honorable conduct, integrity and affability. We have few more polished gentlemen among us than Dr. Knapp, and none who is more considerate of the claims of others, founded on personal worth.

WARREN STONE, M. D.

Dr. Stone was born in St. Albans, Vermont, in February, 1808. He was the youngest of three children; his brother, Chauncey, dying several years ago of the same disease to which he himself fell a victim. He leaves behind a sister much older than himself, and a venerable mother, on whom he lavished to the hour of his death, all the devotion and tender regard of his royal and affectionate nature. She was indeed worthy of his love. From her he inherited the physical development and the noble figure for which he was so distinguished—from her he derived the high intellectual and moral tone that spurred his ambition to fields of noble enterprise beyond his narrow home. It was from her precepts and her examples he imbibed the principles of truth, honesty, philanthropy and self-reliance that appeared so conspicuously in every sphere of his after life. His advantages for school instructions were very limited, but what are they to the solid principles of enlarged thoughts and actions, interwoven into the very growth of his physical nature by a mother so well qualified to educate him both by precept and example! Although apparently so badly prepared to enter on the study of a liberal profession, he exhibited an early preference for medicine. He went from his rural home to be placed as a student under Dr. Twitchell, an eminent physician and surgeon in Keene, New Hampshire. From Dr. Twitchell, a gentleman of reputation and signal ability, he always acknowledged he received the greater part of his professional knowledge. He ever spoke of him with respect and affection, and so on Dr. Stone's first visit to the North they renewed and cultivated a friendship so honorable to professor and pupil, so rare in the present day.

From Keene he proceeded to the medical school at Pittsfield, Massachusetts, where he graduated as a doctor of medicine in 1831. He exhibited in his medical studies much the same disregard for the literature of his profession and books which he retained long after; but to all that was practical and demonstrative he was particularly attentive and well instructed.

In the latter part of his professional life he paid greater attention to the written records of his profession, and there were few more accurate in everything relating to the advance of medicine. Opportunities for practice being few, he took passage October 10, 1832, from Boston, in the brig Amelia, of New Orleans. This voyage was particularly unfortunate. She encountered frequent storms, the cholera appeared on board among the crew and passengers, and at last, on October 30th, the vessel with a valuable cargo and 108 passengers, was beached on Folly, Island, being leaky, and having made an ineffectual effort to put into Charleston harbor.

The passengers and crew were landed on the island, where Mr. Andrew Milne appropriated to their use his two extensive dwellings and other buildings. The city of Charleston sent down the most ample supplies, provisions, clothing and hospital stores, and as they were badly affected with the cholera, dispatched for two other physicians to assist in giving proper attendance. On the seventh of November the physicians employed by the authorities at Charleston were so broken by their exertions that they requested to be relieved from duty, and professor Thomas Hunt, at that time a young and distinguished physician of Charleston, was appointed to take sole charge of Folly Island and of all the passengers and crew of the brig Amelia. Under his administration the disease soon abated, and the mortality, in a short time, was completely extinguished. Dr. Hunt received the most flattering testimonials from the inhabitants and strangers of the island. The Board of Health and City Council of Charleston presented a magnificent silver vase, now in possession of his son, Carleton Hunt, Esq.

Dr. Hunt attended Dr. Stone when he was ill of the cholera, and afterward gave ample accounts of his valuable services in taking care of the sick. The Amelia was burned, and another vessel chartered to carry her passengers to Mobile and New Orleans, where Dr. Stone landed in November or early in December. He was sick, poor, and without sufficient clothing to protect him against the very cold weather of that season. He made ineffectual efforts to procure any kind of labor to provide for his wants, when Dr. Cenas, a physician to the Charity Hospital, procured him employment in a very subordinate capacity in the Charity Hospital. He there gave such evidence of ability and industry, till, we learn, again meeting with Professor Hunt, now removed from Charleston to this city, and appointed resident surgeon of the Charity Hospital, August

31, 1833, he received from Dr. Hunt the following recommendation to the administrators of the Charity Hospital. The result of this application we do not know, but in the following year we find him acting as assistant surgeon under Dr. Picton, and performing the greater part of the surgical duties of the hospital. After urging the necessity of an assistant surgeon, and of an immediate appointment, Dr. Hunt continues:

"I subjoin at the request of Dr. Warren Stone the following certificate and recommendation: I became acquainted with Dr. Stone when he was in attendance on the passengers and crew of the brig Amelia, wrecked in 1832, on Folly Island. It gives me pleasure to state from my own personal knowledge that Dr. Stone is a humane and worthy man, and a well-informed, skillful, and for his age, an experienced surgeon. He is in every respect qualified for the office of Assistant House Surgeon, for which he is a candidate. I respectfully recommend him to your favor as one whose appointment as assistant surgeon would prove valuable to myself and highly advantageous to the public. I am, gentlemen, very respectfully, your obedient servant,

"THOS. HUNT, M. D."

Dr. Stone having now the office of assistant surgeon, and performing the greater part of the services and until 1839, when, by the unanimous and unsolicited action of the board of administrators, and with the sanction of all the medical men, he was elected resident surgeon. Never was so elevated a professional office so meritoriously acquired; never was one so ably and satisfactorily filled. Now was fully inaugurated a career never enjoyed by any surgeon in America.

Known and endeared to the people by his services in the hospital, particularly in the free dispensary, which was filled by a large and anxious crowd every mid-day in the week: elected in 1836 lecturer on anatomy, and in January, 1837, professor of anatomy by the petition of the admiring class, and, on the resignation of Professor Luzenberg, lecturer on surgery, he became at the next session professor of surgery—the leading and most eminent surgeon and physician in the city, the most celebrated and popular professor in the school, until his resignation in the spring of 1872.

In the early years of his residence in the hospital, without many associates and few intimate friends, he devoted his whole time to the study of the cases, and to dissection in the dead-house. The knowledge of anatomy and surgery he had acquired from Dr. Twitchell and the elder professor, Nathan Smith, became in a brief time equal to that of his teachers.

The study of the anatomy of all the regions was so thorough that there was no local injury or disease which he was not capable of diagnosing, no surgical operation he was not prepared to undertake. He pursued such a system of daily post mortems on those who died in the various wards of the hospital that in a few years none were so capable of establishing the real nature or seat of the disease, none were more able to indicate during life, the organs and the tissues most seriously involved.

In conjunction with Dr. William E. Kennedy, an eminent physician of this city, he built, in 1839, an extensive and commodious private hospital on the corner of Canal and Claiborne streets. This private institution was very useful and enjoyed a great reputation, people being brought to it from the city and wide space of the surrounding country. But the proprietors, like most medical men, having no experience in managing the financial and domestic arrangements of so large an establishment, found it very unprofitable. Dr. Kennedy retired in 1845, and Dr. Stone, the most unfit person for conducting any complicated business out of his profession, retained the property, but never devoted it to any purpose profitable to himself. It was here, in 1841, he lost his eye from a specific inflammation contracted from a child. It was a source of great pain and suffering for years, and detracted much from his personal appearance.

In the year 1843 he was married to Miss Johnson, of Bayou Sara, and a few years afterwards built a fine dwelling next to his hospital, where he resided with all the elegance and comforts of a happy home, so congenial to one of his affectionate and devoted nature. Living so long in the world (to the age of thirty-two) without a home, without the society of an affectionate, intelligent lady, never was man so altered in his appearance and manners.

His marriage was followed in a few years by a young family. His devotion to his little children was of the most tender character, and among the few misfortunes that cast their shadows on his path, nothing was borne with so inconsolable and profound affliction as the death of his little children. The people who knew him transiently knew little of the paternal affection that welled up in every throb of that kind and gentle nature of that noble and manly heart. It was the cherished hope of his existence, the long wished for consummation of his devotion to the future of his family, that he might see them elevated by early advantages of education and society above the disadvantages of the difficulties and humiliations of his early life, and that they might stand beside him on the same high platform that he had reached by his own exertions, his own energies and abilities. He educated an accomplished successor to occupy the rostrum which he had himself so long occupied without opposition, and to keep alive that reputation that he wished to transmit.

A year has just elapsed, disease, hopeless disease, was making rapid inroads upon his mental and physical energies. He often complained at home of his inability to deliver his lectures; he made an ineffectual and unsuccessful effort to call in the aid of the one he had educated and prepared to assist him: unexpected opposition manifested itself; all hope of accomplishing his long cherished wishes vanished like a dream; his feelings were deeply wounded by some from whom he anticipated more consideration, and he resigned the professorship he had held for thirty-six years and retired heart-broken with all his long cherished hopes scattered and lost forever. Oh, Warren Stone, how few like thee stood in the world ready to sacrifice much for others, how few like thee would have smothered in silence

the beatings of thy proud heart—would have stood before God uncomplaining, that although not blameless themselves they had been unkindly treated by others.

In politics he was a man of the people and always a leading Democrat. We were always pleased and instructed at his vast display of political knowledge and at the force and ability with which he announced and developed the elevated and stern principles he had adopted as the foundation of his doctrines. What man, seeking appointment, did not besiege him for recommendation, knowing well that no name was more honorable or more influential?

When the war of 1861 was brought upon the South by the mischievous management of Northern and Eastern politicians and clergymen, Dr. Stone went with his party, and, like the other leading members of his profession, sympathized with those among whom he had so long resided. He had a regular commission in the Confederate service, was appointed Surgeon General of the State, and by his advice and labor added valuable aid to the cause of humanity. He visited the battle-field of Bull Run and Shiloh, took his share of the billingsgate and tyranny from Butler, returned the Puritan morality by his skillful services to their wounded Federal officers, and when the war was over, retired to the labors of his peaceful and useful life. During the war the death of Dr. Stone, of Natchez, gave rise to a published report of the death of the subject of this memoir. Professor Hunt, in a letter from Nassau, who held a better pen than this, and who was long more intimately associated with him than the writer, then wrote to his son, Carleton Hunt, Esq., an eminent member of the New Orleans Bar:

"I heard to-day that Dr. Stone died in New Orleans a few weeks since. His death, I have no doubt, was prematurely caused by mental disturbance produced by the war. A New Englander by birth, he still could never tolerate the idea of subjugation of the people of his adopted State by the United States. His mind suffered under the oppressions of Butler and Banks. He lost self-control, and died broken-hearted. Dr. Stone was an extraordinary surgeon, a great observer, and most remarkable, clear, simple, didactic lecturer. He was a man of strong sense, vivid imagination, lively humor, some wit, and interesting and engaging talents. Above all his conspicuous endowments and faculties and acquirements, shone most bright, philanthropy. He studied and practiced his noble profession as a devoted officer of humanity for the purpose of relieving his suffering fellow beings."

The points in our late friend we approach with the greatest diffidence, are the acknowledged excellencies in his intellectual development, his professional characteristics and his high moral and philanthropic character. If the extraordinary development (twenty-three inches in circumference) of the brain be an accepted indication of the degree of power of the intellectual and emotional manifestations, then should he by this evidence have been admitted among the most gifted of mankind! His memory was unsurpassed; what he observed, what he read, what he heard, he seemed never to forget. During the greater part of his life he used no memoranda in his extensive business; no notes in his lectures or addresses, no written records of the vast amount of interesting facts daily submitted to his careful examination. Patients the most transient, returning after a long interval to his care have been astonished and pleased to find that the recollection of their persons, their diseases, and the very prescriptions were fresh in his memory. He read more than was generally credited. His references to historical facts, his wonderful political knowledge in everything that was really important on modern history of the United States and of Great Britain, made him a formidable opponent in a discussion; his knowledge of general literature, and more particularly of the English poets and essayists he often aptly quoted, was an unexpected pleasure to many. In his profession, what he saw and what he learned he never forgot. It was from this vast accumulation, ever at his command, that he contributed those general principles he formed in every department of his knowledge. Indeed, there were few subjects on which he had not adopted opinions or some general principles. His judgment in pronouncing the nature of a case, particularly of one properly surgical, was the most distinguished quality of his mind. The treatment, the operation, the time, the manner of operating and above all, the after treatment, were the points in which he excelled all others of his contemporaries. I saw in Charleston, at the meeting of the American Medical Association, of the most eminent surgeons and physicians in America, an unfortunate fellow from North Carolina, who had attended this and the previous meeting at the North, in 1851, hoping to be relieved of a tumor in the antrum. It was shown to the writer by an eminent professor of surgery, a Philadelphian, who pointed out the indications of what he called fungus hæmatodes, a malignant disease, so pronounced by all the surgeons. It pushed up and disfigured the whole of the left side of the face and of the orbit, drove out the teeth from the alveolar processes, the left side, and produced altogether a shocking deformity of the face. Shortly after my return to New Orleans I found that this man, whom no operator would touch, had arrived at the Charity Hospital and placed himself under the care of Dr. Stone. After thorough examination he pronounced, in spite of all the other diagnoses, that it was non-malignant growth or polypus in the antrum. He proved the truth of his opinion by extracting the growth through the cheek. I witnessed part of the operation and took the tumor in my hand as soon as it was exposed and drawn out. It was a simple fibroid, and the man was recovering rapidly when the erysipelas, then contagious in the hospital, invaded the wound and destroyed the patient's life.

In his frequent consultations with Dr. Wederstrandt he pronounced several obscure and fatal cases of pulmonary disease to be cancer of the lungs, and in two cases of heart disease, one of which occurred lately and baffled the diagnosis of all the experts, he also positively announced what was proved by autopsy, that they were cancerous affections of that important organ. No man in the profession can avoid admiring such uncommon exhibitions of cultivated tact. In the ends of his fingers appeared a *tactus* condition that surpassed all other examples of that wonderful education of touch. He declared the presence of pus when none of us could feel it, and the knife decided the opinion.

On his last visit to London, where he was received with great attention, an eminent surgeon pointed out to him a very obscure case in the neighborhood of a joint that no one could decide. Dr. Stone applied his fingers to it. "Here is pus," said he. The scalpel was brought, and a deep insertion proved the truth of the assertion. His improvements in surgery were many. He did much to inculcate the propriety of opening diseased joints. From the first to the last of his career he insisted on the use of frequent nourishment, of alcoholic and malt stimulants, and of the whole class of medicines and materials considered as tonic and analeptic. He advocated in the medical journals for many years the use of cod liver oil in combination with phosphate of lime in diseases of the the nutritive functions. He was the most persistent and judicious prescriber of mercury in various forms of disease I ever knew. Quinine was probably the medicine he particularly excelled in the use of. He claimed and deserves the reputation of being the first to introduce it in the treatment of yellow fever, and in all malarious, diathier or nervous type he resorted to it with singular success. As a surgeon he was a conservative, and when he visited the bloody fields of Bull Run and Shiloh, his presence contributed to the salvation of many a wounded limb to be consigned to the amputating knife. In the latter battle, Col. Campbell was wounded in the lower third of his right arm. The bone was badly broken, and the eminent surgeons in consultation advised amputation. How gladly I heard of his return from Fort Jackson, where he had been ordered after a brutal exhibition by the brutal Butler. The instant I had him brought to the patient he made an examination and declared: "it shall not come off." He lifted it gently into a pasteboard cradle, and after some exfoliation it was as strong and as useful as ever before. What is to be gained by the relation of personal reminiscences of a skill and experience known and loved by thousands.

We have spoken of his generosity and of the unpaid services that he dispensed to thousands of grateful recipients. He never acknowledged the importunities of street beggars, he rarely made an exhibition of his charity by public subscriptions, yet we have it on the authority of himself and of his excellent lady that every year he provided her with a fund of from fifteen hundred to two thousand dollars to be dispensed by her for the benefit of the poor.

Having completed this brief biographical sketch of Dr. Warren Stone, it will be proper to make a more critical special analysis of the personal character and the intellectual and moral attributes for which he was most distinguished. From his early years he was of a genial and frank disposition, but not hilarious.

He enjoyed all innocent amusements, and although not gifted with original wit or humor, had the keenest perception of what was flavored with either, and a fund of anecdote and quotation with which he was wont to illustrate every point in his discourse that he desired to impress most forcibly on the mind of the listener. Envy and personality he never indulged in, but his honest and truthful nature exhibited a peculiar dislike to presumption, pretension, and the thousand arts by which ignorance, mediocrity and occasionally superior intelligence attempt to impose their thousand arts and practices upon the credulity of mankind. To the lowly, the unassuming, he was peculiarly indulgent. How often have I seen him cast a white ballot for some illy educated candidate for graduation, as if recalling parts of his own history, with the remark: "he ought to be rewarded and encouraged for making so many sacrifices to raise himself to a respectable position."

Few of the unfortunate and clientless of his profession ever sought counsel or aid who did not enjoy his commendation or material encouragement. Of all men of his just and high title to honor, I never saw one so modest and unpretending, although by no means unconscious of his own merits, so overwhelmed by expressions of strong commendation, so charmingly moved by gentle and sincere and grateful declarations of gratitude and admiration for his knowledge and skill.

In the last resolution adopted by the faculty of the medical department of the University of Louisiana, it was recommended that a monument be erected to the memory of Dr. Stone, either in the college buildings or on some part of the college grounds, the most central or convenient position in the city. This suggestion was afterwards also made in the city papers by the Sisters of Charity. I was also informed that an eminent citizen came forward, who offered to subscribe a thousand dollars, and a distinguished clergyman on Dryades street, who proposed to guarantee the same amount. For various reasons the faculty do not wish to receive or become responsible for the funds, and they, therefore, offer all facilities to have responsible citizens appointed to take charge of subscriptions and to select the appropriate style of monument and the inscriptions that the whole public and the friends of Dr. Stone, forming the larger part of our Louisiana public, may be properly represented.

Dr. Stone died December 6th, 1872.

TURF REMINISCENCES.

ANTE-BELLUM NOTES.

The famous contests of Lexington and Lecompte.

Horse races are not what they used to be. The old veteran of the turf regards the flashy affairs of to-day with pretty much the same lofty disdain that our grandfathers entertain for the girls of the period. "They are not what they were when we were young."

The illusive halo that surrounds the past effectually dims the beauty of the present, and your old turfman finds more genuine enjoyment in recounting the glorious contests witnessed in his early manhood, than in attending meetings

HON. P. B. S. PINCHBACK,

EX-LIEUT. GOVERNOR.

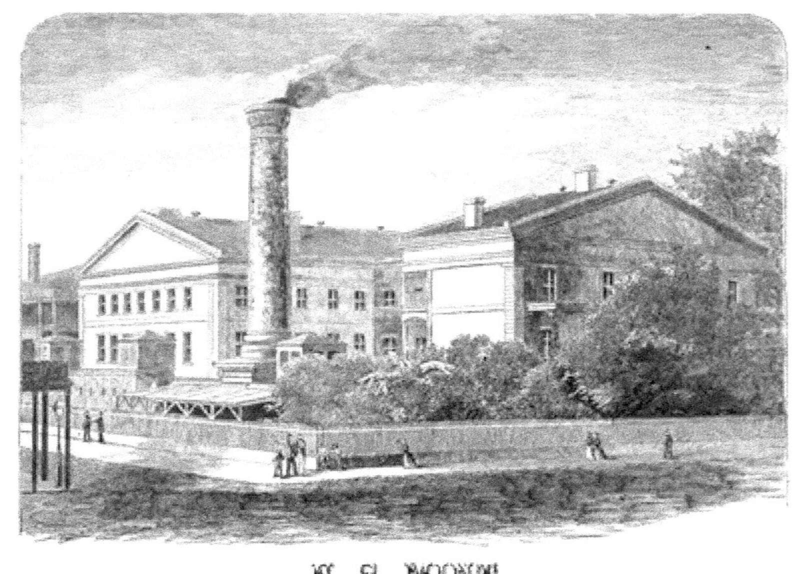

U. S. MINT.

at any of the noted courses in the country. How their eyes brighten with something of the wonted fire of youth, when they meet some friend of the olden time whose presence recalls the sports of *ante-bellum* days, and how like old soldiers they fight over again their battles, dwelling on each interesting incident with the unmistakable gusto with which a *bon vivant* rolls a delicious morsel under his fastidious tongue.

The brightest episodes of the history of the turf in Louisiana occurred before 1855, previous to which there were five courses, upon all of which the music of flying feet was regularly heard with each succeeding year. There was the Eclipse Course at Carrollton, which has not been used since 1845; the Metairie, famed as the scene of Lexington's great victory; the Bingaman Course, over in Algiers; the Louisiana Course, on the Hopkins plantation, about twelve miles below the city, and the Union Course, now the Louisiana Jockey Club Course, and the only one now in existence as a course.

Each year, just previous to the Spring and Fall meetings, people from all parts of the South and West flocked to New Orleans to participate in the excitements of the races and in the gayeties and festivities which were incident thereto. In those days the rotunda on the ground-floor of the old St. Charles hotel was the general rendezvous where gentlemen met to discuss the merits of the different horses and to make their bets—pool selling not having been invented.

Among the throng who nightly gathered there were Col. Wm. Johnson, the Napoleon of the turf; Col. A. L. Bingaman, Col. Jeff. Wells, Dr. Merritt, Y. N. Oliver, Duncan F. Kenner, Capt. W. J. Minor, the brothers Lecompte (Gobsby and Kirkman), Col. McWhorter, Col. Westmore, Jim Valentine, Dr. J. W. Weldon, John L. Cassidy, Alexander Porter, James Cage, H. P. McGrath, Capt. T. G. Moore, old Dr. Burke, John G. Cox, Dick Ten Broeck, Beady Poindexter, Scruggs, and a host of others, most of whom are lying the green turf under.

As may be imagined, there was a delightful Babel in the rotunda every evening, and what with anecdotes, horse talk, bets and coruscations of wit—for some of the gentlemen named above were fine scholars and brilliant conversationalists—the hours were pleasantly away.

In these good old ante-bellum days, when horse-racing was pursued purely as an amusement, and not as a means for accumulating fortunes, turfmen, unlike the proprietors of the equine heroes of to-day, took a personal interest in rearing blooded stock, and were thorough judges of horse-flesh and accomplished riders.

AN AMATEUR RACE.

At one of the race meetings at the Metairie, a discussion arose as to the merits of some of the horses that participated in a race the previous day, and one of the owners of a beaten horse, Col. Wells, remarked, if he had ridden his horse he could have won the race. Duncan F. Kenner, who owned the winner, being somewhat nettled at this statement, proposed that they should enter the same horses for a sweepstake of $1000 each, two mile heats, *gentlemen riders*, Kenner stipulating that he would ride his horse if Col. Wells would ride his. This proposition was eagerly accepted and the race was duly arranged; a third horse to be ridden by an English gentleman, Mr. Holland, being entered, making the stakes $3000.

The day fixed for the race arrived, and as each of the gentlemen had hosts of friends in the city, there was an immense and excited concourse present to witness the performance of their favorites. Betting ran high, and there was much chaffing and fun at the expense of the riders among the throng that swarmed upon the quarter stretch.

Old Dr. Burke, who always took the long chances in betting, observing the English gentleman, with a fine jockey suit of crimson jacket, white corduroys, patent leather, tasseled-top boots, etc., remarked in his quaint way and loud enough to be overheard by the gentleman himself: "I'll bet five dollars to a hundred that the fellow with the shiny boots falls off." The Englishman, with true British pluck, strode up to the Dr. and said, I'll take that bet, sir," and offered to put up the money. The Doctor responded and handed his five over, saying: "You hold the stakes, sir."

A good send off was had, and the three contestants dashed down the quarter stretch, each rider sitting his horse quite gallantly, until making the turn, when the Englishman's inside stirrup breaking, he fell from his horse, which galloped round without him. Dr. Burke, who was intently watching the race, drew a long breath, and, turning to the crowd, raised his spectacles until they rested on his wrinkled brow, and exclaimed, to the amusements of the bystanders: "*I knowed it!*" as if he had previously arranged the affair, and the result was a matter of course.

GENTLEMEN RIDERS.

The heat was won by Colonel Wells, and both riders being pretty well used up, they retired to the weighing room, where they stretched themselves on benches to recuperate. Graves, the well known trainer of Kenner's stable, and a famous rider in his day, upbraided Mr. Kenner for not riding with more skill, and said: "If you can't do better I'll get up and ride myself." Ben Pryor, standing near, tapped him on the shoulder, and said: "Why, Graves, you can't ride; this race is made for *gentlemen riders*." Graves drew himself up pompously and exclaimed, with comic indignation, "Who says I ain't a *gentleman*!"

Old Hark, trainer of Colonel Wells' stable, and who afterwards trained the celebrated Lecompte, congratulated his employer on his success, and remarked, in his patronizing way: "All you got to do, Colonel, is to hold your horse well together, and you wins this race, sure.

Wells, who was still puffing and blowing from the unwonted exertion, said, "Don't bother me, Hark, I wouldn't ride another heat for $10,000." Kenner, who was pretty well exhausted himself, and who had not the remotest idea of riding another heat, thought this an excellent opportunity to try a little game of bluff, and springing nimbly up, he said, "I'm ready now for the next heat," thinking to get a walk over.

After considerable diplomacy on both sides, it was agreed to postpone the race to some future day, and when it came off, was finally won by Kenner's Richard of York—old jockeys riding.

LEXINGTON AND LECOMPTE.

The enthusiasm and excitement in race matters culminated during the celebrated contest between those giants of the turf, Lexington and Lecompte, both foaled in Kentucky, near that famous centre of the Blue Grass country, Lexington. Lecompte was brought South as soon as weaned, and raised on Col. Jeff. Wells' plantation, on Red River, while Lexington was raised by Dr. Warfield, near Lexington, where he was foaled. Both were winners of colt stakes when two years old, Lexington running under the name of "Darley." In their subsequent encounters they made such fame for themselves that the friends of each looked forward eagerly to their meeting in the great Post Stake State race over the Metairie, for which they were both entered as representatives, respectively, of Kentucky and Mississippi, Highlander being entered for Alabama and Arrow for Louisiana.

The city was crowded with people who came from all sections to witness this great contest between the most noted thoroughbreds in America. Each horse had its host of friends and backers, and the night previous to the race the rotunda of the St. Charles Hotel resembled a vast bee-hive. Betting ran up to enormous figures, and the whole town was perfectly ablaze with excitement. Even the newsboys made their little wagers, based on prospective sales, and livery stable keepers and cabmen were in a seventh heaven of ecstasy.

The prices for cabs and carriages were enormous, and it is safe to assert that not a human being who could possibly help himself remained in town when the momentous Saturday arrived. The track was quite sloppy from recent rains, and hence slow time was anticipated.

Highlander having come here with immense reputation, $10,000 having been paid for him by the Alabama party, expressly for this race, had the call in the betting, though no odds were offered.

Lexington was the second favorite, and there was considerable betting as between him and Highlander.

The race was four-mile heats, twelve subscribers, three for each State, $1000 p. p.—total $20,000; each horse to get $1000, if not distanced.

The drum tapped at a good start, Lexington taking the lead, never was headed, and finished winning easily by four lengths, with something to spare. Lecompte second, Highlander third and Arrow distanced. Time—8.08¾. The result of this heat caused a perfect furore and considerable change in the betting, $100 to $60 being offered on Lexington against the field. Highlander's friends, however, still sanguine, believing that he had not been put to his mettle.

In the second heat, Highlander took the lead, and forced the running, Lexington close up. On the back stretch, in the second mile, Lecompte took the lead, and kept it throughout the third mile, Lexington second.

In the fourth mile, in the back stretch, the Kentucky champion went up and ran dead-locked with Lecompte, Highlander distanced well up in the home stretch, Lexington winning the heat and race by several lengths, amid tremendous cheering; time 8.04. The last mile was the fastest, being made in 1.50, which was excellent, considering the wretched condition of the track.

The varying chances of this race, the immense amount at stake, and the interest manifested by every one present—among whom, by the way, was ex-President Fillmore—rendered it one of the most remarkable in turf annals. The 1st of April, 1854, will not soon be forgotten by any of the vast concourse that assembled to witness the contest of the two illustrious sons of Boston.

THE SECOND RACE.

The result of this race caused a vast deal of speculation as to the next meeting of Lexington and Lecompte which was anticipated on the succeeding Saturday, the great four-mile day a purse of $2,000 having been advertised by the Metairie Jockey Club.

These anticipations were realized, and when Saturday, the 8th of April came, the two rivals and Rube appeared to contest the honors. Lexington was largely the favorite, and much money was bet on time, 7.32 being the lowest marked. The track was in tip-top condition. To the utter amazement of all and consternation of many, Colonel Wells' gallant steed won the heat with ease, taking the lead from the start and keeping it throughout, Lexington a good second. The time was unprecedented—7.26 being six seconds and a half better than Fashion's celebrated time when she ran with Boston.

In the second heat Lexington forced the running, taking the lead for two miles, but Lecompte passed him going into the third mile, which was made in 1.46. It may be noted just here that Lexington lost his stride going into the fourth mile, being checked up by his rider who thought the race was over. He immediately recovered, and closing the gap which had been opened on him, made a splendid struggle for the heat, which, however, Lecompte won by several lengths, thus scoring a victory over his great rival in 7.38¾, making the two best consecutive heats on record, Fashion's being 7.32½ and 7.45, and George Martin's 7.33 and 7.43.

THE GREAT RACE AGAINST TIME.

After the above extraordinary race, Mr. Ten Broeck, who had purchased Lexington immediately after the Post Stake, being much nettled, offered to run Lexington against Lecompte's 7.26 time for $10,000, race to take place between the 1st and 15th of April, 1855, over the Metairie Course, he to have two chances; Arrow to be substituted should Lexington be out of fix.

This challenge was accepted by Colonel Calvin Green and Captain John Belcher, of Virginia. The race accordingly came off on the 2d of April, 1855, the track being in superb condition, and the greatest crowd present that ever assembled at the Metairie.

When Lexington appeared, with Gilpatrick on his back, he looked the very picture of a race horse, and Ben Pryor,

ALFRED PHILLIPS, ESQ.

LOUISIANA

STEAM

Sash, Blind and Door Factory,

Nos. 299, 301, 303, 305 & 307 Gravier Street,

NEW ORLEANS.

ROBERTS & CO., ... Proprietors.

his trainer, received and deserved many compliments for the horse's condition. The betting changed from $100 to $80 to two to one in favor of Lexington.

The great antagonist against time took a running start from the draw gates, and passed the stand under full headway, with the horse Joe Blackburn to urge him on. At the second mile Blackburn was withdrawn, and Arrow was shot after him, running two miles, when Blackburn took up the chase, but never got near enough for Lexington to hear him. As the magnificent horse sped onward, and it became apparent that he would win, the excitement was immense, and finally when he dashed under the string in the marvelous time of 7.19¾, the welkin fairly rang again, and the noble horse regarded the tumultuous throng with something of pardonable pride. The first mile was 1.47¼, the second 1.52½, the third 1.51½, and the fourth 1.48¾.

FINAL STRUGGLE OF THE RIVALS.

This exploit of Lexington's aroused the pride of the Red River party, who still thought Lecompte the better horse, and they proposed that the two horses should start in the club purse, $1000 with an inside stake of $2500, to come off on the following Saturday, April 14th, 1855, which was eagerly accepted by Mr. Ten Broeck.

The story of this race, which aroused more excitement than any of the previous contests, and which caused more bitter discussions and hard feelings than any turf event, is soon told.

Lexington was the favorite at odds of 100 to 80, which odds, however, were eagerly taken by Lecompte's backers. At the start Lexington had the track, and for two miles and three quarters they ran side by side, amid tremendous cheering. Coming down the stretch in the third mile, Lexington went to the front and passed the string in the lead. Lecompte gradually closed on him in the back stretch, but at the half mile post Lexington drew away from him, opening a wide gap to the finish, and winning with great ease in 7.23¾.

Lecompte, after the heat, looked very much distressed, had cut his heels and pasterns with his plates, and his owner, Colonel Wells, asked and received permission to withdraw him. The friends of the beaten horse asserted that he had been out of condition, and there were ugly rumors of poisoning, which, however, were never substantiated.

This heat of 7.23¾, though run eighteen years ago, has never been equaled, and it is the nearest approach to the winner's wonderful time of 7.19¾.

Mr. Ten Broeck subsequently bought Lexington under the following circumstances:

Colonel Wells, after the defeat of Lecompte, was thoroughly impressed with the idea that his horse had been poisoned, and named a filly he had by Sovereign, out of Reel, the dam of Lecompte, "Poison," as an expression of that idea. After a race over Mr. Ten Broeck's course, in which Poison was winner, Mr. Ten Broeck offered Colonel Wells $15,000 for Poison and Lecompte, which offer was accepted, and the name of the filly was changed at once to Pryoress, in compliment to Ben Pryor, the trainer of Lexington. They were both taken to England, where Pryoress still is, Lecompte having died shortly after his arrival.

Lexington subsequently went blind, and was sold to Mr. R. A. Alexander, of Kentucky, for $15,000. His purchaser was twitted for buying a blind horse, but replied that he would sell one of Lexington's get for more money, and in the spring of 1864 he sold Norfolk to Mr. Winter, of California, for $15,000.

The blind old monarch, whose royal blood courses in the veins of thousands of the best race horses in America, and who numbers among his progeny such turf heroes as Tom Bowling, Monarchist, Harry Bassett, Asteroid, Norfolk, Lightning, Preakness, Bayonet, Kentucky, Idlewild, Bettie Ward and Annie Bush, still lives, and though twenty-two years old, is as vigorous as ever—the admiration of all Kentuckians.

TOURO INFIRMARY.

Among the many charitable institutions that are an honor to our city, and that succor and shelter our poor and destitute people, is the Touro Infirmary. This institution is situated on Peters, between Calliope and Gaiennie streets. The monotonous appearance of the environs is broken by this massive building rising up to the view. The building is a large, two-story brick one, with brown front, surmounted by a cupola, and it with the garden and outhouses covers half the square. Stone steps leading up to the portico conduct the visitor to the main entrance. The interior of the building is not such as would remind one of a hospital. There is none of the dreariness and sameness about it that is usually found in such institutions. A hall divides the building into four large apartments; those on the first floor are subdivided by folding doors and are used for parlors and offices. The hall and parlors are tastefully fitted up. In the hall hangs a tablet with the following inscription:

Judah, thou art he whom thy brethren shall praise.

This tablet is inscribed to the memory of Judah Touro, through whose benevolence this hospital was founded, May 4, 1854. The portrait of this benefactor of his race is suspended over the parlor mantelpiece. Though old, it has lost nothing of its worth. The soft blue eyes, in which there is something sweet and conciliating, the serene countenance and the pleasant and attractive curve of the mouth, plainly bespeak the distinctive traits of his character. With the poor and helpless of the Jews, his name will, in an especial manner, be held in grateful remembrance and veneration, and with all classes of our citizens in respect and admiration.

This institution is principally intended for the sick Israelites, who are taken in and cared for until they have recuperated their strength; yet, in cases of need, the sick of all religions are provided for. There is also a pay department attached to the institution. In the second story of the building there are four apartments for the sick. These are large and airy, and no disagreeable odor of the sick room about them. There are but seven invalids at present in the infirmary. In the pay department each patient has a neatly furnished room, and everything is at hand that one could desire. Every attention is given to the sick poor as well as the rich. For the insane cells have been long since erected, and the kind treatment bestowed upon them has proved the most successful means of restoring them to their right mind. The sick, when convalescent, can stroll through the fine gardens or recline in the delightful summer-houses.

This hospital has done good service. Thousands who came to it penniless and very nigh death's door have gone away strong and healthy. That this institution is a success, and that its method of treatment is as yet unsurpassed by any in operation in like institutions of our city, is evident from the small mortality that occurred during the epidemic seasons in this hospital when compared to that of other institutions.

The method of treatment in the infirmary, especially for the yellow fever, proved most successful. This institution is highly deserving of patronage of the public, and we regret to say that a very liberal patronage has not been extended to it. Mr. Joseph Levy is the superintendent, and a better and more active one could not be had. It is partly owing to the superintendence of this gentleman and the energy and tact of the board of managers that the institution is in so flourishing a condition. Dr. F. Loeber is the resident physician, a gentleman of great skill and ability in his profession.

THE NEW ORLEANS SAVINGS INSTITUTION.

A CHEF D'ŒUVRE OF ARCHITECTURAL SKILL.

Canal street has received another ornament to the architectural display exhibited in the many edifices of tasteful design on either side of that boulevard, the building of the New Orleans Savings Institution.
surplus fund from the earnings of the bank, the directors, after paying the depositors the interest on their amounts, determined to remove from their old quarters, and to build on a central site an embellishment to our city.

The promenaders of our favorite street have been attracted for some little time to the busy workmen engaged in the erection of a building near the corner of Baronne and Canal streets. As day after day passed, and the proportions began to assume shape and symmetry, the passers-by were held curiously wondering what would be the *finale* of such gorgeous commencement.

The style of the new bank is, throughout, a faithful copy of the Renaissance of Louis Quatorze. The front of iron is florid and ornate, yet rich in the tasty display of that ornamentation which was carried to so great a degree of extravagance in the reign of France's luxurious king. Unlike anything of the kind in this city, the æsthetic eye of the connoisseur can appreciate the graceful curves of the blocking course over the cornice of the front. The cornice proper has the pleasing effect of the Grecian and the enlivening influences of the later adaptations from the classical. Immediately over the door, shaded by the heavy *fronton* of the frame, is a handsomely-finished window in the French style, with a plate glass six feet by twelve, enriched by a handsome engraving, artistically executed.

The entrance next calls for an examination as its details are worthy of more than passing notice. The doors proper are of black walnut, floresque in their carving, and rendered unique by the introduction of two heads, of pleasing features. Each door has, besides the handsomely enriched panes of glass, two antæ or half columns of the united composite and Corinthian order, which add materially to the effect. The deep *renfoncement* of the arched doorway, recalls the architecture of the old Moresque Alhambra of Granada. To those who have studied the builder's art, we would call attention to the effect produced by the *tout ensemble* of this entrance. On reaching the interior of the bank, the visitor is at once struck by the wealth of decoration, and the profuseness of adornment. The counters seem from the workshop of some Antwerp artist. The *grilles* screening the clerks are in walnut, and are beyond all doubt unequaled in the South. Satyrs support in brackets the carved work over the counter, and they are wrought in a style which would do justice to foreign workmen.

The floor is paved with the encaustic tile, the design being in keeping with the other portions of the room. The walls and ceiling have called forth the well-earned praise of amateurs. Medallion portraits of Lee, Washington, Angelo, Bismarck, Humboldt, Maury, DeSoto, Burke, Watt, Newton, Napoleon and Morse, adorn the walls, painted in a manner which does credit to the artist. Near the ceiling there are also paintings representing genre subjects of like merit. In relief to the eye and in aid to the bringing out the effect of the furniture and surroundings, the walls are finished in panels of a chocolate red in harmony with the grand whole. The mantel with a high fronton, embellished by bronze medallions and panels which are really works of art, have called forth the praise they deserve. Over the mantel there is, on a golden background, a painting of three figures representing the "Spinning the Thread of Life," wrought in finished style and worthy of its place.

The immense safe, or vault, apparently would resist the attacks of the cracksmen, with all their tools and appliances. It is from the manufactory of Diebold & Kienzle, at Canton, Ohio, and was sold to the Savings Bank through the efficient agent, Mr. A. Roy. It is eight inches in thickness, the walls being composed of two sub-walls, of ¾ inch iron with concrete between. The lock is one of the most complicated, and at the same time simple in its mechanism, in the United States.

The directors' room, in the rear of the bank, is a commodious apartment, elegantly suited for their purposes. Up a winding stair, the visitor is ushered into the spacious chamber overlooking the business portion of the building, and profusely ornamented in fresco. Diogenes in his tub, and the boarding taker, are drawn on the ceiling with much effect. Around are nautical pictures, displaying the different kinds of water-craft in well drawn lines, and adding by their life a pleasing effect to the room.

Through the well-hole or opening below the working of the clerks can be seen.

ST. PATRICK'S CHURCH.

The ventilator above is an architectural victory. Letting in the light horizontally, the eye below does not suffer that blinding effect produced by the direct rays.

The New Orleans Savings Institution was incorporated in 1855, since which time it has drawn to it the confidence of the public. The amount of deposits now reaches to one million seven hundred thousand dollars.

The present administration is as follows: L. F. Generes, President; Thomas A. Adams, First Vice-President; Thomas Allan Clark, Second Vice-President; Samuel Jones, Treasurer. The directors are Dr. Mercer, George Jonas, David Urquhart, Chas. A. Leeds, C. Schneider, John G. Gaines and Carl Kohn.

The brain from whence came this masterpiece of the builder's art is that of W. A. Freret, Esq., who has been the designer of most of the handsome edifices of the city. His fertile imagination conceived the idea of adopting the Renaissance style, so entirely novel in our community.

The builder to whose care the work was entrusted was a native Louisianian, L. N. Olivier, Esq., and he has accomplished the work in a manner deserving praise. The rich and difficult fresco painting was from the hand of Mr. F. Haug, an artist of merit. W. A. Talen brought his chisel to effect the intricate carvings of the heavy doors and counters. His work would not suffer from a comparison with that of European makers. The heavy front, difficult in the ornamentation and confusing in its details, was from the foundry of Leeds & Co., and is of the best work ever put together. The time and care taken in the preparation of the castings were great. The outside painting and bronzing was the work of H. Rauschenbach, and is in keeping with the rest of the work. Take the structure from door to roof, it has not its equal in the South.

THE TEMPLE SINAI.

Looking back down the line of receding centuries, we find that the chosen Israelites have from time to time given distinguished evidence of devotion to their ancient faith by the rearing of stately and magnificent structures—houses of worship—which have commanded the admiration, and in one instance, at least, the wonder of the world. Of those days when the glory of Solomon brought even Queen Esther a wondering worshiper at his feet, and of the building of his Temple, the like of which will never again be seen—we must turn to the pages of the Bible for information. And there, aided by the sublime and beautiful language of the holy book, let imagination picture the great temple of the Lord at Jerusalem.

In that dark time when, through the power of the Romans, Palestine became a Roman province, the Jews were scattered as thistle down, blown by the wind over the face of the earth. Up to the time of Napoleon I. the condition in Europe of the Jews was fraught with persecutions, humiliations and deep sorrow. When Napoleon took upon his brow the imperial crown, he instituted many happy changes in regard to the government of the Jews, for there were many laws relative to them which were in some respects allied to the notorious black code of the Southern States. Thence up to the time when the Emperor's power began to wane, and until he was finally removed to St. Helena, the sun of prosperity shone with some favor on the Jews. After that event, misfortunes came thick and fast upon their heads, until the revolutions that swept over continental Europe in 1848 again wrought changes greatly ameliorating their condition. In the affairs of to-day, and since the establishment of the German Empire, their fortunes are, indeed, beginning to look bright, and their wealth and their intelligence are being universally recognized. But nowhere have the Jews been received with so much favor as in the United States. Here, the right hand of fellowship has at all times been extended to them; here they are recognized as citizens, and it is but justice to say that in the fulfillment of the duties of citizenship, none hold their duties as more deserving of conscientious regard than the Jews of America. With reference to cultivation and intelligence, the Jews hold deservedly a most enviable position throughout the country.

In the year 1864 a proposed secession from the orthodox church in this city agitated the minds of those who are called the Reform Jews. At the time when the proposition was first made, it did not receive enough attention to authorize the withdrawal from the orthodox church. But in the year 1871, a second call was made by the Reformers, and twenty-six persons answered the call. The result was the determination to build for themselves a temple, which would be the Reform Temple; and immediately one hundred and fifty names were enrolled as members of the new church in prospective.

In the meanwhile, during the New Year and the feast of the Atonement, Minerva Hall was used by the members for the necessary and usual religious exercises of that day. On the 12th November, however, the church was finished, and that event celebrated by a grand ball. The Rev. J. K. Gutheim, one of the most eloquent speakers in this country, who had been a Rabbi for many years in the Rampart street Synagogue, and who was then presiding over the splendid Temple Emanuel in New York, was at once procured as pastor. Since then service and lessons have been held regularly.

The lot on which the temple is situated was purchased from the Grand Lodge of Free Masons, and measures one hundred and twenty feet front on Carondelet street, by one hundred and seventy-five deep, running through to St. Charles street. The temple itself is eighty-three feet wide and one hundred and sixty feet long, leaving on either side a space of twenty-one and a half feet; which space is to be divided out into lots, which will be filled with handsome shrubbery and rare and costly flowers.

THE TEMPLE BUILDING.

The position of the Temple Sinai is extremely well calculated to give effect to its magnificent and well proportioned dimensions. At the distance of many squares from the building the eye can rest upon the gentle acclivity of the broad and elegant building, with marbled steps leading to a wide and beautifully arched portico, which is supported by slender, graceful columns of the Corinthian order.

On each side of the entrance rises an octagonal tower, not obelisk-like steeples, but plain, substantial towers, that might have adorned some Byzantine cathedral, or served as turrets for a Front-de-Bœuf. Each tower has its own eight windows, and countless lesser eyelets lighted up by the rays of the dying sun. Each is fringed with all the circles, curves and scallops of Byzantine and Gothic architecture, and capped by mosque-like green minarets. All this gives it an Oriental look, which the checkered Mosaic work of its red and yellow bricks, like the Mosque of Omar, adds to and strengthens.

Between the towers, above the entrance, stand boldly out the laws of the decalogue, those moral precepts and axioms upon which all systems of philosophy and all religions have built their faith. Graven on marble, printed in characters as immortal as the truth they tell, the strange, straggling and distorted Hebrew letters shine forth as they were received by Moses amidst the thunders of Sinai.

Over the two doors that give entrance to the church a wide marble arch extends with a motto and prayer from the Psalms, "Send thy light and thy truth, they shall guide me."

The beautifully stained and ornamented glass windows are cut in the Gothic style, and were made in Cincinnati. They are colored in dark, rich contrasting tints, and cut diamond shape, each diamond being bound with a leaden fold, which gives them an exceedingly handsome appearance. In the building there are two rows of these windows on each side, each row containing eight windows; then the circular towers gleam brightly in the sunlight as it falls on their many panes of stained glass.

Above the heavy brick raised work on the outside, and the chastely carved oak on the inner parts of each window, is placed a stained glass set, with a five-pointed star, and which is inclosed in a carved oak foil. The elegant manner in which the windows have been made, renders them one of the richest and most beautiful features of the building.

THE INTERIOR OF THE TEMPLE.

The temple is but plainly, simply ornamented; there are none of those curious symbolic signs and mysterious relics to cater to a diseased religious appetite that must be fed on miracles, wonders and mysteries. Down the church centre stretch two long aisles, leading to the pulpit, flanked on either side by large, handsome and comfortable family pews of substantial oak. Short iron pillars, of no particular style, support the gallery, which runs around three sides of the church, and which is like the hanging gardens of Babylon, literally detached from the wall and supported by huge oaken beams beneath. From this gallery thin, yellow Corinthian pillars support a Roman arch going to the roof. From out these pillars branch huge blue dew-drops, each bursting into a triple gaslight.

THE WOODEN DECORATIONS

of the temple are so varied and so exceedingly beautiful, as to make the observer question if there was among us another King David who had spent the years of his life in the collection of many-hued timbers for the adornment of the holy place. In the construction of the pews, as many as seven different kinds of wood have been used. The carvings and inlaid work on the pew fronts are most exquisite—the—well you might call it the back ground or ground-work is of a rich amber-hued timber, inlaid with soft, oily looking brown ovals, surmounted, and as it were bound, with double flutings of a delicate tinted wood, dark, but which has the appearance of the reflection on it of a rose-tinted curtain. The railing of the pew arms is of two fluted rows of wood, light and dark brown.

The pictured windows, set in black oak, soften the sun's rays, which stream through their colored panes with a dim religious light.

At the end of the chancel is the pulpit, the altar and

THE ARK.

In the ark are preserved the laws. It is the holiest place, the sanctum sanctorum, the mercy seat, where none but the High Priest was formerly permitted to enter. The ark is the most ornamental part of the building. Its front being the façade of a Grecian temple, supported by six composite pillars; the doors, two red doors of highly carved wood work; on either hand stand two tall scarlet candelabras, bursting like the golden candlestick each into seven branches, and each branch crowned with a dozen tiny jets of gas. Above it, ever burning, is a red lamp, symbolic of the immortality of the soul; above this are again the ten commandments, this time in golden letters, shining from a blue surface like stars in the heaven to lead us straight.

Before the ark is the pulpit, with a finely worked bible cloth on it; on each side two mighty chairs.

THE ORGAN.

This magnificent instrument has been erected in the temple. It is placed in the forepart of the building. While it is not the largest, it is certainly the most perfect and complete instrument of the kind ever erected in the city. It occupies an immense space, and when the mellow rays of the sun stream in through the stained windows, the deep gold and crimson, and rich dark wood, and carvings of the elegant Gothic structure, appear almost royal in their beauty. The organ was built by Koehnken, of Cincinnati, and contains sixteen hundred pipes, varying from the size of a water-bucket down to the size of one's little finger. The stops are thirty in number. The key-board of the organ is built in the shape of a good sized melodeon, which arrangement enables the organist to sit facing the officiating clergyman, and not with his back to him, as is usually the case. This instrument cost over $6,000.

In but few churches is the choir equaled. The Jews have always possessed a singular taste for and skill in music, and the congregation of Temple Sinai have thought money not wasted which was expended in the acquisition of a good choir. The present choir, which is under the direction of Mr. Leucht, cost the large sum of $5,000, and that, too, when most of the singers have voluntarily given their services.

Every Friday evening the church is filled with Gentiles.

DR. W. N. MERCER.

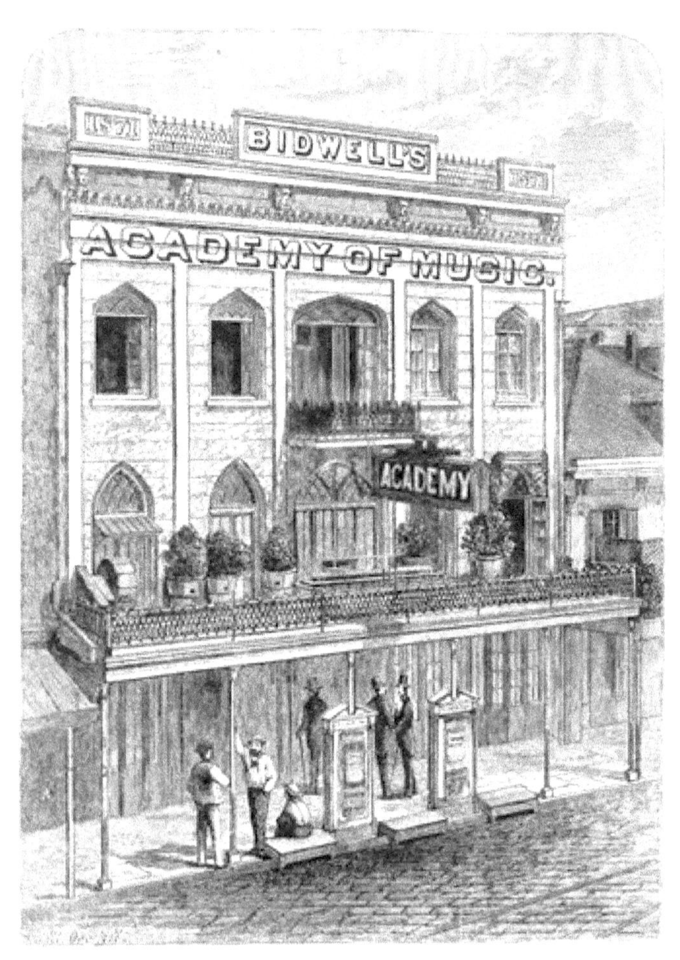

ACADEMY OF MUSIC.

who come here as the only place where, in summer time, really good singing can be heard.

THE SERVICE.

The clergy of the congregation enter—the Rabbi and the Reader—each accompanied by an assistant. Both are dressed in the black canonical robe, not in the ephod, and the robe of scarlet and blue, purple and gold, as commanded of old. The Reader wears a high, brimless, Fez-like hat; the Rabbi, one with the brim at the top, instead of the bottom, such as the undergraduates of Oxford delight in.

A stillness of deep feeling pervades the whole church, and no gossipy whispers or hints about bonnets or back-hair are heard. Suddenly the organ bursts forth into music, its weird voice appealing eloquently to our hearts. A moment after a choir of rich luxuriant voices takes up the dying echo of the organ, and chants in the soft mellifluous tongue of Palestine, the songs that Moses and the Israelites sang centuries ago to the glory of God. The whole congregation turn toward the choir, the Southern nature drinking in the music.

When the music had ceased, the reader read forth the lesson on the euphonious Hebrew, and the Rabbi, in a loud, firm voice, framed a prayer, which the whole congregation joined in, rising from their seats to do so.

Again a burst of song, and then alternate reading in rhythmic and chants, until a final prayer to God broke up the meeting.

As we gazed around us on the congregation, we saw many things to surprise us, whose only knowledge of a Synagogue was from tradition. The men's heads were uncovered, contrary to what we were wont to believe, and the women were no longer separated from the men and imprisoned in the gallery, but were sitting in all the parts of the church, enjoying religious equality. The daughters of Judah, here, have the opportunity their Christian sisters have, with their "dark eyes that flash on you a volley of rays that seem to say a thousand things at once," to tempt our minds to far more earthly thoughts than they should have within this sanctuary, or with their dangerous smiles, leading our thoughts and desires wandering in imagination over other fields than those of Paradise.

THE NEW LIGHT.

In the service also so much seemed changed. No prayer was muttered for the coming of the long expected Messiah, who is to hold dominion over the whole earth. No prayer for their return to that land that God promised Israel as an inheritance for his children. No prayer for the rebuilding of the twice built temple of David.

Tradition has made the Israelite a stickler to forms, a worshiper of old systems, clinging to the history and habits of the past. True it is, that for two thousand years they have clung to their old worship, though persecuted, robbed and murdered. The army of martyrs of the Christian church are but few by the side of the Hebrews, who have died for their religion; yet they who resisted persecution have yielded to the force of time, and the onward march of new ideas.

The main points on which the Reformed Jews differ from the Orthodox Jews, and which, though it separates them in their religious convictions, separates them neither in feelings nor in any other way, are these: the Orthodox Jews are awaiting the coming of a Messiah of David's seed, as promised them in the Bible, who is to be the conqueror of the world, and restore it to peace, prosperity and happiness. In the Reformed Church they do not look forward to any man as the coming Messenger, but consider the whole Jewish people as the Messiah. They have suffered that misfortune and captivity which is promised to the Messiah before he achieves his success.

THE NEW JERUSALEM.

The Orthodox Jews look forward to a return to Palestine; the Reformed Jews do not expect or desire that. True, it was that when God gave them that land, it was flowing over with milk and honey; now it is a dreary, repulsive solitude, where leprosy and a thousand other loathsome diseases flourish. Then it was a terrestial paradise, beautiful with blooming trees, watered by a thousand springs, and with fertile plains. It is not so now. The Israelites of to-day would not, could not dwell there. Some are on the frozen banks of the Neva, some under the tropical sun of Bombay, but few in the land of their fathers. The original Jewish temple, as built by Solomon, was looked on by the Jews as the centre of their religion. After the destruction of the first temple, they were promised a restoration of it. This took place during the reign of Cyrus. But the second temple was also destroyed in the disastrous storming of Jerusalem by the Roman army. The Orthodox Jews expect the rebuilding again of the temple, whilst the Reformed Jews regard the promise of the Almighty as already fulfilled in the restoration of the original temple. Besides these, all those religious customs depending more on the oriental character of the Jews than on any question of morality or ethics, have been swept away by these Reformers, such as the separation of men and women in the church, etc.

LEVITICUS.

In the same manner all those customary laws laid down in Leviticus are regarded, not so much as being divine laws of right or wrong, the breaking of which would be a sin, as simple rules and orders, suiting the then State and country of the Israelites, but which the are now unable to carry out. So it is with all the dietary and sanitary laws of the Bible, many of which are very good sanitary laws, but not binding on the conscience. The mode, too, of making the sacrifice, the peace offering, the sin offering, can no longer be followed, and is necessarily not binding. In the Reformed Jewish Church, the commandments are its canons. Besides these there are three great rules of belief: That there is but one God, a belief in the inspiration of the divine prophets, and in the immortality of the soul, but not in the resurrection of the body. The Reformed Jews do not propose, however, to desert their race. They do not believe in intermarriage between Gentiles and Jews.

With regard to the Sabbath, they still celebrate Saturday as the true Sabbath, but are prepared to give it up and adopt the Christian Sabbath, as they do not regard the commandment of the Lord as hallowing any particular day in the week, but as merely setting aside one-seventh of the week for rest and devotion. Thus has the Jewish Church, from which the Christian Church separated 1860 years ago, dropped almost all these distinctions that separated the two religions, and promises, in a not far distant time, the union of all races and peoples in one common worship.

Thus morally and religiously this congregation has proved a great success. Pecuniarily it has been equally successful. Built at a cost of $160,000, the first two sales of less than one-half the pews, realized the handsome sum of $170,000, $10,000 more than the total cost of the building, and a subscription of more than a thousand dollars from each member of the congregation.

The financial affairs of the Temple are in a most flourishing and promising condition. Fourteen thousand dollars now remain in bank for which there is no use, and the remaining pews are as valuable a piece of property as any in our city. It can not be expected otherwise than that the Temple would be prosperous under the gentlemen who have the management of it. It is to them and their energy and good sense that the congregation and the whole city owes this promising move in the right direction. To these officers too much praise can not be offered. They are at present, M. Frank, President; Julius Weis, First Vice President; Lewis Aleus, Second Vice President; Henry Abrahams, Treasurer; Ferdinand Marks, Secretary; whilst S. Forcheimer, D. Kaufman, J. D. Haas, S. Katz, Pierre Kleppman and Isaac Levy, compose the Board of Trustees.

OUR STREET CARS.

The remark that New Orleans has the best, most complete and pleasantly managed street car system in the country, is rather monotonous. People are as sure to notice that circumstance and comment upon it as the equally notorious fact of the sun rising on the west side of the river. It has been explained innumerable times that our cars are more conveniently constructed than others; that a better style of behavior—courtesy in fact—prevails among the passengers that we don't labor under the nuisance of a conductor, with his vile airs and his perquisites. These things have been dressed up and paraded heretofore in such profusion that it almost amounts to a slight upon the public intelligence to repeat them.

The public may be reassured; we have no designs in that direction. There are so many points of graver interest and more serious importance in this connection, that the inclination to be stupid has no support whatever.

The facts that nine-tenths of our citizens, no matter how remote their domicil, can go from Canal street to within two or three blocks of the objective point; that they can do so as a general rule in comfort and security from any inconvenience whatever—and this at the low rate of five cents; these are of course worthy all acknowledgment. But they are and have been acknowledged for years. Not a day passes, we venture to say, without thousands of eulogies—silent, perhaps—upon the street car system of New Orleans.

Another axiom is that they pay; and yet, with all deference to the enterprising gentlemen who compose the companies, and with our sincere congratulations upon the just reward which attends their labors, we fail to see how this interests the public further than to assure them that the car lines will be perpetuated for their accommodation. People are selfish, and, without the least envy of another's good fortune, are only interested in it so far as it contributes to their own.

From this point of view then—in its capacity as an element of comfort, a factor in the improvement and development of property, and a means of circulating money—we call attention to the street railway system of this city. It has conduced, more than any other cause, to the comfort of this community, to their mutual acquaintance and consequent friendliness of feeling, and, above all, to the appreciation of real estate in every part of the corporation. Population has invariably kept pace with its advances, and substantial improvement marked its increase.

Of a different nature, but no less important, is the influence it has exerted upon the industrial pursuits. Who can compute the number of men supported by these railway enterprises since their inception? Who knows how many mechanics, artisans, laborers, have found, in the innumerable channels of employment thus opened, the one stepping stone by which they have attained independence, perchance fortune! And who ever thinks to-day of the hundreds to whom the street railways are, directly or indirectly, the very breath of life!

For such reasons as these—their benefits to the public, their healthy influence on business and real estate, their humane mission to so many of our poorer class—we feel an abiding interest in the street-car business, and a desire to impart that interest to our readers. The investigations we have been making, and whose results are herewith presented, have proven eminently satisfactory. It will be seen that the leading companies are in a flourishing condition, and fairly keeping pace with the demands of an increasing population.

THE CITY RAILROAD COMPANY.

This company, organized in June, 1860, with a capital of $1,000,000 is the most extensive in New Orleans, comprising six different lines, viz:

The Esplanade line, running to Bayou Bridge, 3¾ miles; the Magazine and the Prytania lines, both running to Pleasant street, 2½ miles; Rampart and Dauphine line, running to the Barracks, 5 miles; the Canal street line, running out to City Park and the Cemeteries, 3¾ miles. All these routes are among the most frequented in New Orleans.

The original cost for constructing and equipping these lines was $997,194.86, viz:

Bonus to city for right of way	$142,966 00
Construction, including cost of materials, etc	559,878 38
Horses and mules	98,329 40
Cars	74,438 73
Real estate, including buildings	146,891 34
Building fixtures	4,022 94
Harness	2,644 13

CAPTAIN WILLIAM McCANN.

THE COTTON EXCHANGE.

In 1866, the Levee Line went into operation (May 16th) involving an outlay for construction, bonus, equipment, etc. of $312,915.68, making the total invested capital of the company $1,312,915.68. The capital stock was consequently increased to $1,300,000.

During the latter part of 1871 the Canal street track was removed from over the canal and placed upon the sides at a cost of some $37,000; and in September, 1872, the company extended the road from the Barracks to the Slaughterhouse. New buildings have been erected, extensions made, etc., at a considerable outlay.

At the Canal street station all the repairs to cars are done, and all feed cut and prepared for the different stations. There is a twelve-horse power engine at this station driving slat planers, mortising machines, hay cutters, etc.

The company has 718 mules and horses and 139 cars, the latter apportioned as follows:

Magazine—28 cars running, 2 extra.
Prytania—17 cars running, 3 extra.
Canal—10 cars running, 6 extra.
Esplanade—18 cars running, 2 extra.
Dauphine—20 cars running, 4 extra.
Levee and Barracks—25 cars running, 2 extra.

This company employs about four hundred men in various capacities.

Its average yearly receipts for the past three years have been $625,132. The average number of passengers transported annually 12,508,616; daily 34,270.

As is to be expected, the City Railroad Company makes money. Looking back over its financial record, we observe that the habit was contracted early in life. In July, 1861, a dividend of 20 per cent. in stock was declared. Since that period, at intervals varying from three to six months, dividends of 6 per cent. gladdened the hearts of the stockholders, culminating in March, 1866, with one of 15 per cent.

After that the capital was increased to $1,300,000, but the dividends continued at similar intervals and an average of four and a half per cent. until April, 1868; since which time they have, with two exceptions, been regularly declared each quarter.

F. Wintz, Esq., is president of the company, having held that position since 1868, and evidently to the hearty satisfaction of his constituents.

A visit to the offices and stables, an inspection of the cars, mules, tracks, etc., furnishes whatever additional evidence may be necessary to show that the affairs of the company are in faithful and competent hands.

THE NEW ORLEANS AND CARROLLTON COMPANY.

This is the oldest railroad corporation in the city, and should perhaps have been placed first on that account. It was chartered in 1833, for seventy-five years; its tenure, therefore, holding 31½ years hence. In May 1866 its original scheme was changed so far as to abolish steam traction and substitute horse power. The stock was then worth $7.50 per share, the par value being $75.

It was about this time that Gen. Beauregard was tendered the presidency of the road, and accepted. His character—of which it is quite unnecessary to speak—inspired the hope that the company's affairs would prosper under him. How well those hopes were founded may be estimated when we say that, in 1871 the stock had risen to $110, par value being $100.

The number of cars used is fifty-nine—fourteen on the Jackson street line, forty on the Carrollton, and five on the branches. Two hundred and forty-nine horses and mules work on the different lines; the stables and car shed of the Carrollton line being at the corner of St. Charles street and Napoleon avenue, and those of the Jackson at St. Charles and Felicity Road. The number of employees, all told, is one hundred and thirty.

As a comparative statement of earnings under the old and new systems, we subjoin the average gross receipts per day (steam power) in 1866, $[illegible]; same in 1872, (horse power) $655.

The number of passengers carried annually, estimated for two or three years past, averages 1,983,[illegible]. Taxes paid by the company last year, $15,[illegible].

The down town terminus for both lines is at Baronne and Canal. The Jackson line runs to the head of Jackson street, the Carrollton to the corner of First and Madison streets in Carrollton. The schedule followed by this company is to run day cars from 5:30 a. m. till 8:30 p. m. every five minutes; after that, until 12:35 every fifteen minutes. It is strictly adhered to, and gives universal satisfaction.

Gen. Beauregard informs us that he has nearly completed ten of Lamm's Fireless Locomotives, which he will introduce at an early day, to run between Napoleon Avenue and Carrollton. The estimated saving is thirty per cent.

Everything about this company moves with the regularity of clockwork. There is hustle, no noise, no mistake. In the whole of last year there was but a single accident, and that a palpably unavoidable one. The spirit of Gen. Beauregard pervades the remotest workings of the complicated machine.

CANAL AND CLAIBORNE COMPANY.

This company, of which Mr. E. J. Hart is President, was organized in 1867, with a capital of $[illegible], and one year later commenced operations. It has three lines—Canal and Common, with termini at the head of Canal street, and corner of Common and Tenth. Girod and Poydras, with the same termini, but different route. Canal and Claiborne, running from the head of Canal street to the depot on Lafayette avenue.

In connection with this line the company has established switches and a car stand at the corner of Elysian Fields and Claiborne street, for the express accommodation of the travelers to and from the lake, and have cars on the arrival of each train ready to receive passengers from the lake.

Forty cars and two hundred and eighteen mules are worked upon the lines of this company, which amount in all to fifteen miles of track. They have two different stables, and there are employed, in all capacities, about one hundred men, whose annual pay roll amounts to $[illegible].

The number of passengers carried for two years past is 6,[illegible].

In this instance, as in those already recorded, the stockholders have been fortunate in their choice of presidents. The name of E. J. Hart is synonymous with business ability and success.

THE CRESCENT CITY COMPANY.

We are bound to admit that our visit to the headquarters of this company resulted in checking all greed for statistics. Not through any failure to receive information, but rather on the Shakespearean plan

—"If music be the food of love, play on; give me excess of it; that surfeiting, the appetite may sicken and so die."

We didn't put the case in just those terms, but we asked for a few items of general knowledge—such as were given in by the others—and we got the whole charter of the company neatly bound in green paper, and, so to speak, mellow with statistics.

The President—we suppose he was the President; he looked like a President—ran his eagle eye over the list of our curiosity, and mastered it in a jiffy. He seemed to take refuge in meagre details; produced his charter, which we clutched in respectful silence, and furtively retired, strong in the conviction of being gorged with sapience.

From the car starter, however, we gleaned the trifling information that the Crescent City Company consists of two lines, named respectively the Tchoupitoulas and New Levee, and the Annunciation and Chippewa. They run from Canal street as high as Louisiana avenue; employ at present about thirty-five cars, and don't put on any airs about it. Which facts, together with the circumstance that they have a charter, ought to be enough for any one.

It may be inquired whether the other companies are not also possessed of charters; and, if so, why they didn't own it. We can't reply. We only know that if they *did* have charters they were base enough to conceal them.

SOME POINTS IN GENERAL.

Referring to the first three companies mentioned in this article, we call attention to their respective schedules. As has been already mentioned, the Carollton Company's cars run during the day every five minutes, and from 8.30 to 12.15 every fifteen minutes. The City Railway Company has a rather eccentric system.

During the period usually occupied in going to and from business their cars run at intervals of two and a half minutes; between those hours, every five minutes; from dark until ten o'clock, every ten minutes; after that, every fifteen minutes.

In the Canal and Claiborne Company, cars on Claiborne street are started every three minutes; cars on Common street every seven minutes; cars on Girod and Poydras streets every eight minutes.

After 8.30 p. m., the schedule averages fifteen minute intervals.

The men employed by them are as follows:

City Railroad Company	400
Carollton Company	130
Canal and Claiborne Company	100
Total,	630

Adopting the low estimate of four to one, it will be seen that more than two thousand people are directly fed and clothed by these three companies alone.

The yearly pay-roll of the Canal and Claiborne Company is put at $59,000. Taking it as a basis, we have:

City Railroad Company	$236,000
Carollton Company	76,300
Canal and Claiborne Company	59,000
Total,	$371,300

circulated annually for labor only! We say nothing of the innumerable other disbursements, amounting in the aggregate to far more than the sum already stated. It is our wish on this occasion to develop the simple fact that three corporations, among the many, pay out annually to a class of people generally poor and dependent on their daily labor, nearly half a million of dollars.

Let some grumbler think of this when next he feels his favorite inclination. At least two thousand human beings in New Orleans are interested, to the extent of bread and meat, in the prosperity of the City, the Carollton, and the Canal and Claiborne Railroad companies.

MORE TO COME.

There are several other companies yet to be recorded, prominent among which are the St. Charles street and the Dumaine street companies. We hope very shortly to add them to the chapter of city railroad enterprise in New Orleans.

In concluding this installment, we beg to return our grateful acknowledgments for the attention received from Gen. Beauregard, F. Wintz, Esq., and E. J. Hart, Esq.; as also from Messrs. P. McBride, C. C. Lewis and J. H. DeGrange, secretaries, respectively, of the companies represented by the first-named gentlemen. Our inquiries were prompted by a motive somewhat better than mere curiosity, and we respect the courtesy which took that fact for granted.

Business of the Department of Customs, Internal Revenue, Naval Office, Post Office, Etc., Etc.

For the Fiscal Year ending June 30, 1873.

The Department of Customs at the port of New Orleans is presided over by Col. James F. Casey. Through him and his subordinates we are enabled to present an authentic statement of the exports and imports of the port for the year ending June 30, 1873, together with other interesting and important statistics.

Department of Customs.

Where it has been found practicable, we have prepared our tables so as to compare the business of the year just closed with that transacted during a series of years preceding.

IMPORTS AND EXPORTS.

Fiscal years.	Imports.	Exports.
1866-7	$11,647,029	$85,126,531
1867-8	11,396,856	60,183,636
1868-9	11,413,902	73,893,812
1869-70	14,993,756	106,660,340
1870-1	19,427,238	99,247,261
1871-2	18,502,708	90,782,975
1872-3	19,906,285	101,994,531

REV. B. M. PALMER.

CITY HOTEL.

CORNER CAMP AND COMMON STREETS.

MERCHANDISE ENTERED FOR TRANSPORTATION IN BOND.

	1871-2.	1872-3.
With appraisement	[illegible]	[illegible]
Without appraisement	[illegible]	[illegible]
Totals	[illegible]	[illegible]

FINES AND SEIZURES.

A remarkable state of facts is developed by the following table of the fines and seizures collected in money since the fiscal year of 1867-8.

1868-9	$175,163 21
1869-70	77,096 56
1870-1	11,413 62
1871-2	9,722 29
1872-3	4,366 50
Total	$277,761 18

This table needs explanation. The fines and seizures collected in the years 1868-9, and 1869-70, were chiefly on account of the frauds on the revenue committed during the administration of Perry Fuller, in the importations of sugar and wine. That for the years of 1869-70 grew out of the wine cases principally. Altogether, the table shows an increasing vigilance in the administration of the custom laws under Col. Casey.

IMMIGRATION.

The subjoined tabular statement is presented more for the purpose of showing what is not and what is. It does not appear that the associations to encourage the immigration of foreign citizens to this State have accomplished much:

STATEMENT of arrival of immigrants and passengers in the District of New Orleans on vessels from foreign ports during the fiscal years ending June 30, 1870, '71, '72, '73.

Where From.	1869-70	1870-1	1871-2	1872-3
Great Britain and Colonies	439	718	960	1007
France	359	188	844	1115
Spain	377	73	102	282
Germany	2616	1952	2475	3352
Italy	383	238	383	202
Austria	48	128	363	660
All other countries	479	503	458	587
Total Immigrants	4799	4151	5601	6811
Add Passengers	1111	1301	1534	1287
Total	5888	5452	7137	7502

Careful inquiry respecting immigrants arriving at this port during the past two years reveals the fact that a large majority were en route for the State of Texas.

How the Office of Collector has been Administered.

Whatever may be said about the political views and conduct of Col. Casey, it will not be denied by the business public that he has administered his office not only with singular success, but also in a manner highly acceptable to importers and exporters. At Washington, the New Orleans Customhouse is regarded as the peer of the one at Baltimore, which is universally admitted to be as nearly perfect in its management as such an institution can be.

Col. Casey became Collector of Customs in the spring of 1869, receiving the office from the hands of Hon. Perry Fuller. There were then on hand a large number of warehouse, transportation and exportation bonds, taken by his predecessor, and for the most part utterly worthless, the obligors being men of straw and in some instances fictitious. There were of those bonds, in the office and uncanceled on the 12th day of April, 1869, as follows:

336 warehouse bonds—duty	$758,471 60
9 re-warehouse bonds—duty	9,294 90
319 transportation bonds—duty	387,438 [illegible]
83 export bonds—duty	113,932 72
39 Mexican bonds—duty	48,370 [illegible]
776 bonds—duty	$1,317,795 91

In contrast with this showing of his predecessor, it is but simple justice to say that Col. Casey has exercised such care in accepting bonds that the Government has not lost a dollar on any bond taken during his administration.

Mr. Fuller left the office with 2,000 entries on each of which there was a deficiency of duty due the Government. On all the entries of merchandise during the past four years there was not, on June 30, due and unpaid one cent of deficiency of duties. Not a warehouse, transportation or export bond was outstanding and uncanceled up to that date.

CIGARS—SMUGGLING.

The smuggling done at this port has always consisted largely of cigars. As will be seen by the following table of cigars imported, this practice has been almost entirely broken up. The fact, of course, can only be negatively ascertained:

Cigars imported 1867	[illegible]
Cigars imported 1868	[illegible]
Cigars imported 1869	[illegible]
Cigars imported 1870	[illegible]
Cigars imported 1871	[illegible]
Cigars imported 1872	[illegible]
Cigars imported 1873, six months	[illegible]

The years named above are calendar years, and the figures prove that the officers of the customs have been vigilant since 1869 in preventing the illicit introduction of cigars into this port.

Surveyor's Department.

The Surveyor of the Port is Hon. J. M. G. Parker. To Special Deputy Surveyor J. J. Maguire, we are indebted for the following statement respecting

THE NUMBER OF VESSELS

arriving at this port during the past year, and for several preceding:

Years.	Coastwise		Foreign Trade		Am. Bottoms.	Foreign Bottoms.
	Sail	Steam	Sail	Steam	Total.	Total.
1864-5	472	151	207	34	728	164
1865-6	497	*468	479	16	1089	364
1866-7	647	691	415	60	1798	354
1867-8	502	735	560	84	1355	415
1868-9	596	[illegible]	530	120	1199	392
1869-70	251	775	847	127	1278	539
1870-1	282	856	678	128	1484	485
1871-2	312	785	786	130	1601	532
1872-3	325	614	[illegible]	116	1277	615

*[These figures include steamers in the Mobile trade.]

The Naval Office.

The Naval Officer of the port in New Orleans is Hon. Charles Delangiman, and his Special Deputy is Mr. E. T. Hurd. As the Naval Officer is in reality the controller of the port, we have chosen to present a statement of the receipts from customs as made up from his records, as follows:

RECEIPTS FROM CUSTOMS.

1864-65	$574,893 68	1869-70	$5,417,823 75
1865-66	4,529,159 58	1870-71	5,805,200 29
1866-67	5,338,366 00	1871-72	5,181,397 85
1867-68	4,378,723 00	1872-73	3,738,849 72
1868-69	4,841,395 12		

It will be observed from the foregoing table that in the customs receipts for the year ending June 30, 1873, as compared with the previous year, there was a falling off of $1,442,547.71. The imports for that year, however, exceeded those of the previous year $1,410,357. With greater importations we have less revenue to the government. This decrease of customs receipts during the last fiscal year is thus accounted for:

1. There was a reduction, under amendments to the tariff laws, of ten per cent. of duty on the amount of duty on all manufactures of cotton, wool, iron, brass, clocks, watches, copper, glass, and on all manufactures of lead, manufactures of metals and metal compositions, and paper.

2. There was also a reduction of the rate of duty on manufactures of tin plate from 25 per cent. to 15 per cent. ad valorem.

3. A large number of articles have been made free of duty, such as tin in bars, blocks or pigs, tea, coffee, and a large variety of articles under the head of drugs, dyes, etc. Of coffee there was imported during the last fiscal year, 31,153,372 pounds, valued at $4,815,791. The duty on this alone would have been $935,567 16.

Department of Internal Revenue.

Col. S. A. Stockdale is the Collector of Internal Revenue for the First District of Louisiana. From his office we have obtained the following statement of the collections made by him during the

FISCAL YEAR ENDING JUNE 30, 1873.

July	1872	$ 235,422 06
August	1872	79,131 27
September	1872	82,054 08
October	1872	122,576 29
November	1872	101,242 16
December	1872	162,239 13
January	1873	107,491 48
February	1873	86,499 39
March	1873	95,428 11
April	1873	83,789 15
May	1873	143,121 01
June	1873	[illegible] 33
Total		$1,261,[illegible] 61

Mr. Stockdale was appointed in the spring of 1869, succeeding Gen. James B. Steedman. During the whole period of his administration he has collected $7,935,166 57.

There has been a falling off in the amount of revenue collected as compared with previous years, resulting from the repeal of the law imposing a tax on sales, and the expiration (last year) of the law imposing a tax on incomes. Formerly licenses were collected on sixty-five different kinds of business and professions; now licenses are exacted only on eleven different kinds, and those eleven all relate to liquor and tobacco.

The cost to the government for assessing and collecting the revenue last year was one and one-half per cent.

Post Office Department.

Mr. Charles Ringgold is Postmaster of the New Orleans office. In consequence of the disorders in the office whilst in the hands of his predecessor, Col. Lowell, it was impossible for us to obtain a statement of the business done during the past fiscal year.

Approximate estimates, however, may be obtained from the following facts:

MONEY ORDER DEPARTMENT.

Average daily payment of orders	$3,000
Average daily receipt of orders	2,500
Average daily receipt of surplus money orders from Louisiana and Mississippi	2,500

REGISTERED LETTERS.

Registered letters received daily	180
Registered letters issued daily	75

LETTERS SENT TO DEAD LETTER OFFICE.

For bad direction, average per month	152
For want of prepayment	356
For illegal stamps, average per month	50

In further illustration of the carelessness of the people in mailing their letters, we mention that recently a letter was received at the New Orleans office embellished with a postal stamp issued by the Confederate States Government, and bearing the face of Jeff. Davis.

STAMP WINDOW.

The average daily sale of stamps, stamped envelopes and wrappers is $500.

Sub-Treasury Department.

The Assistant Treasurer of the United States, in charge of the New Orleans office, is Hon. B. F. Flanders. The Collector of the Port, the Collectors of Internal Revenue in the State, and the Postmaster of New Orleans, are all required by law to make weekly deposits with the Assistant Treasurer of all Government moneys received by them. The collectors of revenues and of customs at Galveston and Brownsville, Texas, and at Mobile, Ala., also make their deposits in the same office. Many other disbursing officers of the Government of the United States make their deposits there also. It is also a medium for the transfer of large amounts of Government money.

It was found impossible to obtain a statement of the business transacted in the office of the Assistant United States Treasury during the past fiscal year. That of the previous year aggregated $25,282,867, and it is thought the year just closed will show approximate figures.

JAMES JACKSON.

The subject of this sketch was born in County Down, Ireland, on the 15th March, 1828, and brought up as a farmer's boy in a family of nine children. His education was confined to those advantages which most farmers' sons receive who make a support by tilling the soil. At a very early age he took charge of the farm and laborers, was a first-class ploughman at the age of 16, and an expert at all kinds of farm labor. He toiled all day, and attended

THE OPERA HOUSE.

night-school to better fit himself for a struggle with the world. Soon as the younger brothers could fill James' place on the farm he bound himself for three years at an agricultural school, his ambition then being to excel as a farmer, when thus occupied. Judge Alex. Porter, of this State, wished an agriculturalist on his plantation, "Bayou Teche." Mr. Jackson was offered and accepted this position with the promise to leave soon as the stipulated term of three years expired. In the meantime Judge Porter died. His eyes had been turned to America as the Mecca of the poor, the industrious and the enterprising. He sailed from Belfast direct for this port on 2d January, 1846, landing here in March. He immediately proceeded to the Porter plantation on Bayou Teche, and delivered some Ayrshire cattle and South Down sheep, which had been purchased for the late Judge Porter. He remained with the late James Porter on said place. Being too ambitious to remain in this sphere, he concluded to try his fortune in this city. Arriving here in December, 1847, expecting to find employment of some kind or other, day by day and month by month he walked these streets, unable to find anything to do, even applying as a day laborer on the new Custom House, foundations of which were then being laid, only to be refused. Not being a "voter," having no friend, relative, or any person he ever knew to refer to, this was very discouraging. The unkind answers received often gave him a heavy heart. At last, through the kind offices of "*Charles Munson*," he was taken on trial with Small and McGill as shipping or out-door clerk in the salt department at a salary of fifty dollars per month. This was small pay; still he managed to save even a portion of this. His rule through life has been to live within his income. His career as a merchant is too well known to require any further remarks. As money was earned, wharves and warehouses on the river were purchased. Some fine stores were built (by his firm, Jackson & Munson) that is an ornament to the city. Becoming a stockholder in the New Orleans City R. R. Co., he was elected a director the second year of its charter. This position he still holds. He was also elected a director in the New Orleans Gas Light Co.; and in 1868 was unanimously elected President of that wealthy corporation, which position he still holds, with profit to the Company and credit to himself. There is not a shareholder dissatisfied with his administration.

Although a strict economist his charities are very liberal. Many families have been aided by his bounty. Soon as able he brought other members of his family here, and procured all a position. One of the brothers occupies a position in St. Louis equal to the subject of this sketch. He has aided several in business. In 1866 he retired from active commercial life, retaining an interest for his capital with the former clerks of the firm. The manner of conducting affairs not being satisfactory, he withdrew, and formed a co-partnership, in 1870, with the junior clerks under the style of Jackson, Kilpatrick & Henderson. This firm having control of Mr. Jackson's salt warehouses, is the prominent firm in that business in this city.

Mr. Jackson has always been devoted to business, and has been rewarded with success. He is considered one of our wealthy merchants. Even when poor his credit was good; whatever he promised was fulfilled. No person was ever known to doubt Mr. Jackson's veracity.

He is still in the prime of life and full of business energy; is distinguished for public spirit, and takes a lively interest in all matters connected with the progress and welfare of the community.

ROBERT ROBERTS, ESQ.

One the most sterling, respectable and enterprising citizens of our city is Mr. Robert Roberts, proprietor of the Louisiana Steam Sash, Blind and Door Factory, located at 230 Gravier street. Although not a native of the place his long residence in New Orleans and active business life, extending for many years back, have led many to believe that he was "to the manor born." Mr. Roberts, however, was born in Liverpool on the 16th of August, 1823, and came to this country when but eight years old. He first landed at Charleston, and from there went to New York state, where he resided for about five years. From New York he came to New Orleans in 1839, and commenced life, as it were, as a house carpenter, working in the Belleville Iron Works as a pattern maker, and afterwards with James A. Bass as a ship-joiner, with whom he subsequently formed a co-partnership and established a steam planing and sawing mill.

In 1856, Mr. Roberts started his present factory in connection with Jas. A. Bass and William Waterman, under the firm name of Waterman & Co. In 1858, Mr. Bass retired from the firm, and Mr. John Brownlee was admitted, thus bringing about a consolidation of the two factories of Brownlee and Waterman & Co. In 1860, Mr. Brownlee died, and Mr. Waterman in 1865. Then it was the firm name was changed to Roberts & Co., the widows retaining the interest of their deceased husbands in the business.

With these few changes, Mr. Roberts has been conducting his business with marked success, and now can boast of one of the largest factories of the kind in the South. The building occupies an entire square of ground, and about seventy persons find employment within its doors. Aside from being a successful business man, Mr. Roberts in the walks of social life is highly esteemed for the many excellent qualities that adorn his character. Charitable, benevolent and generous, we find him always taking part in good works, and in matters of public improvement he is ever ready and willing to give a helping hand. As President of the Mechanics' and Dealers' Exchange, and a Director of the Mechanics' Society, Mr. Roberts has done much towards giving those organizations the high character they enjoy. In 1851 he organized the first fire company in Algiers, the "Pelican." Besides being one of the oldest members of the fire department of the city, Mr. Roberts is also a Mason and an Odd Fellow.

In 1861, Mr. Roberts married Miss Eliza Hammond, of Algiers, and has now two boys and one girl living—two children having died at an early age. On another page will be found a view of Mr. Roberts' handsome residence, located at the corner of St. Charles and Conery streets. Without display, the comforts of an elegant home are here enjoyed, and the hospitalities dispensed by a generous host such as Mr. Roberts is so well known to be.

JOHN M. G. PARKER.

WAS born in Dracut, Massachusetts, September 10th. 1826, and is therefore in the prime of life. He is a descendant in the male line, of an English family of three brothers, who bore honorable parts in the struggles of '76. From them he inherits that fine physique, brusque address, and tenacity of purpose, which so briefly, yet so fitly describe the man. But in all things else, he is strictly the child of America. From constant companionship with her rugged nature, he drew his first inspirations of freedom in her schools; he was taught that respect for law, which is the highest attribute of her citizens; from the study of her institutions, he learned, quoting his own words, "The industrious, intelligent and virtuous citizens form the great bulwark and strength of the Republic."

EARLY LIFE.

Soon after attaining his majority, he was happily united in marriage with a daughter of Dr. Israel Hildreth, of Dracut, a physician of eminence in his profession, and of acknowledged literary abilities.

The medical profession had early engaged the attention of our young friend, but, after a time spent in preparation, he seemed to prefer the more active pursuits of commercial life. Though meeting with serious embarrassments and losses common to mercantile affairs, his teutonic pluck and untiring application, prevented despondency, and wrought out a moderate competence. His first public trust was that of Postmaster of his native town, under President Fillmore. He was also prominently identified with the administration of Buchanan, his efficiency and probity having been recognized in the successive executive changes. These facts show clearly those sterling and original traits of character, which proclaim the self-made man. With respect to such characters, if the touch of nature has been less loving, less accurate in grace, she has given the nobler attribute of individuality.

MILITARY LIFE.

The nation's call to arms found Mr. Parker still continuing to occupy a subordinate federal office, but he soon enlisted as a private in the 30th Regiment Mass. Vols., and, as Lieutenant, assisted in the organization of the regiment, one of the first mustered for what was called the "Butler Expedition."

During the vexatious delays and hardships incident to military life, Lieutenant Parker won the esteem of all his comrades, for gallant conduct under adverse circumstances.

On the 28th of March 1862, the expedition reached Ship Island, where Lieut. Parker performed the duties of Regimental Quartermaster and Postmaster. Following the expedition on the capture of New Orleans, with a valuable mail, he was ordered by General Butler, when in command, to take charge of the Post Office, and to open communication with Washington. He had entered the army with the patriotic desire to contribute the mite of his personal effort to the common defense, but after anxious considerations and urged by the solicitation of friends, he accepted the duty, and took leave of military life.

The Custom House Building was almost a wreck; the furniture of the Post Office destroyed; and its records in indiscriminate confusion. Under these wretched conditions, the work of restoration was prosecuted with such favorable results that more than 2500 letters were rescued from the waste, and nearly all delivered to the proper persons.

For this, and for the arduous services rendered by Mr. Parker, in anticipation of the wishes of the Department, in reorganizing the postal service in several of the Gulf States, he was nominated and confirmed Postmaster at New Orleans. During his incumbency of this office, he introduced a number of improvements to meet the public wants; secured increased postal facilities; endeared himself by the zeal, determination, and uniform courtesy of his administration; and gave to New Orleans, that which she had never known before, a postal service which could be compared with the most efficient in the North. In May 1865, he was removed from office by President Lincoln.

Commenting upon this event, the "Daily Bee" (Democratic) of April 7, 1865, said: "We may only observe with equal emphasis and sincerity, in a strictly non partisan spirit, and from an entirely public point of view, that as far as proved capacity, and eminent zeal and success in the discharge of official duties go to confirm a claim to continued incumbency, that of Postmaster Parker was most valid, indubitable and unquestioned."

The "Times" of April 6th, after refuting the charges that Mr Parker had opposed the President's policy in the reconstruction of Louisiana, proceeds to say;

"But it is a matter of less importance to our citizens that he has been removed on account of any mere party accusations, than that he should be displaced at all. . . . . . We acquit the President of any connivance at injustice in this matter, as there is an obvious impossibility of his knowing everything concerning his subordinates."

Equally flattering comments were made by other journals; and all classes without regard to party distinctions united in unmerited compliment to a deserving officer, by requesting his reinstatement.

Upon the settlement of Mr. Parker's accounts with the Department a balance of $1500, was found in his favor over paid through misinterpretation of the statute. This is the only instance on record. No other Postmaster which New Orleans has ever known, has exhibited the same accuracy in official transactions.

AS A POLITICIAN.

The thanks of the State and of the nation are due to Mr. Parker for his strenuous efforts to create a loyal sentiment and to develop a healthy public taste in Louisiana, at a time when the whirlpool of disloyalty was threatening to engulf the precious fruits of our late sacrifice.

Counseling with a few spirits as fearless as his own, as to the most effective methods of influencing public opinon, he organized the "New Orleans Republican." To it he gave the unflagging service, which springs from singleness of purpose, devotion to principle and love for the Union.

Originally a Whig, when that party ceased to exist, he fell naturally into the ranks of the Democratic party, believing it to be the only national organization, and as an advocate of its political faith, enlisted to fight for the National idea. At this time, for the same reasons given above, he became an ardent supporter of Republican principles. Mr. Parker is still one of the proprietors of the ably conducted journal referred to, in which he has property to the amount of $30,000. Nothing visionary enters his composition. His public course has been eminently practical; yet, with a seeming prescience of coming event, he was among the first to advocate the claims of U. S. Grant, upon the American people.

In November 1867, he organized, as we think, the first political club of the memorable campaign which followed, called the "Pioneer Grant Club" of which he became President. Subsequently he was a delegate to the Convention which nominated President Grant at Baltimore.

For a time he has studiously kept aloof from politics, but it has been in a time when to hold office was a doubtful honor. There are times when communities like individuals go mad. In such times the upright citizen is forced into the character of a quiet observer. Mr. Parker has deemed Republican success of paramount importance to personal ambition, and, on more than one occasion, has voluntarily withdrawn from candidacy for important trusts in the interests of party harmony.

His consistent championship of the interests of the working man must not be forgotten. Indeed, he is naturally their advocate, being constrained by the Democratic principles which have been his constant guide and monitor, and of which he is justly proud.

In a speech delivered at New Orleans after the election of 1868, he said—

"Our population is composed of almost every variety of the human family; and it should be our study to imbue them with a pride of their American citizenship; and this can best be done by securing to them all of the rights and privileges of true Republicanism."

In march 1873 Mr. Parker received the nomination of surveyor of customs at New Orleans and was accordingly confirmed. He entered at once upon his duties with the hearty and general approbation of the entire community. To merchants the appointment is especially pleasing.

To an entire stranger, in the transaction of business, Mr. Parker may sometimes appear harsh, from his anxiety to get at the matter to be considered; but his friends know that his heart is brimming with human sympathy, ready to overflow if the springs be touched.

Of course he has his detractors, and who among us has not? and his faults—and who would have them written in his forehead? We only desire to present the portrait of a lion-hearted friend,—and because of strong convictions, a good hater; a genial companion, an honest citizen, a faithful officer, and withal, a man.

P. F. HERWIG.

Was born in Port-au-Prince in 1839. His father, E. C. Herwig, was U. S. Consul or Charge d'Affaires in the West Indies, and during this time P. F. Herwig was born, and was therefore an American citizen. His father, a native of Baltimore, Maryland, was a large ship owner and merchant, principally engaged in the shipping of mahogany to the United States and Europe, who, after resigning his position in the West Indies and retiring from business, came to New Orleans with his family in 1845.

P. F. Herwig was educated in this city and was first engaged in the manufacture of flour with his father under the style of E. C. Herwig & Son—a large establishment which he conducted until 1862, after which he was extensively engaged in the buying and shipping of cotton in which he was very successful.

In 1865 he was appointed Assistant Assessor of Internal Revenue and served with credit to the Government as well as himself until 1866 when he was appointed at the urgent solicitation of the leading bankers, capitalists and merchants as Government Inspector and weigher of cotton and sugar which he held in partnership with Colonel Casey until the abolition of the Cotton Tax; and this business was conducted in such a manner as met the approval of the government and made both parties very popular with the business community.

Upon the appointment of Col. Casey as Collector of the Port, April 12, 1869, Mr. Herwig was appointed his Chief Deputy, the position he now holds.

In November, 1870, Mr. Herwig was elected by a large majority to the State Senate from the 1st District of New Orleans for four years, and now holds the responsible position of Chairman of the Finance Committee of the Senate. His eldest brother, E. F. Herwig, is largely interested in the planting interest of the State and is also a member of the State Senate, having been elected in Nov., 1872, from the 11th Senatorial District for four years.

His youngest brother, Joseph L. Herwig, has also occupied many offices of honor and trust and is at present State Assessor of the 1st District of New Orleans, the most important district in the State.

The subject of our sketch is a striking instance of the rapid progress of a young man from comparative obscurity to prominence and independence, in the city of his adoption. Energetic, industrious and temperate in habit, reliable and prompt in all his business relations, kind hearted and generous in his nature, it is not surprising to find him in the full enjoyment of the fruits of an exemplary life. Though but a young man Mr. Herwig has shown himself to be eminently fitted for the important and responsible position he now fills, and all unite in according to him the highest praise for the satisfactory and efficient manner in which he discharges his arduous duties.

JUDGE WM. H. COOLEY.

Judge Wm. H. Cooley, late of the Sixth District Court for the parish of Orleans, was born in Pointe Coupée Louisiana. He was educated at Bardstown, Ky., and from his youth was admired by his schoolmates for his intelligence and ready wit.

He studied law at Pointe Coupée, and afterwards became judge of that parish by appointment of Gov. Wells.

In this city he practiced jointly with his father until elected to the bench in 1867.

Judge Cooley commanded a Confederate company during the late war. At the close of the same he returned to New Orleans, and was once more on the war path, this time doing battle with the weapons of intellectual warfare. He was a member of the Radical Convention in 1868, and distinguished himself in that body as a ready debater.

He was endowed by nature with acuteness, and great quickness of apprehension. Whether delivering his opinion to the bar or charging the jury, he showed an admirable perspicuity of statement, combining conciseness with clearness. What costs other minds labor, study and investigation, he saw at a glance.

The intellect of Judge Cooley, and the robust structure of his faculties lead him always to a close grappling with the subject in discussion. He shunned everything collateral and discursive.

The quickness with which he could ascertain his object was fully equalled by the firm grasp with which he held his ground. His strength was in dealing with facts. His power of discrimination was active, and his attention was ever awake. When the writer of these lines first saw Judge Cooley, this gentleman was delivering an oral opinion in an important case. The court-room was crowded, and every eye and ear fixed on the bench. A strain of unbroken fluency came fourth, disposing in luminous order of facts and arguments, reducing into simple arrangement the broken and conflicting statements, weighing each matter and giving out the whole case in every material view with such close reasonings as to satisfy all his hearers.

Judge Cooley was certainly a man of vast talents, a judge of quick perception, of acute penetration, and of masculine common sense.

In private life he was very social and the soul of generosity. None could relate anecdotes better than he, and few could bring more into the stock of entertainment.

THE BLOOD FERTILIZING WORKS OF NEW ORLEANS.

On another page of this book will be found a view of the Blood Fertilizing Works, a new industrial enterprize just established in our city. The buildings are located just in the rear of the Crescent City Slaughter-houses, from which the blood, bones, and offal used in the manufacture of the Fertilizer, are obtained. The machinery used is all of the latest improvement and patented by the Company.

The quality of the Fertilizer manufactured by this Company is pronounced to be the most superior by planters and others who have experimented with it. In addition there is manufactured by this Company an excellent quality of tallow and Neats-foot oil.

No expense has been spared in the construction of suitable and ample buildings and machinery for the successful operation of these works. Mr. L. E. Lemarie, an enterprizing and public-spirited citizen of our city, is the President of the Company and has invested largely in the new enterprize. In the practical operation of the Company he has the assistance of Mr. John Delhonde, the secretary, and Mr. Chas. De Ruyter, the secretary who, with Mr. Chas. Langa, the chemist, are devoting their time and attention to the successful operation of this newly established company. Any one desiring further information relative to the manufactured articles of this Company are referred to Headquarters at No. 27 Peters street, New Orleans, where the President will be glad to give all required information.

MR. THOS. O'CONNOR.

The Chief of the Fire Department was born in New Orleans, June 29, 1829, and was educated in the Public Schools of the city. He started in life as a pattern-maker at the age of 13 years and afterward became a blacksmith. To this calling he devoted himself for a number of years, and, becoming master of his trade, soon found employment as superintendent of the blacksmithing department in some of our largest foundries.

In 1854 he joined Protection Hose Company, No. 19 and in 1857 became a member of Columbia Fire Company, No. 5, and also of the Fireman's Charitable Association. During his connection with No. 5, Mr. O'Connor has filled every office in the gift of the Company and is now its president.

The personal popularity of the young fireman, and his devotion to, and efficient service in the department soon brought him prominently forward as a suitable and worthy member to preside as its chief, and on the 4th of January, 1869 he was elected to that important and responsible position. For this office he was re-elected annually until January, 1872, when he was then re-elected for a term of five years.

As the Chief Engineer Mr. O'Connor commands the confidence of the Fire Department and the respect and esteem of the entire community. Active, energetic and laborious he has succeeded in perfecting the organization of our Fire Department to a degree of efficiency that makes it second to no other in the world.

COL. S. N. MOODY.

NEW ORLEANS GAS COMPANY.

A SONG FOR THE TIMES, WITH A MORAL.

Old farmer Brown came into the house,
  And wrathfully slammed the door,
And flopped himself down into a chair,
  And flopped his hat on the floor.

For farmer Brown was dreadfully wroth,
  And his dander it was up;
And he looked around with an angry scowl,
  And wrathfully kicked the pup.

"I'm tired from head to foot," he said,
  "And hungry as I kin be;
I'd like to have a mouthful to eat—
  Is dinner 'most ready?" said he.

The farmer's wife she was pale and thin,
  And hungry and wan was she;
And her eye was dim and her step was slow,
  And her dress was a sight to see.

"Your dinner is ready," she meekly said,
  "And the dodgers is smoking hot,
But I've scraped the meal all out of the box,
  And the last jint's just from the pot."

"The mischief you have," said farmer Brown,
  Heaving a doleful sigh;
"Thar's plenty of bacon and corn in town,
  And I've no money to buy."

Up spoke the farmer's daughter, Marier—
  And she hadn't spoke before;—
"Thar's cotton out under the shed," said she,
  "Some dozen bales or more."

"Cotton, the devil!" said farmer Brown,
  (It's dreadfully wrong to swear),
"My cotton's all mortgaged for last year's work,
  With never a bale to spare."

"Well, then," his daughter up spoke again,
  "If that won't do for feed,
You've two or three wagon loads or more
  Of Dickson's Prolific Seed."

"Do you think me a beast?" said farmer Brown,
  "I'm neither cow nor steer;
And what if I was? I've hardly enough
  Of seed to plant this year."

Then said his daughter, Marier, again,
  "Thar's guano, lots," she said,
"Thar's twenty sacks full into the barn,
  And barrels under the shed."

"Guano? Oh, Lud!" said farmer Brown,
  "I need all the precious stuff
To put on my cotton land this year,
  And then not have enough."

But when the farmer had eaten his fill,
  He fell into thought profound,
And smoked his tobacco, which cost at least
  Some ninety cents per pound.

CHRISTIAN ROSELIUS.

Christian Roselius was engaged, in New Orleans, during forty-five consecutive years, immediately preceding his death (on the fifth of September, 1873,) in the uninterrupted and active pursuit of the profession of the law. For the half of that long period, simultaneously, performing the duties of a professor of law in the University of Louisiana. Bereft of all adventitious circumstances—of humble parentage—he rose from poverty and obscurity, to an eminent position.

So conspicuous a career deserves noted comment. It will serve a double purpose—as a tribute of respect to the memory of the distinguished departed, mingled with grief and interest, and will offer a bright example, by which the young specially will derive much solace and profit.

HIS EMIGRATION TO AMERICA.

He was born on the 10th day of August, 1803, in Brunswick, a State of Germany, at the distance of a few miles from the free city of Bremen, as well as I can understand in the town of Thedinghausen. He received a good school education, but knew only one language—the German—his maternal tongue. At the age of sixteen he left his native land as a passenger on board of the Dutch brig Jupiter, which sailed from the port of Bremen and arrived in the city of New Orleans on the 18th of July, 1820. William Duby, publisher of the Louisiana *Advertiser*, needing an apprentice to the trade of printing, and learning that there were two young lads on the brig who would suit him, requested one of his acquaintances to accompany him—this credible person, still living, did so and saw the master, the two young men and Duby conversing. The latter told him that his choice had fallen on young Roselius, finding him the more intelligent; that he had paid his passage and taken him for an apprentice. Whether he was regularly bound as an apprentice, I am unable to ascertain. Certain it is that he did serve as such in the printing establishment of Duby two years and a half and immediately afterwards was employed as

A JOURNEYMAN PRINTER,

on wages, in the office of the *Louisiana Courier*, J. C. de St. Romes, the publisher. From the very beginning he was very expert—could simultaneously translate (mentally) advertisements and put up the appropriate type. Subsequently, as editor of the *Halcyon*, he performed the same feat with his editorials, at one and the same time.

It appears that he had incipient ideas of embracing the profession of the law. He had

A PLAIN BED, UNDER HIS PRINTING STAND

in the *Courier* office, and there read law books late in the night. One of his fellow printers, still a survivor, cognizant of this fact, specially adds, "but the stripling printer was always up bright and early at his task of printing." Industry and good conduct were his characteristics. He successfully imitated the early lives of Franklin and Judge Francois Xavier Martin.

HIS CAREER AS AN EDITOR.

In 1827, he and Charles McMicken (subsequently law

partners for a few months) edited, printed and published a literary paper, the *Halcyon*, a small weekly sheet—intended mainly for family reading—in the style of the *Spectator*, interspersed with heavier reading. It was spirited and well edited.

Even at that early day he gives us proof of that good temper, perseverance and fortitude which ever after characterized him and enabled him to mount up the steps of fame. After being engaged in this newspaper six months he published a card of withdrawal, announcing that he had disposed of his interest with some humor, and wrote, "As the abdication of an editorial chair is not of so much consequence as that of a throne, I do not think it worth while to trouble the public with the reasons that have induced me to withdraw." The truth was the paper was not remunerative—it was a pioneer enterprise.

He had reviewed the History of Louisiana, (then just fresh from the press,) by Judge Martin; and there also shows the nascent talent which distinguished him as an artful advocate. It was intended to be laudatory of the author. The writer was forced to admit that the style was not good, but in order to cover the defect he magnified the great value of the materials (as he termed them) contained in the history. The article was a success, at least so far as Judge Martin was concerned, for he expressed himself pleased with it.

At the time he was a student at law in the office of Davezac, and after obtaining his license to practice law, as well as when he was editor, he taught English, for a means of support, in a young ladies' school.

Young Roselius and Alexander Dimitry (the latter, the well-known scholar) after exchanging views, as to the calling in life they should adopt, on the 16th day of December, 1826,

ENTERED AS LAW STUDENTS

the office of Auguste Davezac, who was a prominent practitioner in the criminal court, and spoken of by his contemporaries as a gentleman of taste, wit, and of some eloquence. He did not rank high as a civilian; but these young students had, at the same time, the benefit of the instructions of Workman, (a name familiar to the bar as a thorough jurist with literary attainments) who had an adjoining office.

One of the first books placed in their hands, was Cooper's Justinian, containing an English translation. Dimitry had an advantage over his fellow—he could read the original text. To equalize this, the latter taught the former Latin.

In one year (the facility of the pupil for the acquisition of languages was so great) he could read Roman law authors in the original.

On the 23d day of June, 1828, he was examined in open court, by the Supreme Court, then composed of Judges Matthews, Martin and Porter, and was on that day licensed. Just previous, on the 25th of March, 1828, was adopted that act, the repeal of which is termed by Judge Matthews as sweeping in its effects—tremendously sweeping, and by Etienne Mazureau as

LE GRAND COUP DE BALAI.

In fact, in the absence of any legislative enactment, it left to the French, Roman, and Spanish laws, that authority which the force of reason alone could command. This in no manner abated the study of the systems of jurisprudence of foreign countries; but, inasmuch as our Civil Code is mainly copied from the Code Napoleon, modified by some portions of Spanish jurisprudence and some local provisions, the French civil laws became an object of close study, to which the deceased devoted all the attention and perseverance he was capable of. He studied extensively the French commentators (keeping up with all the new works), and constantly cited them. An attempt is made to depreciate them in saying they are so frequently contradictory. These authors treat of every subject, as if an open question—they go to the sources of the law, from the earliest Roman times, entering extensively, with all the lights before them, in theoretical discussions as to what the law ought to be, or what modifications to it, should exist—then follows the decisions of their courts; but inasmuch as the discussion of the theory occupies so much more of their time, a foreigner may erroneously conclude that the former is of secondary importance, and French jurisprudence in a very unsettled state. These French works, whose researches extend to two thousand years are rarely quoted in the courts of England and of our sister States. The treasures of legal knowledge, locked upon in a foreign language, are in a great measure ignored by them, specially in cases involving the law of contracts, comprising a large portion of the litigation of the country, or in questions in equity jurisprudence.

It is to be regretted that the deceased, with his wide range of experience and profound erudition, did not favor us with an elementary work on our Civil Code.

HIS LOVE OF THE CIVIL LAW

was a passion—the subject of his daily meditations and the favorite topics of his conversations. It is unanimously conceded by the Bar and Bench that in the department of the civil law he was the front figure. He would have graced a seat on the United States Supreme Court Bench; would have materially aided, with the large resources he could have made to bear, in inspiring a taste to the profession in the United States for the study of foreign systems of law, and would have exalted the standard of legal culture.

Fully appreciating the importance of the French language, he soon acquired it, and in his early career, at the Bar, frequently addressed juries in French. He seldom wrote it, for he was cognizant, owing to its niceties, that there are few in this country, although having received a liberal education, who can write it in strict conformity with the numerous rules of grammar, and a less number, with elegance. Even when he was a member of the Legislature, in 1841, the speeches of members who spoke in English were translated, orally, in French when any member so required it. It was a matter of astonishment with what accuracy the clerks of the respective Houses could do so, sentence after sentence, in the same order.

HOTEL DIEU.

HIS BRIEFS.

Many of our ablest lawyers have left no briefs worthy of their reputations; the reports abound with his, carefully prepared, evidencing a thorough examination of both civil and common law authorities, a masterly discussion of all the points, with proper division, and in a clear, accurate and condensed style. Some of the best of them are not reported in full. He did not rest his cases in the appellate court on mere oral argument, for he well knew that in the multiplicity of cases, and in the intricacies of difficult questions, the impressions left might be effaced or not accurately remembered. As specimens of his briefs the Franklin Batture, Williams and Shepherd cases may be referred to. During the summer months he was actively (for he was never idle) engaged in reading the new works on law, keeping step to the march of improvement in jurisprudence, prepared his briefs and cases, to give room for full attention to the new business at the opening of the courts. Never traveled but for the last few years of his life. In 1869 visited his native country where he found only two of his schoolmates survivors. He kept very regular office hours, understanding the great importance of this for success, and his clients always knew where and when to find him, and he had the faculty of rapidly changing his attention from one business to another, so necessary to effect expedition in business.

HIS PERSONAL APPEARANCE AND DEMEANOR.

As to his personal appearance—in his apparel, he was very neat and choice—his face was not handsome—in stature of a medium size. Voice harsh and loud, always pitched to so high a key that it could be heard outside the court room. Such strong lungs, his voice never seemed to be fatigued, although on a strain; in gestures not graceful, making use of the shoulders in gesticulating. He was emphatic, ever confident, very often dogmatic. Showed no quarter to the arguments of his adversaries. (All fortier in re, not much suaviter in modo) scouted them as leading to the most absurd and preposterous results—palpably erroneous. He presented all the phases of the case favorable to his client; he may not have liked to vouch for the soundness of all the views he uttered with such tones of conviction; but he could not take upon himself to decide what alone he might consider as having weight or being decisive—his client must have the benefit of them all. At times this may have been thought that this was a failing. Be it said, he was invariably decorous to the opposite counsel; never ill natured; never betrayed into a personal difficulty. Warded off anything offensive by pleasantry, and derisive argument, but handling his adversary's position without gloves and with the greatest force and ability. Never relaxing his grasp on the difficulties of the case; never dull; more solidity than brilliancy. An admirable temper; proof against all trials, and in this he excelled, which is a secret of success and well worthy of imitation. Never pouted over ill success—blessed with a happy faculty to chase away anxieties or disappointment. Why should he impair his strength and usefulness by brooding over a case, erroneously decided, by a judge who had not had even the sagacity to perceive where the difficulty of the case lay, or over a stupid verdict! This sound philosophy enabled him to push through (with unabated vigor) his heavy labors—never marring in the least a pleasant walk in his orange grove, or a delightful ride on horseback. His contemporaries say that from the beginning of his professional career he attended to his practice with a vigor and energy seldom ever witnessed; he reached the front rank about 1836; from that time he never ceased to have the most lucrative practice and received very large fees. Punctuality and probity characterized him.

HIS HABITS AND BENEVOLENCE.

Many gratuitous professional services has he rendered to the widow, the orphan and to charitable institutions. Members of the bar, in his intimacy, have an idea of their great extent! His obliging disposition, too often, without proper discrimination, betrayed him into the weakness of loaning his signature too freely. This, from an early period, in his professional career and never ceased. A negative, many a time, would be a blessing to him who refuses, as well as to the one who is refused. In him was verified the proverb quoted by Troplong in his work on suretyship; who goes security pays.

His residence, for many years before his death, was in the rural district of Greenville, of late incorporated in the city of New Orleans. His grounds are extensive and adorned and utilized by groves of orange trees. He indulged, at one time, in raising vegetables and gardening; no personal attention on his part; but he delighted to show them to his guests and visitors. Wisely attentive to the means of preservation of health, he arose about daybreak, and when the weather permitted could be seen taking his exercise on a hard trotting horse. During the late epizootic, when means of transportation ceased, he valiantly walked from his residence to his office, a distance of five miles and a half. The habit of punctuality was so strong, and the necessity to his system of a daily dose of law so much felt, the remonstrance of his friends was responded to by a laugh. He was never reduced to flannel and chicken broth.

In his habits he was very domestic—never belonged to a social club; for he avoided any temptation to excess in eating or drinking. Besides, he was economical of his time—careful not to deprive his family of that time which should be allotted to it. In his latter life, running far back, never darkened the door of a drinking saloon, never ate between meals—cultivated moderation in all things. In his young days, fond of the drama, wrote criticisms for the newspapers on plays and actors. Saw a great deal of Booth, the elder, Forrest and Caldwell; he heard Booth, a fine French scholar, perform in a French tragedy, at the Orleans Theatre in this city. Later in life, fond of the opera, a source of relaxation to him.

He possessed an extensive law library, and also a large collection of literary works; of both he made constant use. He

NEVER SUED FOR A FEE

but once, and this, he told me, he regretted. The amount

of the fee was not disputed, but the defendant alleged that he had not employed him, but he had been employed by others interested in having the title established which was in controversy, and his professional services were secured by other parties, who made common cause in the defense of their common title. The defense was maintained, the evidence for the plaintiff—in its nature circumstantial—not being sufficient. He had a nice sense of honor. Marcade (who honored him with a present of his photograph) was his favorite French commentator—his admiration for him unbounded. Our friend had whims at times—for the author be so much idolized is mainly a legal critic.

In his latter years, he did not use tobacco in any shape; his disuse of the weed he attributed to an occurrence which he witnessed in the Criminal Court. Etienne Mazureau, the learned lawyer and powerful speaker, (who has left us a remarkable eulogium, in French, on judge Matthews), being engaged in the prosecution of a criminal case, just at the point of reaching the acme of the pathetic portion of his address, the juicy snuff from the overflowing nose, invaded the throat and threatened to choke him. The ludicrousness of the scene, taught him a lesson of which he availed himself.

He had an iron temperament. He relied so much on this and his temperate habits he was loth to acknowledge that he had ever been sick. He was gay, had a hearty laugh which shook his whole frame; talkative, generally led the conversation. Some were under the impression that he was not a good listener. Always cheerful and blessed with a fine appetite. He entertained once a week distinguished judges and lawyers from other States, and generally men of note received his attention, amongst others, at his festive board. As an instance of the attention he paid to minor matters after being Attorney General, and in the midst of professional engagements in order to improve a defective caligraphy, he found time to take a course of lessons at Dolbear's writing school, and succeeded in writing a legible hand.

THE PROFESSOR.

During twenty-three years he taught the Civil Law in the University of Louisiana. As a lecturer most excellent; could compare favorably with the best professors. In this calling he delighted—very lucid, cogent and animated by his emphatic style, commanded the attention of his hearers. His punctuality on the delivery of his course was exemplary—the students could not depend on the inclemency of the weather or the overflow of the streets, in anticipating a relaxation to their labors. In his conversations some little variety could be detected when referring to his lectures—for there were concentrated his strength, ability and pleasure. He prepared some written lectures, on the Civil Code, for his own use—they are not very extended—the definitions and classifications of the various subjects are strikingly clear and methodical, intending it, as a compendium, to show the actual state of Civil Law—jurisprudence in Louisiana. The introductory lecture, to this course, published in a law magazine, in Montreal, is worthy of his fame.

In his law office were also to be found law students under his charge. He deserves the public gratitude as an instructor of youth; for the impressions left on them follow them in the legislative halls, in courts, and the busy walks of life. His pupils are numerous, found on the Bench and at the Bar,—two of them occupying seats on the Supreme Court Bench of this State. It was his delight to meet them all, and the feeling was warmly reciprocated. He practiced before judges that he had instructed and whose tastes he had formed.

His name stands inseparably connected with the law schools.

ATTORNEY GENERAL.

In February, 1841, he was appointed and confirmed as Attorney General of the State, and served the term of two years. At the time of his appointment, by Governor A. B. Roman, he was a member of the House of Representatives. In 1841, took proceedings against the defaulting banks—a time of great monetary excitement. He had two able and industrious District Attorneys to aid him in the responsible duties of his office. First, Judge T. W. Collens, with whose active co operation gambling houses and other offenses were severely prosecuted.

The offense of gambling was attacked under whatever protean disguise it might assume. Cyprien Dominique Dufour, like his predecessor, prepared the trial of the cases with the greatest care and industry, so that the State had the full benefit of the talents of so distinguished a lawyer as the one whose loss we deplore, and the criminal administration of the State was strikingly effective and successful. He was considerate, firm and just in the discharge of his duties. He shone conspicuously in the prosecution of the State against Williams. It was there contended that the remedy to recover a pecuniary penalty, fixed by statue, is by an action or information of debt. The Supreme Court at first so ruled, but our indefatigable and learned Attorney General applied for a rehearing, accompanied by a masterly brief. Hon. Randell Hunt, the opposing counsel, also displayed, in an answer to it, his learning and excellence, in writing. On a rehearing granted, the Court changed its decision and the State, through its Attorney General, carried the day, but Judge Martin adhered to the opinion he had rendered as the organ of the court.

HIS POLITICAL LIFE.

He was a member of the State Convention of 1845, where were to be found so many able men and lawyers who stood in the front rank of their profession. He took part in the debates. In the succeeding Convention of 1852 he also had a seat. After the adoption of the constitution of that year his friends presented his name to the people as a candidate for Chief Justice of the State. Although he received a heavy vote, he was defeated. Judge Thomas Slidell was the successful candidate.

The excitement of Know-nothingism and party predilections may have had considerable influence on the result, for he had more reputation as a jurist, than the successful candidate. In 1861 he was a member of what is

tered the Secession Convention, having been elected from his Senatorial District by an overwhelming majority. During the canvass he made a vehement speech against secession. He voted against the ordinance of secession, and refused to sign it. His turn of mind was Conservative. He was of opinion that the means for the maintenance of the unity of the Government, and the enforcement of the laws of the United States, passed in pursuance of the Constitution, should not be sought outside of the Constitution, for the latter contains all necessary powers to keep the Government and the States within their appropriate orbits, in this our duplicate form of government. The reconstruction laws of Congress met his decided disapproval. In fact those who mistrust the wisdom of the Constitution, in this, that it did not provide all the necessary powers for its preservation during a civil war and afterwards, are unwittingly not its enlightened friends.

He served in 1841 as a member of the House of Representatives, only for a month, being appointed Attorney General. His heart was not in a political life, but in the profession he adored.

During the military occupation of the city Gen. Shepley tendered him the office of Chief Justice, but he declined. Gov. Wells sent him a commission for the same office. After ascertaining from Gen. Hurlbut that the courts of the State would be held subject to military interference, he did not fancy such an embarrassing or nondescript position. In 1864 he was elected to the State Convention, took his seat for a day, and resigned it by reason of an oath that was exacted from its members.

Our lamented friend departed this life on the 5th day of September, 1873. He has left a daughter and three grandchildren. We all tender them expressions of condolence in their heavy loss.

The names of Roselius and Martin will not be soon forgotten—the latter as the type of the Louisiana Bench; the former as the Louisiana civilian—both honored sons of their adopted State. From the position of journeymen printers, one rose to the Chief Magistracy of the State; the other to the Attorney Generalship. By laborious and persevering application, they improved the gifts of nature, and received the rewards which they richly deserved in enjoying the public confidence and having their names linked with the jurisprudence of Louisiana in their respective spheres. They have acted their parts well, and have done some service to the State. We remain to honor them, and to profit by their examples!

THE PIRATE OF THE GULF.

MORE PIRATICAL DELUSIONS—THE LAFITTE DELUSION.

This name has indeed been the synonym of the pirate in his bloodiest, darkest and most interesting aspects. There is hardly a name in our State annals so familiar to the juvenile, and, indeed, to the senile mind, as that of this brilliant, sanguinary and desperate ruffian, who has been immortalized in verse and prose as the original of those oft-quoted lines of Byron, the possessor of "a single virtue, linked with a thousand crimes."

THE IDEAL LAFITTE.

Innumerable are the Lafittes of history, of romance, of tradition. Every exposed and notable locality, dreary island or desolate inlet, or mysterious nook of a bayou, sets up a claim to association with this mysterious villain. There has not been an ancient, broken-down old sailor, who has lived for the last half century on our desolate coast, who is not suspected by new comers of having been, at one time or another, associated with Lafitte. Lafitte's men have, indeed, like our colored veterans, multiplied with time. They have been the most prolific of pirates. The number of genuine, real, veritable Lafittes who have flourished in our Gulf, has exceeded the Richmonds on the field of Bosworth, as they appeared to the conscience-stricken Richard.

Lafitte has been the generic term for all pirates and all persons engaged in dubious nautical adventures. To destroy this grand and elaborate superstruction of romance and sensational and traditional fiction, is no easy task. It involves, in fact, a very serious responsibility. Popular fancy and love of the marvelous does not yield to such prosaic and cruel contradictions and proofs. Niebuhr, the great Prussian historian, has never been forgiven for his demonstration that Romulus and Remus were never suckled by a wolf, and other fairy stories relating to the early Romans, which so delighted our youthful imaginations, and fixed our attention upon the otherwise dry and sterile story of ancient Rome.

Shall we escape a less severe condemnation by expressing our profound conviction that the only persons of the name of Lafitte, who ever flourished in this section of our great republic, were never pirates, or even nautical characters; never skimmed the Gulf with low, black, rakish cruisers, bearing at their peak the death's-head and cross-bones; never boarded passenger and merchant ships, with cutlasses in hand, and long beards, and grim, savage visages, and, capturing the defenceless vessels, compelled the male passengers to walk the plank, recruited their ranks from the crews, and appropriated the females—the young and beautiful of them as wives and sweethearts, who were, according to the *Ledger*, Mr. Ned Buntline and the Rev. Mr. Ingraham, soon reconciled to the luxuries and wild joys of the Pirates' Home. All these characteristics of the genuine pirate were about as foreign to the personages who figured in our local history under the name of Lafitte, as would be similar exploits on the high road in the Jack Sheppard line, performed by the carpet-bag depredators upon the peace and prosperity of our good citizens.

THE REAL LAFITTE.

Alas! the melancholy fact leaks out that the great head of this supposititious piratical band, who had given such world-wide notoriety to the name of Lafitte, was an intelligent French blacksmith, who kept his forge at the corner of St. Philippe and Bourbon streets, and had no other connections with any transactions on the sea, except as an agent and manager of an association of smugglers and filibusters who combined to defraud the United States Customhouse of duties, and to plunder Spanish commerce under privateering commissions issued by the rebel Spanish State of Columbia. No pirates were they, but first-class smugglers and privateers, who ran a thriving trade by smuggling the goods which they had captured from defenseless Spanish merchantmen, through the Bayou Barrataria up to the point on the other side of the river, now known as Harvey canal, where they would be received and taken care of by Jean Lafitte and his brothers, and brought over to the city by night and then distributed among the stores on the levee, to be retailed to the citizens, to the great disgust of honest traders who [illegible] ot sell like goods at like rates.

LAFITTE AS A PATRIO

This was the extent of the offending of Lafitte and his Barratarians; and not even this much was proved against them, for though arrested and imprisoned by the United States, and indicted, no case could be proved against them, even under the law punishing the violation of our neutrality laws. On the the contrary, it was shown that Lafitte and his followers had rendered most valuable services in the defense of this city in 1814-15 against the British invaders. To estimate the full value of these services, we may state the following conspicuous facts:

1. That Lafitte supplied the raw levies which had been sent to this city to defend it from the British, with the flints which they used so effectively.

2. That he furnished from his associations the most competent cannoniers, who managed the only battery of large guns that aided in repelling the British advance, and in destroying their batteries.

3. That it was through the information furnished by Lafitte, that the United States learned first of the British designs against this city, and through his art and *finesse* that those designs were foiled.

And these are not mere traditions; least of all do they rest upon the imaginings of sensational *raconteurs* and fiction mongers. The proofs thereof are of record in the United States District Court of this city, where the whole subject was thoroughly investigated and ventilated.

EDWARD LIVINGSTON AND JOHN R. GRYMES.

They rest also upon the testimony of Edward Livingston and John R. Grymes, the two ablest lawyers who ever ornamented our bar, and as ardent and true patriots as ever upheld the flag and honor of the Republic. These gentlemen never failed to declare that Lafitte and his associates, so far from being pirates, were in truth gentlemen, men of honor, of most liberal ideas, genial tastes, and only slightly demoralized by an incurable antipathy, which their learned defenders shared, to revenue laws, restrictive tariffs, and other impediments to free trade.

On the part of Col. Grymes this testimony to the estimable qualities of Lafitte was given with peculiar zest and unction, inasmuch as he had had personal experience thereof, in a visit to the Barratarian establishment, to collect a fee which he had earned by a successful defense of Lafitte on an indictment against him in the United States Court. The eloquent and graphic attorney who, by the way, resigned the office of United States District Attorney in order to defend Lafitte against the indictment of the grand jury, preferring a fee of $5,000 in doubloons to the $600 salary of that Federal office, as well as the cause of a persecuted gentleman against a prosecution instigated, as he avowed, by the avarice of merchants who were hostile to the Democratic principle of free trade, gladly accepted the invitation to accompany his client to his Barratarian home, there to receive his fee, in solid Spanish doubloons, and partake of "piratical pot luck."

And a jolly time the jovial counsellor had with Lafitte at Barrataria. The visit was so delightful a one, the company so congenial, the wines so rich and rare, and the viands prepared with such taste and sumptuousness, that Col. Grymes extended his visit for several days longer than he had originally designed, thereby rendering his friends in the city quite anxious about him and especially brother Edward Livingstone, who was to share the fee which Lafitte was to pay.

Finally, however, after a delightful week's sojourn at this so-called "Pirate's Lair," Colonel Grymes returned with the doubloons to the city, and even afterward when interrogated as to Lafitte and his confederates, always declared they were the most perfect gentlemen he had ever meet outside of old Virginia. And from this authority we derived the assurance that Jean Lafitte and his brothers were never pirates not ever seafaring men, but merely shrewd speculators and operators in free trade and privateering; wherein, however, they had no further agency than to receive and dispose of the goods captured under letters of mark by vessels chartered by them, pursuits far less criminal or immoral than such as are now-a-days rewarded with office and Radical honors and prestige.

So far from obtaining these or any other recognition of even the meritorious and invaluable services rendered by Lafitte and his followers in the defense of this city, they met the common fate of such benefactors, of being proscribed and despoiled by certain avaricious officials, who broke up their establishment, seized and appropriated their vessels and property, and utterly empoverished these once rich and prosperous free-traders. They were scattered in every direction. Some of them fled the country, and may have fallen into loose ways and sought to trade upon the name of Lafitte, thereby giving circulation to the fictitious stories and multiplying the name and form of the hypothetical pirate. Others remained in the city and took to honest and regular pursuits, and several prospered and became rich and important personages. Two of them, who were famous fighting men, You and Bluche, managed to secure the admiration and respect of General Jackson to such a degree that he gave the latter, Bluche, a high certificate and recommendation, which procured him an appointment to the command of the fleet of one of the South American republics, and the other old Dominique was the first person the General inquired for on his last visit to the city. He lived to an advanced age, in great poverty, but with undiminished pride in his achievements as a warrior, and at his death was buried in the St. Louis Cemetery, where a pompous tomb was erected over him, and a quotation from Voltaire's Henriade testifies to his

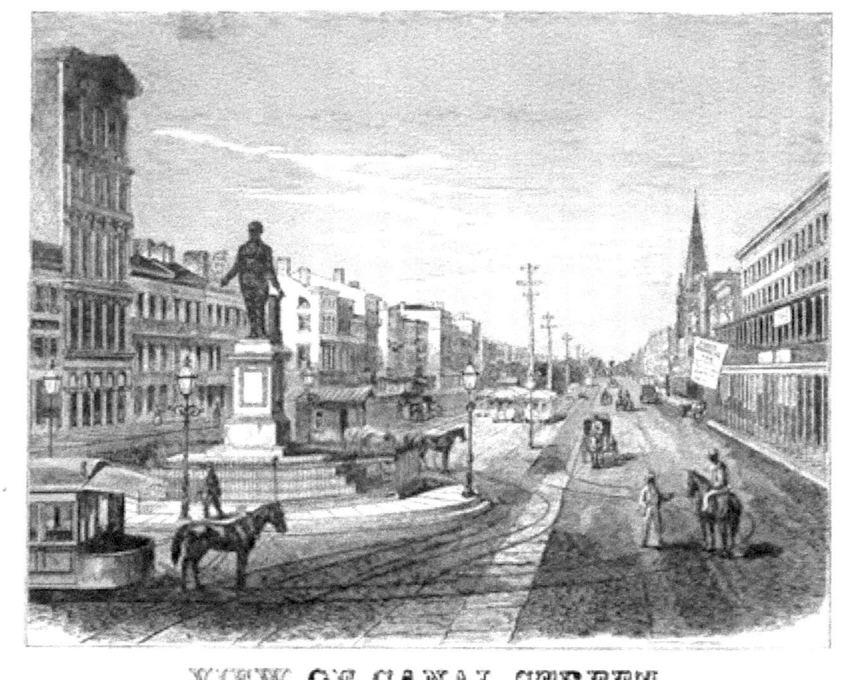

VIEW OF CANAL STREET.

greatness as a hero and warrior, "The victor in a hundred fights on sea and land."

Such is plainly and briefly the real history of the Lafittes and the Barratarians which, however, has been rejected by the multitude, and the far more exciting and attractive version of the *Ledger* novelist school preferred thereto.

Among the most signal and remarkable victims of this delusive version was

THE PRINTER LEGATEE TO THE LAFITTE TREASURE.

About two years ago, a middle aged printer of this city named A. J. Newell, who had saved from his winter's wages enough to buy and equip a small smack, started on a sailing excursion to Lake Borgne. He was all alone. It was well known what was the object of his expedition. It was the repetition of many others he had been in the habit of risking every summer. Though of a silent, unsocial and morose character, he could not conceal from his brother printers the mysterious secret which he had long borne in his breast, and around which all his thoughts, aspirations and hopes clustered. Many years before, in consideration of some kindness rendered by his father, who lived on the sea-coast, to an aged and battered sailor, the grateful tar had made a formal legacy to him of his interest in a vast treasure which had been buried on an island in the gulf by Lafitte's men.

This treasure consisted of countless doubloons which had been captured from a Spanish galleon. Accompanying the legacy was a chart indicating the spot where the treasure was buried. The old sailor after confiding this valuable secret to Newell's father died. The father transferred the legacy and secret to his son, and the latter accepted it with unbounded confidence in its reality, and as soon as he could obtain the means, started with a vessel in pursuit of the buried wealth. Weeks were expended in the search. The topographical similarity of the islands in the gulf, the constant changes in their form and surface by the winds and shifting sands, rendered these perquisitions very laborious, difficult and unproductive. But Newell's confidence was never shaken. He only suspended his search because of the exhaustion of his means. Returning to his trade as printer, he set industriously to work, carefully laying by his savings, and wrapt entirely in his own thoughts, holding little intercourse with his brother printers.

His secret leaked out, and many hints and jokes were indulged in by his companions in regard to his expected wealth. He was not disposed to discredit these stories, but, in fact, seriously intimated that he would, before long, become the possessor of enough money to give them all homes. As soon as he had laid by enough money, he would abandon his case, and steal down to the lakes, and getting aboard would sail away, generally at night, towards the islands outside of the Rigolets. Studying his chart, and carefully selecting the locality, which appeared to be indicated by the charter and descriptive notes, he would land and set to work with spade and shovel to dig the hard sand, persevering therein, until he had penetrated the whole area for several feet deep.

In some of these explorations Newell had the aid and companionship of a friend and partner, but growing suspicious as he became more eager and intent, he finally dissolved his partnership, and in his latter explorations was all alone.

His last adventure was in the summer of 1871. His boat was observed under sail passing through the Rigolets. She was recognized by persons at Fort Pike and Pearl River landing. There was but one person on board. Shortly after the little vessel had passed into Lake Borgne, there came up a heavy blow, and people wondered at the rashness which would venture out in the face of such indications of foul weather. The blow swelled into a storm, that swept the lake of all small craft, driving them into harbors and inlets, and lashed into white foam the great waves, which convulsed and furrowed its usually placid surface; and so it continued to blow until morning.

A bright, clear, calm day succeeded. It revealed the effects of a severe hurricane in several wrecks, and in much damage along shore. Inquiries were naturally made, and much anxiety expressed in regard to the little smack which had ventured so rashly out in the face of the gathering storm. It was not long before this anxiety was heightened by the arrival at the Pearl River Station of a lumber vessel, towing a small smack, which had been picked up floating in the lake, with no person on board. She was identified as Newell's vessel. There were suspicions of robbery and murder, but these were soon dispelled by the recovery of a body which was recognized as that of Newell. There were no indications of violence, and the conclusion of those who examined the vessel and the body was that he had been washed off his vessel by the high waves and drowned. The body was brought to this city and buried with the usual respect always accorded by the craft to their deceased members.

Thus perished a victim for twenty years of a singular delusion, which might have been dispelled by a little sober reflection and examination of well attested facts. It could have been easily ascertained by very simple and easy inquiries that none of the survivors of Lafitte's band had any knowledge of this buried treasure; that, in fact, they were all poor, their accumulations having been swept away by the seizures and confiscations of the United States authorities, and that it could hardly be conceived that this valuable secret would have been kept from all the confederates, or that knowing it, they would not have entered upon the exploration and search in which poor Newell lost his life.

It is an interesting coincidence that Jean Lafitte, the hero of all this mass of delusions and fictions, perished in the same manner as Newell. It was, we believe, in 1817 that, having gathered the remnants of his once large possessions, he chartered a small vessel, to proceed on a trading voyage to St. Thomas. He was never again seen or heard of. There were severe storms in the Gulf about that time, and the vessel was doubtless wrecked in one of them. Not a remnant of her was ever found.

Thus perished Jean Lafitte, the Blacksmith of Bourbon street, who has been so falsely maligned as a desperate and bloody pirate by audacious fiction mongers, intent on making a few dollars, by ignobly pandering to a morbid taste for ruffianly deeds, scenes and characters—that singular preference which our imaginative and excitable people have for sensational and sanguinary fiction over the sober truths and realities of honest and faithful history.

GEORGE A. BRAUGHN.

One of the most successful and promising young lawyers at the bar of this city, is G. H. Braughn, Esq. Thrown much upon his own resources at an early age of life, and deprived of the advantages of a scholastic education, he was forced to rely entirely upon his own exertions for any success in life he might achieve. His present position is ample evidence of how satisfactory his labors have been.

Mr. Braughn was born in Cincinnati, Ohio, on the 11th of October, 1837. His father was of Scotch and his mother of German extraction. In 1849 the former died of cholera, and the latter some time after moved to Kentucky, and there married again. Then it was the ambitious and resolute youth determined to push out for himself, and at the age of fourteen, came to New Orleans, penniless and without friends. He soon found sufficient employment in selling newspapers, setting up ten pins, and serving as a roller boy in the Crescent Job Office, to support himself. Finally he succeeded, in 1856, in obtaining a clerkship in the trunk store of F. Bauer, and after remaining there two years, accepted an offer from H. W. Reynolds & Co., engaged in the trunk business, to become their managing clerk, at a very liberal salary.

In 1860, during the Presidential campaign, young Braughn took an active part in the politics of the day. He was elected Vice-President of the Young Men's Breckenridge Club, and in 1861 was nominated for the Legislature from the the First Ward, but was defeated by B. S. Tappan, Esq.

In the meantime, however, and during his commercial life, Mr. Braughn was unremitting in his studies, reading law under the guidance of the Hon. M. M. Reynolds. But prior to his admission to the bar, the war came on, and the young student joined the Crescent Regiment, and was elected First Lieutenant of Company G. He was engaged in the battles of Mississippi and Tennessee, and afterwards with his regiment was ordered to the Trans-Mississippi Department, where he likewise participated in several engagements, and was promoted to a Captaincy.

At the close of the war, the subject of this sketch resumed his studies, and soon obtained the degree of LL. B. from the Law University of Louisiana. He then commenced the practice of his profession, and soon gave evidence of ability, judgment and tact. Soon after, he was called to preside as Justice of one of the City Courts, and on his retiring from that post, was elected by the Democratic party State Senator from the First District, in 1868. Although in active political life, Mr. Braughn never neglected his law business, and steadily advanced his fame as a lawyer. Finding his business so rapidly increasing, he associated with him Mr. Chas. F. Buck, a talented young gentleman, and together these young lawyers enjoy a practice, in point of profit and importance, second to no other firm in the city. In May, 1872, Gov. Warmoth appointed Braughn to act as Assistant Attorney General, and in this position he was retained by Gov. Kellogg.

The popular Shakspeare Club owes its existence to Mr. Braughn, who was its founder, and for six years its efficient president. He was also Vice-President of the Firemen's Charitable Association for seven terms; Vice-President Y. M. Benevolent Association; Master of Dudley Lodge, F. A. M.; Grand Representative of the Grand Lodges, "Royal York of Friendship," Berlin; "Eclectic Union," of Frankfort on the Main; "Grand Lodge of Saxony," at Dresden. He is also a Director in the Germania Insurance Company, in the Metropolitan Loan and Savings Bank, and is the Attorney of the last as well as of the People's Bank, and the People's Insurance Company.

Working during the day and attending night schools, constitute his early history. With an eager fondness for the stage Mr. Braughn is far above the general run of professionals as an amateur actor. His study of elocution and declamation in this connection is of eminent service to him in his profession, making him a graceful, finished and accomplished speaker; and with his natural ability, close application and personal popularity, future eminence and continued success are easily predicted.

A. SAMBOLA, Esq.

Is a native of the city of New Orleans, in which he has always felt a just pride, and which our citizens fully reciprocate. He was born February 29th, 1836. He received his early education at Spring Hill College, Mobile, Ala., and entered Centenary College at Jackson, La., in 1854, and graduated with credit and honors in 1857. His *alma mater* subsequently, 1868, conferred on him the degree of A. M. After his graduation he entered the office of that veteran lawyer, Hon. Christian Roselius, attended two courses of lectures at the University of Louisiana, received the degree of LL. B., and soon became one of the most active young lawyers in New Orleans.

During this time, and after he returned from college, Mr. Sambola devoted his leisure moments to usefulness in some of the benevolent institutions of the city, particularly the new Lusitanos Benevolent Association, and the Order of S. W. M. Systematic and thorough in the dispatch of business, and conversant with the mother tongues spoken by so many of the people of New Orleans, speaking French and Spanish as well as English, he soon became prominent in these associations.

The war which ensued, drew away Mr. Sambola, like so many thousands of the young men of the country North and South, and he served a member of the Washington Artillery, in the Confederate army, from the early part of 1862, until the close of the war. During this time he participated in many of the engagements that took place in Mississippi, Tennessee, Kentucky, and Georgia.

B. T. WALSHE, ESQ.

ST. LOUIS HOTEL.

Returning to New Orleans, he soon became engaged, as he is now, in a large and lucrative law practice. His fellow-citizens elected him to the House of Representatives, in 1865, and served in the Legislatures of 1866 and 1867. He was elected to the State Senate in 1867, but failed to obtain his seat.

Mr. Sambola, in 1865, resumed his interest in the Order of S. W. M., was soon elected Grand Archon of Louisiana, and afterwards Supreme Archon of the United States, to which office he was recently re-elected at the meeting of the Supreme Conclave in Philadelphia. He is certainly the most efficient and devoted officer that the Order has ever had. While we have spoken of his military and political career as a necessary part of his biography, we will say that he is held in equal and high esteem by the members of the Order in the North, for he knows neither party nor section, in his connection with it, which he evidently regards as a fraternity, or brotherhood, too sacred and intimate for any such considerations.

Mr. Sambola was elected a presidential elector of the State, in 1868, and took an active part in the campaign, and has also, for four years past, been a prominent and very attentive director of our public schools.

He is connected with nearly every benevolent society in the city, and is also a Mason, (30th Degree,) an Odd Fellow, and was Grand Chancellor of the Knights of Pythias. He is also an exempt member of the Fire Department, and a delegate to the Fireman's Charitable Association.

The characteristics of Mr. Sambola are promptness, punctuality and affability, supported by an ever ready good judgment. He is a graceful public speaker, and not a few of our people look with confidence to his future rise and advancement. All heartily regard him as a good citizen, already deserving of public regard for the qualities he has developed in his busy and useful career.

COL. JAMES F. CASEY.

The Collector of the Port of New Orleans, Col. Casey, was born in Union County, Kentucky, in 1829. He was educated at Franklin College, near Nashville, Tennessee. He first engaged in business in St. Louis as a commission merchant, and resided there until the commencement of the war. At its close he invested in a cotton plantation at Friar's Point, Mississippi, and there remained until 1867 when he came to New Orleans to reside. In connection with his present efficient deputy, P. F. Herwig, Esq., Col. Casey embarked in the business of cotton weighing. Upon the election of President Grant, Col. Casey, his brother-in-law, was appointed collector of the Port and re-appointed in 1873. During his administration the business of the Custom House has been conducted in a manner to merit the approbation of the mercantile community. Although politically opposed to a large majority of those with whom he is brought in contact, yet he is highly esteemed and respected. Correct, faithful and honest in the discharge of his official duties, he has earned for himself the name of an efficient and popular Collector.

In his personal relations Col. Casey is very amiable, kind-hearted and generous; ever ready to assist a friend, and with no bitterness or vindictiveness for political opponents. In 1851 Col. Casey married Miss Emma Dent, of St. Louis, and sister of Mrs. Grant. He is now the father of three boys.

JOHN E. LEET,

Was born at Steelville, Crawford County, Missouri, January 4th, 1847. His father was for many years a Circuit Judge, and prominent politician in Missouri, and his grandfather participated in the Whiskey Insurrection and in the Revolution. A more remote ancestor was the famous Puritan Governor of Connecticut, who befriended the English regicides.

At the beginning of the war, Mr. Leet left his school books and enlisted in the Union Army, first as a drummer, then as a private. Serving in the campaign of Arkansas, he was finally captured at Mark's Mill on the 25th of April, 1864, and sent through Shreveport to Tyler, Texas, and afterwards to Camp Gross, at Hempstead. After five months' imprisonment he was paroled, sent to New Orleans, and thence home. His death having been announced, and an obituary notice published, the appearance of young Leet produced quite a commotion at home; but his arrival came too late to secure for him the possession of a young lady's heart and hand, to whom he had been engaged. She thought her affianced dead, and consoled herself by marrying a young and gay Confederate sympathizer.

Somewhat broken in health by his arduous campaigns Mr. Leet, as soon as he had recuperated, entered the Missouri University, at Columbia, and remained there a year. Afterwards he completed his studies in 1870, at the Kentucky Institute, at Lexington, and received his diploma.

Liking New Orleans he determined to make it his future home. But not finding employment immediately, he moved to the parish of Vermillion, where he commenced teaching, and organized the public schools there. Soon after, he leased the newspaper called the *Meridional*, and subsequently purchased it. In May, 1871, he discontinued its publication, and established the Abbeville *Flag*, as a Republican organ. He was a delegate to the Press Convention, and there carried a resolution, pledging in advance all the Republican papers in the State to the re-election of President Grant. In October of the same year, the *Statesman* was established at New Iberia by Mr. Leet, but he soon gave it up for a position on the New Orleans *National Republican*, the organ of Gov. Kellogg and his party. After Gov. Kellogg's inauguration, he appointed Mr. Leet Harbor-master, which position he now holds.

Active, industrious, persevering and intelligent, our young subject has a fair opportunity to make for himself a name and a reputation that will afford the future biographer a wider scope than can possibly be given by one so young as Mr. Leet.

W. H. BELL, Esq.

The present City Surveyor, Mr. W. H. Bell, is a native of New Orleans and is now but [illegible] years of age. Educated as a Civil Engineer and with a thorough knowledge of the topography of the city his appointment to his present office was an eminently proper one. During the years of [illegible] and [illegible] he served as assistant City Surveyor and subsequently filled the office of Street Commissioner for two years. After 1867 he was elected by the Council City Surveyor and with all the various political changes that have occurred since that time he has been retained in his position. This is of itself a testimonial of the highest appreciation of his valuable services and a recognition of his fitness for the position.

During Mr. Bell's term of office he has designed and practically inaugurated a system of drainage for the City of New Orleans, which, when completed, will reclaim a large section of territory and make valuable a number of acres of land that are now only swamps and bayous. The Lake protection levee is a work of his conception and reflects the highest credit upon Mr. Bell as an Engineer.

In all matters relating to the material development of the city he is an ardent advocate and is always foremost in every work that may tend to advance the interests of his native city.

Mr. Bell is modest and retiring in his manners, but firm in the discharge of his duties, and through his long term of official life the tongue of slander has never breathed aught against his reputation. He has before him a bright and promising future and there are hosts of friends who will rejoice to see success crown the efforts of Mr. Bell.

RICHARD M. MONTGOMERY, Esq.

There are but few, if any, of the old residents of New Orleans, who do not know the subject of this sketch. More than a quarter of a century ago he came to this city and since that time has been actively engaged in business and has shared the good and bad fortunes that have attended the city in its past history.

Mr. Montgomery was born in Lexington, Ky., on the 10th of December 18[illegible], and at an early age came to New Orleans where he engaged in the Furniture business in a subordinate capacity. It was not long, however, by industry, economy and business tact, before this young and thriving gentleman was enabled to embark in business on his own account. We find him, then, very soon after at the head of a large and prosperous firm of auctioneers,—which at this date ranks among the first in the city. Associated with his brother R. J. Montgomery, a most estimable gentleman, and occupying the Armory Hall, of historic fame, there is no business firm in the city that enjoys more freely the confidence of the community or is more highly esteemed by the public at large.

Although avoiding participation in all political or public affairs Mr. Montgomery is ever prompt and liberal in contributing to whatever measures that may be inaugurated for the welfare or improvement of the city. He was one of the first patrons of the Canal and Claiborne Streets Rail-Road, and is now one of its most active and energetic directors. Other public institutions receive his support and attention and find in him an efficient and valuable friend.

Socially Mr. Montgomery is free, liberal and warm-hearted, and whilst the number of his friends is legion there is none who can speak of him otherwise than as an honored merchant, an exemplary citizen and a most estimable gentleman.

COLLECTORS OF THE PORT.

Subjoined we give a list of the names of all the collectors of the port of New Orleans, since 1803. Among the names will be found many that will revive old and pleasant recollections, and some that are indissolubly connected with the past glory of our city:

Hore Browse Trist, from December 20, 1803, to Sept. 1 1804.

Wm. Brown, Deputy, Acting, from September 1, 1804, to January 15, 1805.

Wm Brown, from January 15, 1805, to November 15, 1809.

Robert Porter, Deputy, Acting, from November 16, 1809, to January 8, 1810.

Thos. H. Williams from January 8, 1810, to February 1, 1815.

Peter L. B. Dupuy from February 1, 1815, to December 31, 1816.

Beverly Chew, from January 1, 1817 to May 31, 1829.

Martin Gordon, from June 1, 1829, to June 30, 1834.

Jas. W. Breedlove, from July 1, 1834, to June 30, 1839.

Denis Prieur, from July 1, 1839 to July 12, 1841.

Thos. Gibbs Morgan, from July 13, 1841, to October 17, 1843.

Greenberry Dorsey, from October 18, 1843, to April 15, 1844.

M. S. Cucullu, from April 16, 1844, to June 30, 1844.

D. O. Hincks, Deputy, Acting, from July 1, 1844, to July 24, 1844.

Thos. Barrett, from July 25, 1844, to October 12, 1845.

Denis Prieur, from October 13, 1845, to May 13, 1849.

Samuel J. Peters, from May 14, 1849, to November 24, 1850.

Wm. Freret, from Nov. 25, 1850, to August 31, 1851.

Geo. C. Lawrason, from Sept. 1, 1851, to May 22, 1853.

S. W. Downs, from May 23, 1853, to Sept. 14, 1854.

Thos. C. Porter, from Sept. 15, 1854, to March 13, 1857.

F. H. Hatch, from April 1, 1857, to January 31, 1861.*

F. H. Hatch, from February 1, 1861, to Feb. 28, 1861.†

F. H. Hatch, from March 1, 1861, to the arrival of the United States fleet.‡

Geo. S. Denison, Acting Collector from May 16, 1862, to February 28, 1863.

Cuthbert Bullitt, Acting Collector, from March 1, 1863 to November 30, 1863.

Geo. S. Denison, Acting Collector, from December 1, 1863, to June 25, 1865.

Wm. P. Kellogg, Collector, from June 26, 1865, to July 16, 1868.

Acting Collector S. A. Stockdale, from July 17, 1868, to September 21, 1868.

Perry Fuller, Collector, from September 22, 1868, to March 4, 1869.

Wm. C. Gray, Acting Collector, from March 5, 1869, to April 11, 1869.

Jas. F. Casey, from April 12, 1869, to the present time.

*U. S. Collector. †State of Louisiana Collector. ‡C. S. A. Collector.

REV. BISHOP WILMER.

FLASH, LEWIS & CO.,

WHOLESALE GROCERS,

AND DEALERS IN

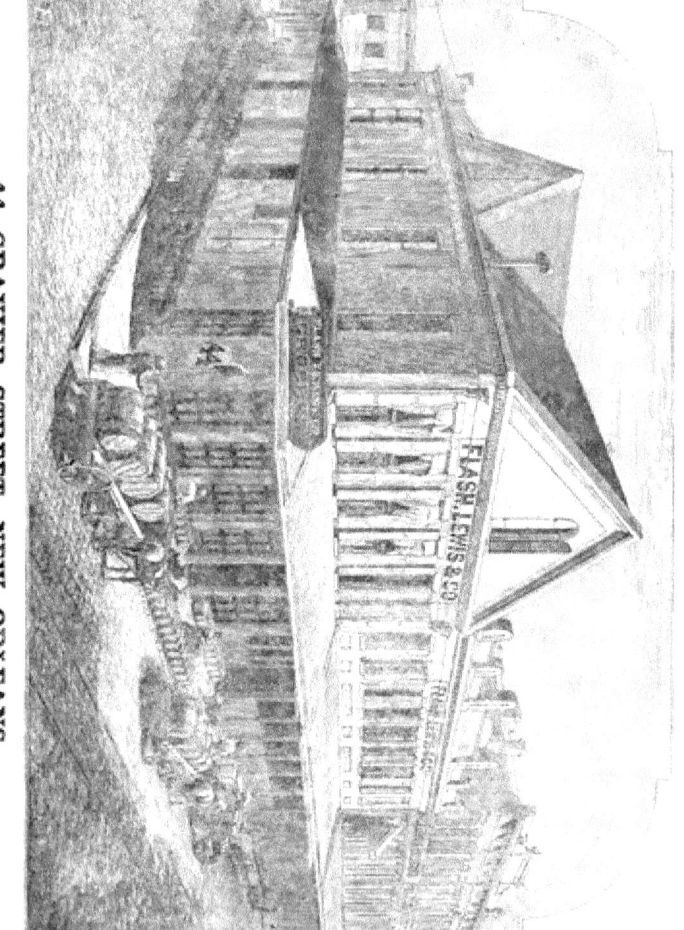

WINES AND LIQUORS.

44 GRAVIER STREET, NEW ORLEANS.

THE NEW OFFICE BUILDING

OF THE

N. O. GAS LIGHT CO.

Exterior.—The new building stands on the West corner of Baronne and Common streets, measuring forty-eight feet front on Baronne, and one hundred and eleven feet six inches on Common, being advantageously placed for view from Canal street. The style can be more nearly assimilated to the better class of suburban houses of Paris, with a touch of French renaissance. A base of Maine Granite reigns on the two street fronts. Above this rises the building, three stories and mansard in height, and divided into two pavilions connected together on Common street and finished exteriorly by curtains receded from the face line. The principal business entrance to the Gas Office is in the cut-off corner of the corner pavilion; the private entrance for the officers and employees is in middle of the long curtain on Common street, from the vestibule of which a door also leads into the inspector's office for business with the gas-fitters, and also leading to the workshops. In the outside curtains are the stairs to the offices for rent on the second and third floors. Still another entrance is obtained from the lot, as yet vacant on Common street, for the reception of meters and other stores.

The walls are faced with Philadelphia pressed bricks, and ornamented with artificial black bricks, and trimmings, cornices and rustic corner pilasters of gray stone; the corner doorway and columns in the double windows being of Alabama limestone and the other parts of artificial stone.

The first story, with its bracketed cornice relieved by encaustic tiles, serves, as it were, as basement to the second and third which are treated as one, divided by a string course. The frieze of the upper cornice is also composed of ornamental tiles.

The whole is crowned by a mansard of different colored slates, with ornamental dormer windows and chimneys of artificial stone, the hips of the pavilions and the mansard cornice being formed of French embossed zinc. A rich cresting finishes the exterior.

Interior.—The general business office, as before stated, is entered through a vaulted doorway forming a semi-circular balcony on the second floor; a somewhat unique arrangement, the nearest approach to which may be found in a curved balcony in the Pavilion Henri IV. of the Louvre.* The general office† is a hexagon, one side containing the entrance, two others containing each two lofty double windows on Common and Baronne streets. Facing the entrance is the vault, and a door into the collector's room, surmounted by a large clock dial; another side is formed by the room of the treasurer and the book-keeper. The sixth side contains a roomy dressing-room with wash-stand, etc., under the main Baronne street stairs, for the clerks. The room is richly frescoed but in subdued tones in what may be called modern Pompeian style. The wainscoting and trimmings of this as well as the treasurer's office are of La. cypress with black-walnut and mahogany panels alternated. The frescoing is by Mr. Eug. Philastre, assisted by Messrs. David & Rocha.

* On each side of the entrance is a bronze statue holding a cluster of gas lights.

† Occupying the 1st floor of the corner pavilion.

The windows, as also all those of the first and second floors on the streets, contain three sash in height and sliding blinds, thereby affording unusual ventilation and facility for keeping off the sun.

The office railing, made by Messrs. McCracken & Brewster, is composed of black-walnut with cypress and mahogany ornamented panels; the parts above the desks are closed with plate glass, frosted and ornamented by Mr. A. J. Burgeon of this city. This railing encloses the public portion in the shape of a hexagon of about half the width of the whole room and paved with ornamental French tiles, in the center of which will stand a drinking fountain in summer, and a stove in winter, the flue for which is under the pavement, thereby avoiding the unseemly stove-pipe.

Passing through a small waiting-room to the right of the pavement, and through a door arranged as a counter, we enter the Treasurer's room, richly papered by Mr. Sielrecht, to which objection may be found that it is too rich for an office.*

* It was originally intended for the Directors' Room.

Next comes the private entrance hall, opening on Common street as above stated, and on the yard. In the rear of the vault is the Collector's room, lighted from the yard, between which and the Treasurer's room a passage leads from the general office, across the private entrance hall to the Inspectors' room and workshops. The portion of the Inspectors' room nearest the street and opening on the private vestibule, is paved and cut off by a railing for the gas-fitters.

The second pavilion on this floor is occupied by the meter-setting shop in front, and repairing shop on the yard. The floor of these is only twelve inches above the sidewalk, allowing the introduction of a half story. From the shops two doors open on a shed in the lot already mentioned, serving for the unloading of goods, washing meters, etc. A goods' elevator and a private staircase lead to the mansard, in which are the ware-room and keeper's room.

In the yard, which is twenty feet by twenty-two feet, are the W.c's, etc. for the employees. From the Collector's room, in an invisible corner formed by the vault, is a small private staircase for the exclusive use of the Company, leading first to the stationary depot over the vault which is lit through the clear glass dial of the clock, thereby affording a supervision over the general office; these stairs next open under the main stairs to the third floor, thus being entirely concealed from the uninitiated. They were rendered necessary by the determination, when the building was well up, of removing the President's and Directors' room from the present Treasurer's Room to the second floor.

Crossing the second floor hall we enter the President's and Superintendent's office, and the Directors' room, the latter occupying the long curtain on Common street, and being sixteen feet wide and thirty-eight feet long. Both these rooms are finished in a rather original style. Above a whimsically paneled walnut wainscoting the walls are divided by pilasters with mahogany and carved walnut panels, into alternately wide and narrow arches, the first either occupied by a corresponding to the openings and chimneys; the others, occupying the piers between, are shortened by small pedestals. The doors are richly carved and the rooms papered in a style to suit the architecture, the smaller arches being filled with a dark Pompeian tapestry, and the larger ones, where not open, by beautiful subject medallions on a light ground.

From the President's office a double letter elevator leads into the Treasurer's room, and speaking-tubes to the general office, Treasurer's and Inspectors' room. Similar tubes also lead from the Inspectors' room to the general office and mansard. Near the Book-keeper's desk in the Treasurer's room a telegraph extends to the gas works of the Company on Locust street.

OFFICES FOR RENT.

From each of the short curtains in the extreme ends of the street fronts, grand staircases lead to the second and third floor halls, along which are ranged some twelve offices, of which five are so arranged as to be subdivided if desired. A portion of the mansard is allotted as waste room for these offices. In the rear of the Common street stairs, but not noticeable to a casual passer-by, are the W.c's and coal bins, each twelve in number. The elevator, which is in the same quarter, gives facility to the introduction of furniture, safes, coal, etc.

In the hall of each floor is a marble wash-stand and drinking fountain and slop sink. The gas meters for the different offices are in two closets in the wall of the second floor hall.

By means of a large iron tank in the mansard, and another on the yard W.c's, rain water is supplied to the different fountains and wash-stands. Mississippi river water is also introduced in the yard, work-shop and lot for more common uses.

After having visited the building an ascension to the flat iron roof will well repay the visitor, from its extensive view of the city and its surroundings, up to and beyond Carrollton.

CANAL STREET AND ITS FUTURE.

Of all our city thoroughfares, the best known abroad is Canal street; and there is no question that it is first in the estimation of the resident population. It has not been many years, however, since it began to enjoy its present repute. It was in the year 1856, that the famous Touro buildings were erected, and in the same year the corner-stone of the Clay Statue was laid. The city, at that time, had just fully recovered from the depression consequent upon the great epidemic of 1853, and the swelling current of renewed prosperity somehow found its way into that channel. The impetus then imparted no subsequent disaster has been able to neutralize. One by one those stately palaces of trade have been reared which now render the beautiful boulevard the wonder and admiration of the visitors, and the delight and pride of the citizens of the Crescent City. We have seen with great pleasure the several improvements which have been this year attempted, and can but add to the architectural beauty and business convenience of this important street. The new savings bank, between Baronne and Carondelet streets, now nearly completed, is eminently calculated to meet both these ends, and already, by the elegance of its proportions, and the taste and finish of its design, is attracting a general and favorable notice. The cornice recently put on the Custom House adds greatly to the effect of that immense structure, and is of no little advantage to the general appearance of the street.

An artistic analysis of the various elements of attractiveness which render Canal street so pleasing to the eye, will show that its two principal charms are breadth combined with a spacious sky and river view and the variety of architectural style exhibited in its buildings. Its present undeniable beauty will be greatly enhanced when all the small and inelegant buildings, which mar the general effect of their more imposing neighbors, have been replaced by others more in keeping with the evident demands of the view.

When the trees which are planted along its various lines of street railways are fully grown, they too will impart an additional charm.

The fact that our system of city railways concentrates all the lines on this thoroughfare, of itself, in a great degree, accounts for its prosperity, and must maintain and increase it.

In the opinion of traveled and competent critics, there is no street in any city of the United States which can compare in grandeur of view with Canal street, as it is even now; and we look forward to a day, when all its possibilities realized, it shall have no superior anywhere.

NEW ORLEANS IN SUMMER.

With no reference to its society or civilization, but to the genial zone in which it is situated and the delights of its climatic properties, New Orleans is unrivaled as a city home in summer. There are no such mornings outside of tropic influences, no such evenings amid torrid heats not aired by tropic breezes. Our sister cities of the North burn to cinders in the dog days

"From morn till dewy eve,"

while night brings no cooling balm, no fragrant scent of orange or magnolia, nothing to cheer, enliven or refresh the spirit weary with its load of summer. Especially, no south wind comes with its cooling kisses of delight, following the red rays of the glaring sun and gladdening the spaces through which they have glinted for long hours with breezy surprise.

Numberless mistaken people wander abroad in search of an indefinable happiness or a vague something which is never found. They populate hotels and seaside resorts for weeks and months, and never overtake an hour of comfort, and hence, are never satisfied with their conquests of many so-called pleasures, which are put down in diaries as triumphs of travel. But when they get back, in the ripe autumn, to the beautiful city, they find their first sensation of real delight, of unalloyed satisfaction, of unspoken and unspeakable gratitude; and as they walk the old familiar streets, glowing with the sense of home and happiness, they feel their real and only employment—the single compensation for the loss of New Orleans in summer to be that one unalloyed recompense—getting back.

Let New Orleans people consider and observe more than they do; imagine and desire less of fashion's glinting nothings, save their money and keep their persons safe, by a rational understanding of this delightful subject—New Orleans in summer.

New Orleans Savings Institution,

INCORPORATED IN 1855.

This Institution has been removed to the new Banking House,

No. 156 CANAL STREET.

INTEREST PAID ON DEPOSITS.

SAM JONES, Jr., Treasurer. L. F. GENERES, President.

DIRECTORS.

DR. W. NEWTON MERCER.
DAVID URQUHART.
J. G. GAINES.
CARL KOHN.
CHRISTIAN SCHNEIDER.
SAML. JAMISON.

L. F. GENERES.
GEORGE JONAS.
T. A. ADAMS.
THOMAS ALLEN CLARKE.
CHAS. J. LEEDS.

E. NORTH CULLOM.

There are some men who, placed in any circumstances, either prosperous or adverse, have within them a spirit that will prompt them to raise themselves above the common herd—to make for themselves names that will shine out in the brightest pages of our country's history. The lives and actions of these men are as bright and shining examples to the youth of the Republic; and to commemorate them, to hand them down to generations yet to come, is a noble and laudable task.

E. North Cullom was born in Opelousas, parish of St. Landry, Louisiana, on the 14th of September, 1825, and is consequently now in his forty-eighth year. His father Francis Cullom, an estimable citizen of Wayne county, Kentucky, was originally a cabinet-maker by trade, but, in the fall of 1825, formed the design of following the legal profession, and accordingly after due preparation, was admitted to practice. In 1832 he removed from Opelousas into the parish of Avoyelles, where he cleared a farm, and settled down to the monotony of rural life, about two miles east of the present town of Holmesville. Meanwhile, Mr. Cullom had been deprived of the tender care of a fond mother, who died, leaving three children, the subject of the present memoir being the eldest, Leonard Davis Cullom, and a daughter, who in a few days followed her to the tomb.

At that time the neighborhood of their farm was a wilderness, the country was as yet thinly settled, and the schoolmaster, that pioneer of civilization, had not as yet blessed it with his presence. Consequently, the young Cullom was for a long time deprived of the advantages and benefits of education. He was employed, however, in the duties of the farm, doing what one of his tender age was capable of performing. He here learned those habits of industry and perseverance for which in after years he has become so remarkable.

When about eleven years old, a schoolmaster established a rural school in the neighborhood, and to him the young Cullom eagerly hastened, to drink at the font of learning, however meagre the stream or unworthy its dispenser. But he was not long allowed to remain. His services being required on the plantation, he was obliged unwillingly to return, after having been under the tuition of the rural pedagogue but nine short months. To him it was a bitter disappointment. Naturally a boy of quick parts, and eager in the pursuit of knowledge, it was with a heavy heart that he resumed his duties on his father's farm.

But the thirst for education within him could not be controlled, and with a joyful heart he again returned to his desk, when about twelve years of age. The school was conducted on the French plan, and while there, the subject of our sketch resided with a French family, and consequently peculiar facilities were presented to him for acquiring a tolerable knowledge of that beautiful language. A youth of Mr. Cullom's quickness and industry could not fail to improve such advantages, and, therefore, he became a tolerable master of the language. He remained there about one year, when he again resumed his labors on the plantation.

His persevering pursuit of education is one of the most remarkable traits in Mr. Cullom's youthful career. In 1841 he was again rejoiced by being placed under the care of a private tutor at his father's residence, under whose auspices he remained for the space of eighteen months. His progress was unusually rapid in all the branches of a preparatory education, and he evinced a particular aptness for the study of geography, grammar and arithmetic, in which branches he excelled.

In 1843 his father removed with his family to a summer residence in the parish of his nativity—St. Landry—about twenty-two miles distant, leaving Mr. Cullom alone on the plantation, to perform the arduous and laborious duties of overseer. It is unnecessary to remark, that he fulfilled them carefully and industriously, ever watchful for the interests of his father, and sparing neither his own time nor labor.

In 1844 he joined his father, and occupied himself in acquiring a thorough knowledge of historical literature, taking for his text-books Plutarch's Lives, Gibbon's Rome, Rollin's Ancient History, Bottas' History of the American War, and similar works of standard and acknowledged excellence. Being passionately fond of literature, he soon made himself a thorough historical scholar.

In the latter part of the summer and fall, he availed himself of the skillful tuition of Charles Singleton, Esq., an eminent practicing lawyer in New Orleans, and from him, ever untiring in his pursuit of knowledge, he acquired a superficial knowledge of Latin, algebra and geometry.

In the spring of 1845 Mr. Cullom entered Franklin College, in his native town, then under the direction of the Rev. John Burke, a ripe and talented classical scholar, and withal a gentleman of kindly disposition and thorough erudition. While here, he bore the highest reputation, both in his association with his fellow students and his strict attention to his scholastic duties. He left it with regret, upon the conclusion of the collegiate session in September, and recommenced his literary reading. He read much and thoroughly; not superficially skimming over the pages of a work, but making himself thoroughly master of its contents, thus laying up a store of useful information which was afterwards of immense benefit to him.

We next find him in the preparatory department of Centre College, at Danville, Kentucky, in March, 1846, where he continued his classical course. He did not pursue the usual collegiate course, but confined himself to Latin, mathematics, moral, political and natural philosophy, logic, chemistry, international law, and other branches which he judged would best fit him for the profession to which he intended to devote his energies, and in the pursuit of which he has since obtained eminence.

Owing to pecuniary difficulty, he was compelled to discontinue his collegiate studies, and entered the law office of Jeremiah T. Boyle, Esq., of Danville, for the purpose of fitting himself for the legal profession. He continued the study of the common law, under the able instruction and guidance of Mr. Boyle, until February, 1848, when he espoused Miss Mary J. Gilmore, of that place. He then established himself as teacher, not neglecting, however, the prosecution of his favorite study of the law.

Aware of the importance of public speaking, he applied himself with energy to the cultivation of oratory. Endowed by nature with very fair oratorical powers, he never failed to exercise them when an opportunity presented itself, and though still young, M. Cullom, in his seat in the Legislature, has attracted attention by his eloquent action and readiness as a debater.

He continued his labors as a teacher until the fall of 1849, and in March of the same year, deeming himself fully qualified, from his thorough course of reading, applied for admission to the bar, and was licensed as a practicing lawyer by Judges John L. Bridges and Samuel Lusk, of Kentucky. He returned to Louisiana in November of the same year, and again applied himself to his studies, under his father, until the 7th of September, 1850, when he was admitted to the bar in the town of Opelousas, by the Supreme Court of Louisiana, Judges P. A. Rost, Thomas Slidell and Isaac T. Preston presiding. On the 1st of March, 1851, he established himself in Opelousas, entering into co-partnership with his father.

And now Mr. Cullom reaped the fruit of his lengthy and laborious course of study. His legal career, since he first opened his office, has been eminently successful. His thorough acquaintance with all the standard works of law has given him a correctness of judgment which seldom errs. Endowed with solid rather than brilliant qualities, he convinces more by the power of logic than the fictitious aids of rhetoric.

Mr. Cullom was very active in benefiting the town of Opelousas, in which he resided. He was one of the first originators of the "New Orleans, Opelousas and Great Western Railroad." He canvassed St. Landry and the neighboring parish with indefatigable energy to further the interests of this road, and made extensive use of the public press to effect the same object.

In February, 1853, we find him entering the lists as a *litterateur*, as editor of the *St. Landry Whig*, which, as its name signifies, was devoted to the dissemination of the principles of the Whig party. Not meeting, however, with that success which he had anticipated, he discontinued it in the following November.

Mr. Cullom was now rapidly becoming a marked man in his parish. On the 13th of October, 1853, the Whig convention showed its appreciation of his devotion to Whig principles by nominating him to represent the parish of St. Landry in the State Legislature, and Mr. Cullom accepting, as the parish was strongly Whig, he was elected without opposition. He accordingly took his seat in the House of Representatives on the 17th of January, 1854.

In 1855, Mr. Cullom became an independent candidate for the Judgeship of the 13th District, and was elected by a handsome majority, both Democrats and Whigs voting for him. In 1860, the Judicial District having been changed, Judge Cullom again became a candidate, and was reelected by a large vote. During the war the judge remained on the bench until the end of his term in 1865. He then ran again for the office, and was elected without opposition, and served until displaced by a Gubernatorial appointment, in the progress of reconstructing the State.

After the war, Judge Cullom immediately renewed his allegiance to the United States Government, and resumed the practice of law in Avoyelles, where he remained until February, 1866, when he came to New Orleans and opened an office here. Very soon after, the Judge was brought very prominently before the political world by a series of well-written letters, published in the New Orleans *Republican*, in which he deprecated the persistent efforts of the white population of the State to keep up the Democratic party, and declared himself a Liberal Republican. In 1872, Judge Cullom labored with zeal to establish a Liberal party in Louisiana, based on a *bona fide* recognition of all the rights of the colored race, and as an acknowledgment of his merits and claims, the convention of the Fusion party in August nominated him as their candidate for Judge of the 5th District Court of the City, and he was elected by a very large majority. This position he now fills with all of that ability and satisfaction that have ever characterized his official career. Honest and upright, kind and generous, a devoted and affectionate husband and father, make up the qualities in an eminent degree of the character of Judge E. North Cullom.

THE COTTON PRESSES OF NEW ORLEANS.

In order to ascertain the extent and importance of the business of recompressing the cotton arriving in New Orleans by rail and river, a *Times* reporter interviewed several leading cotton men, from whom he gleaned the following facts:

THE AMOUNT OF COTTON RECEIVED

at this port is annually over 1,400,000 bales, and the number of bales compressed in this city exceeds 1,200,000. We give approximate figures only, strict accuracy not being necessary for the purposes in view.

About 200,000 bales of the amount shipped to this port are compressed at Memphis, Shreveport and Jefferson, Texas, before being shipped, but the cotton compressed at these places does not give satisfaction, and much of it has to be recompressed after its arrival. This fact has given rise to some dissatisfaction between shippers and brokers.

THE NUMBER OF PRESSES ARE TWENTY-SIX.

The Alabama Press is situated on Tchoupitoulas, between Terpsichore and Robin streets. S. Howard is proprietor.

The Atlantic, M. J. Zaats, proprietor, on Peters street, between Clouet and Montegut, receives about 15,000 bales for compressing.

The Southern Press, on Clara street, between Poydras and Lafayette, has not been in operation the past year.

The Canal Street Press (formerly Wood's Cotton Press), between Villiere and Claiborne streets, J. C. Vanwickle, proprietor, is doing a large business.

HON. JAMES LEWIS,

ADMINISTRATOR OF PUBLIC IMPROVEMENTS.

The Commercial Press is on St. Thomas street, between Richard and Market. Smith & Goldsmith are the proprietors, and have a business of about 80,000 bales.

Cooper's Press, J. P. Conlon & Co., proprietors, situated on the corner of Peters and Thalia streets, does a business of about 25,000 bales.

The Crescent City Press, J. P. Moore, proprietor, is situated on Front street, between Race and Robin.

The Factor's Press, S. Haywood, proprietor, is on Tchoupitoulas street, between Henderson and Robin.

Fassman's Press, on Clio street, between Front and Locust, does a business of about 20,000 bales.

The Fire Proof Press, J. P. Moore, proprietor, is situated on Front street, between Race and Robin.

The Independent Press, S. Boyd & Co., proprietors, is on Front street, between Henderson, Terpsichore and Peters.

The Jackson Press, O'Brien & Co., proprietors, is on the corner of Perdido and Freret streets.

The Kentucky Press, Lipscomb, proprietor, is on Tchoupitoulas street, between Terpsichore and Bellechasse.

The Levee Steam Cotton Press, of which J. C. Denis is President, is on Peters street, between Ferdinand and Montegut. It does a business of about 45,000 bales.

The Louisiana, E. K. Bryant, proprietor, is on St. Thomas street, between Robin and Terpsichore.

The Memphis, J. R. Groves, proprietor, on the corner of Peters and Race streets, compresses annually about 25,000 bales.

The Merchants', F. Eastman, proprietor, on Gravier, between Peters and Front streets, does a large business.

The Mississippi, Hamilton, Lewis & Lynd, is situated on the square bounded by Tchoupitoulas, Religious, Richard and Market streets.

The Natchez Press, L. A. Levy, Jr., proprietor, on Dauphine street, between Montegut and Cotton Press streets, does a business of about 100,000 bales.

The Orleans Press, Sam Boyd & Co., proprietors, on the square bounded by Thalia, Front, Terpsichore and Peters streets, presses a large amount.

The Pelican Press, J. Randolph, proprietor, on Tchoupitoulas street, between St. Mary and St. Andrew, receives annually about 100,000 bales.

The Penn Press, Krumbean & Herndon, proprietors, on the square bounded by Tchoupitoulas, Peters, Terpsichore and Hunter streets, does a business of about 100,000 bales.

The Phœnix Press, H. H. Rainey & Co., proprietors, on Chartres street, between Montegut and Ferdinand, has a business of about 15,000 bales.

The Planters' Press, Robert Abbott, proprietor, is in the square bounded by Annunciation, Constance, Richard and Market streets.

The Shippers' Press, Sam Boyd & Co., proprietors, is situated on Henderson, between Peters and Front streets, and does a large business.

Terrell's Press, K. Terrell, proprietor, is on Chippewa, Orange, St. Thomas and Richard streets, and does a business of 15,000 bales.

The Union Press, A. P. Mason, proprietor, on the square bounded by Terpsichore, Peters, Tchoupitoulas and Henderson streets, has a very good business.

The Virginia Press, Hampton, Lewis & Lynd, proprietors, is on the square bounded by Tchoupitoulas, Peters, Richard and Market streets.

THE NUMBER OF MEN EMPLOYED

by the cotton presses probably exceeds one thousand, including draymen and other laborers.

A compressing gang is composed of fourteen men, including night and day watchmen, a yard clerk, bookkeeper, shipping clerk, cotton rollers, and those who work at the press. From twenty-five to thirty men are employed in a press during the busy season, and get good wages. A gang of cotton rollers, composed of three men to each bale, have been known to receive as high as $150 a week as wages. The cotton rollers and pressmen are generally of the colored persuasion, and as their money comes in fast, they generally spend it freely, only an exceptional few having the foresight to lay it up "for a rainy day."

Altogether the business of compressing cotton is one of our important home industries, and affords employment to many worthy people.

GEORGE STAFFORD LACEY

The present City Attorney was born in the City of Albany, New York, on the 9th day of August, 1820. At the age of sixteen he commenced the study of law in that city with his brother-in-law, Rufus W. Peckham, now one of the Judges of the Court of Appeals, of the State of New York. In 1840 he removed to Louisiana, was admitted to the bar of that State in 1842, and immediately afterwards commenced the practice of law in the city of Baton Rouge. When the seat of government was removed to Baton Rouge, Governor Walker, then the Chief Executive of the State, offered Mr. Lacey a District Judgeship, which he declined. In 1853 he ran for the State Senate, as Senator for the District of East Baton Rouge and Livingston, and, being elected, served the State as her Senator, and as Chairman of the State Judiciary Committee during the years 1853, 1854 and 1855. In 1855 he removed to New Orleans, where, in a short time, he secured a large and lucrative practice, which he has maintained ever since. In 1866 he ran for the office of Attorney General of the State of Louisiana, under the banner of the National Conservative Union Party. In 1870 he was appointed City Attorney of the City of New Orleans, which office he now holds.

Mr. Lacey is an admirable lawyer, and possesses rare talents as an orator.

Notwithstanding the great labors of his profession, Mr. Lacey has found time to devote himself to other studies, and in 1869 he published a work on "The Doctrine of the Real Presence of Christ in the Holy Eucharist." As a representative churchman of the Protestant Episcopal Church in the United States, Mr. Lacey has not only labored in her behalf as an author, but has served her as a Trustee of her General Theological Seminary, and as a Delegate to her General Convention.

THE DRAINAGE OF NEW ORLEANS.

THE topographical features of New Orleans are peculiar to lower Louisiana. The land is highest on the immediate bank of the rivers and bayous, and consequently the rain-water flows from the river to the swamp, as the low back lands are styled before they are cleared and drained.

New Orleans was laid out and settled in 1718. The plan showed a front of eleven blocks (from Custom House to Barrack streets) on the Mississippi River, by a depth of only five blocks from the river to Burgundy street.

Small ditches led the rain-fall into the swamp. The swamp drained slowly into Lake Pontchartrain, by the Bayou Saint John and some smaller Bayous.

This rough natural drainage existed many years without change (except a few private canals), until Louisiana was purchased by the United States in 1803. New Orleans began to increase, as appears by the petition of the City Council on the 20th July, 1805, to the Governor, asking to have the fortifications demolished, and the ditches filled up.

Up to the 19th March, 1845, the street gutters were gradually extended into the swamp, and a few draining canals had been made, viz.: The Melpomene from St. Charles to Willow streets, the Canal Gravier, on Poydras from Baronne street to a branch of Bayou St. John, Canal street from Claiborne street to a branch of Bayou St. John, and Orleans street from Claiborne street to Bayou St. John, St. Bernard from St. Claude street to Bayou St. John, and the old Marigny Canal from Elysian Field street, via Marigny avenue, to the Bayou St. John, in Claiborne from Canal Carondelet to Ursulines streets.

A draining machine was built by the city at Bayou St. John, at the junction of the draining canal on Orleans street.

This machine was built about 1830.

The upper suburbs drained into N. O. Canal, which had cut off the drainage of Bayou St. John.

By an act of the Legislature, approved 19th March 1845, a Draining Company was organized to "drain, fill up, and improve, the territory from the river to Lake Pontchartrain, between Harmony street above, and the Fishermen's Canal, below the city; and went to work as required, by cutting down the forest between the city and the Metairie Ridge, and digging several Draining Canals, viz.: Claiborne, Galvez, Broad, Hagan, Carrollton.

Draining Machines were erected at Claiborne, and, 2d, which was burned, at Melpomene and Claiborne, (2) at New Shell Road and Claiborne, discontinued (3) at Hagan, between Bienville and Conti streets, (4) at Orleans rebuilt, (5) and at London, on Gentilly Ridge, (6) at Bayou St John and Marigny Canal, burnt and not renewed, (7) Dublin Street Draining Machine was inaugurated 4th March, 1870.

By an act of the Legislature of 20th March, 1839, a Special District for Drainage was formed between Claiborne street, Carondelet Canal, Metairie (2) Ridge, Bayou (1) St. John, and N. O. Canal.

By act 18th March, 1858, three Draining Districts were created, each with a separate administration, viz.:

First District—All lands within the river, Julia street, N. O. Canal, Lake Pontchartrain, Bayou St. John, Carondelet Canal, and St. Peter street.

Second District—All lands within the river, Julia street, N. O. Canal, the Lake, Jefferson and Lake Pontchartrain R. R., to the river-bank.

Third District—All lands within the River, St. Peter street, Carondelet Canal, Bayou St. John, the Lake, Lafayette avenue, to the river bank.

Fourth District—River, Florida avenue, Lafayette avenue, and Fishermen's Canal.

Under these different acts, the whole of the territory, from the upper line of Carrollton to Lafayette avenue, has received more or less improvement in its drainage, as will be seen by the following statement of work up to May, 1871:

Protection Levees built, about 19 miles.

Draining Canals dug, about 27 miles.

In 1871 the drainage and protection were assigned to Mexican Gulf Company, which has excavated several Draining Canals, and built several Protection Levees. This work is under the superintendence of W. H. Bell, Esq., City Surveyor, who has projected the plans of a complete system of drainage and protection.

This includes a Superb Levee on the Lake Shore, which, when finished, will extend about 5 miles on the Lake Shore, and will furnish a carriage road, as well as room for a railroad, all fanned by the pure breezes from the Lake, and making a promenade unequaled in the South—the base of levee is 115 feet.

When the land between the Lake and the Metairie Ridge shall be drained by the projected Draining Canals, the Lake front of New Orleans will be studded with residences, which will combine the comforts of City and Lake dwellings.

The work done since 1871 comprises:

1. A Protection Levee on upper line of Carrollton, and along the line of the Jefferson and Lake Pontchartrain R. R. to the Lake 5 miles long, to have a carriage road on it.

2. A Protection Levee from the above down the Lake to New Orleans Canal—3,600 feet.

3. A Protection Levee on each side of the Orleans Draining Canal from the Metairie Ridge to the Lake, with carriage road and street railroads—2¾ miles.

4. Fourteenth Street Draining Canal—1 mile.

5. Poydras Street Draining Canal—1½ miles.

6. Harrison and Taylor Avenue Draining Canal—, mile.

7. London Avenue Draining Canal, from Lake—½ mile.

8. Lower Draining Canal, from Lake—½ mile.

New Canals excavated up to August 1st, 1873, from June 1871—8¾ miles.

Old Canals deepened and widened to August 1st, 1873—7½ miles.

This Company has now 8 Dredge Boats at work with 4 Steam Derricks, excavating the various Draining Canals projected on Mr. Bell's plan.

There are now 7 Draining Machines in operation:

I. N. MARKS, ESQ.,

PRESIDENT FIREMEN'S CHARITABLE ASSOCIATION.

RESIDENCE OF ROBT. ROBERTS, ESQ.,

COR. OF ST. CHARLES & CONERY STS.

1. Dublin Street—2 wheels—1 new.
2. Melpomene Street—1 engine.
3. Bienville Street—2 engines.
4. London Avenue—2 wheels—1 new.

Capacity of three million gallons per hour for each wheel at a lift of 7 feet.

The area to be drained by the above machines is about 30 square miles, and more engines will be required to do it effectually.

But the results of this work are remarkable.

The swamp, which is impassible in most all the year, becomes firm, dry land, and capable of cultivation, thus adding to the available territory of the City. The health of the City is also greatly improved, and when the fresh winds from the Lake come through the openings of new canals and new streets, New Orleans will be a pleasant Summer residence.

The system of open drainage was recommended by the Board of Engineers in 1858, and the present system is according to that report.

The Board recommended underground drainage when the finances of the City would permit it. But experience shows that no system of covered drainage could receive the floods of rain which fall here, sometimes 6 inches in 24 hours.

Wide and deep open Canals are needed to receive these deluges.

SYLVESTER LARNED INSTITUTE.

This is one of the largest Institutions for the education of young ladies in the Southern country. It was first organized in September, 1870, under the auspices of the First Presbyterian Church of this city. The experiment was regarded as so successful that at the close of the first session the Trustees purchased, as a permanent site for the Institute, the large, substantial, and handsome property on Carondelet street, where it has since been located. The main building presents an imposing appearance, and though originally constructed as a private residence, is well adapted for a large and flourishing school. The grounds are kept with taste and order. In the interior arrangements there is an air of cheerfulness and elegance, not always found in school-houses. All the rooms are carpeted and supplied with suitable furniture, including maps, globes, and the like. The school of natural science has been supplied with a small but well selected chemical and philosophical apparatus. A valuable private library and mineral cabinet have been placed in the building for the use of the teachers and students. There is also an abundant supply of pianos for the school of music.

All this has been accomplished in three years, and during that time the attendance has been constantly on the increase. Over two hundred scholars were admitted during the last session, which closed June 27, 1873.

There is a boarding department connected with the Institute. The number of scholars of this class is limited to twenty. No effort is spared to give them the comforts of a pleasant home, and the fullest advantages for intellectual culture.

The aim of the Directors of the Institute is to offer to young ladies superior advantages of instruction in the essential, and in more liberal branches of education. In addition to the full English course in Literature, Natural Science, and Mathematics, much care is bestowed in securing the best talent for the Schools of Ancient and Modern Languages, Vocal and Instrumental Music, Drawing and Painting. Series of Lectures have also been given, during the winter evenings, upon subjects connected with the studies of the Senior Class. For the encouragement and advancement of the scholars, musical soirees are given, from time to time, in the Institute building.

The Institute is under denominational direction, but is not sectarian. All shades of religious belief are represented among the students.

The Principal and Superintendent is Wm. O. Rogers, formerly Superintendent of the City Schools. He is aided by Mrs. A. L. Pargaud, formerly Principal of the State Normal School, and of the Girls' High School as Vice-Principal, together with a full corps of teachers for all the different departments.

THE STATE LINE STEAMSHIP COMPANY, LIMITED.

This Company was started in Glasgow in 1870 by Messrs. Lewis T. Merrow & Co., as Managing Owners, in conjunction with a number of influential Glasgow and Liverpool merchants, and early in 1871 contracts were closed for the six steamers which the company have now running.

These vessels are all of the very highest strength, class, and finish; the saloons being equal to those of any of the first-class lines in the Liverpool and New York trade, while the passages already made evince that they are also not inferior to their competitors in point of speed.

The officers are all gentlemen and seamen, most of them, even down to the fourth officers, have previously had a command.

The disqualification of non-residents in Great Britain, from holding shipping property registered there, caused the original shareholders to form the present Company, under the Limited Liability Act, with a capital of six hundred thousand pounds sterling, by which arrangement those parties wishing to invest can do so in safety.

The intention of the Company is to build six more steamers at once, making a fleet of twelve (when all are completed) of as fine vessels as float the sea.

They will then run a fortnightly line from Liverpool to New Orleans, a weekly one from Glasgow to New York; and if the New Orleans line is a success (as it so far brilliantly promises), it will also be made a weekly service, all the year round, which will give an impetus to the summer trade of the City of New Orleans that cannot but be beneficial, by giving employment to many, and especially of that class who can least afford to be idle. Such enterprises as this Company is, deserve the hearty support of all the inhabitants of this city, and every facility afforded to it in the carrying out their business.

The head offices of the Company are in Glasgow, with Messrs. Lewis T. Merrow & Co. as managers, while its interests are looked out for in Liverpool by Messrs. Ross, Skolfield & Co.; in New Orleans by Messrs. A. K. Miller & Co.; in Bordeaux by Messrs. Laffitte & Vandercruyce, and New York by Messrs. Austin Baldwin & Co.—while several hundred sub-agents are continually at work extending its influence and patronage.

JOHN McDONOGH.

HIS LIFE AND TIMES—INTERESTING EVENTS OF HIS CAREER.

John McDonogh was born in Baltimore, Maryland, in the year 1778, of highly respectable parents of Scotch descent. He received a good education, was quick and apt at acquiring knowledge, and possessed an extraordinary retentive memory, which seldom or ever failed him. Indicating a turn for commercial pursuits, he was placed at an early age in a mercantile house in Baltimore, doing an extensive business both in this country and Europe. He was affable and pleasing in his manners, strictly correct in all transactions. He gained the unlimited confidence of his employers, who, in 1800, sent him as supercargo in one of their ships to Liverpool, with instructions to load her with merchandise suitable for the Louisiana market, and to proceed without delay to New Orleans. He obeyed his instructions, sailed from Liverpool, and arrived at the Balize in the latter part of September, 1800. His ship sailed up the river as fast as winds would permit, and when about twenty miles below the city, he came ashore, hired a horse, and entered the city on the evening of the 3rd of October, 1800,—the next day presenting himself to his consignees. Ere the ship reached port he had disposed of the largest portion of the cargo. Renting a store, he stored the balance of the cargo, which was also disposed of in a very short time. He loaded the vessel for Baltimore and sailed, and on his arrival was greeted by his employers for the success attendant upon this venture.

Shortly after, in 1804, another venture was made, giving McDonogh an interest therein, and he met with far better success. He determined upon making New Orleans his future home. He soon became intimately acquainted with all the city and government officers, merchants and citizens generally, entering into contracts with the Spanish officials to furnish goods for all that part of the country east of the Mississippi and the Floridas, and giving general satisfaction to all.

After the treaty of cession, a former clerk and intimate friend, Shepherd Brown, arrived from Baltimore. Aided by their former employers, they formed a co-partnership, and did an extensive business as John McDonogh, Jr. & Co. After the battle of New Orleans, Brown died; McDonogh attended to the settlement of the affairs of the firm, and carried on the business in his own name.

McDonogh being fond of gayety and parties and of ladies' society, in 1809 he opened a large house at the northwest corner of Chartres and Toulouse streets, furnished it magnificently, had his coaches and horses, gave balls, parties and dinner parties which were attended by the notabilities of the city. Don Almonaster y Roxas, the rich and opulent, was residing here. His daughter, Micaela Leonarda, was the belle, causing, by her handsome face and money, many hearts to beat, amongst others John McDonogh's, who in 1810 demanded her in marriage, the father declining the honor unless McD. would become a Roman Catholic, he (McD.) being a heretic. McDonogh of course retired, and did not renew the demand.

The Baron de Pontalba arriving from France with his title, but an empty purse, sought Micaela, and in 1811 was accepted upon his demanding her in marriage. Don Almonaster caused the marriage contract to be drawn up by Phillippe Pedesclaux, in July, 1811, with the strictest clauses inserted therein. The contract was signed, the marriage consummated, and the Baron and Baroness left for Paris to participate in the festivities and splendor of nobility. The results of that marriage proved unhappy. The causes need not be repeated here, but Micaela was divorced by a decree of *La Cour de Cassation*, and she was once more free. She visited New Orleans in 1846 in relation to the projected buildings on St. Peter and St. Ann streets. The Council of the First Municipality refused to donate to her the banquette in front of her property, and her plan would fail would she not obtain the number of feet needed from the property in the rear. McDonogh owned the largest portion on Chartres and on Jefferson streets. She at at once thought of McD., and meeting him as if by chance in the Louisiana State Bank, approached him, "How are you, McDonogh, have you forgotten me? I am Micaela." After recognition of McD., and some conversation about olden times, she remarked: "McDonogh, would you marry me now?" He, always the polite and gallant gentleman, smilingly said, yes, he would! And shortly they parted, but McDonogh saw her no more. Believing she had by this manœuvre secured McDonogh's good favor, she ordered her builder, Samuel Stewart, to take possession and tear down some 15 or 16 feet of the property of McDonogh. She had caused an act to be drawn up, which she believed McDonogh would sign, by which he abandoned to her this amount of property. McDonogh hearing of the projected tearing down of his property, and thus taking possession, at once applied to the Fifth District Court of New Orleans, Judge A. M. Buchanan presiding, and obtained an injunction, which resulted in Mrs. de Pontalba having to pay damages and costs, besides the repairing of the walls which she had already pulled down. Thus ended his love, if it can be so called, for Mrs. de Pontalba.

After the refusal by Don Almonaster of McDonogh's offer to marry Micaela, for this love was only a momentary passion, *un amour passant*, McDonogh still continued his gay life.

There resided here a Mr. Johnson and family, from Maryland, in 1814. His daughter was then just entering into womanhood, beautiful and magnificent, of a queenly appearance, intellectual and witty, far surpassing Micaela Almonaster in everything but money. McDonogh paid his addresses to this young lady, and was accepted by her, but the father's consent was to be had. McDonogh made the *demande en mariage* in due form, and according to etiquette. The Johnson family were strict Roman Catholics, and McDonogh a heretic. Miss Johnson made no objection to McD. on the score of religion. Not so the father, who acknowledging the honor done to his daughter by McD., of which he was proud, he would consent if McD. would join the Catholic religion. McDonogh declined doing this, stated that no objection was made by the

J. M. G. PARKER, ESQ.,

U. S. NAVAL OFFICER.

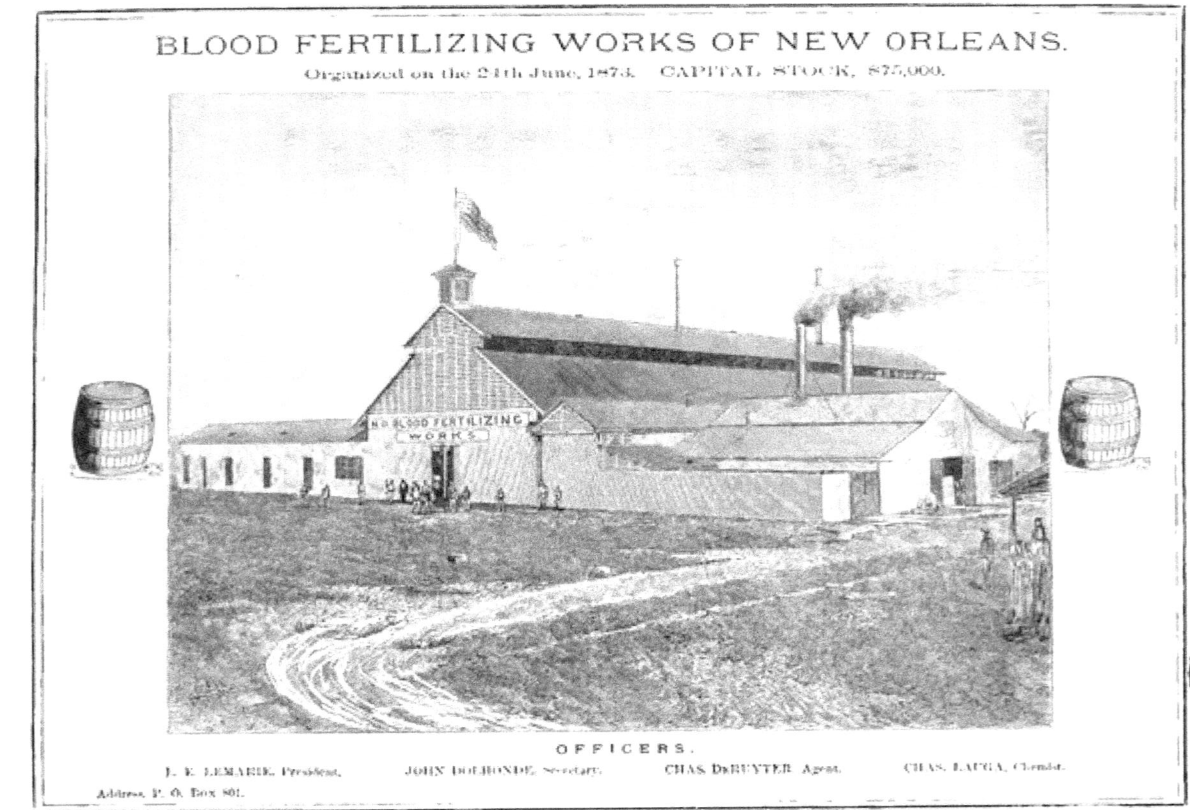
BLOOD FERTILIZING WORKS OF NEW ORLEANS.
Organized on the 24th June, 1873. CAPITAL STOCK, $75,000.
N.O. BLOOD FERTILIZING
WORKS
OFFICERS.
J. E. LEMARIE, President,
JOHN DOLHONDE, Secretary.
CHAS. DeRUYTER, Agent.
CHAS. LAUGA, Chemist.
Address, P. O. Box 801.

daughter, and he would wait some time when, perhaps Mr. Johnson might change his views. Miss Johnson was satisfied with this, hoping, also, that her father would relent.

New Orleans was invaded. McDonogh joined Captain Beale's company of rifles, was at the battle on the 8th of January, 1815. After proclamation of peace McDonogh again renewed his application to the father, with the same result. Miss Johnson then announced that if she were not McDonogh's wife, she would become a nun, and some time after she took the veil, in the Ursuline Church, on Ursulines street, McDonogh being present, as also our worthy fellow citizen, Gen. John L. Lewis, and others, many of whom have since departed this life. From a novice, she became and was for years secluded. Society had lost one of its brightest ornaments.

Many years after, nearly thirty-five years after, Miss J. became the head of one of the religious institutions she had joined. McDonogh, hearing of this, and being made aware that her then position permitted her to receive visitors, respectfully requested permission to pay his respects to her, simply as an old friend. She assented, and McDonogh paid the visit, which was most interesting to both, although no allusion was made to the love of former days. And annually, up to the time of his death in 1850, McDonogh, between the 1st and 6th of January, would make his "visite de bonne année," the New Year's call. McDonogh died in 1850, and in his armoir, carefully preserved, was found a memento of Miss Johnson, in the shape of a pair of beautiful gold embroidered slippers. The lady has since died.

In March, 1819, suffering greatly from piles, a disease with which he had been afflicted for several years, and which had become serious by his mode of living, his old friend and physician, Dr. Flood, said to him "that if he did not quit his balls and parties this disease would kill him, and that in less than three months he would be a dead man." McDonogh was taken aback, asking the Doctor if he were serious in his statement, and receiving a decided reply in the affirmative, McDonogh at once resolved to remove to the other side of the river, and so informed Dr. Flood, hoping to see him in a few weeks in his new domicile. He went from the Doctor's house to his store, made out a correct list or inventory of his furniture, and in an hour after visited the auction store of his old friends Toussaint Mossy & Baillet, and requested them to announce an immediate sale of his furniture. Mossy was astonished, thought McDonogh crazy, inquired the cause, was informed of it, and although Mossy and others remonstrated, McDonogh was firm, and ere the end of March, 1819, saw him installed in his new home.

This house joined a part of a plantation purchased some years before by McDonogh on the other side of the Mississippi River, opposite New Orleans. The house was a two story bricked within posts, a large gallery around it; garden in front and rear, at a distance of a quarter of a mile from the river bank. It has since disappeared by the caving in of the levee. McDonogh, anticipating this, had built, at some distance from the house, two brick buildings, which were to serve as wings to a house which he intended to build for his residence.

From 1819 to 1850 McDonogh never was idle, early and late he was at work. His business called him daily to the city. He had his rents to collect, his notes to pay. He attended the auction sales and bought real estate, and to attend to this business he would cross the Mississippi in a skiff manned by one of his slaves. Prior to 1835 there were no steam ferries plying between New Orleans and the opposite side. The planters and the largest portion of the inhabitants had their own skiffs, and since the establishment of steam ferries none landed within a half a mile of his residence. No weather, however threatening or tempestuous, would prevent him from crossing in this skiff, to fulfill any engagement which he had made. He was always punctual to the hour and minute, and his skiff was always ready, even when it was doubtful if the steam ferry would venture. After completing his business in the city, he would recross, and has never been known, since his removal, to have passed a night in the city.

McDonogh corresponded with many of the eminent men of the day, such as Henry Clay, Daniel Webster, John M. Clayton, Wm. M. Meredith, Judges Story and McLean, and many others, besides corresponding with the various departments, both of the United States and of the State, in regard to land and other claims in which he was interested. He frequently wrote articles upon the important questions of the day, which were published in the newspapers here, and republished in the leading papers throughout the country. The late Peter K. Wagner would often request him to write his views in regard to questions of vital importance to the city and State. He did so, and the articles were published in the New Orleans *Courier*.

John McDonogh was no miser. His whole career, his will, refute the idea that he was a miser. He declined giving money for frivolous purposes. He refused to have his biography written, as it was money the writer wanted. He declined being interviewed, as it is now called, for money was at the bottom of it. Hence he was called a miser. Whatever may have been his views in regard to the disposition of his property, and the apparent ridiculous mode he desired to have them carried out, it was his hobby; he was entitled to it, as much as it was the hobby of those who entertained the idea of obtaining money from him, no matter by what means. He was no "miser." He hoarded no moneys. At the time of his death he owed $166,000, payable in January and February, 1851, $100,000 of which was due the Citizens' Bank of Louisiana, the balance, $66,000, for several properties which he had purchased from Destrehan's estate and other parties.

He had but $10,500 cash in bank to meet this amount due. His property he left to the cities of Baltimore and New Orleans. Baltimore has profited by this legacy and reveres his name. New Orleans received a similar legacy. What has become of the amount? She has nothing to show of the results—why * * * * *Quien sabe?* New Orleans reviles his memory, and verifies the the French proverb, "*Faites du bien à Bertrand il vous le rend*," etc. What a contrast between the two cities.

McDonogh was charitable, not as some people would have the term charity applied, by placing their names on a list, with a large amount affixed opposite, and when the hour comes the subscription is not come-at-able, but the name and amount has been blazoned forth in the newspapers. He cared nothing for this kind of notoriety. Samuel J. Peters, the late and lamented fellow-citizen, has testified, after McDonogh's death, to his charities—a number of which were bestowed secretly through him. McDonogh sent his charities under cover, under the signature of "anonymous," requesting simply an acknowledgment of their reception through the papers. It was nothing to him whether the city believed him charitable, there was "One above who knew it."

McDonogh, though a great friend of the African race, was no abolitionist. He never believed in the social and political equality of the negro. He was no amalgamationist. He always believed the white superior to the negro race. He favored the American Colonization Society to Liberia; was one of its founders and ardent supporters. He was opposed to setting slaves free and to remain in the State; he advised that they be sent at once to Liberia. That he was right the sequel proves it. He believed this to be a white man's government and none other.

McDonogh died at his house on the evening of the 26th of October, 1850, (Saturday,) and was buried on Sunday evening, the 27th of October, 1850, in the burial ground which he had projected. His funeral was attended by several friends, who, though few in number, had always entertained a high regard for him; also, a large concourse of persons attracted by simple curiosity. The funeral service was performed by the Rev. Mr. Whitall, of the Episcopal church. A few months prior to his death he had become a communicant, and frequently attended service in the Bethel Church, corner of Levee and Esplanade streets.

His will was opened and probated in the Fifth District Court of New Orleans, Judge A. M. Buchanan, presiding. The contest by the heirs in the Federal courts lasted up to 1858, when the cities took possession. Some time after this a codicil, in the shape of a note for $100,000, in favor of Francis Pena, payable four years after his death, was presented. This was a surprise. On examination it was found to be wholly written, signed, and dated by McDonogh; it was not strange or unintelligible, it was in his bold handwriting. It had been in the possession, for years prior, of that highly respected fellow-citizen, Rezin D. Shepherd, who held it for safe keeping, to be handed Pena at the proper time. When the time arrived Mr. Shepherd placed it in the hands of the lamented distinguished member of the New Orleans bar, E. A. Bradford, who attended to the recovery of the amount.

Although it appears strange, yet, when it is known that Francis Pena was the illegitimate issue of McDonogh and Carmelite Pena, by whom he also had a daughter, the whole is easily understood. Subsequently, Carmelite, the mother, married Louis Vanley, foundryman, in the employ of Jedediah Lewis, and she lived for years previous and after McDonogh's death, on St. Joseph street, between Camp and St. Charles, on right hand side going to the rear of the city.

McDonogh caused both Francis and the daughter to be educated, Rezin D. Shepherd being his agent and acting for him, paying the annual fee for tuition. On the return of the daughter from school, McDonogh had selected for her residence, the family of a Mr. Joseph Weber, living in the two story brick building southeast corner of Camp and Julia streets, but the mother opposed it and caused the daughter to live with her. The daughter married a dry goods merchant, named Leauthier, living at the northwest corner of Julia and Camp streets, and McDonogh, on the marriage day, gave her a large sum of money, and in 1848, Leauthier and wife left for France.

Francis P. was of a sort of roving character, fond of excitement. He was in the Texan war for independence; subsequently joined a company of trappers in Missouri. His mother was, however, careful of his rights, and got McDonogh to give the document alluded to, with the understanding that it was to remain in the hands of R. D. Shepherd.

No one who knew McDonogh and sees Francis or Mrs. L., can be mistaken as to the paternity of McD. Mrs. L. was a proficient of the fine arts, and Francis P. is ever on the alert as an utilitarian.

Tea is now extensively raised in Hindostan, the exports to England, in 1872, exceeding sixteen millions of pounds. The Indian teas are of rare flavor, and are used by the English shopkeepers to mix with the Chinese. The culture in India is now carried on by joint stock companies, which are now paying from ten to twenty per cent. dividends.

The ownership of one-fourth of England's land by a score or so of families has a likeness in California, where there are eleven hundred owners of fifteen million acres—over thirteen thousand acres each. This land is now used only for grazing, and rated at a comparatively low valuation; but its appreciation is liable to make a few thousand Astors out there within a few years.

The fact that brandy can be made economically from sawdust, and the extent to which this manufacture is carried on in Sweden, is generally considered astonishing; still more so, however, is the statement of a recent chemist that brandy or alcohol can be distilled from quartz rock. This furnishes the subject of a paper in the Chemical News.

A remarkable invention, by Mr. Siemens, of Dresden, is that of the simplest form known of steam motor, and believed to be very applicable to the minor industries, such as sewing-machines, the lathe, etc. This is an engine without a boiler, piston, valves, or other machinery, being merely an elongated, pear-shaped vessel, which is set in rotation, and possesses considerable power.

The English war department is said to be contemplating the construction of a gun which shall weigh sixty tons, and require a charge of two hundred pounds of gun powder, by means of which it will be able to throw a shot over half a ton in weight. The "Woolwich Infant," which is the largest gun, weighs thirty-five tons, requires a charge of one hundred and ten pounds, and carries a seven hundred pound shot.

WM. P. KELLOGG,

GOVERNOR

WM. PITT KELLOGG.

William Pitt Kellogg was born in Vermont, in the year 1830, and was educated at Norwich University. At the age of eighteen he removed with his parents to Illinois, studied law, and in 1848, when barely of age, was admitted to the bar. He cast his first vote for John P. Hale for President, and in 1856 was chosen one of the Fremont electors by the Republican Convention of Illinois. He became a personal and political friend of Abraham Lincoln, and supported him in his unsuccessful contest with Stephen A. Douglas for the U. S. Senatorship in 1858.

In 1860 he was again chosen one of the Republican Presidential electors from Illinois, and cast his vote for Lincoln. Shortly after Mr. Lincoln's inauguration he nominated Mr. Kellogg Chief Justice of Nebraska. The war came on, and Chief Justice Kellogg tendered to President Lincoln his sword and his resignation. The sword was accepted, the resignation not. He went back to Illinois on leave of absence, raised the 7th Illinois Cavalry, was elected Colonel, and served in Missouri, where he had much rough-and-tumble fighting, and, on one brisk skirmish, defeated Gen. M. Jeff. Thompson, the present Chief Engineer of Louisiana, then in the Confederate service. His leave of absence expired, he resumed his position on the Supreme Bench of Nebraska, and resigned to participate in the Presidential campaign of 1864. He was a delegate from Nebraska to the Republican Convention which renominated Mr. Lincoln, and actively supported both Lincoln and Andrew Johnson, the Republican candidate for Vice-President.

Soon after his second inauguration Mr. Lincoln appointed Judge Kellogg Collector of the Port of New Orleans. His commission was signed only a few hours before the fatal visit to Ford's Theatre, and was the last civil commission signed by President Lincoln. In 1868 Mr. Kellogg, whilst still Collector of the Port, was elected to the U. S. Senate by the reconstructed Legislature of Louisiana. In the Senate he succeeded in passing many measures for the advancement of the material interests of Louisiana. He was nominated by the Republican Convention at Baton Rouge in 1872 for Governor of Louisiana, which position he now holds.

HON. JAMES LEWIS.

Born at Woodville, in the State of Mississippi, in the year 1832, and raised at Bayou Sara, Louisiana, Mr. Lewis has, by his steadiness of purpose, strict integrity and indomitable energy, worked himself up to a highly honorable and conspicuous position for a man so young—he is only 41 years of age—and to whom all avenues to public distinction were shut out up to within the last few years. When the war broke out Mr. Lewis went with R. L. Hodge into the Confederate service. Mr. Hodge, whose memory still lives in the name of one of our popular steamboats, was the Second Lieutenant of the "Shreveport Grays," Dreux's batallion, a company of which Gen. Williamson, late Reform candidate for Governor, was the First Lieutenant. Following the company in the first Virginia campaign up to the time the gallant Dreux was killed at the head of his command, Mr. Lewis then returned to this city with his patron, Mr. Hodge, and became steward of the Confederate transport De Soto, which place he retained until he heard the news of President Lincoln's emancipation proclamation. While on board the De Soto, he was present at the fighting about Columbus, at the fall of Island Number Ten and New Madrid; but when his heart was gladdened by the liberation of his race, knowing that the cause of freedom needed all its friends, he made his way by a devious and dangerous route to this city, over which he found the flag of the Union waving, and at once resolved to be a soldier. In conjunction with some other colored men he petitioned the commanding officer for permission to raise what proved to be the first colored troops that ever entered the army of the United States. The petition was granted. Gen. Lovell's order raising a regiment of colored troops for the Confederate service was substantially reissued by General Butler in September, 1862, and Mr. Lewis at once raised two companies of colored infantry. At the head of one of these he was mustered into the First Native Guards as Captain of Company K. The regiment was first ordered to the Opelousas country, where it operated against the Confederate General Mouton; thence it was sent to Fort St. Philip; thence to Baton Rouge; thence to Port Hudson, where it became famous, and where "the colored troops fought nobly," and demonstrated that they were fit not to be slaves, but to be freemen.

Resigning his commission upon the Red River expedition, on account of mistreatment from a superior officer, Col. Lewis again returned to the city in March, 1864, and became a Permit and Custom House broker, a vocation he pursued industriously to the satisfaction of his customers up to the opening of the coast trade and the coming of reconstruction. With this latter era his public life began. Receiving the appointment of traveling agent of the educational department of the Freedmen's Bureau, he devoted his whole time, his talents, and his energies to the establishment of schools for the instruction and elevation of his down-trodden race. In this capacity he journeyed all over the State, carrying light into dark places and opening up schools on every hand, wherever he went. At that time this sort of business was no inviting feat; not by any means were his trips pleasant picnic excursions. His life was in constant peril, and in many places he moved about in the very jaws of death. On one occasion, in St. Landry, he was captured and nothing but the interposition of some friendly Masons saved his neck. But the seeds he planted, the love of learning he instilled, brought forth good fruit which his people are now only beginning to taste.

When Senator Kellogg became Collector of the Port, he appointed the first colored man to a civil position in the Federal service in Louisiana, when he made Col. Lewis Assistant Superintendent of the Custom House. This place the latter held up to the time that Perry Fuller, turned him out because he refused to vote for Seymour and Blair. In 1869 Mr. Lewis became a Sergeant of the Police, and discharged his duties with such fidelity, impartiality and integrity, that he was promoted within less than a year to the position of Captain of Police in recognition of his services. In this capacity he extorted even the admiration of the Democrats, a thing most difficult for a colored man to do at any time. The report of the Metropolitan Board for 1870, in the course of a long article commending the manner in which Capt. Lewis had discharged his duties in the Fifth Precinct, remarks:

"Under Captain Lewis, the force of this precinct attained a high state of discipline and efficiency; a remarkable degree of order was maintained throughout the year, few burglaries were committed, and the force have earned the good-will and respect of the community. In many respects the management and efficiency of the fifth precinct police might be emulated by other precincts to the advantage of the department."

In the summer of 1870 when Capt. Lewis received the commission of Administrator of Police, Superintendent Badger refused to accept his resignation on the ground that the city could not dispense with his services at that exciting time.

CAPTAIN T. P. LEATHERS.

Thomas P. Leathers was born in Kenton county, Ky., on the 14th of May, 1816. He was of that stock of stalwart men of whom old Simon Kenton, after whom the county was named, was a notable representative. The Captain and all his brothers stood six feet and two in their stockings, and were of gigantic build and great muscular power. Thomas P. Leathers came down the Mississippi with his brother on the Sunflower in the fall of 1836, and, as mate, engaged in the Yazoo river trade. After "learning the ropes," and seeing the great profitableness of the cotton transportation business, he united with his brother and brother-in-law, Capt. Sanford, in building the Princess No. 1, which, in 1840, started in the Natchez, Vicksburg and New Orleans trade. This boat was run with great success till 1846, so that Capt. Leathers—for he had now become a full captain—was encouraged to build a new and expensive boat, which was the

NATCHEZ No. 1.

The first Natchez was run with great success, from 1846, for two years, when the ambition of Capt. Leathers aspiring to a larger and finer boat he sold her to Capt. John Pierce, and again repaired to Cincinnati to build.

NATCHEZ No. 2.

This was in 1848, and the second Natchez entering the old trade, ran steadily and profitably until 1852, in conjunction with the the Princess No. 4, in which Capt. Leathers had acquired an interest. The second Natchez, in her turn, became insufficient for the demands of Capt. Leather's ambition, and in 1852, he sold her for the coast trade, and set to work on a still larger and finer boat, which was

NATCHEZ No. 3.

Her career was, however, a brief one. Six weeks after she had begun her trips she was burned at the wharf in this city, in the great conflagration which originated with the Belcher, and destroyed some ten or twelve boats. Captain Leathers was on board with his family when this fire occurred, and narrowly escaped with his life. His younger brother was not so fortunate. Sleeping in the Texas so soundly that he could not be awaked, he perished in the flames. Captain Leathers immediately proceeded to Cincinnati, and in due time returned with

NATCHEZ No. 4.

Her career was a profitable one from 1856 to 1859. But not suiting the always expanding and progressive views of Captain Leathers, he had her machinery transferred into another and new hull, selling the old hull for a wharfboat at Natchez, and thus constructed towed her down to that city in 1860.

NATCHEZ No. 5.

This boat was run down to the fall of New Orleans in 1862, on the eve of which she was taken up the Mississippi to the Yazoo, where she was burned during some of the fierce battles in that neighborhood.

Then followed the long interruption of the war when Captain Leathers abandoned the river, and never came within sight of it, until the war was over.

After peace and the resumption of business, Captain Leathers became interested successively in the Magenta and General Quitman. The latter being old and somewhat infirm, was sunk and lost at Morgan's Landing in 1868. He then ran the Belle Lee for six months, chartered the Ames for the cotton season of 1868, and after this began the construction of the

NATCHEZ No. 6.

Of this boat Capt. Leathers owns seven-eighths and his engineer one-eighth. It has always been a peculiarity of Capt. Leathers' management that he has retained the same experienced and tried officers for twenty years, always paying large salaries to "keep a good thing when he had it," to use his favorite maxim. The expense of running this boat is about $18,000 per month in the business season, and $10,000 in the summer or dull months. Capt. Leathers during his career has brought to this city

TWO MILLION BALES OF COTTON.

The number brought last year on the Natchez was 5,000. In the year 1861 her predecessors brought to this city 110,000 bales of cotton, or more than six millions of our product. His average annual business has been about one hundred thousand bales. At the same time Captain Leathers has transported, with a safety and a degree of comfort and luxury never enjoyed on any other boat in the world, many thousands of passengers. It is his proud boast that he never had an explosion or lost a life on any boat commanded by him. The admirable system of order, elegance and comfort enjoyed by all who travel on his boat has been the theme of constant praise and surprises throughout the Southwest, ever since he embarked in the business in which, it may be truly said, he has attained an eminence reached by few in their several spheres of ambition and effort.

SOULE RESIDENCE.

COL. GEORGE SOULÉ.

This gentleman, distinguished in the educational annals of New Orleans, and the presiding officer of an influential college, designed and incorporated for the education of the future merchants of this great metropolis, was born at Barrington, Yates County, in the State of New York, May 14, 1834. His great-grandfather, grandfather, father and mother, were natives of New York, and of German and French extraction. His father, a substantial farmer, belonged to that progressive class of tillers of the soil, who believed that agriculture, the nursing mother of the arts, had not yet reached its highest state of development and perfection, and who accordingly availed himself of all the improvements with which the discovery of occult laws of nature, and the multiplication of mechanical inventions, in our day, have enriched this great and controlling branch of industry. His mother, a woman of fine intellectual powers, is said to have found ample opportunities for their constant exercise in the economy that properly belongs to a farmer's homestead. His father died when the subject of this sketch was but three years old, leaving three sons, Andrew, George, and Stephen.

George, at the age of eleven years, his brothers and the family, including their grandfather, moved to the far West, and settled in Illinois, about fifty miles north of Chicago. He had no taste for a farmer's life, but a decided passion for books, and, at this early period, avowed his determination to aim at something higher than was attainable by the sturdy pioneer settlers on the prairies of Illinois. Accordingly, at the age of fifteen years, he bid farewell to his rural occupations, for the purpose of prosecuting his education with a view to a more extended sphere of usefulness. At the age of nineteen years he graduated at the Sycamore (Illinois) High School.

In 1854 he removed to St. Louis, Missouri, where he continued, under private tutors, his scientific studies, and became quite a proficient in Natural Philosophy, Mathemation and Chemistry. While at St. Louis he attended a course of Lectures at McDowell's Medical College, and gave some attention to the study of medicine, but, for want of means, was forced to abandon his medical course.

During much of the time, while prosecuting his education, he was compelled to engage in various occupations in order to obtain the necessary means to meet his expenses, and, while acting as a collector for a Commission and Grocery House in St. Louis, made himself acquainted with the whole routine of office business and mercantile affairs, and, in the latter part of 1855, resolved to devote his life to the profession of teaching the commercial sciences. In order to prepare himself more thoroughly for this duty, he entered, in the beginning of 1856, Jones' Commercial College, at St. Louis, and in the Fall of the same year, he graduated in Commercial Science and Commercial Law, removed to New Orleans, and in December, 1856, founded the Commercial College, which bears his name.

For the next two years he realized, as a teacher and practical accountant, but little more than was sufficient, to meet his rent and absolute necessities. These two years were the dark periods in the history of the institution. During this time he devoted much attention to reading, observation, inquiry, and the storing of his mind with practical information, which could be turned to immediate and future account. A Commercial College of high order was a desideratum in this metropolis, and he was ambitious to meet, in all respects, the popular demands in respect to such an institution.

In 1859 his ability and fidelity as a first-class teacher of commercial science were generally recognized, and secured for him extensive patronage, and a good and constantly increasing income, up to the Spring of 1862, when he entered the service of the Confederate States, leaving the management of his institution to one of his instructors, who closed it upon the surrender of New Orleans to the Federal Army.

He entered the Southern Army as Captain of Company A, Crescent Regiment, from New Orleans, and served through the war with much reputation. At the battle of Shiloh he was captured, and spent five months, as a prisoner of war, on Johnson's Island. He was twice promoted, first to the rank of Major, and then to that of Lieutenant Colonel.

In 1864, by reason of the casualties of war, his regiment was consolidated, and he was appointed Superintendent of the Labor Bureau for the Trans-Mississippi Department of the Confederate States of America, which position he held until the surrender of the Confederate Army. He then returned to New Orleans, and, on the 10th July, 1865, re-opened his Commercial College, and prosecuted with renewed energy the great enterprise to which he had originally dedicated himself. During the war he had lost his library, his college furniture, and what money he had left in bank, and on his return was again forced to commence his operations from a new stand-point, which afforded but little encouragement except to a man of indomitable energy, who was determined to command success by his own merits.

From the re-opening of his institution to the present time his popularity, as a conscientious, faithful instructor, has steadily increased, and in consequence of the judicious management of his institution, in all its departments, it now enjoys the confidence of the Southern people to an almost unlimited extent, and annually sends forth large numbers of educated young gentlemen, well instructed in the principles of Commercial Law, Political Economy, of Banking, Exchange, of the History of Commerce, and all the duties which belong to a thorough accountant and an accomplished merchant.

The institution was chartered by the State Legislature in 1861. It is a member of the International Business College Association, and reciprocates scholarship with all the colleges of "the Association," located in thirty-six of the principal cities in the States and the Canadas. It employs nine Instructors, and matriculates upward of three hundred pupils annually.

In 1866 his business as a teacher, and practicing and consulting accountant, convinced him of the need of a more thorough and comprehensive treatise on Commercial and Exchange Computations, Accounts, Partnership Settlements, and Commercial Science and Customs, than had yet been published, and he therefore determined to address himself to the labor of preparing and publishing such a work, and actually commenced it at that time, but the war intervening, caused a suspension of the work during its continuance; but, on the conclusion of hostilities, he resumed the important undertaking, devoting to it all the time he could command from his professional duties, and, in 1872, he gave to the public the long meditated and skillfully elaborate treatise, in the shape of a large octavo volume of 800 pages, executed in the best style of the American press, under the title of Soule's "Analytic and Philosophic, Commercial and Exchange Calculator."

This work is pronounced by competent mathematicians, accountants, and business men, to be the great arithmetical production of the age. It employs new and comprehensive methods of computation, using reasons instead of rules, and embracing thousands of problems extending over the whole field of business life. It also contains some 300 pages of matter of special interest to merchants and practical accountants, and abounds with important discussions and information pertaining to the laws of trade, the customs of merchants, and the history of commercial affairs. "It undoubtedly places the author," says Professor Cundiff of Kentucky, "in the first rank of mathematicians."

In 1860 Col. Soule married Miss M. J. Reynolds, a native of Mobile, Ala., by whom he has had eight children, of whom six are living, five sons and a daughter. He is well entitled to the reputation he has certainly acquired of being one of the most successful and distinguished educators in the Southern States. To the manners of a courtly gentleman he unites the modesty of the man of true science.

MAYORS OF NEW ORLEANS.

The following is a list of the Mayors of New Orleans who have occupied the office since the acquisition of Louisiana by the United States in the year 1803. Previously the office corresponding to that of Mayor was held under appointment by the French Government, and it was by the first Legislature, that met in 1804, that the office of Mayor was created:

Pitot, James, Mayor from 16th June,		1804 to 1806.
Watkins, John,	from	1806 to 1807.
Mather, Jos.	"	1807 to 1812.
Girod, N.,	"	1812 to 1815.
McCarthy, Aug.,	"	1815 to 1820.
Roffignac, J.,	"	1820 to 1828.
Prieur, Denis,	"	1828 to 1838.
Genois, C.,	"	1838 to 1840.
Freret, Wm.,	"	1840 to 1844.
Montegut, E.,	"	1844 to 1846.
Crossman, A. D.,	"	1846 to 1854.
Lewis, John L.,	"	1854 to 1856.
Waterman, Chas. M.,	"	1856 to 1858.
Stith, Gerard,	"	1858 to 1860.
Monroe, John T.,	"	1860 to 1862.
Shepley, G. F., (Acting Military),	May,	1862.
Weitzel, G., "	July,	1862.
French, Jonas H., "	Aug.,	1862.
Deming, H. C., "	Sept.,	1862.
Miller, Jas. F., "	Nov.,	1862.
Hoyt, Stephen, "	July,	1864.
Quincy, S. M., "	May,	1865.
Kennedy H.,	from	1865 to 1866.
Monroe, J. T.,	"	1866 to 1866.
Heath, E., Military Appointee,		1866.
Conway, J. R.,	from	1866 to 1868.
Flanders, B. F.,	"	1868 to 1872.
Wiltz, L. A.,	"	1872 to 1874.

SHERIFFS.

PARISH OF ORLEANS.

BY GOVERNORS OF STATE.

George W. Morgan, from March, 1813, to 5th March, 1835.

Frederic Buisson, from 5th March, 1835, to 1st October, 1838.

Charles F. Hozey, from 1st October, 1838, to 30th December 1840.

Manuel Cruzat, Coroner of the Parish of Orleans, acting ex-officio Sheriff, from 30th December, 1840, to 10th March, 1841.

OFFICE DIVIDED.

APPOINTMENTS BY GOVERNOR A. B. ROMAN.

Valerien Allain, Sheriff Parish of Orleans from 10th March, 1841, to 20th March, 1843.

John L. Thielen, Sheriff of the District Court, from 10th March, 1841, to 20th March, 1843.

L. A. Dubois, Sheriff of the Commercial Court, from 10th March, 1841, to 20th March, 1843.

[illegible] Bouligny, Sheriff of the Criminal Court, from 10th March, 1841, to 20th March, 1843.

APPOINTMENTS BY GOVERNOR ALEX. MOUTON.

D. Augustin, Sheriff of the Parish of Orleans, from 20th March, 1843, to 24th March, 1846.

A. S. Lewis, Sheriff of the District Court, from 20th March, 1843, to 24th March, 1846.

Emile Lasere, Sheriff of the Commercial Court, from 20th March, 1843, to 5th June, 1845.

Armand Guyol, Sheriff of the Commercial Court, from 5th June, 1845, to 24th March, 1846.

H. D. Peire, Sheriff of the Criminal Court, from 20th March, 1843, to 24th March, 1846.

BY ELECTION.

CONSOLIDATED.

John L. Lewis, from 24th March, 1846, to 2d December, 1851.

James P. Freret, from 8th December, 1851, to 29th November, 1853.

M. Marigny, from 30th November, 1853, to 3d November, 1855.

Jos. Hufty, from 30th November, 1855, to 29th March, 1856.

(Sampson Bridgman, Deputy Sheriff, acting interim.)

John M. Bell, from 29th March, 1856, to 16th November, 1857.

F. T. Parker, from 17th November, 1857, to 23d November, 1861.

OFFICE DIVIDED.

Adolph Mazureau, Sheriff Criminal Court from 23d November, 1861, to 14th June, 1862.

John P. Walden, Sheriff Civil Courts, from 23d November, 1861, to 14th June, 1862.

INTERREGNUM ON ACCOUNT OF WAR.

BY MILITARY AUTHORITY.

James E. Dunham, from 21st October, 1862, to 21st March, 1864.

Alfred Shaw, from 21st March, 1864, to 21st July, 1865.

Charles Bienvenu, from 21st July, 1865, to 12th May, 1866.

BY ELECTION.

Harry T. Hays, from 12th May, 1866, to 23d November, 1867.

BY MILITARY AUTHORITY.

George W. Avery, from 23d November, 1867, to 1st July, 1868.

BY ELECTION.

Thos. L. Maxwell, Sheriff Civil Courts, from 1st July, 1868, to 27th November, 1870.

E. S. W[illegible], Sheriff Criminal Court, from 29th June, 1868, to 23d November, 1870.

C. S. Sauvinet, Sheriff Civil Courts, from 28th November, 1870, to 21st November, 1872.

J. A. Masicot, Sheriff Criminal Court, from 23d November, 1870, to 21st November, 1872.

W. P. Harper, Sheriff Civil Courts, from 21st November, 1872, to —

Isaac W. Patton, Sheriff Criminal Court, from 21st November, 1872, to —

CHRIST'S CHURCH,

CANAL STREET, NEW ORLEANS.

THE FAIR GROUNDS.

The entrances to the Fair Grounds about three miles from the Clay Statue are reached by the street cars which pass down Canal to Rampart, down Rampart to Esplanade, and down Esplanade towards and near Bayou St. John, being the pleasantest railroad ride afforded by the city cars, as well as a delightful drive for carriages. By the Gentilly gate, or the Mystery entrance, the visitor is introduced to a park of 120 acres, (formerly the old Creole Race Course,) studded with magnificent oaks, thickly overgrown with grass, containing a fine tract in complete order, and all the buildings required for fairs, fetes, and exhibitions of all kinds. The race course is an ellipse exactly one mile in measurement, and from the nature and elevation of the ground is usually in good condition. Within the ellipse are the Club House of the Fair Grounds, a platform for music and dancing, and a base ball park. The Public Stand, built by the Jockey Club on the south side of the course, is considered the best stand on the continent, being an enormous three story pile of graceful and substantial carpentry, two stories high, with comfortable seats for more than five thousand people, with ample promenades, broad and easy staircases, roomy saloons, and commanding a view of the whole course and enclosure. The view from the ample and lofty cupola takes in the whole city and its suburbs, a lovely mingling of rivers, bayous, lakes, swamps, forests, gardens, streets, shipping, spires, and railroad trains.

The main building is appropriated to the exhibition of fine and delicate manufactures, paintings, statuary drawings, musical instruments, machinery for household uses, needle work, furniture &c. It is of brick, 300x95 feet, two stories high, amply supplied with light and ventilation from large doors, lofty windows, and numerous skylights through its slate roof. The cost of the building was $70,000.

At each side of the main building at a distance of fifty yards, is a wooden building 306x80 feet, used for agricultural products, and implements, machines and mechanical inventions, often in full operation, and competing articles of produce or manufacture. The largest engines and machines are stored and exhibited under a shed near the principal buildings which covers an area of nearly nine hundred square yards. Extensive stables on the north side will accommodate more than a hundred horses, and on the same side adjoining the grounds is the live-stock farm of Mr. Slocomb, containing many specimens of thorough-bred and imported animals. The deer park is on the east side and was improved by Mr. Slocomb at his own personal expense.

Six acres in the south east corner are appropriated to the Flower Gardens and Nurseries, under the charge of Mr. Joseph Muller, by whose care and judicious management, the garden has become a special attraction. This garden now affords to visitors an exhibition of vigorous tropical shrubs, flowers, plants and trees not to be found elsewhere north of the Gulf of Mexico. The walks are shelled and the grounds symetrically laid out. The number of specimens is increasing and the whole garden is undergoing constant improvement.

Attached to the garden and furnished from it is the Floral Hall, a walled circular arena, 60 feet in diameter, sheltered by canvass and cooled by numerous fountains. Here during the regular public exhibitions are seen banks and pyramids of the rarest and most beautiful flowers and vines that grow in the garden, field or forest.

The Fair Grounds reflect credit upon the Association, for their enterprise, zeal and public spirit. They are seconded in their laudable and industrious efforts by a generous public. Such cooperation will accelerate the attainment of the great objects which all should have in view, the maintenance of the dignity of labor, the vindication of the worth of brains, and the practical promotion of the prosperity of our State.

MECHANICS' AND AGRICULTURAL FAIR ASSOCIATION.

This body was incorporated in April 1866, "to promote and foster improvements in all the various departments of agriculture" and for "the promotion and development of the mechanical arts and home manufactures in all branches; the rearing, development, and improvement of the races of useful animals; the general advancement of rural economy; the encouragement of household manufactures and the dissemination of useful knowledge upon such subjects by offering inducements and premiums therefor."

The first officers of the Association were: G. W. Race, Esq., President; Messrs. C. H. Slocomb, P. A. Rost, and H. R. Swasey, Vice-Presidents; T. D. Harper, Secretary and Treasurer; and I. G. Seymour, C. Pattbeff, J. O. Nixon, Luther Homes, Charles Pride, L. Folger, T. N. Blake, G. W. Sizer, L. W. Pilié, David H. Fowler, John Pemberton, J. W. Tilton, Isaac N. Marks, Thomas O. Moore, E. E. Kittridge, J. H. Overton and J. Hardesty, Directors.

The first fair was held on the New Fair Grounds in the Fall of 1866, the second in January 1868, the third and fourth early in 1869 and 1870. The buildings of the Association were burnt in the Spring of 1871 and the Fair, necessarily postponed, was held in the Fall of that year. The Fair of April 1872 was eminently successful, giving renewed promise of a brilliant future. Besides diplomas and other rewards, premiums to the value of more than twenty thousand dollars were distributed.

The Association is to continue twenty five years. There is no room to doubt that its success and marked influence will secure a renewal of its term.

Its officers for 1872, (chosen May 1st) were I. N. Marks, President; C. H. Slocomb, N. E. Bailey, and James Jackson, Vice-Presidents; Luther Homes, Secretary and Treasurer; and Williamson Smith, L. Folger, J. A. Blaffer G. W. Dunbar, A. W. Merriam, Joseph L. Harris, C. A. Miltenberger, John Giddes, G. A. Breaux, A. Fortier, E. A. Tyler, G. G. Garner, W. B. Schmidt, E. M. Rusha and Frederick Wing, Directors.

CRESCENT CITY SUGAR REFINERY.

On Tchoupitoulas street, between Julia and St. Joseph streets, occupying about half a square, is the enormous eight story brick building, which, with several subsidiary brick structures adjoining, constitute the Crescent City Steam Sugar Refinery, the most substantial, best managed and perhaps the largest manufactory of refined sugars in the world. Steam power is ingeniously applied wherever manual labor can be saved, so that with no more than one hundred laborers, results are accomplished, which, with less ingenuity, might require five times as many. The crude sugar as it comes from the plantation is hoisted by steam to the eighth story, and the molasses is pumped by steam from a tank or reservoir in the basement. From the top the sugar passes downward through the "blow ups," the bag filters, coolers, vacuum kettle, mixer, drainers, cutters and mill, by a succession of automatic processes, some of which are the invention of Adam Thompson, Esq., the enterprising sole proprietor, whose earnest study has long been to improve upon every mechanical contrivance by which time and labor can be saved. His establishment has thereby become the model refinery and the special admiration of all practical engineers.

No chemicals are used here in the process of refining, the sugar being whitened and purified entirely by filtration through charcoal. Of these charcoal filters Mr. Thompson has twenty-eight in operation, and intends soon to add twenty-three more. They are cylinders sixteen feet high, and four feet in diameter, compactly filled with bone black through which the liquid filters in about thirty-six hours. The charcoal, after having been used for several charges of liquid, is washed and revivified by burning in a furnace, which renews its purifying properties as often as may be required. Fifty tons of charcoal are in constant use. When in full operation four hundred and fifty barrels of sugar or five hundred barrels of molasses are used, the most of which is imported from Cuba.

The Louisiana molasses cannot be refined by charcoal filtration, as it contains sulphur, which prevents the whitening action of the bone black. Mr. Thompson has therefore provided eight centrifugal mills through which it is passed for refining and deodorizing.

Water is supplied by eight "drove wells," one of which is 140 feet deep. From these are filled very large tanks and cisterns in all parts of the establishment, extending to the eighth story and roofs. Pipes descend from these in all directions, so that in case of fire, the whole can be flooded in a few seconds. An extensive cooperage supplies the manufactory with barrels, &c., for refined sugars and syrups, besides making large numbers for the outside market.

The products of this establishment have become noted in American and foreign markets and the demand for them has so increased as to make an enlargement necessary. For his enterprise, energy and talents, the liberal and public-spirited proprietor merits the gratitude of all our citizens, and he is held in especial esteem by all who seek the development of Southern resources.

NEW ORLEANS,

Natchez AND Vicksburg Packet.

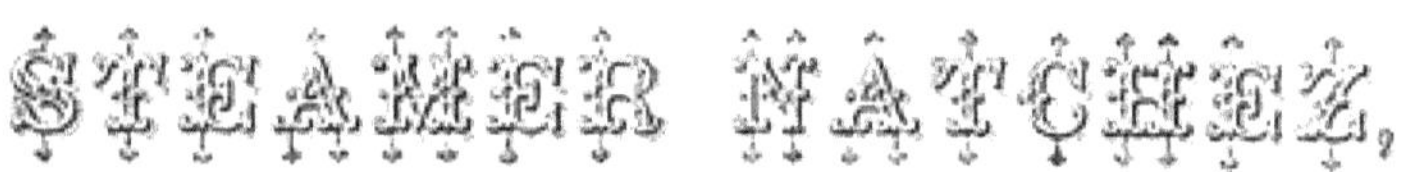

Captain T. P. Leathers, Master.

Length of Hull, .	307 Feet.	Eight Boilers, 34 feet long---
Width of Beam, .	44 "	40 inches diameter and 2 Flues.
Depth of Hold, .	10 "	Two 34 inch Cylinders, 10 feet Stroke.
Diameter of Wheel, .	44 "	Extreme Height, 119 feet, 6 inches.
Length of Bucket .	16 "	Capacity for 5,500 bales cotton.

CRESCENT MUTUAL INSURANCE COMPANY.

CORNER OF CAMP STREET AND COMMERCIAL ALLEY.

Incorporated in 1849.

ASSETS, $732,129 40.

THOMAS A. ADAMS, President. *SAMUEL B. NEWMAN, Vice President.*
HENRY N. OGDEN, Secretary.

RESIDENCE OF E. A. TYLER, ESQ.,

565 St. Charles Street, New Orleans.

Factors' & Traders Insurance Co.

39 CARONDELET STREET.

OFFICERS.

HARMON DOANE, President. MOSES GREENWOOD, Vice Pres. EDWARD A. PALFREY, Secretary.

TRUSTEES.

J. LEVOIS & JAMISON,

J. LEVOIS,

Commission Merchant.

3 Rue de Chateaudun,

PARIS.

126 CANAL STREET,

NEW ORLEANS.

Importers of

Foreign Dry Goods

and

GENERAL DEALERS IN

American Dry Goods

AND

NOTIONS,

AT

WHOLESALE AND RETAIL.

TABLE OF CONTENTS.

ASSOCIATIONS.

PAGE.
Fair Grounds 349
Fireman's Charitable 40
Hancock Literary 47
Howard Charitable 48
Mechanic's 59
St. Andrew's Literary 253
Touro Infirmary 263

BIOGRAPHICAL.

Abram, H 112
Adams, T. A 68
Bayne, T. L 108
Bidwell, D 151
Bartlett, N 184
Blanchard, A 183
Bailey, G. W. R 240
Benton, E. R 61
Brickell, E. W 174
Bell, W. H 304
Beaughn, G. H 304
Conway, J. R. (Mayor) (Portrait) 31
Campbell, J. A 31
Casey, J. F 307
Cavaroc, C 91
Collens, T. W 103
Curto, G 188
Cooley, W. H. (Portrait) 298
Clapp, T 147
Clarke, T. A 107
Cullom, F. N 215
Collignon, G 172
Castellanos, H. C 163
Chiapella, A 174
Davidson, J 149
De Ferriet, G 43
Day, J. I 123
Deere, G. H 132
Edwards, D. (Portrait) 213
Flanders, B. F. (Portrait) 43
Fourchy, P. (Portrait) 61
Fosdick, G. A. (Portrait) 55
Foster, A 119
Freret, J 127
Fosdhey, C. G. (Portrait) 232
Fitzgerald, C 211
Gayarré, C. (Portrait) 20
Gibson, R. L 40
Gaines, Mrs. M. C 155
Hatch, F. H. (Portrait) 104
Howard, H 96
Howard, C. T. (Portrait) 107
Harper, W. P 244
Hodgson, W. I. (Portrait) 111
Herwig, P. F 267
Holcombe, W. H 203
Hunt, R 115
Higby, L. J 231
Heunen, A 127
Hay, A 132
Huntington, E. W 270
Irwin, P 121
Jamin, L 115
Jacobs, H. S 131
Kellogg, W. P 331
Kennedy, S. H 164
Kennedy, P. J. (Portrait) 224
Kennedy, T. H 27
Kenner, D. F 167
Knapp, Jas 288
Lewis, Jas 351
Lacey, Geo. S 319
Leet, J. K. (Portrait) 307
Lafitte 259
Leacock, W. T 141
Leathers, T. P 332
Lewis, J. L., Mayor (Portrait) 23
Lusher, R. M 216
Mott, R 24
Moynahan, C 168
Moynahan, J 35
Marks, I. N 116
Maybin, J. A 120
Monroe, I. T., Mayor (Portrait) 139
McCann, W 244
McCloskey, H. (Portrait) 175
McEnery, J 207
Mercer, W. N 187
Moody, S. N 220
McConnel, J 183
Montgomery, R. M 308
McDonogh, J 321
Mulligan, T 215
New, J. H 128
Ogden, H. N 211
Oglesby, J. H. (Portrait) 38
O'Conor, T 283
Palmer, B. M 63
Phillips, A 100
Prevost, E 168
Perche, N. J 179
Price, J. B 151
Parker, J. M. G 284
Packard, S. B 90
Reynolds, L. E 152
Roselius, C 278
Randolph, W. M 109
Rozier, J. A 136
Ringgold, C 115
Roberts, R 283
Seymour, I. G 135
Sambola, A. (Portrait) 304
Summers, F. H 32
Semmes, T. J 163
Sloo, T 123
Soulé, P 335
Smith, G. (Portrait) 228
Stone, Dr. W 251
Tucker, J. T 67
Tagon, J 43
Taylor, M 23
Tyler, E. A 55
Turnbull, A. M 247
Van Wickle, J. C 99
Whittaker, J. S 109
Whittaker, D. K 153
Whittaker, Mrs. M 124
Wimmer, J. P. B 128
Wiltz, L. A. (Portrait) 69
Wiltz, P. S 67
Walshe, B. T 119
Zacharie, J. W 185

CARNIVAL SOCIETIES.

King of the Carnival 68
Knights of Momus 304
Mystick Krewe of Comus 48
Twelfth Knight Revelers 192

CHURCHES.

First Presbyterian 47
St. John Baptist 163
Synagogue, Carondelet street 92
Temple Sinai 267

FACTORIES.

Cotton Seed Oil Works 39
Crescent City Sugar Refinery 128
La. Cotton Factory 326

INSURANCE COMPANIES.

La. Equitable Life 28
N. O. Insurance Co 163

MISCELLANEOUS.

Algiers 19
Academy of Sciences 92
Crescent City 7
Ferries 163
Carrollton 136
N. O. Gas Light Co 311
N. O. and its drainage 320
Sylvester Larned Institution 323
Shakespeare Club 168
St. Louis Hotel 163
Clay Statue 173
History of New Orleans 11
Battle Ground 227
Turf Reminiscences 256
N. O. Savings Institution 264
Street Cars 252

PUBLIC BUILDINGS.

Exposition 87
Mosque 264
Touro Alms House 39
New Masonic Temple 36

PUBLIC INSTITUTIONS.

City Water Works 41
City Markets 131
Gas Light Co 78

PUBLIC SQUARES.

Annunciation 344
City Park 253
Coliseum Place 50
Douglas Square 130
Jackson Square 249
Lafayette Square 59
Tivoli Circle 78
Washington Square 112

THEATRES.

Academy of Music 151
Opera House 248

TRADE AND COMMERCE.

Chamber of Commerce 192
Bulk Grain trade 196
N. O. & Spanish America 199
Fort St. Phillip Canal 256
Custom House 276
A. B. Griswold & Co 290
Collectors of the Port 308

LIST OF ILLUSTRATIONS.

Asylums. PAGE.

Poydras 213
St. Ann's 197

Banks.

America 137
Accommodation 192
Citizens 93
Louisiana National 17
Mutual National 153
N. O. Savings Institution 313

Churches.

Cathedral 220
Christ 337
Immaculate Conception 81
Saint Patrick 265
Temple Sinai 125
Trinity 37

Factories.

Edward's Foundry 253
Louisiana Ice 301
Louisiana Cotton 185
Louisiana Sash 261
Lane's Cotton Mills 145
N. O. Blood Fertilizing 325

Hotels.

City 257
St. Charles 33
St. Louis 305

Insurance Offices.

Crescent Mutual 343
Factors and Traders' Ins. Co 347
Louisiana Equitable (Life) 333
Merchants' Mutual 109
N. O. Insurance Association 113

Portraits.

Beauregard, P. G. T 109
Bell, W. H 24
Braughn, G. H 284
A. S. Badger 32
Campbell, J. A 96
Casey, Jas. F 236
Cullom, E. N 240
Fitzenreiter, Chas 128
Harper, W. P 224
Herwig, P. F 176
Kellogg, W. P 328
DeLacey, Geo. S 49
Leathers, T. P 80
Lewis, Jas 316
Marks, I. N 320
McCann, W 272
Mercer, W. N 268
Moody, S. N 288
O'Connor, Thos 127
Palmer, B. M 276
Parker, G. M 324
Patton, I. W 232
Phillipps, A 209
Pinchback, P. B. S 256
Pike, W. S 112
Price, J. B 48
Roselius, C 208
Stone, Dr. Warren 16
Turnbull, B. M 141
Walshe, B. T 201
Witte, L. A 64
Willmer, Bishop 308

Public Buildings.

Charity Hospital 201
City Hall 245
Cotton Exchange 273
Court Houses 229
Custom House 69
Hotel Dieu 293
Mechanics' Institute 117
Mint 257
Odd Fellows Hall 65
Parish Prisons 317

Residences.

Ellison, Jos 57
Oglesby, J. H 231
Schmidt, W. B 45
Roberts R 321
Slocomb, C 149
Soulé, G 181
Tyler, E. A 345
Walshe, B. T 249

Schools.

Peabody Normal 241
Sylvester Larned 285

Steamers.

Alabama (Steamship) 297
Natchez (Steamboat) 341

Stores.

Blessing, S. T 77
Flash, Lewis & Co 309
Gonzales, F. A 65
Griswold, A. B. & Co 105
Grunewald, L 237
Hart, E. J. & Co 161
Hedrick, M. S 317
Holmes, D. H 29
Leeds & Jamison 349
Montgomery, R. M. & B. J 329
Morespue Building 141
Schmidt & Zeigler 53
Slocomb & Baldwin 41
Story Building 133
Touro Building 93
Tyler, E. A 89
Walshe, B. T. (Exterior) 97
Walshe, B. T. (Interior) 129

Theatres.

Academy of Music 229
National 189
Opera House 281
St. Charles 209
Varieties 69

Views.

Bird's Eye of City 5
Canal Street 204
Clay Statue 153
Cotton Exchange 273
Fair Grounds 180
French Market 13
Gas Office 293
Grain Elevator 61
Jackson Square 225
Jockey Club House 225
Lake Protection Levee 181
La. State Lottery Office 177
Orleans Cotton Press 121
Race Course Stand 157
Row Boat Club 109
Shakespeare Club 165
Slaughter Houses 221
Steamboat Landing 21
Sugar Sheds 49

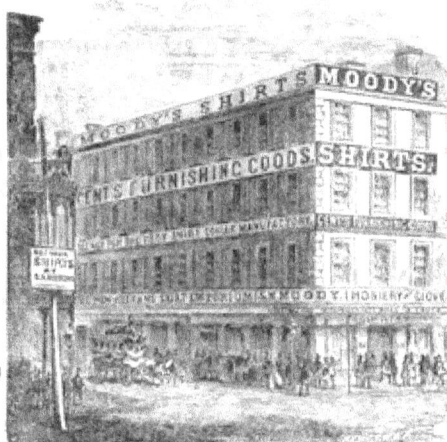

www.ingramcontent.com/pod-product-compliance
Lightning Source LLC
Chambersburg PA
CBHW032307280326
41932CB00009B/731

* 9 7 8 3 7 4 3 3 1 5 0 1 3 *